RUSKIN: THE CRITICAL HERITAGE

RUSKIN

THE CRITICAL HERITAGE

Edited by

J. L. BRADLEY
Formerly Department of English
University of Maryland

ROUTLEDGE & KEGAN PAUL
LONDON, BOSTON, MELBOURNE AND HENLEY

First published in 1984
by Routledge & Kegan Paul plc
39 Store Street, London WC1E 7DD, England,
9 Park Street, Boston, Mass. 02108, USA,
464 St Kilda Road, Melbourne,
Victoria 3004, Australia, and
Broadway House, Newtown Road,
Henley-on-Thames, Oxon RG9 1EN, England
Printed in Great Britain by
Redwood Burn Limited, Trowbridge, Wilts
Compilation, introduction, notes and index
© J. L. Bradley 1984
No part of this book may be reproduced in
any form without permission from the publisher,
except for the quotation of brief
passages in criticism

Library of Congress Cataloging in Publication Data

Ruskin, the critical heritage.
(The Critical heritage series)
Includes bibliographical references and index.
1. Ruskin, John, 1819–1900.   2. Art criticism—Great
Britain—History—19th century.   I. Bradley, J. L.
II. Series.
N7483.R8R87   1983   709   83–11102
ISBN 0–7100–9286–5

General Editor's Preface

The reception given to a writer by his contemporaries and near-contemporaries is evidence of considerable value to the student of literature. On one side we learn a great deal about the state of criticism at large and in particular about the development of critical attitudes towards a single writer; at the same time, through private comments in letters, journals or marginalia, we gain an insight upon the tastes and literary thought of individual readers of the period. Evidence of this kind helps us to understand the writer's historical situation, the nature of his immediate reading-public, and his response to these pressures.

The separate volumes in the *Critical Heritage Series* present a record of this early criticism. Clearly, for many of the highly productive and lengthily reviewed nineteenth- and twentieth-century writers, there exists an enormous body of material; and in these cases the volume editors have made a selection of the most important views, significant for their intrinsic critical worth or for their representative quality—perhaps even registering incomprehension!

For earlier writers, notably pre-eighteenth century, the materials are much scarcer and the historical period has been extended, sometimes far beyond the writer's lifetime, in order to show the inception and growth of critical views which were initially slow to appear.

In each volume the documents are headed by an Introduction, discussing the material assembled and relating the early stages of the author's reception to what we have come to identify as the critical tradition. The volumes will make available much material which would otherwise be difficult of access and it is hoped that the modern reader will be thereby helped towards an informed understanding of the ways in which literature has been read and judged.

B.C.S.

For E. P. B.

Contents

Acknowledgments

For a book in the Critical Heritage Series a thorough bibliography can be of considerable assistance; thus it is unfortunate that, in the case of Ruskin, no such volume exists. However, two bibliographies pave the scholar's way: the first is 'A Complete Bibliography of the Writings in Prose and Verse of John Ruskin, LL.D. with a List of the Most Important Ruskiniana', compiled by Thomas J. Wise and James P. Smart, edited by Thomas J. Wise (2 vols, London, 1893; reprinted 1966); the second is in vol. 38 (pp. 109-96) of the 'Works'. And to both, especially to the latter, I am under obligation. Of much aid in identifying various reviewers were the three monumental volumes comprising 'The Wellesley Index to Victorian Periodicals'; similarly, that admirable journal, the 'Victorian Periodicals Review', proved most helpful.

Various Victorian scholars kindly responded to my inquiries. Dr Jean Halladay of Old Dominion University, Norfolk, Virginia, granted me access to her unpublished dissertation on the critical reception of a large corpus of Ruskin's work; and Dr Russel Kacher liberally shared with me his wide knowledge of Ruskin and permitted me to consult his significant thesis on critical attitudes towards many of Ruskin's social writings. To such other Victorians as Jeremy Maas, Joanne Shattock, Brian Maidment, George Landow, Samuel Brown, Herbert Sussman, and Lockett Thomson, I am also indebted for their aid and interest. Further co-operation and help were given by librarians at the Lilly Library (University of Indiana), the Enoch Pratt Free Library (Baltimore), the University of London Library, and the University of Bristol Library. In particular the following expedited my way: W.E. Mackey of the Trinity College (Dublin) Library, Miss Kathleen Phillips of the Boston Public Library, William Joll of Thomas Agnew & Son Ltd, D. Taylor of the Central Library,

Manchester, and Patricia Swetman of the Yeovil Public Library.

Much of the research for this volume was carried out in that Taj Mahal of libraries, the Library of Congress, Washington, D.C., where, without exception, I received friendly and informative assistance. But it is to the following members of that august institution who did so much on my behalf that I would express particular appreciation: Mrs Andrew Robison, Messrs Nelson, Wilgus, Calvan, T. Martin, Shields and Burney, as well as members of the Newspaper Room staff. Seldom has a scholar received so much help so unstintingly given.

Finally, my appreciation extends to the General Research Board of the University of Maryland for granting financial assistance towards the completion of this volume.

A Note on the Text

All selections derive from original sources with the occasional misprint silently emended. Lengthy quotations from Ruskin, omitted in the interests of space, will be found in 'The Library Edition of the Works of John Ruskin' (39 vols, London, 1903-12), edited by E.T. Cook and A.D.O. Wedderburn. Volume and page references to this edition, hereafter referred to as 'Works', are supplied in the text at the appropriate places. Omissions in the texts of individual selections are noted by ellipses.

Introduction

I

Ruskin the Controversialist

Both consciously and unconsciously Ruskin was a controversialist. Born into the post-Napoleonic age when England
was emerging as the world's strongest industrial power, he
was swept and buffeted by the frenzied currents of
aesthetic, social, and religious activity for some sixty
years, each one a salient part of what is termed the
'Victorian Age'. For Ruskin published his first work, a
poem after the style of Wordsworth, in 1830 when he was
eleven and his last, issued between bouts of tormenting
insanity, at seventy. He is the quintessential Victorian
intellectual racked and ravaged by the times with a fer-
ocity not visited even upon his master,Thomas Carlyle.
True, much of his agony can be ascribed to emotional disorders, but his responses to sundry Victorian malaises are
those of a gifted individual abnormally aware of the
turbulent problems about him.
     Yet Ruskin is no controversial prose stylist: not for
him any daring experiments in prose expression. Unlike
his contemporaries writing the novel - Dickens, Thackeray,
the Brontës - he did not so much extend the frontiers of a
literary form as draw upon an ageless tradition of prose
expression that enabled him to articulate his particular
message. Analysis of Ruskin's style, regardless of whether
he often delivered himself (as early on) in an extrava-
gantly romantic vein or (as later) in a pellucidly
classical manner, suggests that he looked back as he wrote
rather than forward or about him. Whilst the Bible from
first to last dominates his prose, echoes of seventeenth-
century divines, the satires of Horace, the authority of
Milton, the elegance of Addison, the majesty of Johnson,

the richness of Scott (to mention only a few) pulse
through his writing to constitute not a mere pastiche but,
after submission to the Ruskin crucible, a mode of
expression at its finest carefully fashioned, traditionally
disciplined, and instinct with a sensitivity unique in the
long tradition of which he is so distinguished a standard-
bearer.

However, the controversial Ruskin does appear when he
writes as a youth of seventeen a stirring if unnecessary
defence of Turner, who had been savaged by 'Blackwood's'.
(1) But it was with the appearance of 'Modern Painters I'
in 1843 that the startling variation of response that was
to characterize so much criticism of Ruskin's work down
through the decades makes its appearance. From that time
it is apparent that his views and his modes of expression
are frequently to draw from his critics extremities of
praise or condemnation as acute as some of his own utterances on the numerous subjects he dealt with in the course
of a long life.

But it is perhaps Ruskin's Tory-Socialism which, but
slenderly evident in his young manhood and remaining
relatively dormant until the 1850s, raised many a hackle
in the mercantile world when its doctrines were promul-
gated in the second volume of 'The Stones of Venice' (1853)
and, more forthrightly, in 'Unto this Last' (1860, 1862) as
well as by letters and lectures to working men in the
sixties and seventies. These earned him, with a few
honourable exceptions, almost uniform hostility from the
conservative press and from the adherents of the Manchester
School of economics. And it is to Ruskin's lasting credit
that he carried his campaign into the heart of *laissez-
faire* England by lecturing, fearlessly and powerfully, at
such bastions of unalloyed capitalism as Manchester and
Bradford. In sum, it might be said that throughout a
long career Ruskin attracted contention.

The Critical Selections

In addition to the controversial nature of Ruskin's
writings is their immense bulk, a matter of millions of
words as set forth in the 'Works'. This in itself creates
a problem of selectivity in relation to Ruskin's critical
reception across the decades. Coupled with the bulk is
the extraordinarily varied subject-matter which became,
with the passage of time, maniacally diverse. For Ruskin
was emotionally unbalanced from his earlier years, and
whilst his revolutionary pronouncements of the forties and
fifties concerning artistic England and the social

manifestos of the sixties are his dominating motifs, much
other matter intrudes. Furthermore, in the midst of the
latter decade, when Ruskin was on the lecture platform,
he came to regard it as a forum for discussion of any
subject catching his fancy. Later, the written word became
alarmingly discursive as is evident in the prodigality
of 'Fors Clavigera' where, side by side, is found matter so
unrelated as the St George's Company, the character of
Mazzini, the poetry of Tennyson and Wordsworth, the
author's spiritual problems and the fallacies of his art
instruction. Even more markedly disparate subjects are
found jostling one another by dipping anywhere into 'Fors'.
Such excessiveness and dissimilarity of material are bound
to impose upon the selection of critical response.
    What sort of reviews did Ruskin receive? And who
reviewed his work? A full response to these questions
would necessitate book-length studies rendered the more
exacting by virtue of his spanning the entire Victorian
period. Even his dates, of birth 1819, of death 1900,
fit so perfectly as to render him chronologically the
archetypal Victorian, with his first work coming on the
threshold of Victoria's accession and his last within a few
years of her death: thus he moves from the Victorian sun-
rise through its brightest years and subsides in its
twilight. However, despite the enormity of the span, which
was accompanied by a multifariousness of critical positions,
it is possible to suggest, in broad outline, the form taken
by criticisms of his writings, though in doing so it is
well to ponder some of the variations on the critical motif:
for instance, how would a Tory quarterly of the forties
review 'Modern Painters I' or a Catholic periodical
consider 'The Seven Lamps of Architecture', or a *laissez-
faire* journal or a liberal newspaper 'Unto this Last'? Of
significance, too, is the changing face of reviewing itself,
for in his early career Ruskin was scrutinized by the polymaths of the 'Edinburgh Review', 'Blackwood's' and the
'Quarterly Review': such critics, biased in various ways -
social, economic, spiritual - were allowed a great deal of
space and were well paid to fill it up. Until roughly mid-
century these 'heavy' journals held sway but were challenged by, and in many cases ceded their positions to, new
quarterlies and monthlies as well as by rising weeklies,
forthnightlies, and dailies - one thinks of the 'Athenaeum',
the Spectator', and the 'Saturday Review' in particular -
whose notices were brief, pithy, pointed. The reasons for
the shift were several, among them the increasing tempo of
mid-century life which left little opportunity for
leisurely consideration of the long essay-reviews often
over-stuffed with lengthy quotation. The later Victorian

critics, too, tended to differ from the Wilsons and
Jeffreys of earlier years in that they were not polymaths
so much as specialists in English literature although, like
all critics at all times, they were prone to idiosyncrasies
and prejudices that showed in their writing. Suffice to
say, then, on this point, that Ruskin ran the gamut of
critical reviewing but found it, because of harbouring so
many unorthodox ideas himself, harder going than many.

I have tried to spread the following critical selections
across journals of varied sorts; but if some publications
are represented more than once it is because the grasp
and awareness of the journal in question were firmer and
more acute than other notices that came under consideration
for inclusion. I have also tried to avoid long synopses
of Ruskinian argument although occasionally, as in the
case of 'Modern Painters II' (No. 4), it has seemed helpful to explicate a particular line of his reasoning.

While cognizant that it is not possible to please all
readers constantly, a selection of reviews has been made of
Ruskin's salient publications in the forties and fifties
(those decades when he emerged as the aesthetic arbiter
of a growing segment of the rising middle classes) and
the sixties (when 'social' Ruskin comes fully forth).
After that, from approximately 1870 onwards Ruskin, to
judge from the numerous essays assessing his relation to
the age - rather than specific criticisms of specific
works - becomes an 'institution', a constantly hovering
presence over the Victorian movement of mind. So the
criticism of Ruskin, again speaking in broad terms,
appears to resolve itself into two main parts: the first
focusing upon the individual publications as they streamed
forth; the second concerning the place of the man and his
work in the age.

II THE 1840S

'Modern Painters I, II'; 'The Seven Lamps of Architecture'

With the arrival in May 1843 of the initial volume of
'Modern Painters' Ruskin, publishing as 'A Graduate of
Oxford', provoked an assortment of critical responses
characteristic of the pathfinder and revolutionary; thus
it is well that his admirable editors, Cook and Wedderburn,
wisely temper their originally enthusiastic account of the
book's reception. (2) In retrospect, a wider reading of
reviews, together with modest sales, suggests a limited
critical success for this singular work, although
Wordsworth, Charlotte Brontë, and Mrs Gaskell as well as

some reviewers appreciated the heretical views so boldly
expressed and were alive to the epoch-making and insurgent
quality of the book. One such was the anonymous critic,
perhaps Ruskin's friend, Dr Croly, of the mildly voiced
conservative journal, 'the 'Britannia' (3) who wrote:

> This is the bold title of a bold work, a general
> challenge to the whole body of cognoscenti, dilettanti,
> and all haranguers, essayists, and critics on the art of
> Italy, Flanders, and England, for the last hundred years.
> Of course, it will raise the whole *posse comitatus*
> of the pencil in arms. The phalanx of the pen will be
> moved against the Oxford graduate; the 'potent, grave,
> and reverend signors' who fill the reviews with profound
> theorems which defy all readers, and the haunters of
> exhibitions for the purpose of seeing their own por-
> traits, and laughing at those of every one else, will
> anathematize the new heresy; and yet we should not be
> surprised if the time should arrive when the contro-
> versialists will be turned into converts, and the heresy
> be dignified with the honours of the true belief. Our
> space allows of scarcely more than a sketch of this
> volume, which we pronounce to be one of the most inter-
> esting and important which we have ever seen on the
> subject, exhibiting a singular insight into the true
> principle of beauty, order, and taste - a work calcu-
> lated more than *any other* performance in the language
> to make men enquire into the nature of their sensations
> of the sublime, the touching and the delightful, and to
> lead them from doubt into knowledge, without feeling the
> length of a way so scattered over with the flowers of an
> eloquent, forcible, and imaginative style.

But readers of this prescience and sensitivity were rare in
1843, and as strongly as the reviewer advocated Ruskin's
cause as forcefully was it repelled by the entrenched
critical establishment, for even a casual reading (if that
be possible) of 'Modern Painters I' demonstrates Ruskin
tilting against the accepted aesthetic canons of the day.
With the arrogance and misplaced confidence of youth he
spared very few. He set aside the authority of many of
the ancients and disdained the pronouncements of Sir George
'where-is-your-brown-tree' Beaumont, demanding that the
artist look clearly and incisively at Nature. He asserted
the claims of the 'modern', invariably anathema to the
established powers, the more strongly by alleging in his
sub-title the 'superiority' of contemporary painters over
their predecessors. And by singling out Turner for special
'superiority' he further antagonized many who, whilst

cognizant of that painter's genius, nevertheless experienced difficulty in apprehending his more experimental work. All this, linked with the supreme self-confidence radiated by a young man of twenty-four, did nothing to mollify his elders and, by their own lights, his aesthetic betters.

An early broadside, within six months of publication of 'Modern Painters I', came from the powerful 'Blackwood's' (No. 1), nicknamed 'Maga', a Tory journal founded in 1817 in opposition to the Whiggish 'Edinburgh Review'. (4) Its politics and perspectives were ultraconservative and its devastation of the young Ruskin an early example of how the fundamental inclinations of publication can inform its critical approaches.

Ruskin's reviewer was John Eagles (see p. 34) who, in a thickly textured piece of criticism, accused him of 'malice', prejudice, fallaciousness, disrespect for tradition and finally placed him in the 'Fudge School' of language. Neither does Ruskin's 'monomania' for, and 'nonsensical praise' of, Turner pass without notice, a thread of hostile criticism that runs through the majority of reviews of this first volume.

A briefer brace of criticisms in the 'Athenaeum' (No. 2) raps Ruskin for his worship of Turner and it might be added as an example of what that artist was subjected to in the name of criticism, that in May 1842 the art critic of the 'Athenaeum' had spoken of Turner as choosing 'to paint with cream or chocolate, yolk of egg, or currant jelly, - here he uses his whole array of kitchen stuff'. The hostility of this journal, to become in the fifties one of the most powerful publications for the growing literate middle class, is marked by its censure, too, of Ruskin's 'modernism' and of those contemporary painters working for 'Brummagem picture-markets', an allusion to the increased interest in art taken by the rising middle-class merchants of the Midland cities, a group akin to John James Ruskin, the author's father. Yet it is said on excellent authority that the 'Athenaeum', particularly under John Francis who was well entrenched in the forties, was impeccably honest and brought integrity to reviewing. (5)

It fell, however, to a middle-of-the-road quarterly that for some years steered a wise course between the Scylla of the 'Edinburgh Review' and the Charybdis of the 'Quarterly Review' to grant Ruskin a piece of balanced, encouraging criticism. In the 'North British Review' (No. 5) of 'Modern Painters I, II' one observes a liberal journal of diverse topics and non-denominational religious articles in its happiest light. Addressed mainly to Scottish readers, the 'North British' had as contributors

such men as Dr John Brown, David Masson, Herbert Spencer,
Charles Kingsley, and John Tulloch. Also it can be
claimed that this magazine, commendably free from the
partisan intellectual strife raging in Edinburgh and
London, especially at this point in its development,
sought balance and equilibrium in what it published.

But for all the critical honesty of this estimable
quarterly it should be noted that Dr John Brown, the
reviewer, already an admirer of Ruskin and to become a
close friend, may seem unduly generous. Be that as it
may, his initial remarks reveal additional aspects of
Ruskin's critical reception as Brown claims the 'larger
Reviews' neglect the two volumes, and those periodicals
representing the literature of the Fine Arts 'almost without exception have treated it with the most marked injustice and the most shameful derision'. And it is only near
the end of the long article that Brown seemingly takes
Ruskin to task, but for stylistic reasons only; yet the
apparent caveat is significant in that the objections he
raised were not his own but the consequence of editorial
intervention, a practice common in Victorian reviewing.
A letter of appreciation from Ruskin to Brown clarifies
the point:

> Nevertheless, for my own part, I *was* glad to hear *you*
> had not written the passages in question, for, though
> preparing to consider them and benefit by them as I
> best might, I was a little aghast at the request that
> I would never be eloquent any more; for I do think
> that some things cannot be said except passionately
> and figuratively. (6)

Other publications beyond those already mentioned who
reviewed 'Modern Painters I, II' showed some variation in
their responses. The 'Art-Union' (June 1843) delivered itself of 500 vituperative words on the first volume whereas the 'Foreign and Colonial Quarterly' (October 1843),
noting Turner as the 'hero' of the book, is reasonably
receptive to Ruskin's main arguments. 'Fraser's (March
1846), with a touch of its earlier rebelliousness, is
generally favourable although, as with the 'Gentleman's
Magazine' (November 1843), asserting that far too much
space is given to quotation. The 'Westminster Review'
(August 1843) remarks the volume's extravagance, especially over Turner, but its notice is too brief to carry
much authority.

As regards 'Modern Painters II', the 'Athenaeum'
(25 July 1846), whilst hostile to Ruskin, half-praises
the book as a 'perturbative volume', whereas

'Douglas Jerrold's Weekly Newspaper' (18 July 1846) lauds
it as a publication forcing people to think, though joining
in the chorus against Turner as 'eccentric'. The
'Westminster Review' (June 1846) quietly, but disappoint-
ingly, gives the book one sentence postponing the review.

Pausing briefly, then, in the mid-forties to ponder
Ruskin's relation to his critics, what becomes most evident
is the impossibility of generalization beyond the obvious.
Certainly, most reviewers opposed his deification of
Turner and his extravagance of language whilst a small
handful hailed him as the saviour of art criticism and
heralded his energetic championing of some of the moderns.
Very few, on the other hand, dealt ably with the second
volume, an exception being the 'Foreign Quarterly Review'
(No. 4) whose dissection of Ruskin's aesthetic theories is
intelligent and clearly reasoned. Out of conflicting
evidence, allowing for various biases and bearing in mind
how limited Ruskin's appeal would at best be - at this
time - it appears that these controversial early writings
received no more than a mixed reception.

With the advent of 'The Seven Lamps of Architecture'
(1849) Ruskin, by now a recognized figure within the limitations of the aesthetic landscape, attracted from a bur-
geoning world of criticism a good many more reviews than
heretofore. In this volume Ruskin himself is now more
temperate, less arrogant, and he writes, save for a dis-
tressing lapse into religious bigotry, with a generosity
and moderation suggestive of a more meditative mind at
work. Neither does his press seem to range so extremely in
comment, although John James Ruskin's enthusiasm for the
book's reception needs modification. (7)

Several of Ruskin's old antagonists, for example,
'Blackwood's' (September 1851) and the 'Athenaeum'
(1 September 1849), reared up, although the latter's
response was tempered with some reluctant praise on this
occasion of 'The Seven Lamps'. But Ruskin aroused the ire
of practising architects who saw his theories as impracticable, although the 'simply nauseous' of a significant
journal of that profession, the 'Builder' (19 May 1849),
did little to focus the opposition. Later, in November-
December 1851, this same magazine will indulge in some
ponderous levity at Ruskin's expense when it runs a series
of articles, Architecturus to his Son, using decidedly
different lamps as the basis of its pseudo-criticism.

A short but balanced notice in the 'Examiner' (No. 6)
represents the more measured criticism of this phase of
Ruskin's work, and it is the more significant as taking the
author's side in stressing the necessity for finer, more
telling, contemporary architecture. The criticism, too,

compels attention with its stress on Ruskin's writing as a
moral influence, an emphasis that is to grow steadily
stronger through the century. In contrast is the sharply
derisive comment in the 'Rambler' (No. 8). As the critic
berates Ruskin for dogmatism, laments his narrowness of
education, and deplores his 'peculiar style', the basis of
hostility surely attaches in some measure to the critic's
own biased belligerence. For the 'Rambler', born less than
a year before this review, was itself a child of controversy. Founded in an attempt to mollify the spiritual
distress of Catholic converts anguished by the spiritual
upheavals of the forties, the magazine was generous in its
diversity of subjects but pointedly attacked facets of
Catholicism in the past considered sacrosanct. It is not
surprising that in Ruskin and Capes (the reviewer) Greek
met Greek for both were born for controversy; and from the
battle between the author and the critic an illuminating
document pertinent to mid-nineteenth century thought
emerges.

While in the delighted words of one journal, 'John Bull'
(25 May 1849), 'a hymn to architectural loveliness', 'The
Seven Lamps' was the subject of a judicious, discriminating
review in the 'Dublin University Magazine' (No. 7) which is
of consequence for its clear vision of the wider implications of the book. After a good deal of sensible
balancing of the pros and cons of 'The Seven Lamps' the
reviewer directs the reader beyond the importance of the
stones of a building to those abstractions that may result
from contemplation of its form and design and thus stresses
something central to any understanding of Ruskin's
aesthetic: his insistence upon commencing any study with
fundamental and practical details and reasoning from those
to higher aesthetic and philosophical concerns.

Thus it is these criticisms, varied in their perspectives, which convey the diversity of opinion of Ruskin's
work and his growth into an important figure, within a
limited circle still, in the world of art criticism. So
far, his work has been heavily in the humane disciplines;
but in the next decade a shift in emphasis will become
apparent.

III THE 1850S

'Pre-Raphaelitism'; 'The Stones of Venice I-III'; 'Modern
Painters III-IV'; 'The Political Economy of Art'; Ruskin in
the 1850s

The controversy that swirled about Ruskin in the forties
was as nothing compared with the storms he generated in the
early fifties when he chose to champion the Pre-Raphaelite
Brotherhood, that short-lived but influential movement born
in 1848 which, although closely related to painting,
spilled over into other forms of artistic expression. That
Ruskin came to their defence is not surprising for both he
and the Brotherhood were young, unorthodox men challenging
established canons and sharing some common artistic tenets.
The immediate occasion of Ruskin's defence arose from a
fierce attack in 'The Times' in May 1851 upon Millais's
picture 'Christ in the House of His Parents' - an onslaught
so savage that the artist begged his friend, the poet
Coventry Patmore, to intercede for him and the movement.
Seizing the cudgels, Ruskin countered with two letters to
'The Thunderer', both upholding the PRB and the work of
Millais and Holman Hunt in particular; and he was to write
again three years later to the same newspaper in favour of
these same artists. In fact, Ruskin remained their
defender for some time to come.
    The pamphlet, 'Pre-Raphaelitism', emanating from the
strife of aesthetic combat, appeared in November 1851 and
brought a storm upon Ruskin and the Brotherhood as seen in
the criticism of the 'Art-Journal' (No. 9) where the movement is termed 'a pseudo-system of art' and the pamphlet
itself a 'maundering medley', 'absurd', and appalling in
'tone'. Such terminology abounds in other reviews of 'pre-
Raphaelitism' as well. Indeed, most criticisms are closer
to invective than to any other form of literary expression
and suggest that Ruskin's relations with his critics, which
seemed to have softened a little at the end of the forties,
were again as strained as ever.

The three volumes comprising 'The Stones of Venice' -
the first appeared in 1851 and was followed by the second
and third in 1853 - are considered by many readers to be
Ruskin's most orderly and methodical piece of work -
perhaps because so much is placed in near 50 appendices.
Certainly 'The Stones' is the most carefully ordered
and composed of Ruskin's various multi-volumed works.
Free from diffuseness, it traces the rise and fall of the
Venetian republic whilst maintaining from start to finish

a firm, undeflected course. It is a work of spectacular
sweep and magnitude whose themes and motifs are sustained
throughout in singular equilibrium even if its initial
volume does not engage as its successors do. An obstacle
to fuller appreciation of 'The Stones I' lay in its highly
specialized contents: sub-titled 'The Foundations', the
book is an essay on the arch line, the roof, the capital
the shaft, and other elements strictly architectural,
although these individual passages are flanked by two
superb chapters, the first, The Quarry, outlining the
main direction and themes of the whole work, the other,
The Vestibule, taking the reader, in some of Ruskin's
most compelling prose, to the edge of a Venice arising
from the waves.

It is hardly surprising, therefore, that many reviewers
were once again baffled by Ruskin's approach to his subject,
although this was not so with 'Fraser's' critic (No. 10)
who, whilst remarking the architectural professionalism of
the first volume, explicates Ruskin's aims and goals in
the work as a whole. The review is admirable in its
common sense and clarity and for its freedom from the
slanted attack of, for instance, the 'Athenaeum'
(22 March 1851) and the 'Guardian' (18 February 1852),
a powerful, largely High Church weekly whose critic
opposed Ruskin's arguments with displeasing vigour.

On the other hand, several reviews suggest his large
influence and wider readership among the educated middle
classes. Unfortunately, however, too many criticisms,
even favourable to the author, incline to summarize the
architectural chapters, supplementing them with long
quotations. But much criticism, either hostile or misdirected, must have been for Ruskin somewhat offset by the
'Church of England Quarterly' (July 1851) celebrating the
advancement of his reputation or by Coventry Patmore's
praiseworthy if verbose comment in the 'British Quarterly
Review' (May 1851). In sum, the criticism attaching to the
1851 volume seems more palatable than much Ruskin received
in the forties; but it was not until two years later that
the power and quality of this central work of the age
became truly apparent.

The appearance within three months of each other of the
second and third volumes of 'The Stones of Venice' (in
July and October 1853) considerably enhanced Ruskin's
reputation for the books were widely reviewed both by the
established journals and in magazines and papers less
directed to the *cognoscenti* than to the educated middle-
class public. The challenge of the 'Athenaeum' and the
'Spectator' - joined in 1855 by the 'Saturday Review' -
to the established quarterlies and monthlies was under way,
and it is tempting to record their generally favourable

evaluations of Ruskin's huge work. But one publication in particular, 'The Times' (No. 11), which in
those years rarely reviewed books, gave the pair of volumes three long, searching criticisms which collectively
constitute a uniquely comprehensive inquiry. They are of
singular concern in that the critic boldly confronts
Ruskin's 'false or turgid imagery', his exaggeration, and
his mode of classification and places his philosophy below
his criticism and his morality; but he sees the second
volume as beneficial to art and 'to higher things than art'
and would encourage the diffusion of the books. So high
is his estimate of Ruskin that he believes no other man
living could have written 'The Stones of Venice'.
Especially noteworthy is the reviewer's approach to the
'philosophy of the imperfect' so central to Victorian
thought and so surprisingly overlooked by most of the
critics: the sixth chapter of the second volume, entitled
The Nature of Gothic, embodies this salient aspect of
Victorianism and is as vital to an understanding of the
age as a thorough knowledge of 'Sartor Resartus', 'In
Memoriam', and 'Middlemarch'. Of interest, too, is the
manner in which the critic, by disputing facets of Ruskin's
arguments, succeeds in extracting the very core of them for
the reader. Whether the reviews be by George Meredith or
by another, they are masterpieces of their kind.
    Ruskin himself (see p. 143) considered the 'Times'
articles the finest evaluations of his work to date, and
that they are so full attests to his ever-growing importance as an aesthetic presence. It is to be noted as well
that the literate middle classes read 'The Times' when
they did not regularly read the quarterlies, so the
attention given the volumes clearly suggests the developing concern of the more 'ordinary' reader for architecture
and painting in mid-Victorian England.

When 'Modern Painters III' appeared in January 1856 it bore
the daunting sub-title 'Of Many Things', and with good
reason for the reader is conducted through the most
bewildering maze of topics in this *embarras de richesses*
as its variegated contents embrace Greatness of Style, the
True and False Ideal, the Pathetic Fallacy (so widely
misunderstood by modern critics), and sundry discussions
upon landscape, classical and medieval. In many
respects Ruskin's canvas is a dazzlingly Spenserian one
enriched by a plethora of references to Shakespeare, Scott,
Homer, Holbein, Pope, Turner, Masaccio and others: the
list is endless and the names are used in appropriate
allusion.
    Once more the leading weeklies treated him quite

roughly, although the 'Saturday Review' (23 February 1856)
tempered its severity, whilst his old enemy, the 'Athenaeum'
(26 January 1856), berated him for fallaciousness and
imperiousness. But of the many criticisms, one stands pre-
eminent and that is the short notice by George Eliot in the
'Westminster Review' (No. 13). Complementing the admiration for Ruskin apparent in her correspondence, the future
novelist, recognizing the multifariousness of the book,
shows a critical sagacity rare in any age as she acknow-
ledges, without dwelling on, some weaknesses and states her
critical credo in these words: 'We value a writer not in
proportion to his freedom from faults, but in proportion
to his positive excellences - to the variety of thought he
contributes and suggests, to the amount of gladdening and
energizing emotions he excites.' And her just, compassionate perspective upon Ruskin's realism, his moral bent, and
his fineness of style render this short notice of considerably greater critical significance than many longer ones.
    The month before George Eliot's review of 'Modern
Painters III' came out there appeared, in the 'Quarterly
Review' a lengthy criticism (No. 14) of the first three
volumes of 'Modern Painters' and of Ruskin's 'Academy
Notes' for 1855. The reviewer was Lady Eastlake who
resented Ruskin's unfavourable treatment of her husband's
picture, 'Beatrice', in the 'Notes'. But it was not only
a wife's loyalty and the innate conservatism of the
'Quarterly' that led to this scurrilous piece of invective
posing as criticism. The rancour of Lady Eastlake lay
deeper than mere political, aesthetic, and 'domestic'
conviction; it went back several years to her close
friendship with Effie Ruskin, the annulment of whose
marriage to Ruskin had taken place in 1854. In the drawing-
room gossip and argument over the guilt and innocence of the
parties concerned, Lady Eastlake was a strong partisan of
Effie's.
    A reading of her masterly piece of illogicality shows
the depth to which personal attack can descend and trenchantly reveals one of the unacceptable sides of Victorian
criticism. After grudgingly remarking Ruskin's 'popularity' and turning it against him, Lady Eastlake assaults the
man, his character, and his work on one front after another
to the point where the reader can only read on appalled. (8)
    Never one to do anything by halves, Ruskin, against the
wishes of his parents, took to the lecture platform in the
fifties with a zeal and eagerness manifest by his frequent
appearances during that decade. Among his more striking
performances were the two lectures given on 10 and 13 July
1857 at the Manchester Art Treasures Exhibition and
entitled 'The Political Economy of Art' (republished with

additions in 1880 as 'A Joy for Ever'). They are of
particular significance for they form a link in content
between the social message implicit in 'The Nature of
Gothic' and those so central to 'Unto this Last' (1860,
1862); and in form, the fine sweeping passages and arresting images look back to 'The Stones of Venice II, III' even
as Janus-like they anticipate the disciplined metaphorical
clarity of 'Unto this Last'.

The importance of 'social affection' is Ruskin's main
argument in the lectures and, for him, this means that the
national economy hinges on the wise arrangement of labour,
a paternalistic government, and a humane discernment of
personal relationships. The laissez-faire, or 'let-alone
principle', he sees as the principle of death. Having set
forth these heterodox views before the Manchester School of
economics he relates them to his beliefs about the role and
place of art in society. Needless to say, the two lectures
bristle with provocative ideas revolving around the central
ones.

The critical reaction to 'The Political Economy of Art'
was, by and large, not impolite, perhaps because many
reviewers did not take his economic theories too seriously:
to many he seemed a rank amateur out of his depth in such
matters and therefore easily dismissed But, in this
instance, Ruskin moves with measured tread through the
labyrinth of arguments he sets forth: beautifully written
as the two lectures are, they do not crackle as many a
page of 'Modern Painters'. Indeed, the modulated tenor
of Ruskin's remarks appears to have reached the critic of
the 'Athenaeum' (No. 18) even if the 'Manchester Examiner
and Times' (No. 17) not surprisingly dismisses much of
what he says as 'arrant nonsense'.

Contrasting views on Ruskin's position in the fifties were
taken some years ago, by R.H. Wilenski and Professor
J.D. Jump: in two provocative pieces of writing - one an
appendix to a biography, (9) the other an article, (10)
assessing Ruskin's reputation through the eyes of the
'Spectator', the 'Athenaeum', and the 'Saturday Review' -
the two scholars came to quite different conclusions about
Ruskin's influence during the decade. However, with the
advantage of greater hindsight than the two earlier
critics enjoyed, it is now clear that Professor Jump, with
his firm conviction that Ruskin was held in respect 'by the
general cultured public and its representative critics',
was closer to the mark than Mr Wilenski.

Such, then, is the background against which one may
reflect upon Ruskin's reputation in that period when he
leaned towards social questions, although broader estimates

invariably focus upon his aesthetic writings as seen by
the passages from the 'Eclectic Magazine' (No. 19) that
point out, with almost too much reference, his genius in
leading the age 'to discern the beauty and glory of this
universe as no generation ever did before'. In addition,
much of import is remarked of his style as well, but the
article returns with deep conviction to his adoration of
the beautiful in Nature. 'Fraser's' (No. 20) ranges
freely across the Ruskinian landscape and is informative
on his qualifications as leader in the cause of art. At
the same time, the critic unflinchingly notes his weaknesses. That such full attention is given the man and his
work at this juncture is surely testimony to his importance even if the 'Edinburgh Review' (No. 21), on the other
hand, is decisively and aggressively antagonistic, denying
Ruskin the standing of 'an oracle of Art' and stooping to
personal attack. Yet the estimate, although unpleasantly
partisan, is a searching if late, determined, objection
from an old reactionary enemy carrying at the time of
writing not quite such strong ammunition as in the past
and now in competition with rising waves of recently
arrived periodicals. 'Blackwood's' (No. 22), whilst
hardly in the highest satirical vein, at least suggests
Ruskin's significance by attempting parody, a fact that
did not escape him when he wrote to his father in August
1858:

> As for the 'Blackwood', I am only annoyed because I
> think you will be a little so; for me the stimulus of
> a little mean abuse and rascality of that sort is at
> present rather good; for I have got into slightly too
> cool a state for writing well in.... writing sometimes
> requires *impatience,* and if you send me the 'Blackwood'
> it will be just a nice little spur for me. (11)

Ruskin had some ups and downs in the fifties as the
Pre-Raphaelite débâcle suggests, but considerable evidence
supports his position as a cultural influence beyond the
rarefied intellectual circle of London. The plethora of
reviews in journals, from the most **dignified** quarterlies
down to daily newspapers, testify that his audience was a
wide one growing wider all the time.

IV THE 1860S

'Modern Painters V'; 'Unto this Last'; 'Essays on
Political Economy'; 'Sesame and Lilies'; 'The Crown of Wild
Olive'; 'The Queen of the Air'; Ruskin in the 1860s,
'Lectures on Art' (1870)

Since 1854 Ruskin had given his services intermittently at
the Working Men's College, that admirable institution
designed to broaden the aesthetic interests and hone the
sensibilities of the less privileged rather than to assist
them towards greater material ends. He had, also, by the
end of the decade brought the huge cycle of 'Modern
Painters' to an end when, under parental pressure, he
produced the fifth volume in 1860. Containing some of
Ruskin's most enduring prose, 'Modern Painters V' (See
Nos 23 and 24 for differing views) is suffused with a sadness and melancholy suggestive of the writer's concern for
the national well-being, a concern especially apparent in
that memorable chapter, The Two Boyhoods, which deals with
the early lives of Giorgione and Turner and which draws
vivid pictures of the squalor and deprivation rife in
eighteenth and nineteenth century England.
By 1860, too, Ruskin was an accomplished lecturer and
had already, as noted earlier, carried his social beliefs
into the world of laissez-faire economics; but he is now
increasingly to deliver his convictions through the medium
of the shorter essay. Thus between September and November
1860 his four papers, 'Unto this Last', appear sequentially
in the 'Cornhill Magazine', at that time under the nervous
editorship of Thackeray. Both as book (which came out
under the same title in 1862) and as 'Cornhill' contributions, 'Unto this Last' once more set Ruskin down in an
arena as controversial as that generated by 'Pre-
Raphaelitism'. The response was overwhelmingly hostile as
evinced in Nos 25 and 28 where a leading weekly and a
leading quarterly attacked fiercely: and their response to
the essay and book alike were widely reflected in other
publications of the time.
Yet at least one 'democratic' newspaper, 'Lloyd's
Weekly Newspaper' (No. 26), counter-attacked, and that as
the voice of many thousands of readers. More surprising,
perhaps, is that the 'Press' (No. 27), a progressively
conservative journal, allowed 'Unto this Last' such an
easy passage. Not surprisingly, the 'Cornhill' discon-
tinued the essays with the fourth instalment and the book,
for some years subsequent to publication, failed to sell.
But 'Unto this Last' is not easily dismissed. One of

Ruskin's own favourites, it is, in spite of its unattainable goals, an exquisitely written work persuasive in its simplicity and clarity. Certainly, its message, which runs counter to the beliefs of the Manchester School, could not in its time either enchant or convince, but the common sense implicit in its reiterated theme of 'social affection' and the manner in which its statements are set forth are nothing if not winning - particularly when read today.

Ruskin followed 'Unto this Last' with a series of articles on political economy published in 'Fraser's Magazine' as 'Essays on Political Economy' and subsequently, in substantially different form, as a book entitled 'Munera Pulveris' in 1872. The 'Essays' once more assert the individual, the human being, but this time Ruskin is less the opponent of laissez-faire and more the pleader for new definitions of old concepts. The review in the 'London Review' (No. 29) is significant in its acceptance of Ruskin's power and authority; and whilst denigrating his political economy and lamenting his inability to 'master the phenomena of social life', it nevertheless sees him as an immense influence over unthinking masses. Regarded also as the 'most subtle critic since Coleridge', Ruskin, in the eyes of the reviewer, is clearly a force to be reckoned with.

Two further lectures of the sixties appeared in 1865 under the title 'Sesame and Lilies'. Dealing with subjects so seemingly disparate as libraries and women's education, they caught the eye of Anthony Trollope (No. 30), by that time a recognized novelist. His review attracts for its acknowledgment of Ruskin's influence and of his having a very large circle of readers. And Trollope's distinction between the teachings of Carlyle and Ruskin is notable as the comment of one major artist upon the work of two others of great distinction.

Both the 'Saturday Review' and the 'Fortnightly Review' (Nos 32 and 33) reflect the hostility afforded 'The Crown of Wild Olive' when it appeared in 1866. Ruskin's imprecations upon the Victorian age and man came forth with ever increasing vehemence, and in such harsh figures as the 'Goddess of Getting-on' and 'Britannia of the Market', to the point where he was not so much dismissed as a crank as savagely attacked. One expects such treatment from the 'Saturday Review' but it is singularly revealing that Trollope in the 'Fortnightly', although as a fellow-writer sensitive to Ruskin's visual power, his 'beauty of language' and the excellence of his 'early work', should berate him for 'false teaching' and 'illogicality'.

During the later sixties, though by ordinary standards

prolific enough, Ruskin, because he was suffering both
physical and emotional distress induced by his hopeless
passion for Rose La Touche, produced what was for him
relatively little. In 1869, however, 'The Queen of the
Air', a study of Greek myth, appeared and, perhaps because
it is removed from political economy, met with a favourable
reception from the press (No. 34) and in particular from
Carlyle who wrote on 17 August, 1869:

> Last week I got your 'Queen of the Air' and read it.
> Euge! Euge! No such Book have I met with for long
> years past. The one soul now in the world who seems to
> feel as I do on the highest matters, and speaks *mir aus
> dem Herzen* exactly what I wanted to hear! As to the
> natural history of those old Myths, I remained here and
> there a little uncertain, but as to the meanings you put
> into them, never anywhere. All these things I not only
> 'agree' with, but would use Thor's Hammer, if I had it,
> to enforce and put in action on this rotten world. Well
> done, well done! and pluck up a heart, and continue
> again and again. (12)

That Ruskin was recognized as a prominent intellectual
figure in the sixties, even if many contended with him, is
attested to by the essay (No. 35) by William Michael
Rossetti (for whom see No. 15) and another by Justin
McCarthy (No. 36): both assess Ruskin broadly and stress
his influence upon and relation to the times. Rossetti,
interestingly enough, follows a number of hostile critics
in regretting Ruskin's apparent departure from the field of
art, whilst McCarthy is unstinting in his respect and
enthusiasm for Ruskin and his work, comment the more
pertinent as coming from someone not a specialist in
aesthetics.

When Felix Slade, the wealthy collector and donor to the
British Museum, endowed Chairs of Fine Art at Oxford,
Cambridge, and University College (London) simultaneously,
it was fitting that Ruskin should be offered the professorship at his own university, a post he accepted with
considerable pride. Slade's triple gift is in itself
recognition of the importance of Art in a university
syllabus even if, at Oxford especially, more than one eye-
brow was raised.
    It is of value to record the critical reception (Nos. 37
and 38) to these initial Oxford lectures because they
contain some of Ruskin's finest work and, lamentably, are
among the last of his sustained and formulated pieces of
writing. He held the professorship from 1870 to 1878

(the golden years of his tenure) and was re-elected in 1883
but resigned soon after. He entered upon the first period
of his Oxford responsibilities with immense enthusiasm,
seeing himself from the very commencement as the spokesman
for the Humanities; and it has more than once been aptly
remarked that he fulfilled the four necessary conditions of
a professorship: research, ornament, professional teaching,
and general instruction. Frequently humorous and certainly
often unconventional on the lecture platform, Ruskin was, as
many records show, a highly successful university speaker.

All the while, too, he was pouring forth the thousands upon
thousands of words of that strange, inexplicable blend of
autobiography, vituperation, poignancy, prophecy, and
didacticism known as 'Fors Clavigera'. In addition, he
was involved in many other enterprises, was writing inter-
minably to the press and to friends and, tragically,
moving towards those fits of insanity that plagued the last
quarter of his life. Yet withal he remains a solitary
figure of dignity and magnitude.

V RUSKIN 1872-1900

In the last thirty years of his life Ruskin published two
major works, 'Fors Clavigera' and 'Praeterita', as well as
a number of still unrecognized short masterpieces such as
The Storm Cloud of the 19th Century and My First Editor.
Both 'Fors' and the incomplete but exquisite autobiography,
'Praeterita', subsequently came out in book form, but were
not widely reviewed: in the case of 'Fors' the diversity
and diffusion of content discouraged criticism and
'Praeterita' simply suffered an ill-deserved neglect. Save
for an attempt here and there, such 'criticism' of these
works as did appear amounted to little more than a summary
of contents as scrutiny of the 'Pall Mall Gazette' in the
eighties bears witness. Similarly, the numerous collec-
tions of Oxford lectures were little more than desultorily
noted.

Writing to Emerson on 2 April 1872 advising him to read
Ruskin's works, Carlyle remarked: 'if you can manage to get
them (which is difficult here, owing to the ways he has
towards the bibliophilic world!) (13) Controversial as
ever, Ruskin decided with the appearance of 'Fors' (the
first letters comprising it came out in 1871) to publish
and market his own books and to that end appointed George
Allen his publisher and general factotum. By thus
eliminating middlemen Ruskin incurred the displeasure of
the book trade. Furthermore, after 1874 he refrained

from sending review copies to the press with the obvious
result that the sale of his works declined. (14) His
procedures were, however, subsequently amended, and
accommodation with the booksellers was reached, and by the
early eighties his sales appear to have improved. Whilst
Ruskin's departure from the customary methods of book
marketing did not eliminate his sales, available figures
suggest that they were for some years inhibited.

On the other hand, Ruskin was the subject of numerous
articles by various men of letters in the latter third of
the nineteenth century and some of these are among Nos
39-49. For although much of Ruskin's later writing
apparently dissuaded reviewers from considering it, and
his methods of publication discouraged critical attention,
he nevertheless became a legend in his own time and
provoked intellectual inquiry. It is true that much about
him is in the form of artless reminiscence; perhaps he
will be found among 'Studies of English Authors' or as
'Master' in some formless encomium; or his residence will
be marked out as one of 'London's Literary Homes'. But
interspersed among such ephemeral writings are many perceptive estimates that suggest his vast influence upon his age
and the respect in which he was held. All the essays given
to Ruskin in Nos 39-49 are broad and far-reaching and come
from intellects strikingly different one from another;
again, each shows an individual critical inclination and
perspective upon its subject. Each, too, seems honest and
straightforward and, above all, does not shirk from the
recognition of defects in Ruskin's work. In fact, the
concluding essays form a fitting critical compendium
directed towards what is perhaps the greatest body of work
produced by a Victorian figure.

It is fitting that selections from Charles Locke
Eastlake's chapter on Ruskin in 'A History of the Gothic
Revival' (No. 39) should introduce those essays relating
the author to his age. This revival, termed by Lord Clark
in 1950 'the most widespread and influential artistic
movement which England ever produced' stirred both spiritual and secular controversy throughout the Victorian years
and was responsible for the construction of innumerable
churches and other buildings up and down the country.
Ruskin's relation to the Gothic Revival is complex in the
extreme, because his architectural theories were frequently
misunderstood and his spiritual stance shifted over the
years as is evinced, for example, in the subsequent repudiation of his anti-Catholicism manifest in the earliest
edition of 'The Seven Lamps of Architecture'. But
Eastlake's estimate, written a bare generation after that
volume, achieves importance as it sketches Ruskin's contri-

bution to the movement, defines his position as 'a lost
leader' in the Gothic Revival and, beyond that, weighs his
impracticability, impetuousness, and faulty reasoning
against his fineness of language, his contributions to the
field of pictorial art, and his keen observation of nature.
Eastlake also claims many disciples for Ruskin, converts
who previously regarded Augustus Welby Pugin as their
Messiah in the movement. The chapter is a discerning one
by a man whose study of the Gothic Revival remained the
classic textbook for almost a century.

J.J. Jarves's brief 'pen-likeness' of Ruskin (No. 40)
compels both for its stress upon Ruskin the controversialist and as an evaluation from the pen of a well-known
American art historian. Jarves, whom Ruskin knew but did
not especially care for, effected the initial meeting
between Ruskin and Charles Eliot Norton, the distinguished
Harvard Professor of Fine Art and one of Ruskin's many
correspondents. Norton, it may also be remarked, was on
friendly terms with the major Victorians and was responsible for conveying many of their ideas and writings to the
New World. But Jarves himself is, although not of Norton's
prominence or stature, an important figure in his devotion
to Ruskin, even though he differed from him in his views,
for instance, on Turner. Jarves's relations to Ruskin
point towards the rarely considered problem of Ruskin and
nineteenth century America which is a signally important
chapter in aesthetic history and has to date yielded at
least one book of considerable scope and quality. (15)

The introductory comments of Alexander Wedderburn (No.
42) prefacing his review of Ruskin's public letters rest
their significance in the placing of Ruskin's greatest
work in the pre-1860 years and the conviction that when he
turned more markedly to social criticism he lost his
audience; yet that surely might be challenged for Ruskin
doubtless widened his audiences through the medium of the
lecture in the 1860s. Similarly, such letters as 'Time
and Tide' and 'Fors Clavigera' - both post-1860 - compelled
large numbers of readers, thus enlarging Ruskin's audiences.
The point is perhaps a moot one; but Wedderburn's attention
to an audience is in itself a register of the seriousness
with which Ruskin was taken.

Vernon Lee's chapter (No. 43) on Ruskin from 'Belcaro'
is a distinctly subjective assessment of his quest for
beauty, of his endless moralization, of the subtlety of his
teachings, and of his artistic iconoclasm. But she queries
his 'impossible system', asserts his anachronistic position
and, in passing, comments on his 'mystic symbolism'. Due
close attention, however, are her final paragraphs
(pp. 383-5) maintaining that, despite his irrelevancies,

his self-contradictions, and his sterile morality, he 'has
made art more beautiful and men better without knowing it'.
Severely censorious the chapter may be, yet from it can be
distilled a fine sense of Ruskin's immense, if provocative,
contribution to his age and, by extension, to the present
time.

That William Morris's preface (No. 44) to the publication of 'The Nature of Gothic' by the Kelmscott Press (16)
was a supreme achievement should come as no surprise. It
is apparent, too, that whilst acknowledging Ruskin's
aesthetic prominence Morris directs his comment on the
great chapter to 'ethical and political' issues, for the
welfare of mankind must aspire to the 'happiness of labour'.
And his eulogium of 'Unto this Last' - a book as important
to Morris as Carlyle's 'Past and Present' was to Ruskin -
is a moving tribute to Ruskin's role as sage and prophet in
a turbulent society.

The influence of Ruskin upon Morris went back to the
latter's Oxford days in the mid-fifties, as a fellow-
student, later to become Canon Dixon, vividly recorded.

It was when the Exeter men, Burne-Jones and he [Morris]
got at Ruskin, that strong direction was given to a true
vocation - 'The Seven Lamps', 'Modern Painters', and
'The Stones of Venice'. It was some little time before
I and others could enter into this; but we soon saw the
greatness and importance of it. Morris would often
read Ruskin aloud. He had a mighty singing voice, and
chanted rather than read those weltering oceans of
eloquence as they have never been given before or since,
it is most certain. The description of the Slave Ship
or of Turner's skies, with the burden 'Has Claude given
this?' were declaimed by him in a manner that made them
seem as if they had been written for no end but that he
should hurl them in thunder on the head of the base
criminal who had never seen what Turner saw in the sky.
(17)

At that time, too, Morris defended Ruskin from the onslaughts of Elizabeth Rigby (see No. 14), and in subsequent
years he alluded frequently and respectfully to the writing
and thoughts of his master. In many respects Morris stood
in relation to Ruskin as the latter had to Carlyle,
although the two men never became close in friendship: both,
of course, were romantic idealists who sought man's
amelioration, and both, in characteristic nineteenth-
century fashion, might be said to have achieved at least
some success through failure.

Value attaches to Saintsbury on Ruskin (No. 45) if only

because he writes of 'the Ruskinian heresy', a term indicating that, in the latter years of the century, much of
Ruskin's thought was under attack from a younger generation
of aesthetes. Saintsbury recalls Ruskin's career in brief
chronology and asserts that Ruskin, more than any other
individual, was responsible for the national improvement
in artistic appreciation, discernment, and judgment. As
Saintsbury remarks:

> whereas from the thirties to the sixties, it was almost
> impossible to buy anything new that was not complacently
> hideous, from the sixties to the nineties it has always
> been possible to buy something that was at least grace-
> ful in intention.

And, although anathema to him, Saintsbury grants the power
of such writings as 'Unto this Last' and maintains that
after aesthetic Ruskin lost ground social Ruskin regained
it. Perhaps this is a trifle facile and has a touch of
the professional critic about it; but it is not wholly
bereft of truth for, certainly, many thoughtful men,
Tolstoy among them, came to respect the compassionate
socialism of Ruskin's later years.

Saintsbury's remarks also register as coming from a
powerful, if not always totally acceptable, critical voice
of the era, one that would seem at near odds with, say,
the critical principles of Arnold or, indeed, of Ruskin
himself. For Saintsbury was much the impressionist, a
critic striving to convey the charm, the pleasure, and the
grace of literature. His is an approach decried in the
present time of ephemeral critical trends, but it is to be
considered in its attempts to generate enthusiasm, awareness, and perception. To communicate elegance, taste,
loveliness, and culture are by no means the only ends of
criticism, but they surely belong to its intricate processes and are not easily disdained.

Termed by his son the 'happy humanist', Frederic
Harrison, even for a Victorian, was a man of unusually wide
and varied interests; and his remarks on Ruskin (No. 47)
constitute a trenchant analysis of his subject's prose
style. Harrison's examination is down to earth, clear,
and in the spirit of the best of the 'new criticism' of
some few years ago. It is an analysis that encourages
the reader to accept the primacy of the text for it
directs him to specific passages and to a consideration of
one of the means by which an artistic effect is obtained
instead of encouraging a fanciful weaving of esoteric and
transient critical theory.

Harrison's consideration assumes additional consequence

because his relations with Ruskin extended over several
decades, and whilst the two men were not intimates, there
existed between them a mutual regard. From the days of
the Working Men's College, where Ruskin lectured and
Harrison instructed in History, through the effusions of
'Fors Clavigera', some of whose extravagances were challenged by Harrison, to the end of Ruskin's life, the two
remained in intellectual relationship. Thus Harrison
observed his subject over many years so that it is no
accident that the best brief introduction to Ruskin is
Harrison's book published in the English Men of Letters
Series.

It is surely right that the final essay on Ruskin
(No. 49) should be by Leslie Stephen who, although no
slavish admirer of his work, was an observer of it for
some years. His essay, John Ruskin, written a few months
after the subject's death is notable for its summarizing
quality as it ranges across Ruskin's 'good style', his
explorations into aesthetics, his ability to provoke
thought about art in new ways, and his passionate sincerity.
Much of this may seem familiar, but it is Stephen's distinction that in suggesting the relationship between
Ruskin's work and society he brings to the essay a freshness and originality peculiarly his own and pertinent to
the time immediately following Ruskin's death. Conveyed
also to the reader is a sense of the idea of Ruskin as
part of and integral to his society. Similarly, Stephen
looks at the social and political inclinations of Ruskin's
writings, expressing the opinion that they play a lesser
role than the aesthetic in his career. His conviction
that Carlyle is more effective in that sphere than Ruskin
should not be ignored any more than his passage on Ruskin
as symbolist. The essay is a distinguished one and serves
the further purpose of setting forth its subject, in weakness and in strength, as he appeared at the end of a long
career to a fine intellect.

Without over-pleading for a particular approach to
Ruskin, the foregoing suggest a diversity of reasons for
adulatory or adverse or mixed criticism that he received
in the last third of his life. Sometimes certain strengths
or weaknesses are found that cut through several selections;
on the other hand, individuality of perspective, originality of reasons for this or that viewpoint, are not lacking
either. All, however, conduce to the efforts of a rapidly
changing time to ascertain the position and stature of one
of its most prolific and controversial authors.

A NOTE ON RUSKIN IN OUR OWN TIME

It is a deplorable fact that with his death in 1900
Ruskin's reputation suffered a decline from which it is
only now recovering - and that in limited fashion. (18)
Although he remains England's finest art critic and one of
its most acute social observers, as well as the individual
endowed with the most capacious, and perhaps capricious,
mind of his century, readers have simply neglected him.
True, editions of 'The King of the Golden River' and of
'Sesame and Lilies' occasionally appear, but the significantly enduring works - 'Modern Painters', 'The Stones of
Venice', 'Unto this Last', 'Praeterita', and sundry other
pieces - have received very short shrift. Unfortuantely,
too, Ruskin does not lend himself to selections or antholo-
gies; his finest work is closely wrought and excerpting
from individual chapters or passages is invariably a
deterrent to the cadence and movement of his prose as well
as a violation of the train of thought.
   The reasons for Ruskin's fall from grace are severally
attributed to his heavy moralizing, his dictatorial style
(how many paragraphs commence with the commanding
'Observe...'), his lack of humour, his didacticism, his
arrogance, and his bewilderingly varied subject-matter.
Then, too, the irresponsible manner in which he often
jumps from one topic to another - a glance at the synopsis
of any 'Fors Clavigera' letter illustrates the point -
renders him unattractive to potential readers; and it is
undeniable that a fair quota of rubbish is unhappily interspersed among too many of his writings. Again, prejudice
against his character repels readers, and although this
may appear to be an odd reason for neglecting an author it
seems an active one in Ruskin's case. Nevertheless, it is
lamentable that such an impressive body of superb prose,
searching art criticism, and social comment pertinent as
much in our times as in its own, should suffer such rebuffs.
   With marked shifts in sensibility, the development of
the cult of personality, and a distinct move away from
Victorian reticence, Ruskin was resuscitated in the 1930s
under, as Professor F.G. Townsend has aptly noted, (19)
the aegis of the late R.H. Wilenski whose 'John Ruskin: An
Introduction to Further Study of his Life and Work' (1933)
is an innovative examination of his subject as psychological enigma. Dispensing with the pieties of Victorian
biography apparent in the sturdy but reserved studies of
W.G. Collingwood (20) and Cook and Wedderburn (21) and the
briefer introductions of Frederic Harrison (22) and
A.C. Benson (23) Wilenski, by drawing up some illuminating
Synoptic Tables juxtaposing the 'Events', 'Productions',

'Repute', and 'Health' of Ruskin and by facing biographical fact heretofore discreetly put aside, set the stage
for a series of books having as their concentration
Ruskin's unconsummated marriage to Effie Gray and his subsequent unfulfilled passion for Rose La Touche. Parenthetically, it should be noted to Wilenski's credit that he was
early to deal with the symbolic relationship formulated by
Ruskin between Rose and Carpaccio's 'St Ursula'. However,
supplemented by editions of letters and diaries (24)
published over the next twenty-five or thirty years Ruskin
scholarship leaned heavily on the dramatic disclosures of
his private life. One admirable exception, however, is the
late Derrick Leon's 'Ruskin, the Great Victorian' (1949).
Because of its author's premature death, the book is marred
by typographical and other faults; but it remains to date
the most ambitious study of Ruskin, one that assimilates
with unique sensitivity all that could be garnered about
its subject to date. Leon also possessed a finely honed
critical awareness so that his biography is that most
rare of studies, a volume setting forth its subject as
man and artist in aesthetic equilibrium.
     Two other books of consequence appearing about the same
time as Leon's were Peter Quennell's 'John Ruskin: The
Portrait of a Prophet' (1949) and Joan Evans's 'John Ruskin'
(1954), both the works of distinguished belles-lettrists.
Their biographies make use of the Ruskin-Rose débâcle but
tend to place it in appropriate perspective. Neither
Mr Quennell nor Miss Evans could be termed textually
incisive, but their urbane studies suggest to the reader a
Ruskin who is not simply a psychiatric problem. They were
followed by John Rosenberg's 'The Darkening Glass' (1961)
and, recently, Joan Abse's 'John Ruskin: The Passionate
Moralist' (1980), two books of merit, if limited in scope,
the first confined to a handful of works, the second circumscribed by the emphasis pronounced by its sub-title. A
worthy addition to Ruskin biography is John Dixon Hunt's
'The Wider Sea' (1982), a sweeping study that draws heavily,
and in the main wisely, upon postwar editions of Ruskin's
letters. Professor Hunt's perspective is orthodox,
scrupulous in scholarship, and ambitious in scope. Criti-
cally, 'The Wider Sea' is perforce limited in its perceptions so that little original light is cast upon Ruskin's
writings. However, the author commendably marshals much
recent material and presents, as a totality, the
'literary navvy work' produced singly by various editors
in the last thirty years or so. So as matters now stand,
it is Leon's book, warts and all, that remains the central
study of Ruskin.
     Moving away from the biographical, there are some note-

worthy contributions of the last several years that deal
with Ruskin's aesthetic. The first of these was H. Ladd's
'Victorian Morality of Art' (1932), a pioneer work of merit
which creditably tried to disentangle Ruskin's aesthetic
theories from the mass of his writings; it was superseded
in 1971 by George Landow's 'Aesthetic and Critical Theories
of John Ruskin', a study that moves farther than Ladd's
into the higher and more esoteric realms to elucidate
Ruskinian theory. Landow's book is signally enhanced by
an uninhibited enthusiasm complemented by an intellectual
incisiveness that renders it a pleasure to read. The
author is especially successful in placing Ruskin's
theories in historical perspective, in weaving together the
strands of his Evangelical faith, his theories of Typical
and Vital Beauty, and his social views, and ultimately
clarifying Ruskin's seemingly inextricable concept of the
Imagination. The book is a major landmark in the history
of aesthetics. Another valuable work of distinction is
Professor Townsend's monograph 'Ruskin and the Landscape
Feeling' (1951) which deals in the main with 'Modern
Painters' and charts the direction of Ruskin's mind during
the vital years, 1843-60, the time of composition of those
five remarkable volumes. Yet another work, the initial
essay of 'The Last Romantics' (1949), by Graham Hough, is
central to an understanding of Ruskinian aesthetics with
its emphasis upon the visual and its anticipation, with
Wilenski, of the importance of symbolism in his writing, a
facet of investigation that is at the present time
receiving much scholarly attention. A further publication
of worth is Robert Hewison's 'John Ruskin: The Argument of
the eye' (1976) which descends directly from Graham Hough
and explores at length the importance of vision in Ruskin's
work. To be added to the aforementioned are hosts of
shorter articles within the last ten or twelve years
attesting to the growth of interest in his voluminous
oeuvre. And renewed inquiry into Turner has also height-
ened concern for Ruskin as has a dawning recognition of
the latter as artist in his own right, a felicitous example
being Paul Walton's 'The Drawings of John Ruskin' (1972).
In sum, there is a developing interest, mainly academic,
in many facets of Ruskin. It is the greater pity, therefore, that many more readable, well-edited, texts are
unavailable and that the academic world so obviously
neglects the pedagogical strength of Ruskin's writings.

NOTES

1   In vol. 40, October 1836, 543-6.
2   'Works' 3: xlii f.
3   3 December 1843.
4   For uniformly sound accounts of some of the journals
    mentioned in this volume the reader is referred to the
    'Wellesley Index to Victorian Periodicals',
    W.E. Houghton et al., 3 vols, London, 1966, 1972, 1979.
5   E.E. Kellett, The Press, in 'Early Victorian England',
    2 vols, London, 1934, II, 78-9.
6   'Works' 36: 67.
7   'Works' 3: xxxvi-xxxvii.
8   An excellent account of Lady Eastlake's relations with
    Effie and John Ruskin and her role in their marital
    disharmony is given in the highly readable 'Millais and
    and the Ruskins' by Mary Lutyens, London 1967.
9   R.H. Wilenski, 'John Ruskin', New York, n.d., 369-83.
10 J.D. Jump, Ruskin's Reputation in the Eighteen-fifties:
    The Evidence of the Three Principal Weeklies,
    'Publications of the Modern Language Association of
    America', vol. 63, June 1948, 678-85.
11 'Works' 14: 146.
12 'Works' 19: lxx.
13 'Works' 27: lxxxvii.
14 'DNB' Supplement I, xl.
15 Roger B. Stein, 'John Ruskin and Aesthetic Thought
    in America, 1840-1900', Cambridge, Mass., 1967.
16 Founded by Morris in the very early nineties.
17 J.W. Mackail, 'The Life of William Morris', 2 vols,
    London, 1912, I, 48-9.
18 Although schools and universities fail to teach Ruskin
    today, increasingly his writings are subjected to
    academic research. It is not possible nor desirable
    to enumerate here the numerous writings of recent
    years devoted to him; but the reader is referred to
    Professor F.G. Townsend's excellent biblio-critical
    article in 'Victorian Prose: A Guide to Research' ed.
    David DeLaura, Modern Language Association of America,
    New York, 1973, 219-48. The article deals at length
    with editions of Ruskin's work, selections from it,
    biolographical studies, editions of letters and
    journals, and criticism; the essay comes down to the
    year 1971. For post-1971 Ruskin bibliography readers
    might wish to consult the annual bibliographies of the
    'Publications of the Modern Language Association of
    America' and of 'Victorian Studies'. What follows in
    this section is simply a series of brief allusions to
    some of the more important works on Ruskin in more
    recent times.

19   Townsend, 'Victorian Prose', 222.
20   W.G. Collingwood, 'The Life of John Ruskin', 2 vols, 1893. Revised, abbreviated, and published in one volume in 1900.
21   The introductions to various volumes of 'Works' contain full biographical material. Also, in 1911, E.T. Cook published his two-volume biography which derives largely from the aforementioned introductions.
22   Frederic Harrison, 'John Ruskin', English Men of Letters Series, 1902.
23   A.C. Benson, 'Ruskin: A Study in Personality', 1911.
24   Of the various volumes of Ruskin's letters published in the post-war years, among the more significant are: 'The Order of Release, ed. Admiral Sir William James (1947), biased and poorly edited but important; 'Ruskin's Letters from Venice, 1851-1852', ed. J.L. Bradley (1955); 'The Letters of John Ruskin to Lord and Lady Mount-Temple', ed. J.L. Bradley (1964); 'The Winnington Letters of John Ruskin', ed. Van Akin Burd (1969); three volumes edited by Emily Lutyens, 'Effie in Venice', **'Millais and the Ruskins'**, **'The Ruskins and the Grays'** (1965, 1967, 1972 respectively); these volumes are enlivened by perceptive commentary and linking passages between the letters; 'The Ruskin Family Letters', ed. Van Akin Burd (1973). Joan Evans edited 'The Diaries of John Ruskin' (3 vols, 1956, 1958, 1959) and H.G. Viljoen published in 1971 'The Brantwood Diary of John Ruskin', a significant document in relation to Ruskin's later years.

Chronological Table

1819	John Ruskin born 54 Hunter Street, London (8 February).
1825	First Continental tour.
1826	Begins writing verse. Reads Bible, under mother's aegis, continuously, and commences lifelong reading of Homer and Scott.
1830	First tour of the Lake District. First publication, a poem 'On Skiddaw and Derwent Water', in the 'Spiritual Times'.
1831	Attends a school conducted by the Reverend Thomas Dale. Takes drawing lessons.
1832	Receives gift of Samuel Rogers's 'Italy', illustrated by Turner.
1834	First prose work published - on the colour of the waters of the Rhine - in Loudon's 'Magazine of Natural History'.
1835	Visits Venice for the first time.
1836	Falls in love with Adele Domecq, daughter of one of his father's partners in the sherry trade. Writes, but does not publish, a reply to 'Blackwood's' criticism of Turner. Matriculates as a gentleman-commoner at Christ Church, Oxford.
1837⎱ 1838⎰	Publishes The Poetry of Architecture in the 'Architectural Magazine'.
1839	Wins Newdigate Prize for poetry. Meets Wordsworth.
1840	Receives, on twenty-first birthday, a private income of £200 per annum and Turner's 'Winchelsea'. Leaves Oxford due to illness. In Rome meets Georgiana Tollemache (later Lady Mount-Temple), his main confidante over his love for Rose La Touche.
1841	Writes 'King of the Golden River' for Euphemia (Effie) Chalmers Gray whom he later marries.
1842	Receives double fourth at Oxford
1843	Publishes 'Modern Painters I'.

1846   Publishes 'Modern Painters II'.
1847   Experiences an unreturned affection for Charlotte
       Lockhart, daughter of Scott's biographer.
1848   On 10 April marries Effie Gray.
1849   Publishes 'The Seven Lamps of Architecture'.
1850   Publishes his collected poems.
1851   Publishes 'The Stones of Venice I', 'Pre-
       Raphaelitism' and 'Notes on the Construction of
       Sheepfolds'. Meets the young Millais. Friendship
       with Carlyle ripens. Turner dies in December.
1853   Publishes 'The Stones of Venice II, III'. Summer
       holiday in Scotland with Effie, Millais and latter's
       brother. Lectures in Edinburgh.
1854   Annulment of his marriage to Effie who subsequently
       marries Millais. Defends Pre-Raphaelites in letters
       to 'The Times'. Teaches at Working Men's College.
       Develops friendship with Dante Gabriel Rossetti
       and at about this time makes acquaintance of his
       brother, William Michael Rossetti, as well.
1855   Initiates 'Academy Notes'. Meets Tennyson.
1856   Publishes 'Modern Painters, III, IV', and 'The
       Harbours of England', a commentary on marine
       drawings which were produced by Turner and Thomas
       Lupton the engraver. Meets Charles Eliot Norton.
1857   Publishes 'The Elements of Drawing' (addressed to
       'My dear Reader') and 'The Political Economy of
       Art' (lectures). Over the next twenty years is to
       lecture a great deal.
1858   Agrees to give drawing lessons to Rose and Emily
       La Touche. Spiritual crisis in Turin.
1859   Publishes 'The Elements of Perspective' and 'The
       Two Paths', the latter a series of lectures.
       Visits Miss Bell's school at Winnington for the
       first time.
1860   Publishes 'Modern Painters V'. 'Unto this Last'
       serialized in 'Cornhill Magazine' (August-November).
1862   Publishes 'Essays on Political Economy' in 'Fraser's
       Magazine' (June 1862 - April 1863): publication
       suspended. Revised, the essays appear in 1872 as
       'Munera Pulveris'.
1864   Death of his father, John James Ruskin. Delivers
       more lectures including Traffic and Of Kings'
       Treasuries.
1865   Publishes 'Sesame and Lilies' (lectures).
1866   Publishes 'The Crown of Wild Olive' (lectures);
       also 'The Ethics of the Dust', a series of
       dialogues originating in Winnington. Emotionally
       distraught over his relations with Rose La Touche.

1867   Publishes 'Time and Tide, by Weare and Tyne', an
       Epistolary series devoted to social questions.
       Experiences giddiness and slightly impaired vision.
1868   A time of extreme emotional difficulty in regard to
       Rose La Touche.
1869   Publishes 'The Queen of the Air'.
1870   Delivers, in February, his inaugural lecture at
       Oxford, as first Slade Professor of Fine Art, which
       address forms part of the 'Lectures on Art' offered
       in the Hilary Term.
1871   Begins, in January, the epistolary series, 'Fors
       Clavigera', which appear monthly until 1878 and
       intermittently thereafter. Seriously ill at Matlock.
       Purchases Brantwood in the Lake District. Develops
       interest in the St George's Fund for social amelior-
       ation. Margaret Ruskin, his mother, dies aged 90.
1872   **Publishes two series of Oxford lectures:** 'Aratra
       Penetelici' (on sculpture) and 'The Eagle's Nest'
       (on science and art).
1873   Delivers some ornithological lectures, mainly at
       Oxford, which are ultimately published as 'Love's
       Meinie'. Ten further lectures, on Tuscan art, later
       appear as 'Val d'Arno'.
1874   Modification of his spiritual views.
1875   Begins part-publication of 'Mornings in Florence'.
       Initiates 'Proserpine', a botanical series. Also
       commences part-publication of the geological
       lectures to become 'Deucalion'. Dabbles in
       spiritualism. Death of Rose La Touche, aged 27.
1877   Whistler v. Ruskin case, with latter too ill to
       attend. Various treatises on art and drawing
       published. Suffers from giddiness.
1878   Guild of St George legally constituted. Attacked
       by serious mental illness.
1879   Resigns Slade professorship.
1880   Publishes Fiction, Fair and Foul in '19th Century
       Magazine'; also 'Arrows of the Chace' (miscellaneous
       correspondence) and the initial part of 'The Bible
       of Amiens".
1881} Further attacks of mental illness.
1882}
1883   Re-elected to Slade professorship and delivers
       lectures which become 'The Art of England' (1884).
       Notes his brains are 'always on the over-boil'.
1884   Delivers The Storm-Cloud of the 19th Century, one
       of his most exquisitely wrought and self-revealing
       lectures. Publishes Oxford lectures entitled 'The
       Pleasures of England'. Increasing mental turmoil.

1885   Commences his last work of greatness, the auto-
       biography 'Praeterita' which runs intermittently in
       parts until July 1889. Mental attacks once more,
1887   Struggles, after yet further mental onslaughts, to
       work. 'Hortus Inclusus' (letters) published.
1888   Makes final Continental journey from which he is
       brought home by his cousin, Joan Severn, very
       seriously disturbed. The rest is silence.
1900   Dies 20 January and is buried in Coniston churchyard.

'Modern Painters I'

1843

1. THE REVEREND JOHN EAGLES, FROM AN UNSIGNED REVIEW,
'BLACKWOOD'S MAGAZINE'

October 1843, vol. 54, 485-503

The Reverend John Eagles (1783-1855), artist and author,
attended Winchester and Oxford. From 1831 until his death
he contributed frequently to 'Blackwood's'. Eagles had
already in that magazine, in October 1836, written an
article, The Exhibitions, severely criticizing Turner.
This had aroused the young Ruskin's ire and he wrote a
sharp response - unpublished until after his death - which
is found in 'Works' 3: 635-40. Eagles appears to have been
an 'all-purpose' critic (not uncommon in the earlier nineteenth century) for his evaluations and articles range
across such diverse subjects as the wrongs of women, the
lectures of Thackeray, government, the maintenance of the
poor, church music and, of course, artistic studies and
exhibitions. In the 'Dictionary of National Biography' he
is remarked upon as 'a critic of the old-fashioned school,
to which he loyally adhered in artistic as in other
matters'. This might well explain, in part, the tenor of
the following review. See Introduction, p. 6.

We read this title with some pain, not doubting but that
our modern landscape painters were severely handled in an
ironical satire; and we determined to defend them. 'Their
superiority to *all* the ancient masters' - that was too
hard a hit to come from any but an enemy! We must measure
our man - a graduate of Oxford! The 'scholar armed,' without doubt. He comes, too, vauntingly up to us, with his
contempt for us and all critics that ever were, or will be;

we are all little Davids in the eye of this Goliath.
Nevertheless, we will put a pebble in our sling. We saw
this contempt of us, in dipping at hap-hazard into the
volume. But what was our astonishment to find, upon looking further, that we had altogether mistaken the intent of
the author, and that we should probably have not one
Goliath, but many, to encounter; while our own particular
friends, to whom we might look for help, were, alas! all
dead men. We found that there were not 'giants' in those
days, but in these days – that the author, in his most
superlative praise, is not ironical at all, but a most
serious panegyrist, who never laughs, but does sometimes
make his readers laugh, when they see his very unbecoming,
mocking grimaces against the 'old masters' – not that it
can be fairly asserted that it is a laughable book. It has
much conceit, and but little merriment; there is nothing
really funny after you have got over that he 'looks with
contempt on Claude, Salvator, and Gaspar Poussin.' This
contempt, however, being too limited for the 'graduate of
Oxford,' in the next page he enlarges the scope of his
enmity; 'speaking generally of the old masters, I refer
only to Claude, Gaspar Poussin, Salvator Rosa, Cuyp,
Berghem, Both, Ruysdael, Hobbima, Teniers (in his landscapes,) P. Potter, Canaletti, and the various Van Somethings and Back Somethings, more especially and malignantly
those who have libelled the sea.' Self-convicted of malice,
he has not the slightest suspicion of his ignorance;
whereas he *knows* nothing of these masters whom he maligns.
Still is he ready to be their general accuser – has not
the slightest respect for the accumulated opinions of the
best judges for these two or three hundred years – he puts
them by with the wave of his hand, very like the unfortunate gentleman in an establishment of 'unsound opinions,'
who gravely said – 'The world and I differed in opinion –
I was right, the world wrong; but they were too many for
me, and put me here.' We daresay that, in such establish-
ments, may be found many similar opinions to those our
author promulgates, though, as yet, none of our respectable
publishers have been convicted of a congenial folly. We
said, that he suspects not his ignorance of the masters he
maligns. Let it not hence be inferred that it is the work
of an ignorant man. He is only ignorant with a prejudice.
We will not say that it is not the work of a man who
thinks, who has been habituated to a sort of scholastic
reasoning, which he brings to bear, with no little parade
and display, upon technicalities and distinctions. He can
tutor *secundum artem*, lacking only, in the first point,
that he has not tutored himself. With all his arrangements
and distinctions laid down, as the very grammar of art, he

confuses himself with his 'truths,' forgetting that, in
matters of art, truths of fact must be referable to truths
of mind. It is not what things in all respects really are,
but what they appear, and how they are convertible by the
mind into what they are not in many ways, respects, and degrees, that we have to consider, before we can venture to
draw rules from any truths whatever. For art is something
besides nature; and taste and feeling are first - precede
practical art; and though greatly enhanced by that practical cultivation, might exist without it - nay, often do;
and true taste always walks a step in advance of what has
been done, and ever desires to do, and from itself, more
than it sees. We discover, therefore, a fallacy in the very
proposal of his undertaking,when he says that he is prepared 'to advance nothing which does not, at least in his
own conviction, *rest on surer ground than mere feeling or
taste.*' Notwithstanding, however, that our graduate of
Oxford puts his 'demonstrations' upon an equality with 'the
demonstrations of Euclid,' and 'thinks it proper for the
public to know, that the writer is no mere theorist, but
has been devoted from his youth to the laborious study of
practical art,' and that he is 'a graduate of Oxford;' we
do not look upon him as a bit the better judge for all that,
seeing that many have practised it too fondly and too ignorantly all their lives, and that Claude, and Salvator, and
Gaspar Poussin must, according to him, have been in this
predicament; and more especially do we decline from bowing
down at his dictation, when we find him advocating *any
'surer ground than feeling or taste.*' Now, considering that
thus, *in initio*, he sets aside feeling and taste, the reader will not be astonished to find a very substantial reason
given for his contempt of the afore-mentioned old masters;
it is, he says, 'because I look with the most devoted veneration upon Michael Angelo, Raffaelle, and Da Vinci, that
I do not distrust the principles which induce me to look
with contempt,' &c. We do not exactly see how these great
men, who were not landscape painters, can very well be compared with those who were, but from some general principles
of art, in which the world have not as yet found any very
extraordinary difference. But we do humbly suggest, that
Michael Angelo, Raffaelle, and Da Vinci, are in their practice, and principles, if you please, quite as unlike Messrs
David Cox, Copley Fielding, J.D. Harding, Clarkson Stanfield, and Turner - the very men whom our author brings forward as the excellent of the earth, in opposition *to all* old
masters whatever, excepting only Michael Angelo, Raffaelle,
and Da Vinci, to whom nevertheless, by a perverse pertinacity of their respective geniuses, they bear no resemblance whatever - as they are to Claude, Salvator, and

Gaspar Poussin. We do not by any means intend to speak
disrespectfully of these our English artists; but we must
either mistrust those principles which cause them to stand
in opposition to the great Italians, or to conceive that
our author has really discovered no such differing principles, and which possibly may not exist at all. Nor will
we think so meanly of the taste, the good feeling, and the
good sense of these men, as to believe that they think
themselves at all flattered by any admiration founded on
such an irrational contempt. They well know that Michael
Angelo, Raffaelle, and Da Vinci, have been admired, together with Claude, Salvator, and Gaspar Poussin, and they
do not themselves desire to be put upon a separate list.
The author concludes his introduction with a very bad
reason for his partiality to modern masters, and it is put
in most ambitious language, very readily learned in the
'Fudge School,' - a style of language with which our
author is very apt to indulge himself; but the argument it
so ostentatiously clothes, and which we hesitate not to
call a bad one, is nothing more than this, (if we understand it,) - that the dead are dead, and cannot hear our
praise; that the living are living, and therefore our love
is not lost; in short, as a *non-sequitur*, 'that if honour
be for the dead, gratitude can only be for the living.'
This might have been simply said; but we are taken to the
grave - with 'He who has once stood beside the grave,'
&c.; we have 'wild love - keen sorrow - pleasure to pulse-
less hearts - debt to the heart - to be discharged to the
dust - the garland - the tombstone - the crowned brow -
the ashes and the spirit - heaven-toned voices and heaven
- lighted lamps - the learning - sweetness by silence -
and light by decay;' all which, we conceive, might have
been very excusable in a young curate's sermon during his
first year of probation, and might have won for him more
nose-gays and favours than golden opinions, but which we
here feel inclined to put our pen across, as so we remember
many similarly ambitious passages to have been served,
before we were graduate of Oxford, with the insignificant
signification from the pen of our informator of *nihil ad
rem*. As the author threatens the public with another, or
more volumes, we venture to throw out a recommendation,
that at least one volume may serve the purpose and do the
real work of two, if he will check this propensity to
unnecessary redundancy. His numerous passages of this kind
are for the most part extremely unintelligible; and when
we have unraveled the several coatings, we too often find
the ribs of the mummy are not human. We think it right to
object, in this place, to an affectation in phraseology
offensive to those who think seriously of breaking the

third commandment - he scarcely speaks of mountains without taking the sacred name in vain; there is likewise a
constant repetition of expressions of very doubtful meaning in the first use, for the most part quite devoid of
meaning in their application. One of these is 'palpitating.' Light is 'palpitating,' darkness is 'palpitating' -
every conceivable thing is 'palpitating.' We must, however,
in justice say, that by far the best part of the book, the
laying down rules and the elucidating principles, is
clearly and expressively written. In this part of the work
there is greater expansion than the student will generally
find in books on art. Not that we are aware of the advancement of any thing new; but the admitted maxims of art are,
as it were, grammatically analysed, and in a manner to
assist the beginner in thinking upon art. To those who
have already *thought*, this very studied analysis and
arrangement will be tedious enough.

In the Definition of Greatness in Art, we find - 'If I
say that the greatest picture is that which conveys to the
mind of the spectator the greatest number of the greatest
ideas, I have a definition which will include as subjects
of comparison every pleasure which art is capable of conveying.' Now, there are great ideas which are so conflicting as to annul the force of each other. This is not
enough; there must be a congruity of great ideas - nay, in
some instances, we can conceive one idea to be so great,
as in a work of art not to admit of the juxtaposition of
others. This is the principle upon which the sonnet is
built, and the sonnet illustrates the picture not unaptly.
'Ideas of Power' are great ideas - not always are ideas of
beauty great; yet is there a tempering the one with the
other, which it is the special province of art to attain,
and that for its highest and most moral purposes. In his
'Ideas of Power,' he distinguishes the term 'excellent'
from the terms 'beautiful', 'useful,' 'good,' &c., thus -
'And we shall always, in future, use the word excellent,
as signifying that the thing to which it is applied required a great power for its production.' Is not this
doubtful? Does it not limit the perception of excellence
to artists who can alone from their practice, and, as it
were, measurement of powers with their difficulties, learn
and feel its existence in the sense to which it is limited.
The inference would be, that none but artists can be
critics, as none but artists can perceive excellence, and
we think in more than one place some such assertion is
made. This is startling - 'Power is never wasted; whatever
power has been employed, produces excellence in proportion
to its own dignity and exertion; and the faculty of perceiving this exertion, and appreciating this dignity, is

the faculty of perceiving excellence.' 'It is this faculty
in which men, even of the most cultivated taste, must
always be wanting, unless they have added practice to reflection; because none can estimate the power manifested in
victory, unless they have personally measured the strength
to be overcome.' For the word strength use difficulty, and
we should say that, to the unpractised, the difficulties
must always appear greatest. He gives, as illustration,
'Titian's flesh tint; 'it may be possible that, by some
felicitous invention, some new technicality of his art,
Titian might have produced this excellence, and to him
there would have been no such great measurement of the
difficulty or strength to be overcome; while the admirer
of the work, ignorant of the happy means, fancies the
exertion of powers which were not exerted. In his chapter
on 'Ideas of Imitation,' he imagines that Fuseli and
Coleridge falsely apply the term imitation, making 'a distinction between imitation and copying, representing the
first as the legitimate function of art – the latter as
its corruption.' Yet we think he comes pretty much to the
same conclusion. In like manner, he seems to disagree with
Burke in a passage which he quotes, but in reality he
agrees with him; for surely the 'power of the imitation'
is but a power of the 'jugglery,' to be sensible of which,
if we understand him, is necessary to our sense of imitation. 'When the object,' says Burke, 'represented in
poetry or painting is such as we could have no desire of
seeing in the reality, then we may be sure that its power
in poetry or painting is owing to the power of *imitation*.'
'We may,' says our author, 'be sure of the contrary; for
if the object be undesirable in itself, the closer the
imitation the less will be the pleasure.' Certainly not;
for Burke of course implied, and included in his sense of
imitation, that it should be consistent with a knowledge
in the spectator, that a certain trick of art was put upon
him. And our author says the same – 'Whenever the work is
seen to resemble something which we know it is not, we
receive what I call an idea of imitation.' Again – 'Now,
two things are requisite to our complete and most pleasurable perception of this: first, that the resemblance be
so perfect as to amount to a deception; secondly, that
there be some means of proving at the same moment that it
is a deception.' He justly considers 'the pleasures resulting from imitation the most contemptible that can be
received from art.' He thus happily illustrates his meaning – 'We may consider tears as a result of agony or of
art, whichever we please, but not of both at the same
moment. If we are surprised by them as an attainment of
the one, it is impossible we can be moved by them as a

sign of the other.' This will explain why we are pleased
with the exact imitation of the dewdrop on the peach, and
why we are disgusted with the Magdalen's tears by Vander-
werf; and we further draw this inevitable conclusion, of
very important consequence to artists, who have very
erroneous notions upon the subject, that this sort of imitation, which, by the deception of its name, should be
most like, is actually less like nature, because it takes
from nature its impression by substituting a sense of the
jugglery. This chapter on ideas of imitation is good and
useful. We think, in the after part of his work, wherein
is much criticism on pictures by the old masters and by
moderns, our author must have lost the remembrance of what
he has so well said on his ideas of imitation: and in the
following chapter on Ideas of Truth. 'The word truth, as
applied to art, signifies the faithful statement, either
to the mind or senses, of any fact of nature.' The reader
will readily see how 'ideas of truth' differ from 'ideas
of imitation.' The latter relating only to material objects, the former taking in the conceptions of the mind -
may be conveyed by signs or symbols, 'themselves no image
nor likeness of any thing.' 'An idea of truth exists in
the statement of *one* attribute of any thing; but an idea
of imitation only in the resemblance of as many attributes
as we are usually cognizant of in its real presence.'
Hence it follows that ideas of truth are inconsistent with
ideas of imitation; for, as we before said, ideas of imitation remove the impression by an ever-present sense of
the deception or falsehood. This is put very conclusively
- 'so that the moment ideas of truth are grouped together,
so as to give rise to an idea of imitation, they change
their very nature - lose their essence as ideas of truth -
and are corrupted and degraded, so as to share in the
treachery of what they have produced. Hence, finally,
ideas of truth are the foundation, and ideas of imitation
the distinction, of all art. We shall be better able to
appreciate their relative dignity after the investigation
which we propose of the functions of the former; but we
may as well now express the conclusion to which we shall
then be led - that no picture can be good which deceives
by its imitation; for the very reason that nothing can be
beautiful which is not true.' This is perhaps rather too
indiscriminate. It has been shown that ideas of imitation
do give pleasure; by them, too, objects of beauty may be
represented. We should not say that a picture by Gerard
Dow or Van Eyck, even with the down on the peach and the
dew on the leaf, were not good pictures. They are good if
they please. It is true, they ought to do more, and even
that in a higher degree; they cannot be works of greatness

- and greatness was probably meant in the word good. In
his chapter on Ideas of Beauty, he considers that we
derive, naturally and instinctively, pleasure from the
contemplation of certain material objects; for which no
other reason can be given than that it is our instinct -
the will of our Maker - we enjoy them 'instinctively and
necessarily, as we derive sensual pleasure from the scent
of a rose.' But we have instinctively aversion as well as
desire; though he admits this, he seems to lose sight of
it in the following - 'And it would appear that we are
intended by the Deity to be constantly under their influence, (ideas of beauty;) because there is not one
single object in nature which is not capable of conveying
them,' &c. We are not satisfied; if the instinctive desire
be the index to what is beautiful, so must the instinctive
aversion be the index to its opposite. We have an instinctive dislike to many reptiles, to many beasts - as apes.
These *may* have in them some beauty; we only object to the
author's want of clearness. If there be no ugliness there
is no beauty, for every thing has its opposite; so that we
think he has not yet discovered and clearly put before us
what beauty consists in. He shows how it happens that we
do admire it instinctively; but that does not tell us what
it is, and possibly, after all that has been said about it,
it yet remains to be told. Nor are we satisfied with his
definition of taste - 'Perfect taste is the faculty of
receiving the greatest possible pleasure from those
material sources which are attractive to our moral nature
in its purity and perfection.' This will not do; for taste
will take material sources, unattractive in themselves,
and by combination, or for their contrast, receive pleasure
from them. All literature and all art show this. That
taste, like life itself, is instinctive in its origin and
first motion, we doubt not; but what it is by and in its
cultivation, and in its application to art, is a thing not
to be altogether so cursorily discussed and dismissed. The
distinction is laid down between taste and judgment -
judgment being the action of the intellect; taste 'the
instinctive and instant preferring of one material object
to another without any obvious reason,' except that it is
proper to human nature in its perfection so to do. But
leaving this discussion of this original taste, taste in
art is surely, as it is a thing cultivated, that for which
a reason can be given, and in some measure, therefore, the
result of judgment. For by the cultivation of taste we are
actually led to love, admire, and desire many things of
which we have no instinctive love at all; so that the
taste for them arises from the intellect and the moral
sense - our judgment. He proceeds to Ideas of Relation, by

which he means 'to express all those sources of pleasure,
which involve and require at the instant of their perception, active exertion of the intellectual powers.' As this
is to be more easily comprehended by an illustration, we
have one in an incident of one of Turner's pictures, and,
considering the object, it is surprising the author did
not find one more important; but he herein shows that, in
his eyes, every stroke of the brush by Mr Turner is important - indeed, is a considerable addition to our national
wealth. In the picture of the 'Building of Carthage,' the
foreground is occupied by a group of children sailing toy-
boats, which he thinks to be an 'exquisite choice of incident expressive of the ruling passion.' He, with a whimsical extravagance in praise of Turner, which, commencing
here, runs throughout all the rest of the volume, says -
'Such a thought as this is something far above all art; it
is epic poetry of the highest order.' Epic poetry of the
highest order! Ungrateful will be our future epic poets if
they do not learn from this - if such is done by boys
sailing toy-boats, surely boys flying a kite will illustrate far better the great astronomical knowledge of our
days. But he is rather unfortunate in this bit of criticism; for he compares this incident with one of Claude's,
which we, however, think a far better and more poetical
incident. 'Claude, in subjects of *the same kind*,' (not, by
the by, a very fair statement,) 'commonly introduces people
carrying red trunks with iron locks about, and dwells, with
infantine delight, on the lustre of the leather and the
ornaments of the iron. The intellect can have no occupation
here, we must look to the imitation or to nothing.' As to
the '*infantine delight*,' we presume it is rather with the
boys and their toy-boats; but let us look a little into
these trunks - no, we may not - there is something more in
them than our graduate imagines - the very iron locks and
precious leather mean to tell you there is something still
more precious within, worth all the cost of freightage;
and you see, a little off, the great argosie that has
brought the riches; and we humbly think that the ruling
passion of a people whose 'princes were merchants, and
whose merchants princes,' as happily expressed by the said
'red trunks' as the rise of Carthage by the boys and boats;
and in the fervour of this bit of 'exquisite' epic choice,
probably Claude did look with delight on the locks and the
leather; and, whenever we look upon that picture again, we
shall be ready to join in the delight, and say, in spite
of our graduate's 'contempt,' there is nothing like leather. If the boys and boats express the beginning, the red
trunks express the thing done - merchandise 'brought home
to every man's door;' so that the one serves for an 'idea

of relation,' quite as well as the other. And here ends
section the first.

The study of ideas of imitation are thrown out of the
consideration of ideas of power, as unworthy the pursuit
of an artist, whose purpose is not to deceive, and because
they are only the result of a particular association of
ideas of truth. 'There are two modes in which we receive
the conception of power; one, the most just, when by a
perfect knowledge of the difficulty to be overcome, and
the means employed, we form a right estimate of the faculties exerted; the other, when without possessing such
intimate and accurate knowledge, we are impressed by a
sensation of power in visible action. If these two modes
of receiving the impression agree in the result, and if
the sensation be equal to the estimate, we receive the utmost possible idea of power. But this is the case perhaps
with the works of only one man out of the whole circle of
the fathers of art, of him to whom we have just referred -
Michael Angelo. In others the estimate and the sensation
are constantly unequal, and often contradictory.' There is
a distinction between the sensation of power and the
intellectual perception of it. A slight sketch will give
the sensation; the greater power is in the completion, not
so manifest, but of which there is a more intellectual
cognizance. He instances the drawings of Frederick Tayler
for sensations of power, considering the apparent means;
and those of John Lewis for more complete ideas of power,
in reference to the greater difficulties overcome, and the
more complicated means employed. We think him unfortunate
in his selection, as the subjects of these artists are not
such as, of themselves, justly to receive ideas of power,
therefore not the best to illustrate them. He proceeds to
'ideas of power, as they are dependent on execution.'
There are six legitimate sources of pleasure in execution
- truth, simplicity, mystery, inadequacy, decision, velocity. 'Decision' we should think involved in 'truth;' as
so involved, not necessarily different from velocity.
Mystery and inadequacy require explanation. 'Nature is
always mysterious and secret in her use of means; and art
is always likest her when it is most inexplicable.' Execution, therefore, should be 'incomprehensible.' 'Inadequacy' can hardly, we think, be said to be a quality of
execution, as it has only reference to means employed.
Insufficient means, according to him, give ideas of power.
We otherwise conclude - namely, that if the inadequacy of
the means is shown, we receive ideas of weakness. 'Ars est
celare artem' - so is it to conceal the means. Strangeness
in execution, not a legitimate source of pleasure, is
illustrated by the execution of a bull's head by Rubens,

and of the same by Berghem. Of the six qualities of execution, the three first are the greatest, the three last
the most attractive. He considers Berghem and Salvator to
have carried their fondness for these lowest qualities to
a vice. We can scarcely agree with him, as their execution
seems most appropriate to the character of their subjects
– to arise, in fact, out of their 'ideas of truth.' There
is appended a good note on the execution of the 'drawing-
master,' that, under the title of boldness, will admit of
no touch less than the tenth of an inch broad, and on the
tricks of engravers' handling.

Our graduate dismisses the 'sublime' in about two
pages; in fact, he considers sublimity not to be a specific term, nor 'descriptive of the effect of a particular
class of ideas;' but as he immediately asserts that it is
'greatness of any kind,' and 'the effect of greatness upon
the feelings,' we should have expected to have heard a
little more about what constitutes this 'greatness,' this
'sublime,' which 'elevates the mind,' something more than
that 'Burke's theory of the nature of the sublime is incorrect.' The sublime not being 'distinct from what is
beautiful,' he confines his subject to 'ideas of truth,
beauty, and relation,' and by these he proposes to test
all artists. Truth of facts and truth of thoughts are here
considered; the first necessary, but the latter the highest: we should say that it is the latter which alone constitutes art, and that here art begins where nature ends.
Facts are the foundation necessary to the superstructure;
the foundation of which must be there, though unseen, unnoticed in contemplation of the noble edifice. Very great
stress is laid upon 'the exceeding importance of truth;'
which none will question, reminding us of the commencement
of Bacon's essay, 'What is truth? said laughing Pilate,
and would not wait for an answer.' 'Nothing,' says our
author, 'can atone for the want of truth, not the most
brilliant imagination, the most playful fancy, the most
pure feeling (supposing that feeling *could* be pure and
false at the same time,) not the most exalted conception,
nor the most comprehensive grasp of intellect, can make
amends for the want of truth.' Now, there is much parade
in all this; surely truth, as such in reference to art, is
in the brilliancy of imagination, *in* the playfulness,
without which is no fancy, *in* the feeling, and *in* the very
exaltation of a conception; and intellect has no *grasp*
that does not grasp a truth. When he speaks of nature as
'immeasurably superior to all that the human mind can conceive,' and professes to 'pay no regard whatsoever to what
may be thought beautiful, or sublime, or imaginative,' and
to 'look only for truth, bare, clear downright statement

of facts,' he seems to forget what nature is, as adopted
by, as taken into art; it is not only external nature, but
external nature in conjunction with the human mind. Nor
does he, in fact, adhere in the subsequent part of his
work to this his declaration; for he loses it in his 'fervour of imagination,' when he actually examines the works
of 'the great living painter who is, I believe, imagined
by the majority of the public to paint more falsehood and
less fact than any other known master.' Here our author
jumps at once into his monomania – his adoration of the
works of Turner, which he examines largely and micro-
scopically, as it suits his whim, and imagines all the
while he is describing and examining nature; and not un-
frequently he tells you, that nature and Turner are the
same, and that he 'invites the same ceaseless study as the
works of nature herself.' This is 'coming it pretty
strong.' We confess we are with the majority – not that we
wish to depreciate Turner. He is, or has been, unquestionably, a man of genius, and that is a great admission. He
has, perhaps, done in art what never has been done before.
He has illuminated 'Views,' if not with local, with a
splendid truth. His views of towns are the finest; he led
the way to this walk of art, and is far superior to all in
it. We speak of his works collectively. Some of his
earlier, more imaginative, were unquestionably poetical,
though not, perhaps, of a very high character. We believe
he has been better acquainted with many of the truths of
nature, particularly those which came within the compass
of his line of views, than any other artist, ancient or
modern; but we believe he has neglected others, and some
important ones too, and to which the old masters paid the
greatest attention, and devoted the utmost study. We have
spoken frequently, unhesitatingly, of the late extraordinary productions of his pencil, as altogether unworthy his
real genius; it is in these we see, with the majority of
the public, 'more falsehood and less fact' than in any
other known master – a defiance of the 'known truths' in
drawing, colour, and composition, for which we can only
account upon the supposition, that his eye misrepresents
to him the work of his hands. We see, in the almost adoration of his few admirers, that if it be difficult, and not
always dependent, on merit to attain to eminence in the
world's estimation, it is nearly as difficult altogether
to fall from it; and that nothing the artist can do,
though they be the veriest 'ægri somnia,' will separate
from him habitual followers, who, with a zeal in proportion to the extravagances he may perpetrate, will lose
their relish for, and depreciate the great masters, whose
very principles he seems capriciously in his age to set

aside, and they will from followers become his worshippers,
and in pertinacity exact entire compliance, and assent to
every, the silliest, dictation of their monomania. We subjoin a specimen of this kind of worship, which will be
found fully to justify our observations, and which, considering it speaks of mortal man, is somewhat blaspheming
Divine attributes; we know not really whether we should
pity the condition of the author, or reprehend the passage.
After speaking of other modern painters, who are so superior to the old, he says: 'and Turner - glorious in conception - unfathomable in knowledge - solitary in power -
with the elements waiting upon his will, and the night and
the morning obedient to his call, sent as a prophet of God
to reveal to men the mysteries of his universe, standing,
like the great angel of the Apocalypse, clothed with a
cloud, and with a rainbow upon his head, and with the sun
and stars given into his hand.' Little as we are disposed
to laugh at any such aberrations, we must, to remove from
our minds the greater, the more serious offence, indulge
in a small degree of justifiable ridicule; and ask what
will sculptor or painter make of this description, should
the reluctant public be convinced by the 'graduate,' and
in their penitential reverence order statue or painting of
Mr Turner for the Temple of Fame, which it is presumed
Parliament, in their artistic zeal, mean to erect? How
will they venture to represent Mr Turner looking like an
angel - in that dress which would make any man look like a
fool - his cloud nightcap tied with rainbow riband round
his head, calling to night and morning, and little caring
which comes, making 'ducks and drakes' of the sun and the
stars, put into his hand for that purpose? We will only
suggest one addition, as it completes the grand idea, and
is in some degree characteristic of Mr Turner's peculiar
execution, that, with the sun and stars, there should be
delivered into his hand a comet, whose tail should serve
him for a brush, and supply itself with colour. We do not
see, however, why the moon should have been omitted; sun,
moon, and stars, generally go together. Is the author as
jealous as the 'majority of the public' may be suspicious
of her influence? And let not the reader believe that
Mr Turner is thus called a prophet in mere joke, or a
fashion of words - his prophetic power is advanced in
another passage, wherein it is asserted that Mr Turner not
only tells us in his works what nature has done in hers,
but what she will do. 'In fact,' says our author, 'the
great quality abour Mr Turner's drawings, which more especially proves their transcendant truth, is the capability
they afford us of reasoning on past and future phenomena.'
The book teems with extravagant bombastic praise like this.

Mr Turner is more than the Magnus Apollo. Yet other English artists are brought forward, immediately preceding
the above panegyric; we know not if we do them justice, by
noticing what is said of them. There is a curious description of David Cox lying on the ground 'to possess his
spirit in humility and peace,' of Copley Fielding, as an
aeronaut, 'casting his whole soul into space.' We really
cannot follow him, 'exulting like the wild deer in the
motion of the swift mists,' and 'flying with the wild wind
and sifted spray along the white driving desolate sea,
with the passion for nature's freedom burning in his
heart;' for such a chase and such a heart-burn must have a
frightful termination, unless it be mere nightmare. We see
'J.D. Harding, brilliant and vigorous,' &c., 'following
with his quick, keen dash the sunlight into the crannies
of the rocks, and the wind into the tangling of the grass,
and the bright colour into the fall of the sea-foam -
various, universal in his aim;' after which very fatiguing
pursuit, we are happy to find him 'under the shade of some
spreading elm;' yet his heart is oak - and he is 'English,
all English at his heart.' But Mr Clarkson Stanfield is a
man of men - 'firm, and fearless, and unerring in his
knowledge - stern and decisive in his truth - perfect and
certain in composition - shunning nothing, concealing nothing, and falsifying nothing - never affected, never morbid, never failing - conscious of his strength, but never
ostentatious of it - acquainted with every line and hue of
the deep sea - chiseling his waves with unhesitating knowledge of every curve of their anatomy, and every moment of
their motion - building his mountains rock by rock, with
wind in every fissure, and weight in every stone - and
modeling the masses of his sky with the strength of tempest in their every fold.' It is curious - yet a searcher
after nature's truths ought to know, as he is here told,
that waves may be anatomized, and must be *chiseled*, and
that mountains are and ought to be *built* up rock by rock,
as a wall brick by brick, no easy task considering that
there is a disagreeable 'wind in every fissure, and weight
in every stone' - and that the aerial sky, incapable to
touch, must be 'modeled in masses.' All this is given
after an equally extravagant abuse of Claude, of Salvator
Rosa, and Poussin. He finds fault with Claude, because his
sea does not 'upset the flower-pots on the wall,' forgetting that they are put there because the sea could not -
with Salvator, for his 'contemptible fragment of splintry
crag, which an Alpine snow-wreath' (which would have no
business there) 'would smother in its first swell, with a
stunted bush or two growing out of it, and a Dudley or
Halifax-like volume of smoke for a sky' - with Poussin,

for that he treats foliage (whereof 'every bough is a
revelation!') as 'a black round mass of impenetrable paint,
diverging into feathers instead of leaves, and supported
on a stick instead of a trunk.' A page or two from this,
our author sadly abuses poor Canaletti, as far as we can
see, for not painting a tumbled-down wall, which perhaps,
in his day, was not in a ruinous state at all; it is a
curious passage – and shows how much may be made out of a
wall. Pyramus's chink was nothing to this – behold a
speciment of 'fine writing!' 'Well: take the next house.
We remember that too; it was mouldering inch by inch into
the canal, and the bricks had fallen away from its
shattered marble shafts, and left them white and skeleton-
like, yet with their fretwork of cold flowers wreathed
about them still, untouched by time; and through the rents
of the wall behind them there used to come long sunbeams
gleamed by the weeds through which they pierced, which
flitted, and fell one by one round those grey and quiet
shafts, catching here a leaf and there a leaf, and gliding
over the illumined edges and delicate fissures until they
sank into the deep dark hollow between the marble blocks
of the sunk foundation, lighting every other moment one
isolated emerald lamp on the crest of the intermittent
waves, when the wild sea-weeds and crimson lichens drifted
and crawled with their thousand colours and fine branches
over its decay, and the black, clogging, accumulated limpets hung in ropy clusters from the dripping and tinkling
stone. What has Canaletti given us for this?' Alas,
neither a *crawling* lichen, nor *clogging* limpets, nor a
tinkling stone, but 'one square, red mass, composed of –
let me count – five-and-fifty – no, six-and-fifty – no, I
was right at first, five-and-fifty bricks,' &c. The picture, if it be painted by the graduate, must be a curiosity – we can make neither head nor tail of his words. But
let us find another strange specimen – where he compares
his own observations of nature with Poussin and Turner.
Every one must remember a very pretty little picture of no
great consequence by Gaspar Poussin – a view of some
buildings of a town said to be Aricia, the modern La
Riccia – just take it for what it is intended to be, a
quiet, modest, agreeable scene – very true and sweetly
painted. How unfit to be compared with an ambitious description of a combination of views from Rome to the Alban
Mount, for that is the range of the description, though,
perhaps, the description is taken from a poetical view of
one of Turner's incomprehensibles, which may account for
the conclusion, 'Tell me who is likest this, Poussin or
Turner?' Now, though Poussin never intended to be like
this, let us see the graduate's description of it. We know

the little town; it received us as well as our author,
having left Rome to visit it.

Egressum magnâ me accepit Aricia Roma.

Our author, however, doubts if it be the place, though
he unhesitatingly abuses Poussin, as if he had fully intended to have painted nothing else than what was seen by
the travelling graduate. 'At any rate, it is a town on a
hill, wooded with two-and-thirty bushes, of very uniform
size, and possessing about the same number of leaves each.
These bushes are all painted in with one dull opaque brown,
becoming very slightly greenish towards the lights, and
discover in one place a bit of rock, which of course would
in nature have been cool and grey beside the lustrous hues
of foliage, and which, therefore, being moreover completely in shade, is consistently and scientifically painted of
a very clear, pretty, and positive brick red, the only
thing like colour in the picture. The foreground is a
piece of road, which, in order to make allowance for its
greater nearness, for its being completely in light, and,
it may be presumed, for the quantity of vegetation usually
present on carriage roads, is given in a very cool green-
grey, and the truthful colouring of the picture is completed by a number of dots in the sky on the right, with a
stalk to them, of a sober and similar brown.' We need not
say how unlike is this description of the picture. We pass
on to –

[Quotes from 'Not long ago' to 'blaze of the sea', 'Works'
3: 278-80.]

In verity, this is no 'Compana Supellex.' It is a riddle!
Is he going up or down hill – or both at once? No human
being can tell. He did not like the 'sulphur and treacle'
of 'our Scotch connoisseurs;' but what colours has he not
added here to his sulphur – colours, too, that we fear for
the 'idea of truth' cannot coexist! And how, in the name
of optics, could it be possible for any painter to take in
all this, with the '*fathomless intervals*,' into an angle
of vision of forty-five degrees? It is quite superfluous to
ask 'who is likest this, Turner or Poussin?' There immediately follows a remark upon another picture in the
National Gallery, the 'Mercury and Woodman,' by Salvator
Rosa, than which nothing can be more untrue to the original. He asserts that Salvator painted the distant mountains,
'throughout, without one instant of variation. But what is
its colour? *Pure* sky-blue, without one grain of grey, or
any modifying hue whatsoever; – the same brush which had

just given the bluest parts of the sky, has been more
loaded at the same part of the palette, and the whole
mountain thrown in with unmitigated ultramarine.' Now the
fact is, that the picture has, in this part, been so injured, that it is hard to say what colour is under the
dirty brown-asphaltum hue and texture that covers it. It
is certainly not blue now, not 'pure blue' - unless pictures change like the cameleon. We know the picture well,
and have seen another of the same subject, where the mountains have variety, and yet are blue. We believe a great
sum was given for this picture - far more than its condition justifies. We must return - we left the graduate
discussing ideas of truth. There is a chapter to show that
the truth of nature is not to be discerned by the uneducated senses. As we do not perceive all sounds that enter
the ear, so do we not perceive all that is cognizable by
the eye - we have, that is, a power of nullifying an impression; that this habit is so common, that from the
abstraction of their minds to other subjects, there are
probably persons who never saw any thing beautiful. Sensibility to the power of beauty is required - and to see
rightly, there should be a perfect state of moral feeling.
Even when we think we see with our eyes, our perception is
often the result of memory, of previous knowledge; and it
is in this way he accounts for the mistake painters and
others make with respect to Italian skies. What will Mr
Uwins and his followers in blue say to this, alas -
Italian skies are not blue? 'How many people are misled by
what has been said and sung of the serenity of Italian
skies, to suppose they must be more blue than the skies of
the north, and think that they see them so; whereas the
sky of Italy is far more dull and grey in colour than the
skies of the north, and is distinguished only by its intense repose of light.' Benevenuto Cellini speaks of the
mist of Italy. 'Repose of light' is rather a novelty - he
is fond of it. But then Turner paints with pure white -
for ourselves we are with the generality of mankind who
prefer the 'repose' of shade. 'Ask a connoisseur, who has
scampered over all Europe, the shape of the leaf of an
elm, and the chances are ninety to one that he cannot
tell you; and yet he will be voluble of criticism on every
painted landscape from Dresden to Madrid' - and why not?
The chances are ninety to one that the merits of not a
single picture shall depend upon this knowledge, and yet
the pictures shall be good and the connoisseur right.
One man sees what another does not see in portraits. Undoubtedly; but how any one is to find in a portrait the
following, we are at a loss to conceive. 'The third has
caught the trace of all that was most hidden and most

mighty, when all hypocrisy and all habit, and all petty
and passing emotion - the *ice, and the bank, and the foam
of the immortal river - were shivered and broken, and
swallowed up in the awakening of its inward strength,'* &c.
How can a man with a pen in his hand let such stuff as
this drop from his fingers' ends?

In the chapter 'on the relative importance of truths,'
there is a little needless display of logic - needless,
for we find, after all, he does not dispute 'the kind of
truths proper to be represented by the painter or sculptor,' though he combats the maxim that general truths are
preferable to particular. His examples are quite out of
art, whether one be spoken of as a man or as Sir Isaac
Newton. Even logically speaking, Sir Isaac Newton may be
the *whole* of the subject, and as such a whole might require a generality. There may be many particulars that are
best sunk. So, in a picture made up of many parts, it
should have a generality totally independent of the parti-
cularities of the parts, which must be so represented as
not to interfere with that general idea, and which may be
altogether in the mind of the artist. This little discussion seems to arise from a sort of quibble on the word
important. Sir Joshua and others, who abet the generality
maxim, mean no more than that it is of importance to a
picture that it contain, fully expressed, one general
idea, with which no parts are to interfere, but that the
parts will interfere if each part be represented with its
most particular truth - and that, therefore, drapery
should be drapery merely, not silk or satin, where high
truths of the subject are to be impressed.

'Colour is a secondary truth, therefore less important
than form.' 'He, therefore, who has neglected a truth of
form for a truth of colour, has neglected a greater truth
for a less one.' It is true with regard to any individual
object - but we doubt if it be always so in picture. The
character of the picture may not at all depend upon form -
nay, it is possible that the painter may wish to draw away
the mind altogether from the beauty, and even correctness
of form, his subject being effect and colour, that shall
be predominant, and to which form shall be quite subservient, and little more of it than such as chiaro-scuro
shall give; and in such a case colour is the more important truth, because in it lies the sentiment of the picture. The mystery of Rembrandt would vanish were beauty of
form introduced in many of his pictures. We remember a
picture, the most impressive picture perhaps ever painted,
and that by a modern too, Danby's 'Opening of the Sixth
Seal.' Now, though there are fine parts in this picture,
the real power of the picture is in its colour - it is

awful. We are no enemy to modern painters; we think this a
work of the highest genius - and as such, should be most
proud to see it deposited in our National Gallery. We further say, that in some respects it carries the art beyond
the old practice. But, then, we may say it is a new subject. 'It is not certain whether any two people see the
same colours in things.' Though that does not affect the
question of the importance of colour, for it must imply a
defect in the individuals, for undoubtedly there is such a
thing as nature's harmony of colour; yet it may be admitted, that things are not always known by their colour;
nay, that the actual local colour of objects is mainly
altered by effects of light, and we are accustomed to see
the same things, *quoad* colour, variously presented to us -
and the inference that we think artists may draw from this
fact is, that there will be allowed them a great license
in all cases of colour, and that naturalness may be preserved without exactness - and here will lie the value of
a true theory of the harmony of colours, and the application of colouring to pictures, most suitable to the intended impression, not the most appropriate to the objects.
We have often laid some stress upon this in the pages of
'Maga' - and we think it has been too much omitted in the
consideration of artists. Every one knows what is called a
Claude glass. We see nature through a coloured medium -
yet we do not doubt that we are looking at nature - at
trees, at water, at skies - nay, we admire the colour -
see its harmony and many beauties - yet we know them to be,
if we may use the term, misrepresented. While speaking of
the Claude glass, it will not be amiss to notice a peculiarity. It shows a picture - when the unaided eye will
not; it heightens illumination - brings out the most delicate lights, scarcely perceptible to the naked eye, and
gives greater power to the shades, yet preserves their
delicacy. It seems to annihilate all those rays of light,
which, as it were, intercept the picture - that come between the eye and the object. But to return to colour - we
say that it must, in the midst of its license, preserve
its naturalness - which it will do if it have a meaning in
itself. But when we are called upon to question what is
the meaning of this or that colour, how does its effect
agree with the subject? why is it outrageously yellow or
white, or blue or red, or a jumble of all these? - which
are questions, we confess, that we and the public have
often asked, with regard to Turner's late pictures - we do
not acknowledge a naturalness - the license has been
abused - not 'sumpta pudenter.' It is not because the
vividness of 'a blade of grass or a scarlet flower' shall
be beyond the power of pigment, that a general glare and

obtrusion of such colours throughout a picture can be
justified. We are astonished that any man with eyes should
see the unnaturalness in colour of Salvator and Titian,
and not see it in Turner's recent pictures, where it is
offensive because more glaring. Those masters sacrificed,
if it be a sacrifice, something to repose - repose is *the*
thing to be sacrificed according to the notions of too
many of our modern schools. It is likewise singular, after
all the falsehoods which he asserts the old masters to
have painted, that he should speak of 'imitation' - as
their whole aim, their sole intention to deceive; and yet
he describes their pictures as unlike nature in the detail
and in the general as can be, strangely missing their
object - deception. We fear the truths, particulars of
which occupy the remainder of the volume - of earth, water,
skies, &c. - are very minute truths, which, whether true
or false, are of very little importance to art, unless it
be to those branches of art which may treat the whole of
each particular truth as the whole of a subject, a line of
art that may produce a multitude of works, like certain
scenes of dramatic effect, surprising to see once, but are
soon powerless - can we hope to say of such, 'decies
repetita placebunt?' They will be the fascinations of the
view schools, nay, may even delight the geologist and the
herbalist, but utterly disgust the imaginative. This kind
of 'knowledge' is not 'power' in art. We want not to see
water anatomized; the Alps may be tomahawked and scalped by
geologists, yet may they be sorry painters. And we can
point to the general admiration of the world, learned and
unlearned, that a 'contemptible fragment of a splintery
crag' has been found to answer all the purposes of an impression of the greatness of nature, her free, great, and
awful forms, and that depth, shades, power of chiaro-
scuro, are found in nature to be strongest in objects of
no very great magnitude; for our vision requires nearness,
and we want not the knowledge that a mountain is 20,000
feet high, to be convinced that it is quite large enough
to crush man and all his works; and that they, who, in
their terror of a greater pressure, would call upon the
mountains to cover them, and the holes of rocks to hide
them, would think very little of the measurement of the
mountains, or how the caverns of the earth are made.
Greatness and sublimity are quite other things.

We shall not very systematically carry our views,
therefore, into the detail of these truths, but shall just
pick here and there a passage or so, that may strike us
either for its utility or its absurdity.

With regard to truth of tone, he observes - that 'the
finely-toned pictures of the old masters are some of the

notes of nature played two or three octaves below her key,
the dark objects in the middle distance having precisely
the same relation to the light of the sky which they have
in nature, but the light being necessarily infinitely
lowered, and the mass of the shadow deepened in the same
degree. I have often been struck, when looking at a
camera-obscura on a dark day, with the exact resemblance
the image bore to one of the finest pictures of the old
masters.' We only ask if, when looking at the picture in
the camera, he did not still recognize nature - and then,
if it was beautiful, we might ask him if it was not *true*;
and then when he asserts our highest light being white
paper, and that not white enough for the light of nature -
we would ask if, in the camera, he did not see the picture
on white paper - and if the whiteness of paper be not the
exact whiteness of nature, or white as ordinary nature?
But there is a quality in the light of nature that mere
whiteness will not give, and which, in fact, is scarcely
ever seen in nature merely in what is quite white; we
mean brilliancy - that glaze, as it were, between the object and the eye which makes it not so much light as
bright. Now this quality of light was thought by the old
masters to be the most important one of light, extending
to the half tones and even in the shadows, where there is
still light; and this by art and lowering the tone they
were able to give, so that we see not the value of the
praise when he says -

'Turner starts from the beginning with a totally different principle. He boldly takes pure white - and justly,
for it is the sign of the most intense sunbeams - for his
highest light, and lamp-black for his deepest shade,' &c.
Now, if white be the sign of the most intense sunbeams, it
is as we never wish to see them; what under a tropical sun
may be white is not quite white with us; and we always
find it disagreeable in proportion as it approaches to
pure white. We never saw yet in nature a sky or a cloud
pure white; so that here certainly is one of the 'fallacies,' we will not call them falsehoods. But as far as
we can judge of nature's ideas of light and colour, it is
her object to tone them down, and to give us very little,
if any, of this raw white, and we would not say that the
old masters did not follow her method of doing it. But we
will say, that the object of art, at any rate, is to make
all things look agreeable; and that human eyes cannot bear
without pain those raw whites and too searching lights;
and that nature has given to them an ever present power of
glazing down and reducing them, when she added to the eye
the sieve, our eyelashes, through which we look, which we
employ for this purpose, and desire not to be dragged at

any time - 'Sub curru nimium propinqui solis.'

After this praise of white, one does not expect - 'I
think nature mixes yellow with almost every one of her
hues;' but this is said merely in aversion to purple. 'I
think the first approach to viciousness of colour in any
master, is commonly indicated chiefly by a prevalence of
purple and an absence of yellow.' 'I am equally certain
that Turner is distinguished from all the vicious colourists of the present day, by the foundation of all his
tones being black, yellow, and intermediate greys, while
the tendency of our common glare-seekers is invariably to
pure, cold, impossible purples.'

> Silent nymph, with curious eye,
> Who the *purple* evening lie,

saith Dyer, in his landscape of 'Grongar Hill.' The
'glare-seekers' is curious enough, when we remember the
graduate's description of landscapes, (of course Turner's,)
and his excursions; but we think we have seen many purples
in Turner, and that opposed to his flaming red in sunsets.
He prefers warmth where most people feel cold - this is
not surprising; but as to picture 'is it true?' 'My own
feelings would guide me rather to the warm greys of such
pictures as the "Snow-Storm," or the glowing scarlet and
gold of the "Napoleon" and the "Slave Ship."' The two
latter must be well remembered by all Exhibition visitors;
they were the strangest things imaginable in colour as in
every particle that should be art or nature. There is a
whimsical quotation from Wordsworth, the 'keenest-eyed.'
His object is to show the strength of shadow - how 'the
shadows on the trunk of the tree become darker and more
conspicuous than any part of the boughs or limbs;' so, for
this strength and blackness, we have -

> At the root
> Of that tall pine, the shadow of whose bare
> And slender stem, while here I sit at eve,
> Oft stretches tow'rds me, like a long straight path,
> Traced *faintly* in the greensward.

'Of the truth of space,' he says that 'in a real landscape, we can see the whole of what would be called the
middle distance and distance together, with facility and
clearness; but while we do so, we can see nothing in the
foreground beyond a vague and indistinct arrangement of
lines and colours; and that if, on the contrary, we look
at any foreground object, so as to receive a distinct impression of it, the distance and middle distance become

all disorder and mystery. And therefore, if in a painting
our foreground is any thing, our distance must be nothing,
and *vice versa*.' 'Now, to this fact and principle, no
landscape painter of the old school, as far as I remember,
ever paid the slightest attention. Finishing their foregrounds clearly and sharply, and with vigorous impression
on the eye, giving even the leaves of their bushes and
grass with perfect edge and shape, they proceeded into the
distance with equal attention to what they could see of
its details,' &c. But he had blamed Claude for not having
given the exactness and distinct shape and colour of
leaves in foreground. The fact is, the picture should be
as a piece of nature framed in. Within that frame, we
should not see distinctly the foreground and distance at
the same instant: but, as we have stated, the eye and mind
are rapid, the one to see, the other to combine; and as a
horse let loose into a field, runs to the extremity of it
and around it, the first thing he does - so do we range
over every part of the picture, but with wondrous rapidity,
before our impression of the whole is perfect. We must not,
therefore, slur over any thing; the difficulty in art is
to give the necessary, and so made necessary, detail of
foreground unostenstatiously - to paint nothing, that
which is to tell as nothing, but so as it shall satisfy
upon examination; and we think so the old masters did
paint the foregrounds, particularly Gaspar Poussin - so
Titian, so Domenichino, and all of any merit. But this is
merely an introduction, not to a palliation of, but the
approbation and praise of a glaring defect in Turner.
'Turner introduced a new era in landscape art, by showing
that the foreground might be sunk for the distance, and
that it was possible to express immediate proximity to the
spectator, without giving any thing like completeness to
the forms of the near objects.' We are now, therefore,
prepared for an absurd 'justification of the want of drawing in Turner's figures,' thus contemptuously, with regard
to all but himself, accounted for. 'And now we see the
reason for the singular, and, to the ignorant in art, the
offensive execution of Turner's figures. I do not mean to
assert that there is any reason whatsoever for *bad* drawing,
(though in landscape it matters exceedingly little;) but
there is both reason and necessity for that want of drawing which gives even the nearest figures round balls with
four pink spots in them instead of faces, and four dashes
of the brush instead of hands and feet; for it is totally
impossible that if the eye be adapted to receive the rays
proceeding from the utmost distance, and some partial impression from all the distances, it should be capable of
perceiving more of the forms and features of near figures

than Turner gives.' Yet what wonderful detail has he required from Canaletti and others? - But is there any
reason why we should have '*pink* spots?' - is there any
reason why Turner's foreground figures should resemble
penny German dolls? - and for the reason we have above
given, there ought to be reason why the figures should be
made out, at least as they are in a camera obscura. We
here speak of nature, of 'truth,' and with him ask, it may
be all very well - but 'is it true?' But we have another
fault to find with Turner's figures; they are often bad in
intention. What can be more absurd and incongruous, for
instance, than in a picture of 'elemental war' - a sea-
coast - than to put a child and its nurse in foreground,
the child crying because it has lost its hoop, or some
such thing? It is according to his truth of space, that
distances should have every 'hair's-breadth' filled up,
all its 'infinity,' with infinities of objects, but that
whatever is near, if figures, may be 'pink spots,' and
'four dashes of the brush.' While with Poussin - 'masses
which result from the eclipse of details are contemptible
and painful;' and he thinks Poussin has but 'meaningless
tricks of clever execution' - forgetting that all art is
but a trick - yet one of those tricks worth knowing, and
yet which how few have acquired! Surely our author is not
well acquainted with Hobbima's works; that painter had not
a niggling execution. 'A single dusty roll of Turner's
brush is more truly expressive of the infinity of foliage,
than the niggling of Hobbima could have rendered his canvass, if he had worked on it till doomsday.' Our author
seems to have studied skies, such as they are in Turner or
in nature. He talks of them with no inconsiderable swagger
of observation, while the old masters had no observation
at all; - 'their blunt and feelingless eyes never perceived it in nature; and their untaught imaginations were
not likely to originate it in study.' What is the *it*, will
be asked - we believe it to be a 'cirrus,' and that a
cirrus is the subject of a chapter to itself. This beard
of the sky, however, instead of growing below, is quite
above, 'never formed below an elevation of at least 15,000
feet, are motionless, multitudinous lines of delicate
vapour, with which the blue of the open sky is commonly
streaked or speckled after several days of fine weather.
They are more commonly known as "mare's tails."' Having
found this 'mare's nest,' he delights in it. It is the
glory of modern masters. He becomes inflated, and lifts
himself 15,000 feet above the level of the understanding
of all old masters, and, as we think, of most modern
readers, as thus: - 'One alone has taken notice of the
neglected upper sky; it is his peculiar and favourite

field; he has watched its every modification, and given
its every phase and feature; at all hours, in all seasons,
he has followed its passions and its changes, and has
brought down and laid open to the world another apocalypse
of heaven.' Very well, considering that the cirrus never
touches even the highest mountains of Europe, to follow
its phase (query faces) and feature 15,000 feet high, and
given pink dots, four pink dots for the faces and features
of human beings within fifteen feet of his brush. We will
not say whether the old masters painted this cirrus or
not. We believe they painted what they and we see, at
least so much as suited their pictures – but as they were
not, generally speaking, exclusively sky-painters, but
painters of subjects to which the skies were subordinate,
they may be fairly held excused for this their lack of
ballooning after the 'cirrus;' and we thank them that they
were not 'glare-seekers,' 'threading' their way, with it
before them, 'among the then transparent clouds, while all
around the sun is unshadowed fire.' We lose him altogether
in the 'central cloud region,' where he helps nature
pretty considerably as she 'melts even the unoccupied
azure into palpitating shades,' and hopelessly turns the
corner of common observation, and escapes among the 'fifty
aisles penetrating through angelic chapels to the shechi-
nah of the blue.' We must expect him to descend a little
vain of his exploit, and so he does – and wonders not that
the form and colour of Turner should be misunderstood, for
'they require for the full perception of their meaning and
truth, such knowledge and such time as not one in a thousand possesses, or can bestow.' The inference is, that the
graduate has graduated a successful phæton, driving Mr
Turner's chariot through all the signs of the zodiac. So
he sends all artists, ancient and modern, to Mr Turner's
country, as 'a magnificent statement, all truth' – that
is, 'impetuous clouds, twisted rain, flickering sunshine,
fleeting shadow, gushing water, and oppressed cattle' –
yes, more, it wants repose, and there it is – 'High and
far above the dark volumes of the swift rain-cloud, are
seen on the left, through their opening, the quiet, horizontal, silent flakes of the highest cirrus, resting in
the repose of the deep sky;' and there they are, 'delicate, soft, passing vapours,' and there is 'the exquisite
depth and *palpitating* tenderness of the blue with which
they are islanded.' Thus *islanded in tenderness*, what
wonder is it if Ixion embraced a cloud? Let not the modern
lover of nature entertain such a thought; 'Bright Phœbus'
is no minor canon to smile complacently on the matter; he
has a jealousy in him, and won't let any be in a melting
mood with the clouds but himself; he tears aside your

curtains, and steam-like rags of capricious vapour – 'the
mouldering sun, seeming not far away, but burning like a
red hot ball beside you, and as if you could reach it,
plunges through the rushing wind and rolling cloud with
headlong fall, as if it meant to rise no more, dyeing all
the air about it with blood.' This is no fanciful description, but among the comparative views of nature's and of
Turner's skies, as seen, and verified upon his affidavit,
by a graduate of Oxford; who may have an indisposition to
boast of his exclusive privilege....

Accordingly, in 'the effects of light rendered by
modern art,' our author is very particular indeed. His
extraordinary knowledge of the sun's position, to a
hair's-breadth in Mr Turner's pictures, and minute of the
day, is quite surprising. He gives a table of two pages
and a-half, of position and moment, 'morning, noon, and
afternoon,' 'evening and night.' In more than one instance, he is so close, as 'five minutes before sunset.'

Having settled the matter of the sky, our author takes
the earth in hand, and tosses it about like a Titan. 'The
spirit of the hills is action, that of the lowlands,
repose; and between these there is to be found every
variety of motion and of rest, from the inactive plain,
sleeping like the firmament, with cities for stars, to
the fiery peaks which, with heaving bosoms and exulting
limbs, with clouds drifting like hair from their bright
foreheads, lift up their Titan hands to heaven saying,
"I live for ever."' We learn, too, a wonderful power in
the excited earth, far beyond that which other 'naturalists' describe of the lobster, who only, *ad libitum*,
casts off a claw or so. 'But there is this difference
between the action of the earth and that of a living creature, that while the exerted limb marks its bones and ten-
dons through the flesh, the excited earth casts off the
flesh altogether, and its bones come out from beneath.
Mountains are the bones of the earth, their highest peaks
are invariably those parts of its anatomy, which in the
plains lie buried under five-and-twenty thousand feet of
solid thickness of superincumbent soil, and which spring
up in the mountain ranges in vast pyramids or wedges,
flinging their garment of earth away from them on each
side.'... Salvator Rosa could not paint rock; Gaspar
Poussin could not paint rock. A rock, in short, is such a
thing as nobody ought to paint, or can paint but Turner,
and all that, after his description of rock, we believe;
but were not prepared to learn that 'the foreground of the
"Napoleon" in last year's Academy,' is 'one of the most
exquisite pieces of rock truth every put on canvass.' In
fact, we really, in ignorance to be ashamed of, did not

know there was any rock there at all. We only remember
Napoleon and his cocked-hat - now, this is extraordinary;
for as *we* only or chiefly remember the cocked-hat, so he
sees the said cocked-hat in Salvator's rocks, where we
never saw such a thing, though 'he has succeeded in cover-
ing his foregrounds with forms which approximate to those
of drapery, of ribands, of *crushed cocked-hats*, of locks of
hair, of waves, of leaves, or any thing, in short, flexible or tough, but which, of course, are not only unlike,
but directly contrary to the forms which nature has impressed on rocks.' And the nature of rocks he must know,
having the 'Napoleon' before him. 'In the "Napoleon" I can
illustrate by no better example, for I can reason as well
from this as I could with my foot on the native rock.'
What rocks of Salvator's, besides the No. 220 of the Dulwich gallery, he has seen, we cannot pretend to say; we
have, within these few days, seen one, and could not discover the 'commas,' the 'Chinese for rocks,' nor Sanscrit
for rocks, but did read the language of nature, without
the necessity of any writing under - 'This is a rock.'
Poor Claude, he knew nothing of perspective, and his
efforts 'invariably ended in reducing his pond to the form
of a round O, and making it look perpendicular;' but in
one instance Claude luckily hits upon 'a little bit of
accidental truth;' he is circumstantial in its locality -
'the little piece of ground above the cattle, between the
head of the brown cow and the tail of the white one, is
well articulated, just where it turns into shade.'

After the entire failure of all artists that ever lived
before Turner in land and skies, we are prepared to find
that they had not the least idea of water. When they
thought they painted water, in fact, they were like 'those
happier children, sliding on dry ground,' and had not the
chance of wetting a foot. Water, too, is a thing to be
anatomized, a sort of rib-fluidity. The moving, transparent water, in shallow and in depth, of Vandervelde and
Backhuysen, is not the least like water; they are men who
'libelled the sea.' Many of our moderns - Stanfield in
particular - seem naturally web-footed; but the real
Triton of the sea, as he was Titan of the earth, is Turner.
To our own eyes, in this respect, he stands indebted to
the engraver; for we do not remember a single sea-piece by
Turner, in water-colour or oil, in which the water is
liquid. What it is like, in the picture of the Slave-ship,
which is considered one of his very finest productions, we
defy any one to tell. We are led to guess it is meant for
water, by the strange fish that take their pastime. A year
or two ago were exhibited two sea-pieces, of nearly equal
size, at the British Institution, by Vandervelde and

Turner. It was certainly one of Turner's best; but how inferior was the water and the sky to the water and sky in Vandervelde! In Turner they were both rocky. We say not this to the disparagement of Turner's genius. He had not studied these elements as did Vandervelde. The two painters ought not to be compared together; and we humbly think that any man who should pronounce of Vandervelde and Backhuysen, that they 'libelled the sea,' convicts himself of a wondrous lack of taste and feeling. Of their works he thus speaks - 'As it is, I believe there is scarcely such another instance to be found in the history of man, of the epidemic aberration of mind into which multitudes fall by infection, as is furnished by the value set upon the works of these men.' Of water, he says - 'Nothing can hinder water from being a reflecting medium but dry dust or filth of some kind on its surface. Dirty water, if the foul matter be dissolved or suspended in the liquid, reflects just as clearly and sharply as pure water, only the image is coloured by the hue of the mixed matter, and becomes comparatively brown or dark.' We entirely deny this, from constant observation. Within this week we have been studying a stream, which has alternated in its clearness and muddiness. We found the reflection not only less clear in the latter case, but instead of brown and dark, to have lost its brownness, and to have become lighter. To understand the 'curves' of water being beyond the reach of most who are not graduates of Oxford; and painters and admirers of old masters being people without sense, at least in comparison with the graduate, he thus disposes of his learned difficulty:- 'This is a point, however, on which it is impossible to argue without going into high mathematics, and even then the nature of particular curves, as given by the brush, would be scarcely demonstrable; and I am the less disposed to take much trouble about it, because I think that the persons who are really fond of these works are almost beyond the reach of argument.' The celebrated Mrs Partington once endeavoured, at Sidmouth, to dispose of these 'curves,' and failed; and we suspect a stronger reason than the incapacity of his readers for our author's thus disposing of the subject. We believe the world would not give a pin's head for all the seas that ever might be painted upon these mathematical curves; and that, in painting, even a graduate's 'high mathematics' are but a very low affair. But let us enliven the reader with something really high - and here is, in very high-flown prose, part of a description of a waterfall; and it will tell him a secret, that in the midst of these fine falls, nature keeps a furnace and steam-engine continually at work, and having the fire at hand, sends up rockets -

if you doubt - read:- 'And how all the hollows of that foam burn with green fire, like so much *shattering chryso-prase*; and how, ever and anon, startling you with its white flash, a jet of spray leaps hissing out of the fall, like a rocket, bursting in the wind, and driven away in dust, filling the air with light; and how, through the curdling wreaths of the restless, crashing abyss below, the blue of the water, paled by the foam in its body, shows purer than the sky through white rain-cloud, while the shuddering iris stoops in tremulous stillness over all, fading and flashing alternately through the choking spray and shattered sunshine, hiding itself at last among the thick golden leaves, which toss to and fro in sympathy with the wild water, their dripping masses lifted at inter-vals, like sheaves of loaded corn, by some stronger gush from the cataract, and bowed again upon the mossy rocks as its roar dies away.' 'Satque superque satis' - we cannot go on. There is nothing like calling things by their con-traries - it is truly startling. Whenever you speak of water, treat it as fire - of fire, *vice versa*, as water; and be sure to send them all shattering out of reach and discrimination of all sense; and look into a dictionary for some such word as 'chrysoprase,' which we find to come from χρυσός gold, and πράσον a leek, and means a precious stone; it is capable of being shattered, together with 'sunshine' - the reader will think the whole passage a 'flash' of moonshine. But there is a discovery - 'I be-lieve, when you have stood by this for half an hour, you will have discovered that there is something more in nature than has been given by Ruysdaël.' You will indeed - if this be nature! But, alas, what have we not to undergo - to discover what water is, and to become capable of judging of Turner! It is a comfort, however, that he is likely to have but few judges. Graduate has courage to undergo anything. Ariel was nothing in his ubiquity to him, though he put a span about the world in forty minutes; 'but there was some apology for the public's not under-standing this, for few people have had the opportunity of seeing the sea at such a time, and when they have, cannot face it. To hold by a mast or rock, and watch it, is a prolonged endurance of drowning, which few people have courage to go through. To those who have, it is one of the noblest lessons in nature.' Very few people, indeed, and those few 'involuntary experimentalists.'

We are glad to get on dry land again, 'brown furze or any thing' - and here we must question one of his truths of vegetation: he asserts, that the stems of all trees, the 'ordinary trees of Europe, do not taper, but grow up or out, in undiminished thickness, till they throw out

branch and bud, and then go off again to the next of equal
thickness.' We have carefully examined many trees this
last week, and find it is not the case; in almost all, the
bulging at the bottom, nearest the root, is manifest.
There is an early association in our minds, that the birch
for instance is remarkably tapering in its twigs. We would
rather refer our 'sworn measurer' to the factor than the
painter, and we very much question whether his 'top and
top' will meet the market. We are satisfied the fact is
not as he states it, and surely nature works not by such
measure rule. We suspect, for nature we should here read
Turner, for his trees, certainly, are strange things; it
is true, he generally shirks them. We do not remember one
picture that has a good, true, *bona fide*, conspicuous tree
in it. The reader will not be surprised to learn that the
worst painter of trees was Gaspar Poussin! and that the
perfection of trees is to be found in Turner's 'Marley,'
where most people will think the trees look more like
brooms than trees. The chapter on the Truth of Turner concludes with a quotation - we presume the extract from a
letter from Mr Turner to the author. If so, Mr Turner has
somewhat caught the author's style, and tells very simple
truths in a very fine manner, thus:- 'I cannot gather the
sunbeams out of the east, or I would make *them* tell you
what I have seen; but read this, and interpret this, and
let us remember together. I cannot gather the gloom out of
the night-sky, or I would make that teach you what I have
seen; but read this, and interpret this, and let us feel
together.' We must pause. Really we do not see the slightest necessity of an interpretation here. It is a simple
fact. He cannot extract 'sunbeams' from cucumbers - from
the east, we should say. The only riddle seems to be, that
they should, in one instance, remember together, and in
the other, feel together; only we guess that, being night-
gloom, people naturally feel about them in the dark. But
he proceeds - 'And if you have not that within you which I
can summon to my aid, if you have not the sun in your
spirit, and the passion in your heart, which my words may
awaken, though they be indistinct and swift, leave me.'
We must pause again; here *is* a riddle: what can be the
meaning of having the sun in one's spirit? - is it any
thing like having the moon in one's head? We give it up.
The passion in the heart we suppose to be dead asleep, and
the words and voice harsh and grating, and so it is
awakened. But what that if, or if not, has to do with
'leave me,' we cannot conjecture; but this we do venture
to conjecture, that to expect our graduate ever to *leave*
Mr Turner is one of the most hopeless of all Mr Turner's
'Fallacies of Hope.' But the writer proceeds with a *for* -

that appears, nevertheless, a pretty considerable *non-sequitur*. 'For I will give you no patient mockery, no laborious insult of that glorious nature, whose I am and whom I serve.' Here the graduate is treated as a servant, and the writer of the letter assumes the Pythian, the truly oracular vein. 'Let other servants imitate the voice and the gesture of their master while they forget his message. Hear that message from me, but remember that the teaching of Divine Truth must still be a mystery.' 'Like master like man.' Both are in the 'Cambyses' vein.'

We do not think that landscape painters will either gain or lose much by the publication of this volume, unless it be some mortification to be so sillily lauded as some of our very respectable painters are. We do not think that the pictorial world, either in taste or practice, will be Turnerized by this palpably fulsome, nonsensical praise. In this our graduate is *semper idem*, and to keep up his idolatry to the sticking-point, terminates the volume with a prayer, and begs all the people of England to join in it - a prayer to Mr Turner!

2. GEORGE DARLEY, TWO UNSIGNED REVIEWS, 'ATHENAEUM'

3 and 10 February 1844

George Darley (1795-1846) was a poet, critic, and graduate of Trinity College, Dublin. Although he was a capable mathematician, Darley's primary interests were aesthetic. Establishing himself in London in the early 1820s, he contributed to the 'London Magazine', edited the work of Beaumont and Fletcher, and became drama and art critic on the 'Athenaeum'. See Introduction, p. 6.

(a)

There is too much reasoning in this book, without the higher qualities of reasoning, which are clearness and conclusiveness, subordination of parts, and able summation of the whole: perhaps we should have said, too much parade of logic and too little real power. Yet it is a clever book - neither less nor more. It exhibits what may recommend it to many readers, some characteristics of Hazlitt's style - boldness and brilliancy, bigotry amidst liberality, and great acuteness amid still greater blindness. Whether

the author be an Oxford Graduate or no, he appears beyond
doubt an under-graduate in Criticism, - a very 'freshman;'
sanguine and self-confident, he would cut the Gordian
knot with a bulrush, like one of those ambitious youths who
undertake the trisection of an angle, or the duplication
of the cube, while they are still tingling from the
schoolmaster's rod, and have scarce surmounted the *pons
asinorum*. Were his age, indeed, as green as his judgment,
good result might hereafter flow from his energies, well
directed; but we suspect his opinions to be inveterate,
however immature. He declares himself an artist; the being
which, when not a prodigious advantage, is a prodigious
disadvantage to any writer on art: professional prejudices,
pet systems - *idola specûs* - corporate or selfish interests, narrow artistic principles, or none, almost always
characterize the criticism of an artist: his 'soul lives
in an alley,' even if one of palaces; and even if it takes
the air by times, its route is, like that of a steam-engine,
along a given track-way; but with a certainty and celerity
so far forth unrivalable. We should guess our author a
water-colourist, too, from the tone of his critiques; this
we do not charge as a positive disqualification, however:
Reynolds, who painted little besides portraits, wrote
better upon high Art than Barry, who seldom painted anything beneath historical subjects. The volume before us
illustrates, at all events, our former position. Here we
find an artist-critic pronouncing - what? let us put his
infallible dogma, like a papal bull, into a decree by
itself. Not that the old landscape-painters are neither
unmatched nor unmatchable - not that they are full of imperfection, are quite mis-appreciated, and much over-
praised - not that they are inferior to the moderns - our
author does not allege this - but, that they are all but
utterly contemptible; that they possess one bare and
second-rate merit alone! that, on the other hand, there is
scarce one perfection which the moderns want, scarce a
defect which they have; and that, in brief, Mr. J.W.
Turner is supreme Art personified, the God of Landscape-
painting incarnate! To characterize such hyperbolical sentiments, the very expressive, though vulgar, adage becomes
feeble - our enthusiast 'goes' the whole *hoggery* itself at
a mouthful. We cannot call his paradoxes mere madness -
they exhibit too much method; but among what may be entitled sane absurdities, none half so preposterous were ever
put forth by an otherwise sensible person. Are we to
believe the everlasting hills stand upon false bases? Are
brilliant meteors to shine hereafter as fixed stars of the
firmament, instead of those immortal luminaries which have
hitherto borne the name? True, the world has sometimes

persisted many ages in an error; but when Sabeanism was
exploded the sun and moon were not pronounced 'contemptible,' nor were men bid fall down and adore - fire-flies!
    It is plain enough, however, what produced this volume
of heterodox criticism. Extreme opinions make a great
'sensation;' they require less mental grasp to comprehend
them, far less mental power to sustain them - excitement
being a source of inspiration. The rabid democrat will
disembogue a thundering cataract of foam upon aristocrati-
cal abuses; the patrician will pour forth a vial of sparkling froth and wrath upon that hydra-headed monster, re-
publicanism: how many persons can see the merits *or* defects of each extreme; how few its merits *and* defects; how
much fewer still can by potent reasoning and persuasive
eloquence make others see them! We have heard it argued
very plausibly, that Michael Angelo was no painter - heard
him cried down into a mere terrific caricaturist, his sublime proved ridiculous, his imaginativeness fond extravagance - *id est*, when his censors fell into caricature,
extravagance, and the ridiculous-sublime themselves. They
could with like ease prove, to the uninitiated, Wilkie a
better manipulator than Teniers, a greater dramatist than
Raffael, a richer humourist than Hogarth, a skilfuller
sketcher than Rembrandt, a sweeter colourist than Correggio, &c. &c.; but we have seldom indeed met even a professed connoisseur able to appreciate the Florentine or
the Scottish master precisely, and seldomer still to make
readers appreciate him. Hear Fuseli talk of Michael, and
Mengs of Raffael, you will think them the so-called arch-
angels become artists; hear our Oxford Graduate talk of
Mr. Turner, and you will suspect that either St. Luke, the
patron of painting, must have rapt the artist into the
seventh heaven, or St. Luke, the patron of lunatics, must
have carried off the author! What more light-headed rhodomontade could be scrawled, except upon the walls, or
hallooed, except through the wards, of Bedlam, than the
annexed passage presents us? It is just not blasphemous
because it is crack-brained:-

[Quotes from 'With respect to' to 'revelation to mankind',
'Works' 3: 629-31.]

    That this elsewhere rational writer was in his 'lunes'
when composing the above passage is clear from its palpable incongruities: if opinions are not to be pronounced
upon the works of a man who has walked with Nature three-
score years, if we are neither to praise nor blame him,
why all the opinions and praises poured forth upon him and
his work by our author? If we are to impress the public

with respect for Mr. Turner's pictures, will our Oxford
logician tell us *how*, without praise and opinions? One
sentence contains a wish that Mr. Turner would not do such
and such things; the next sentence denies all wish even to
form a wish regarding any such things; and the next sentence again wishes that 'he would follow out his own
thoughts and intents,' - though these should lead him
peradventure (for all he does *must* be right) to do the
very things wished *not* to be done by the first sentence!
Here's a choice specimen of Oxonian dialectics; here's a
sample of the 'reasoning power' which often distinguishes
this volume. We have scarce been just to the above passage
however: will our readers believe their eyes when they see
that the fourth consecutive sentence exhibits another
aberration, nay, a double aberration within half a sentence, two aberrations entangled together? Peruse it once
more - 'But we request, in all humility, that those
thoughts may be seriously and loftily given.' What! you
will not presume to form even so much as a *wish* - yet you
request! You will not presume to form even an *idea* 'respecting the *manner* of anything proceeding from his hand,'
yet you have an idea its manner should be serious and
lofty! Again, you desire he would proceed 'without reference to any human authority,' yet you refer him 'in all
humility' to your own hint! Nay, as we live, both the next
sentences give each other the logical lie too: let us
repeat them. 'In all that he says we believe, in all that
he does we trust.' - 'It is therefore that we pray him to
utter nothing lightly, to do nothing regardlessly.' Why,
for Idol-Bel and Dagon's sake, if you trust in all he does
can't you let him do as he pleases? How is it possible he
can utter anything lightly or regardlessly if he *be* such
an impeccable? Moreover, when he can paint histories of
the universe, and give lessons to future time, how can you
suppose he will descend to illustrate Boboli Gardens and
Annuals of the Season? When both a psalmist and a prophet
- an evangelist into the bargain - wherefore insinuate
with 'all humility' that he whistles off 'hymns' after a
light fashion, and vents 'revelations' in a regardless
manner? We will answer our own question: Mr. Turner's
doxologist, desirous that his last paragraph should out-
do all the rest, yet exhausted by his antecedent efforts,
has here wrought his eloquence up to an unnatural pitch;
and hence cannot, in his paroxysm of panegyric, distinguish between genuine heartfelt praise and wild hallelu-
jahs. He reminds us of a Whirling Dervish, who at the end
of his well-sustained reel falls, with a higher jump and a
shriller shriek, into a fit.
    We shall quote, for more than amusement's sake, a few

other of the inconsistencies promiscuously and plenteously
scattered through the volume. The chief purpose - to heap
terms of abuse, and derision, and disdain upon the Old
Masters* - is often fulfilled with a verve and a glibness
as if the author had been a graduate of Billingsgate,
instead of Oxford: *tone* he declares 'the first and nearly
the last concession' they must expect from him; and even
this merit he conjectures the probable result of some
'mere technical secret, gained at the expense of a thousand falsehoods and omissions'. But his preface - written
after his book we surmise - makes a very different last
concession from the first: 'Let it be remembered that only
a portion of the work is now presented to the public; and
it must not be supposed because in that particular portion
I have spoken in constant depreciation, that I have no
feeling of other excellencies, of which cognizance can
only be taken in future parts of the work.' What his
future parts may accomplish we cannot tell; what his immediate efforts should, seems plain - a second volume,
parallel to the first, and a running recantation of its
errors. Such a prose palinode would cost such an adept at
self-conviction little trouble. Here we have another brief
specimen: 'Power is never wasted..... A nut may be cracked
by a steam-engine, but it has not, in being so, been the
subject of the power of the engine!' No, nor if the Carron
Foundry at full work cast a single toy-cannon, power is
not wasted. If, indeed, our Oxford logician's head were
cracked, like the nut, by a steam-engine, we might admit
the power wasted; because the fracture seems superfluous.
Again, we find truths pronounced 'valueless in proportion
as they are general,' though pronounced a page earlier
right in practice! Now for some few other examples of
Turneromania, and volcanic eruptions from the crater of a
fervent imagination:-

[Quotes with omissions from 'Turner - glorious in conception' to 'infinite and the beautiful', 'Works 3: 254-7.]

   Speaking of Mr. Turner's 'War' he has the hardihood to
assert -

[Quotes from 'There was not one hue' to 'glowing absorbing
light', 'Works' 3: 288-9.]

   The same painter's *palpitating* light (?) seems to have
inflicted a sort of sun-stroke on its worshipper:-

[Quotes from 'There is the motion' to 'but never dies',
'Works' 3: 308.]

All this said of painted light! As Addison's school-
mistress exclaimed - 'Bless us! eight volumes about
potatos!' But even Mr. Turner's *figures* are defended; it
is shown that geology might be lectured upon from one of
his landscapes as from Nature herself; while his hills are
complimented by the somewhat awkward encomium that we
never get to their top 'without being *tired* with our walk.'
'Cuyp, on the other hand, could paint close truth of
everything except ground and water [at p. 189 he painted
false *skies*] with decision and success; but then, he has
not the slightest idea of the word beautiful.' 'A pencil-
scratch of Wilkie's, on the back of a letter, is a greater
and a better picture - and I use the term picture in its
full sense - than the most laboured and luminous canvas
that ever left the easel of Gerard Dow.' With what justice
might the Modern Painters cry out on reading these ludicrous exaggerations - Heaven defend us from such a defender as this!

Sound opinions resemble pine-trees; the roughest shaking only strengthens their hold: we do not dislike to have
our most deep-implanted, long-cherished convictions blus-
tered against every now and then, with all the force of
new-sprung enthusiasm for other tenets - if ours be rotten
at root, the sooner they are eradicated the better, we
would gladly get rid of them. Nay, let us make a large
concession, in proof of our being unprejudiced; it has
always been our opinion, that but few *landscapes* by the
ancient masters deserve to rank among first-rate productions of art. Seldom, indeed, did we meet upon our rather
excursive tours, from Brittany to Bohemia, from the Baltic
to the Mediterranean, a painted land or water piece half
so beautiful as a bed of March violets, or the sparkle of
a mountain-rill; one glimpse at ocean through a pocket
spyglass gave us more pleasure than all the 'Marines' by
Joseph Vernet in the Louvre, a blank Alpine heath had for
us more varied charms than all the bottle-green landscapes
Paul Brill ever produced. We shall go yet farther with our
concessions: even Claude's performances have often left
little deeper impressions upon us than so many glass-
windows - they are panes of pictorial glazing, smooth,
transparent, and bright surfaces, which seem less to de-
lineate the aerial perspective than to let it through them
from the scene itself behind, such is their magic mechanism, - but display, in general, few merits besides. Had
our author been content to reduce popular reverence on
this subject within just bounds, we should have approved
his efforts, but when he pronounces Claude, Salvator,
and Poussin 'contemptible' - when in the same unscrupulous
style he bespatters all the old landscapists with foul

epithets, like a 'Legion Club,' it only proves his language stronger than his judgment. We love straightforward
opinions expressed in strenuous diction - always understood, however, that the boldness should not spring from
the blindness - else we hate them as so much hollow noise,
we regard them as so many oracles uttered by Roger Bacon's
brazen head - trumpet-tongued impostures. Laughably
enough, this railer and perpetual scoffer at these
Ancient Masters protests against ridicule being thrown
upon his modern idols! He observes, with extreme sore-
ness, -

[Quotes from 'There is nothing so high' to 'or the dinner
table', 'Works' 3: 277.]

Yet his own very next paragraph is a tissue of Sardonic
jests about Poussin's 'La Riccia,' amongst which 'brick-
red' takes the place of Scotch sulphur, and *dots in the
sky with a stalk to them* that of English spinach and
eggs! A few pages onward we find this polite critique:
'There is no man living more cautious and sparing in the
use of pure colour than Turner. To say that he never per-
petrates anything like the blue excrescences of foreground,
or hills shot *like a housekeeper's best silk gown* with
blue and red, which certain of our celebrated artists consider the essence of the sublime, would be but a poor compliment'; and again, speaking of Turner's 'Mercury and
Argus,' 'the reader can scarcely fail to remember at once
sundry works in contradistinction to this, with great
names attached to them, in which the sky is a sheer piece
of *plumbers' and glaziers' work*, and should be valued per
yard, with heavy extra charge for ultra-marine; skies, in
which the raw, meaningless colour is shaded steadily and
perseveringly down, passing through the pink into the
yellow, *as a young lady shades her worsted*, to the successful production of a *very handsome oil-cloth*, but certainly not of a picture.' This is the philosophical
reasoner who would not condescend to a jest? this is the
thin-skinned critic who deprecates the shafts of ridicule!
Why, not merely his most amusing passages, but far the
most effective portions of his volume - those which will
convince and seduce and cajole many readers where his
argument would fail - are the numberless burlesque simi-
litudes and ludicrous analogies sprinkled through his
critiques, to disparage by all means, whether foul or
fair, the Ancient Masters!
But more of this hereafter.

(b)

Modern artists may deem it their interest to decry old
pictures, as competing with their own productions, and
lowering their market prices: that this has been, and is
often done, both at home and abroad, we ourselves can
testify - we have heard the leperous distilment drop word
by word into a purchaser's ears, till we could perceive
his taste was poisoned. Miserable selfishness! wise enough,
perhaps, for its generation, but short-sighted for the
future welfare of Art, if painters feel any care about it.
They do not see that depreciating those time-honoured
works, from which their profession derives its chief glory,
descredits *it*, and therefore degrades themselves. Let
modern poets lead the ignorant world to think Spenser a
frigid, allegorical fancymonger, Milton a sounding brass,
full of pompous blare and flare, like Azazel's trumpet,
Shakespeare a false god - a mere quintessence of dust,
whom patriotism, prejudice, and custom have deified - were
it possible such opinions could be held, and modern poets
could be so asinine as to bray them forth with effect,
would not the poetic art itself fall into disrepute? would
not its present and future cultivators lose the ancestral
honours those names reflected upon their order? But in the
semi-poetic art, Painting, the world is still more per-
suadeable, because perplexed by the merits of mechanism,
about which craftsmen alone can decide. Painters, we fear,
will learn too soon that their vocation has need of all
its past renown, when Middle-Class patronage has made them
wholesale manufacturers for those Brummagem picture-
markets - the Art-Unions.
    We do not impute to our author any sordid or self-
interested motive of the kind above-said: indeed, he bows
himself almost as prostrate before the shrines of Michael-
angelo and Raffael, and other demi-deified historic painters, as before the image of Turner, which he hath set up:
it is only their brethren Landscapists he would pelt down
from their pedestals or disfigure where they stand. Let
him, and his aiders and abettors, if he has such among the
craft, reflect whether this may peradventure tend to its
eventual profit or loss. Once sacrifice the outworks, and
the citadel itself, maugre its many towers of strength,
will be endangered. A Cambridge Graduate might ere long
come forward, and prove the whole Art a terrible waste of
power, toil, and time, - employing super-eminent genius
like Raffael's and Michael's to produce 'illustrations' on
perishable plaster, panel, canvas, or paper, and even
Turner's omnipotential abilities to decorate our drawing-
rooms, dazzle our eyes, and at best instruct the mind by

an immeasurable roundabout through the senses. Art, like
religion, has its free-thinkers no less than implicit
believers: thus, we can get but one response from discri-
minative, unbiassed critics, when we ask their opinion of
Mr. Turner's gorgeous performances - silence and a shrug!
Were our author to change sides (which fanatics oftenest
do), we should in all likelihood find him delitigating
just as copiously and as loudly against his present idol;
perhaps somewhat after this fashion - 'He has debauched
his visual taste by the use of stimulant colours - such is
the common fate both of schools and individual painters,
they begin with a small indulgence and end with inordinate
excess:- his pictures, to say the most of them, are a
beautiful splish-splash of splendid tints - they resemble
dishes of gold and silver fish, in a sauce of ultramarine,
and garnished with marigolds, orange-peel, &c. If to produce a maximum of effect by a minimum of means be the
touchstone of artistic power, how many among these brilliant things would it not prove brazen counterfeits? All
the richest and brightest pigments mingled together to
produce a mere luxurious *olla podrida* for the corrupt
ocular taste, is, so far forth, a mark of artistic incom-
petence. Some of his pictures have no extractable meaning -
others an absurd one when found: thus a man up to the mid-
leg in ruddle, his eyes fixed on a distant bell of gam-
boge, means "War," "The Exile and the Rock Limpet,"
"Buonaparte at St. Helena," everything and nothing!' We
warrant, too, our convert could, if the maggot bit him,
spin as fine a harangue about Claude's wonderful works as
Turner's.

But reverting to the subject of new fangledness *versus*
old-fangledness. Has it never struck this exclaimer
against antiquated taste, that if there be persons who
admire old things because they are old, there be other
persons likewise, who admire new things because they are
new? Aye, and that the lovers of novelty, compared with
their antagonists, might count ten noses for one? Whilst
here and there a bookish, baldpate old gentleman, whose
brain is as barren as the dust on his shelves - a dilettante medal-hunter, or greyheaded mouser in archæological
nooks and burrows, amidst vermin, darkness, and dirt -
while a score or two, perhaps, of such oddities make up
that class of respectable laughing-stocks called antiquarians - perverse, we will add, and preposterous creatures,
who, like certain among Dante's condemned wretches, seem
to have their heads turned backwards; upon the other hand,
all the frivolous and all the fickle, all the superficial
and all the sensual - *id est*, the major portion of mankind,
detesting what the aforesaid small minority loves (and for

the self-same profound reason, because old things are old)
- idolize whatever exhibits the gloss and glitter of new
manufacture about it, however garish and futile, trashy
and flashy the production. Let us ask this *Wotton*, so fain
to do fierce bettle for Modern Pictures, whether he thinks
a spick-span florid gewgaw, from the easel of a fashionable artist, in a frosted-gilt frame, or a dull antique in
a worm-eaten rim of deal, would have more admirers? His
candour, we doubt not, will admit - the gewgaw. Well might
Platonic philosophers make a butterfly an emblem of the
Soul! It illustrates that of most human beings.

Such is an Englishman's bias to be gulled, that rather
than remain long undeluded by some one else, he gulls himself. We cannot but believe our author has got wilfully
into a labyrinth, that he may enjoy the pleasure of transient bewilderment, and of bewildering others who may
follow him. His own ingenuity will get him out - perhaps
into a deeper and deeper still: it was our province to
warn the green geese from the decoy whither the wild goose
whistled them. Yet we may have taken superfluous trouble -
it had been enough perchance to state his pictorial creed,
which declares that the most erratic genius among all
Modern Painters exhibits in his works a consolidated fund
of perfections without the shadow of a single fault! Monomania could scarce go much farther - after this the
Ancient Masters might feel such idle breath could not
blast their laurels were it ever so freezing and blustrous.

Nevertheless, as we said at first, the book before us
contains a great deal of cleverness, and a good deal of
truth, even amidst its manifold inconsistencies. Thus,
although it begins with pronouncing Claude, Salvator, and
Poussin contemptible, it ends with eating up about half
that oracle: 'All others [except Backhuysen and Vander-
velde] of the ancients have real power of some kind or
another, either solemnity of intention as the Poussins, or
refinement of feeling as Claude, or high imitative accuracy as Cuyp and Paul Potter, or rapid power of execution,
as Salvator; there is something in all which ought to be
admired, and of which, if exclusively contemplated, *no
degree of admiration, however enthusiastic, is unaccount-
able or unnatural.*' Then follows a caper of the genuine
Quixote justifying his exception abovesaid: 'But Vandervelde and Backhuysen have *no* power, no redeeming quality
of mind; their works are neither reflective, nor eclectic,
nor imitative; they have neither tone, nor execution, nor
colour, nor composition, nor any artistical merit to recommend them; and they present not even a deceptive, much
less a real resemblance of nature.' Hey, hey, the devil
rides upon a fiddlestick! as Falstaff says to his hostess

in a pasty, what next? But the second volume promised, and
which we hope may come, even if from the moon, will no
doubt repeal this fulmination against Vandervelde and
Backhuysen, or at least publish another bull to correct
the present infallible decree. Let us hope likewise, that
the author will, meantime, should he have the power, take
the trouble of acquainting himself with those Ancient
Masters whom he criticizes, for he appears by his confes-
sions, voluntary and involuntary, *quam proximè* ignorant
about them. How such a grand-tourist as he proclaims himself should not say one word of the sublime Pitti Salvators, Nicolas Poussin's 'Great Flood,' Gaspar's *chefs-
d'oeuvre* in San Martino, the Brera Giorgione, the Fesch
Rembrandt, the Camuccini Titian, various fine Claudes and
magnificent Cuyps throughout England, numberless other
splendid landscapes everywhere, puzzles conjecture, or
rather is plain enough: we will not call him as he calls
Canaletti, a 'shameless asserter of whatever was most convenient to him,' but his little information respecting the
Old Masters qualified him well to condemn them, because
much knowledge had made him far more cautious - or had
given him, if no qualms of criticism, perhaps some of conscience. He finds just the basis that suits his temple
raised to divine Mr. Turner - his *Turnerion* - with a cella
behind it for all other Modern Painters - in a few Claudes,
most of which abler connoisseurs than ourselves deem
second-rate, or apocryphal, specimens, and a few Salvators,
Poussins, &c. which *he* deems first-rate, whether apocryphal or not, at the London and Dulwich Galleries. Yet
even on this narrow ground we might perplex his self-
complacence by a very simple question - where is the oil-
picture from Mr. Turner's hand equal to the worst Claude
of the National Collection? Let him spend no more logic
demonstrating what vile things the old Landscapes are, how
and why and wherefore they are beneath the modern, - but
just point us out that one oil-work of his impeccable that
can justly compete *even* with the 'St. Ursula!'

This brings us near our conclusion. We apprehend the
Oxford Graduate, despite his enormous apparatus of axioms,
postulates, lemmas, categories, divisions, and subdivisions, has omitted the true principles of landscape-
painting, or if mentioned, has misunderstood their value
and virtue. He seems to think landscapes should be,
throughout their details, little facsimiles of real
objects, and that no other merit surpasses minute faithfulness. He cannot conceive, for example, the 'St. Ursula,'
with its buckram waves, hopping figures, and false perspective, nevertheless a far more excellent work than 'The
Exile and the Rock Limpet,' were this as faithful as he

imagines it. He professes, indeed, a noble disdain of servile imitation in art, but half his book is a ding-dong against the Ancient Masters on its sole account - Salvator's rocks are not stratified, Poussin's leaves not botanical, Cuyp's clouds not cirrostrate, &c. - none of those artists exhibit what he and the newspaper critics call 'truthfulness to nature.' He would have geologic landscape-painters, dendrologic, meteorologic, and doubtless entomologic, ichthyologic, every kind of physiologic painter, united in the same person; yet alas for true poetic art amidst all these learned Thebans! No, landscape-painting must not be reduced to mere portraiture - portraiture of inanimate substances - *Denner*-like portraiture of the Earth's face, with all its wrinkles and pimples, line by line, shade by shade. As we have said elsewhere, if people want to see Nature let them go and look at *herself*; wherefore should they come to see her at second-hand on a poor little piece of plastered canvas? We disapprove the 'natural style' in painting, not because we dislike Nature, but because we adore her; she is so far above any imitation of her, that the very best disappoints us and dissatisfies. Ancient landscapists took a broader, deeper, higher, view of their art: they neglected particular traits, and gave only general features: thus they attained mass, and force, harmonious union, and simple effect, the elements of grandeur and beauty. Modern artists travel more - peregrination is now easier than it was to the ancients, and commoner: of course modern landscapes are, for this reason, more varied in subject, more accurate in details, - to which likewise the number of illustrated volumes and the extension of 'physiologic' knowledge conduce: such merits and all they involve, do those they adorn honour enough, without any need to attempt exalting them by disparaging their predecessors. Our author himself does not deny the latter super-eminent *tone*, perhaps unaware how much his term would embrace - tone of composition as well as of colour; they possess both equally, and how much its tone of composition elevates or depresses a work, he might learn by a comparison between the general outlines of Paradise Lost and those of Paradise and the Peri.

We shall end with a pretty long quotation to prove he has mistaken himself no less than the Ancient Masters; his forte is the very reverse of sound reasoning, *videlicet* - fine writing. Popular taste runs, now-a-days, a vast deal too headlong towards *Description*, that lowest among literary merits; but albeit page succeeds page of eloquent skimble-skamble in this vein, albeit the 'pure and holy' slang of sentimentalism often bespots his best descriptive passages, still they are his happiest, and preferable, because spontaneous ebullitions, to the beautiful balderdash elaborated with such efforts by many a renowned provider of it for public consumption:-

[Quotes from 'It had been wild' to 'into the blaze of the sea', 'Works' 3: 278-80.]

Note

* Rubens, indeed, obtains grace - because like Turner.

3. WALT WHITMAN, UNSIGNED REVIEW, 'BROOKLYN EAGLE'

22 July 1847

Walt Whitman (1819-92) was editor of the 'Brooklyn Eagle' when he wrote the following comment which, although brief, is characteristic of the Whitman style in demonstrating an appreciation of Ruskin's early work. Then, too, both Whitman and Ruskin tilted against established artistic canons. In later years Ruskin was to express great admiration for 'Leaves of Grass'.

The first dip one takes in this book, will, in all probability, make him pleased with the dashy, manly, clearhearted style of its author. He tells us in the preface that he began his writing from a feeling of indignation at the shallow and false criticism of the periodicals of the day, on the works of a certain artist. That his writing is entirely devoid of selfish or partial motives we feel confident; no other than a sincere man could make such eloquence as fills these pages. The widest expanse of the ideal, and the most rigid application of mechanical rules, in art, appear to have been mastered by the author of 'Modern Painters.' As for artists, we should suppose such a work would be invaluable; and to the general reader it will present many fresh ideas, and afford a fund of intellectual pleasure. Indeed it is worthy of the reading of every lover of what we must call intellectual chivalry, enthusiasm, and a high-toned sincerity, disdainful of the flippant tricks and petty arts of small writers.

'Modern Painters II'

1846

4. FROM AN UNSIGNED REVIEW, 'FOREIGN QUARTERLY REVIEW'

July 1846, vol. 37, 380-416

Even the 'Wellesley Index' fails to identify the reviewer of the article, Nature in Art, that dealt at length with the two initial volumes of 'Modern Painters'. The part here excerpted is one of the very few clearer efforts to articulate the aesthetic philosophizing that informs 'Modern Painters II'.

...It is to be lamented that the Oxford Graduate should have been dazzled by the fantastic lights of this eccentric painter. He is a man of so much good faith, so valuable as an observer of nature, as a teacher in art, that we cannot see him wandering in pursuit of the *ignis fatuus* without regret. Let him, indeed, discover what he can in Turner, and use that painter for his illustrations as he will; but while, with scarcely an exception, – for one or two rare words of condemnation are no sufficient caveat, – he advances the painter as the great exemplar, those whom he might teach will be deceived; betrayed either into mistaking the madness of Turner for sober truth; or, revolting from such a specimen, will dismiss the teacher as utterly unworthy of attention: that, undoubtedly he is not.

In his second volume he is emancipated from these specialties. A graver sense of his vocation seems to have grown upon him. He speaks, we think, in a tone of maturer judgment and greater modesty; is less bent upon making out a case for a client, than on extracting the principles of art. Thus he announces his new mission:

[Quotes from 'It is not now' to 'sleep with baby murmurings', 'Works' 4: 28-9.]

Even from this short specimen it may be gathered that the Oxford Graduate has grown more lofty in his language. The greater part of the second volume is theoretical; it therefore deals less in that precise observation of nature in which the writer is so-happy. He is by no means so well able to grapple with abstract reasoning, or to bind himself to the one path of logical sequence, and his argument is a great deal more marred by dogmatic assumption and sermonising apostrophes. He still assumes art to be nothing but an auxiliary to the Church and to the Religious Tract Society. 'Man's use and function,' he says, '(and let him who will not grant me this follow me no further, for this I propose always to assume) is to be a witness of the glory of God, and to advance that glory by his reasonable obedience and resultant happiness.' He vehemently denounces those men who 'insolently call themselves utilitarians,' and who speak 'as if houses, and lands, and food and raiment, were alone useful.'

[Quotes from 'This Nebuchadnezzar curse' to 'however distant', 'Works' 4: 30-1.]

This second volume may be designated as an analysis of Beauty, in which also the writer includes the Sublime. It contains much valuable matter, the whole of which may be traced to that part of the argument that the writer has drawn from the direct contemplation of real things; learning from them, and from them alone, by the aid of an acute and cultivated perception, their proper and intimate significance. The indifferent portion, as in the case of the previous volume, but perhaps more obviously, consists of such part as the author has derived from assumptions as to what art ought to be, or ought to teach, and this part of the book it is which is shadowy and unsubstantial in its nature, hazy or turgid in style. The two portions are so distinct, although frequently crossing each other, that you might suppose them to be read by the author in different tones of voice; one in the tone of a person explaining some novel and favourite theory, with earnestness, but with the moderate and rational manner of an intellectual man in congenial society; the other in a tone of voice resembling the mechanical solemnity and eloquence of the pulpit. The better portion however is so valuable, that the reader readily accepts the book as it stands. It is, like the previous one, a valuable contribution to the theory of art.

According to the writer Beauty is something which depends upon an instinct of moral perception. 'I wholly
deny,' he says, 'that the impressions of Beauty are in any
way sensual - they are neither sensual, nor intellectual,
but moral.' The faculty receiving them he designates the
theoretic faculty from the Greek *theoria*: he objects to
the term aesthetic as indicating sensuous feeling. Of
course men receive impressions through their senses; but,
according to our author, the senses are of different ranks,
superior and inferior. The inferior senses may be distinguished by this test, that in respect of their unlimited
use man may be said to be intemperate; but that in respect
of the higher senses indulgence cannot be called criminal
or intemperate. The inferior pleasures, upon prolongation,
are self-destructive, and destructive also to life; they
are incapable of existing continually with other delights
or perfections of the system. There is another test: their
proper function is to subserve life as instruments of our
preservation. Such are taste and smell; of which the
pleasure can only be artificially, and under high penalty,
prolonged. But the higher pleasures, 'the pleasures of
sight and hearing, are given as gifts; they answer not any
purpose of mere existence, for the distinction of all that
is useful or dangerous might be made, and often is made by
the eye, without its receiving the slightest pleasure of
sight.' This is a very gross assumption; but let it pass.

[Quotes from 'Herein, then, we find' to 'of the thing de-
sired', 'Works' 4: 46-7; and from 'As it is necessary' to
'servant of lust', 'Works' 4: 48-9.]

The rude and uneducated senses, however, are not true
in their impressions; repeated trial and experience are
necessary to arrive at principles in some sort common to
all. But, if we rightly understand the author; those principles once attained, a 'true verdict' is elicited, and a
final 'authority' is thenceforth established. There seems
to us to be a great fallacy in this position. It may be
said of every impression of the sense that it contains a
truth. No doubt, cultivation of the sense attains to further truth; but perhaps at no stage can it be declared
that the truth so attained is final. The Oxford Graduate
takes for an illustration, the sense of the palate, which
at first perceives only coarse and violent qualities; but
from experience 'acquires greater subtlety and delicacy of
discrimination, perceiving in both agreeable or disagreeable qualities at first unnoticed, which, on continued
experience, will probably become more influential than the
first impressions; and whatever this final verdict may be,

it is felt by the person who gives it, and received by
others as a more correct one than the first.' The object
of this analogy is to take the business of judicial decision out of the hands of the ignoble vulgar, and to repose
it in trust with the initiated few, thus establishing an
authority. But, we say, the finality cannot at any time be
predicated. No doubt taste changes; and therefore a second
verdict may be fuller than the first. But it is not more
absolutely correct or finally true than the first, or the
third than the second, and so on; each has a truth in it,
each successive one more truth; but none is perfect. The
error usually lies in asserting a partial verdict as if it
were complete. To predict of an orange that its colour is
golden is true; to say also that its taste is acid is more
true. We advance in truth when we add predications that it
is sweet, and the sweet is agreeable; that there is bitter
in the skin. At each stage the verdict has been incomplete,
but has been true, so far as it went. Even where the
original verdict is reversed, the process is not different.
We say, for instance, that a green fig is sickly; which is
true; for to the unaccustomed palate it produces sensations of nausea. We say, secondly, that it is luscious;
but that is not more true than the former assertion. Discrimination of taste, in fact, is the result not only of
instant perception, but also of comparative knowledge,
which adds to the estimate. You might even extend the
verdict on the orange by saying that its bitter is wholesome; that its seed will reproduce the plant, and so
forth, and those predictions are substantial additions to
your own judgment on the orange; but at no point, unless
you have exhausted the whole evidence of knowledge that
can be brought to bear upon the fruit, have you attained
what can be called a final verdict; at no point can your
'authority' be so complete as to overbear and supersede
the growth of floating opinion. It is necessary to make
this reservation, because 'authority,' like some other
assumptions, enters by implication, or directly, largely
into the Oxford Graduate's work. Authority is *primâ facie*
evidence of what the author calls the verdict, to stand in
lieu of experience until that be acquired, but no longer.

Putting these things together, as the Chinese say, the
Oxford Graduate's position seems to be this. The sense of
Beauty does not consist in the sensuous perceptions,
neither is it worked out by an operation of the intellect
regarding fitness for the purposes of utility, nor does it
depend upon ideas of association. The senses are the
mediums for perceiving it, and therefore it is necessary
that the senses be trained, or they will convey false conclusions. But having trained the senses or the sensuous

perceptions, we are enabled to pronounce upon what is good,
and to deliver a verdict on the Beautiful. When we are in
that state, and the higher, permanent, or self-sufficient
pleasures of sense are perceived and are 'gathered together, and so arranged as to enhance each other, as by
chance they could not be,' they incite 'the perception of
the immediate operation of the intelligence which formed
us;' out of that perception arise joy, admiration, and
gratitude - gratitude, namely, to the Omnipotent, for the
benefit vouchsafed. This definition, if so it can be
called, seems to imply that a sense of the Beautiful must
depend, in part, upon a knowledge of the true religion,
and therefore to imply that none can have a sense of the
Beautiful but Christians; indeed, the writer almost says
as much. Without true religious faith, the 'sense of
Beauty sinks into the servant of the lust' - the sense of
Beauty is degraded. So says the author. It may be so. What
we are now considering, however, is not the proper function of the sense of Beauty, but its essence; and the
phrase just quoted is tantamount to an admission, that,
although without the true faith, the sense of Beauty may
be degraded, it still exists, to endure that degradation;
which would upturn the whole argument.

But we will not rest the question upon separate phrases.
It may be doubted whether the world waited for a sense of
the Beautiful until the Christian dispensation, whether it
is not a much more primitive thing; one, ruder or more
cultivated, inherent in human nature. For the same reason
the author is no doubt right in denying that the sense of
Beauty is based on complex intellectual operations or
critical ideas as to fitness or association. He is right,
no doubt, in regarding it as instinctive; wrong, we think,
in complicating it with other sentiments; for, indeed, all
instinctive sentiments are perfectly simple. The instinct
of appetite - as that, for example, of a child for food,
is a perfectly simple feeling, and goes direct to its
object. It is true too, we think, that Beauty moves in us
sensations of joy, admiration, and kindness; sentiments
which need no very profound explanation. Admiration is a
feeling that always accompanies a sense of goodness in any
object when it exceeds the level ratio of that object as
it is commonly presented to us. Joy is a feeling that
accompanies every agreeable condition of the senses. The
kindness, perhaps, may need a little more consideration;
though it is undoubtedly moved by the aspect of Beauty.

It is to be observed, that the author continually uses
the word 'pleasure;' one which is objectionable, because
it is frequently applied to trivial and inferior classes
of satisfaction, and it is also of a far too small and

limited meaning for the present purpose....
The Oxford Graduate reckons two kinds of Beauty - what
he calls 'Typical Beauty,' and 'Vital Beauty.' Typical
Beauty consists in the external qualities of bodies, which
are instinctively perceived to be Beautiful, and which he
thinks he has 'shown to be in some sort typical of the
Divine attributes;' wherefore he calls it 'typical.' Vital
Beauty consists in 'the appearance of felicitous fulfilment of function in living things, more especially of the
joyful and right exertion of perfect life in man.' His
analogy between the elements of Typical Beauty and the
Divine attributes is forced and fantastical. He treats the
several kinds in separate chapters under these heads:-
'Infinity, or the type of Divine Incomprehensibility,' (in
which consists the beauty of vague and indeterminate
things, curves, gradations of shade, unlimited vastness,
&c.); 'Unity, or the type of Divine Comprehensiveness;'
'Repose, or the type of Divine Permanence;' 'Symmetry, or
the type of Divine Justice;' 'Purity, or the type of
Divine Energy;' 'Moderation, or the type of Government by
Law' - 'which is the girdle of Beauty.' Purity is made out
to be the type of Divine Energy, because impurity is a
term suggested by the human sense of decay, or interference with organic function.
As a specimen of this portion may be taken, in brief,
the idea evolved in the chapter on unity. There are
various kinds of unity - 'subjectional unity,' where different things are subjected to one influence; 'original
unity,' where different things, like the branches of trees,
and the petals of flowers, spring from the same origin;
'unity of sequence,' where many links are necessary to one
chain - 'in spiritual creatures it is their own constant
building up by true knowledge and continuous reasoning to
higher perfection, and the singleness, the straightfor-
wardness of their tendencies to more complete communion
with God;' and there is the unity of membership or essential unity, 'which is the uniting of things separately
perfect into a perfect whole.' Unity cannot exist between
things similar to each other, unless they are united by a
third, different from both; thus, two similar things, the
arms, are united by a third different, the trunk, forming
one perfect body. Out of the necessity of this unity
arises that of variety; which is not pleasing in itself,
but becomes so, as a means of harmony:

[Quotes from 'Receiving [therefore] variety only as' to
'human heart conceived', 'Works', 4: 99-100; and from 'The
same great feeling' to 'of their sorrow', 'Works' 4: 101.]

In Unity of Sequence, variety is exemplified by the melodies of music; 'wherein by the differences of the notes, they are connected with each other in certain pleasant relations. This connexion, taking place in quantities, is proportion.'
Vital Beauty, the appearance of felicitous fulfilment of function in living things, is thus introduced:

[Quotes, with omissions, from 'I have already noticed' to 'essence is in God only', 'Works' 4: 146-8.]

The changes are rung on the fulfilment of function, in vegetation, in animals, and in man. But in respect of principles, the whole of this portion, beyond the first enunciation, is very vague and unsubstantial. It includes, however, many valuable observations drawn from nature; especially those on the fallacy that the Ideal is something abstract and different from nature, instead of being the perfection of actual forms, from the study of which it is to be deduced.
The sublime we have said is included by the writer in Beauty; and properly so. His Typical Beauty is to a great extent intended as a substitute for it. Burke's idea that the sense of the Sublime is based in dread is well confuted.

[Quotes, with omissions, from 'The fact is that' to 'it to be so', 'Works' 3: 128-30.]

This is too general to serve any purpose. The adjective 'Sublime' surely has some separate meaning, which Burke aimed at defining, though we think he failed. He regarded it as antithetical to Beauty: the Oxford Graduate would wipe it out of the vocabulary, or allow it only a very general use in the study, not of natural objects, but of the human mind. Both appear to us to be wrong. Sublimity we take to be a quality as distinct as the having a name in the vocabulary can make it; but we do not agree with Burke in ascribing it to a sense of dread. In a broad sense, in the 'sublimest' sense, nothing that we observe in the universe can be pronounced bad or destructive, save by a narrow assumption which has reference simply to our own finite nature and limited observation. That which destroys the individual does but work the preservation of the universal: fruits are destroyed to feed animals: whole generations of creatures perish that others may live - whole races die, as we find in the volume of geology, and help to build up a new surface of the globe, for more perfect races. But although the sense of individual

destruction may deeply impress the mind, undoubtedly the
predominant sense here is one of power and permanency, of
immortality. Does not this explain our admiring sense of
the sublime? Our feeling may be thus explained: although
the vast [the sublime] agencies of the universe crush and
destroy the individual, they keep up for ever the immortal
universe in which we live: we are proportionately impressed by the greatness of the interests at stake, we
feel a gratitude proportionate to the vastness of the
beneficent results; although our individual and small
interest is nullified. This feeling is thoroughly unselfish; it therefore exalts us in our own estimation. We
feel that we, petty men as we are, sympathise with the
universal; and we also, magnanimous, great, and of sublime
aspirations, can set aside our own small interests. Nature
acts with the concurrent approval of man; whose sense of
his own magnanimity exalts him to a companionhood with
immortal beneficence.

A large section of the book is devoted to an analysis
of imagination; which fails in distinctness; yet it is
valuable for insisting on the fact that imagination is not
something distinct and opposed to truth, but is the intuitive perception of truth; also for some useful distinctions between Imagination and Fancy, and for some illustrations of the mode in which the mind operates under the
process of composition. Where the author deals with practical working he is usually happy. It is still where he
gets into theoretical analysis that he appears to us most
liable to error.

We think that he might have made a valuable addition to
this portion of his work, by adding a more emphatic and
substantial assertion of the fact, that the quality of
Imagination is necessary to the painter, even in the most
humble 'walks of art.' No picture can be well painted
without the active exertion of the imagination: it is for
the want of it that mere mechanical copying fails to catch
the traits of life; because the most salient and characteristic traits of vitality never remain sufficiently long
before the observation to suffer the mechanical process of
copying. The mere copyist always imitates something else in
which those highly characteristic but fugitive traits have
disappeared. This, like most essential truths, is true of
all arts as well as painting. Our meaning will be best explained by a physical illustration. In every muscular
action, especially in that which is vigorous and sudden, it
will be observed that the greatest contraction of the muscle
takes place immediately before the action is perceived.
Thus, in the action of walking, the most vigorous contraction of the muscles named glutei will be perceived, by
resting the hand behind the hip, to occur immediately

before the retraction of the leg; that most vigorous contraction of the muscles subsides immediately into a minor
action, while the act of retracting the leg is continued.
These sharp and vigorous contractions of the muscle endure
only for an instant of time. In the same way, on any sudden
demand for attention, any sudden emotion of surprise, the
eyelids are vigorously opened and constrained. They cannot
be retained so above a few seconds, for not only does the
strain become painful to the eyeball, but the muscles lose
the energy necessary for that sharp and vigorous action.
The painter must learn these actions entirely from observation on subjects in a state of *bonâ fide* activity: he never
sees them in the model which he sets before him to copy.
Could the model produce them for a moment, the thing would
be gone before the painter could turn his eye to the canvass; and no reward would enable the hireling to reproduce
the effect many times in succession. The artist, therefore,
who trusts slavishly to his model, who copies that modified and secondary action of the muscles, which is more
susceptible of being permanently sustained, not only fails
to impart perfect truth to his figures, but actually
asserts falsehood. He places his men and women under circumstances which require the most sudden and vigorous
action of the muscles – running for instance – but throws
the muscles merely into the secondary state of excitement:
he undertakes to make designs of startling events, but
gives to his eyes a fixed stare instead of that sudden
glance which is seen and gone in an instant. Hence in the
vast majority of inferior artists, especially in the
English school, that want of real vitality which is their
curse. Of course, the power of catching these fugitive
traits implies great readiness and fulness of observation,
retentive memory for the particular class of facts, the
power of recalling them by force of imagination, and perfect mastery of hand in drawing. The excessive rarity with
which our artists see the figure in a naked state, excepting in the shape of inanimate models, is, no doubt, a
fearful difficulty in their way.

It would be a great mistake to suppose that the power
of imagination upon which we insist, is necessary solely
in inventive pictures; it is no less needed in portraiture.
The traits which impart vitality – the glance of the eye
in the sudden turn to look at you – the fixing of the
mouth – the breathing of the nostril – the contour of the
cheek harmonising with the features, the action of the
limbs, the posture of the whole body; all have disappeared
by the time the 'sitter' is comfortably placed. The artist
can copy from his 'sitter' no more than the general forms
and the position of the features; the nicer traits of
vitality must be caught from observation, retained in the

mind of the artist, and impressed upon the canvass from
memory. The general form of the 'sitter,' indeed, may be
traced upon the canvass by the process of copying; but the
perfect figure must be brought out by the process of imagination. The artist must imagine the original, not as he
sees him sit before him, but as he has seen him in an animated condition; and that imagined figure, not the sleepy
creature before him, must be the figure in his picture.

We are now in a condition to understand what is the
nature of art - what is the mission of art. Nature in art
is the seizing and collecting those traits which are
essential to the particular subject in hand. In the case
of an historical picture, the essentials are the traits of
the predominant passions concerned in the event. Commonly
the landscape and other accessories are not essentials,
but merely form the *situs in quo*. They may be given by the
process rather of representation, than of copying. It will
suffice, though they fall negatively far short of perfect
imitations, if they do not contain positive contradictions
to truth or possibility in reference to the function which
they have to perform in the picture; for instance, a stone
pillar, which has to support a roof, must be perpendicular,
must look of sufficient strength to support that roof; but
it does not much matter whether it exactly imitate marble
or any other kind of substance, so that it be of sufficient solidity for its purpose. As you come nearer, however, to the immediate agents under the influence of the
passion, you must have more perfection: the human forms
must be more developed and more complete in their parts;
and to avoid abrupt transitions, the dresses of the forms,
though less elaborated, must also be more marked out than
the remoter accessories. These rules will be well illustrated by the simplest of all great paintings, those of
Raphael.

In other kinds of painting of course the application of
the rule varies: in landscape, for instance, the chief
attention will be turned to the natural objects; the
figures will sink to the position of accessories. To draw
attention to them by too great elaboration or prominency,
or to draw attention by the same means to the mere accessories of architecture and foliage in an historical design,
would derogate from the concentrated unity of the picture.
The natural in art, therefore, is not the making a perfect
transcript of all the objects which in nature might be
included in the view circumscribed by the frame, but is
the seizing on those vital traits which are essential to
the main action of the piece.

The mission of art is to fulfil the same function with
beauty in nature. It reflects external existences, retains

those which are transitory for our slower view, impresses
the consciousness of them more emphatically upon the perception, seals the sense of existence, of goodness. It
enhances, then, our happiness by the same direct means as
that in which it is enhanced by the sense of existence
itself. To see a beautiful form illustrated by Titian; an
exalted sentiment illustrated by Raphael; or a fine landscape by Ruysdael, raises the same sentiments in us that
the objects would themselves excite in nature, with this
difference: the same things in nature might be attended by
circumstances that would disturb us, and deprive us of the
proper and deliberate observation. In the case of landscape the sense of sight would be divided by the sense of
hearing; in the case of the nobler sentiment our own emotions might prevent a complete perception of the picture;
and other subjects than picturesque beauty might disturb
the attention in the presence of Titian's lady. Painting
retains to us such spectacles for deliberate and undis-
turbed contemplation. The effect is no doubt enhanced, too,
by some reference to the skill of the human being who
executed it.

The sight of beauty, or of those things which elevate
the mind, beget congenial feelings on the part of the
observers. Familiarity with graceful aspects tends sym-
pathetically to induce graceful action, and graceful
habits of action tend to induce, by an inverse process,
the graceful habits of mind from which in part they
originate: in part we say, for grace is partly physical.
He who is familiar with art, therefore, in its highest and
best aspect, as a reflex of nature, will be a happier and
a better man.

Such we take to be a very rude and hasty sketch of the
theory of art. We cannot think that the Oxford Graduate
has fully developed it; but we are prepared emphatically
to declare that his work is the most valuable contribution
towards a proper view of painting, its purpose and means,
that has come within our knowledge. Probably he printed
too soon; but we cannot regret that he did so, since the
comparatively trivial motive that first spurred him, seems
to have urged him far forward in a path of much usefulness.

His third volume, we are given to understand, is to
elucidate his views by copious references to the works of
the great masters, and is to be illustrated by engravings;
and the first volume is to be reprinted to be uniform with
the other two. To that we have no objection; but we still
hope some day to see a work of larger scope and maturer
execution from the same hand.

By the bye, we should like to know what lights the
Oxford Graduate draws from photography.

'Modern Painters I, II'

1843, 1846

5. DR JOHN BROWN, FROM AN UNSIGNED REVIEW, 'NORTH BRITISH
REVIEW'

February 1847, vol. 6, 401-30

Dr John Brown (1810-82), a good friend of Ruskin's for
many years, received his MD from Edinburgh in 1833. Brown
had studied art before he studied medicine and throughout
his life he wrote on both literary and medical matters. He
is perhaps best known for 'Rab and His Friends', a collection of informal essays. Brown's review of 'Modern
Painters I, II' drew an appreciative letter from Ruskin
('Works' 36: 66-8); of particular interest is the fact
that the criticism is marked by the nineteenth-century
system of editorial interpolation, for p. 94 ll. 17-20 are
not by Brown as Ruskin's letter suggests. See Introduction
duction, pp. 6-7.

This is a very extraordinary and a very delightful book,
full of truth and goodness, of power and beauty. If genius
may be considered (and it is as serviceable a definition
as is current) that power by which one man produces for
the use or the pleasure of his fellow men, something at
once new and true, then have we here its unmistakable and
inestimable handiwork. Let our readers take our word for
it, and read these volumes thoroughly, giving themselves
up to the guidance of this most original thinker, and most
attractive writer, and they will find not only that they
are richer in true knowledge, and quickened in pure and
heavenly affections, but they will open their eyes upon a
new world - walk under an ampler heaven, and breathe a
diviner air. There are few things more delightful or more

rare, than to feel such a kindling up of the whole faculties as is produced by such a work as this; it adds a
'precious seeing to the eye,' - makes the ear more quick
of apprehension, and, opening our whole inner-man to a new
discipline, it fills us with gratitude as well as admiration towards him to whom we owe so much enjoyment. And
what is more, and better than all this, everywhere
throughout this work, we trace evidence of a deep reverence and godly fear - a perpetual, though subdued acknowledgment of the Almighty, as the sum and substance, the
beginning and the ending of all truth, of all power, of
all goodness, and of all beauty.

Not the least valuable effect of such productions is
the temper of mind into which they put, and in which they
leave the reader - the point of sight to which they lead
him being as precious as the particular sights which they
disclose, so that he finds, in the unknown writer, a com-
panion, a teacher, a friend, who makes him a sharer in his
own strong feelings and quick thoughts - hurries him away
in his own enthusiasm - opens to him the gate Beautiful,
and shews him the earth and every common sight transfigured before him, - what is base, and personal, and
evanescent, yielding to what is eternal, spiritual, divine,
- and leaves him there more than delighted, instructed,
strengthened, ennobled under the sense of having not only
beheld a new scene, but of having held communion with a
new mind, and having been endowed for a time with the keen
perception, and the impetuous emotion of a nobler and more
penetrating intelligence.

We can have no stronger or more lamentable proof of the
low state of the public understanding and taste, as
regards painting and the other ideal arts, or of the
ignorance that prevails as to their true scope and excellence, and the kind of faculties required for the intelligent enjoyment of their productions, than in the reception which this remarkable book has met with from what is
called the literary world. The larger Reviews, as far as
we have seen, have taken no notice of it whatever, though
it contains more true philosophy, more information of a
strictly scientific kind, more original thought and exact
observation of nature, more enlightened and serious enthusiasm, and more eloquent writing than it would be easy to
match, not merely in works of its own class, but in those
of any class whatever. It gives us a new, and we think,
the only true theory of beauty and sublimity - it asserts
and proves the existence of a new element in landscape
painting, placing its prince upon his rightful throne - it
unfolds and illustrates, with singular force, variety and
beauty, the laws of art - it explains and enforces the

true nature and specific function of the imagination, with
the precision and fulness of one having authority, - and
all this delivered in language which, for purity and
strength and native richness, would not have dishonoured
the early manhood of Jeremy Taylor, of Edmund Burke, or of
the author's own favourite Richard Hooker.

On the other hand, those periodicals which are considered to represent the literature of the Fine Arts, and
to watch over their progress and interests, almost without
an exception, have treated it with the most marked injustice and the most shameful derision. We rejoice, in spite
of all this neglect and maltreatment, that it is finding
its way into the minds and hearts of men. This is better
shown by the first volume having come to a third edition,
than by any [sic] the most elaborate patronage from the
press. The national literature is in this case a good
index to the national mind and feeling; so that it is not
to be wondered at, that such productions as Charles Lamb's
Essays on the Genius of Hogarth, and on the Barrenness of
the Imaginative Faculty in the productions of Modern Art*
- Hazlitt's works on Art - those of Sir Charles Bell and
his brother John, should rarely occur, and be not much
regarded, and little understood, when they do, in a
country where Hogarth was looked upon by the majority as a
caricaturist fully as coarse as clever - where Wilkie's
Distraining for Rent could get no purchaser, because it
was an unpleasant subject - where, to this day, Turner is
better known as being unintelligible and untrue, than as
being more truthful, more thoughtful, than any painter of
inanimate nature, ancient or modern - where Maclise is
accounted worthy to illustrate Shakspeare, and embody
Macbeth and Hamlet, as having a kindred genius - and where
it was reserved to a few young self-relying unknown Scottish artists to purchase Etty's three pictures of 'Judith,'
the 'Combat,' and the 'Lion-like Man of Moab,' at a price
which, though perilous to themselves, was equally dis-
graceful to the public who had disregarded them, and
inadequate to the deserving of their gifted producer....

We have left ourselves no space for the second volume,
which though about one third in size is as to argument and
general interest fully more deserving and more admissible
of analysis than the first. There is much truth in it, and
something new as well as true, not in the way of any absolute new theory, but in completing and harmonizing many
truths into one system, and dismissing many errors. The
argument, as we have already explained, of this volume, is
Beauty, as art in all its functions has to deal with it.
It discusses, 1st, The Theoretic faculty as concerned with
the pleasures, the accuracy of the impressions of sense;

2d, False opinions upon beauty, that it is not itself but
something else, truth, usefulness, association, symmetry,
&c. 3d, Beauty as typical of God's attributes - his
Infinity - his Unity, of his absolute Repose, of his Justice, of his Purity, of his moderation as the type of
government by law. 4th, Of vital beauty as relative, as
generic, as human. This brings him to imagination as the
master power in the painter, that which makes him one, or
rather that condition of his whole nature which makes him
look upon all nature, and feel it with the eye and the
mind of a painter, and gives him the vision and the
faculty. This chapter we could have wished to have delayed
ourselves and our readers over, it is so original, so
good. The author proves here, as elsewhere, that he has
himself the power he speaks of, and knows its high office.
It is well to remember that genius and imagination and
invention are not peculiar in their essence to men like
Homer, Milton, Michael Angelo, Hogarth, John Bunyan, or
Turner. No one man has any faculty which any other man has
not at least the rudiment of, and it is this that renders
it possible for a great genius to make known any of his
thoughts, his peculiar thoughts, to any and to all men;
and what we would wish to impress on our readers is, that
they, every one of them, have *some* imagination, *some*
fancy, *some* relish for and longing after the beautiful,
the tranquil, the clear; they had the first two in childhood, they will have them again in old age, and it is to
be hoped, cheered and enlightened by the others; and their
exercise, in this, as in all cognate things, will increase,
and rouse into conscious action and enjoyment, even the
minimum of either. The people among whom and from whom
Shakspeare rose, are capable, so to speak, or may be made,
capable of Shakspeare....

In conclusion, whatever be the estimate our readers may
form of the scientific, philosophical, literary, intellectual, and moral worth of this performance, and of the
degree of success with which the author has made out his
positions against the elder landscape painters and in
favour of the moderns, and whatever may be the place each
man shall assign to the extraordinary painter who occupies
so much of the mind and of the matter of the author, whatever be the general judgment formed of the true value of
this author's subject, and of the merits of his treatment
of it, all thoughtful, sober-minded men must be agreed as
to the necessity that is laid upon each one of us for ourselves, and for our neighbour, to do and be everything
that may help to counteract the master-evil of our times -
the fearful influence which the present, the actual, the
immediate, the seen and temporal, is every day getting

over every man.

God has multiplied this nation, and is multiplying it, in numbers, in intelligence, in power, with a rapidity of increase the limit and the result of which he himself alone can tell; but he has not, in proportion, 'increased its joy;' its goodness is behind its greatness, and it is one of the pillars of his throne - one of the conditions of his own existence, as it is of theirs, that his rational creatures, made in his own image, should find rest and happiness nowhere but in him; that the child should never be a happy child away from his father; and that it is not many wise men, not many mighty, not many noble, but only 'the pure in heart' who see him and are blessed. What is the only cure for all this no man need be ignorant of, it is shining down upon him like the sun at noon; but this is not our province. What we assert, and are prepared to prove is, that in the right exercise of the impersonal emotions, in the full understanding and feeling of imaginative works, we have a natural counter-poise to these domineering, overbearing tendencies, and that, as already mentioned, it is not less true that Painting and all the Ideal arts may be made to confer to morality and magnanimity not less than to delectation.

We have made no observation on the merits merely lite-rary of this work. The faults both of substance and of form are all resolvable into the fact of the author's being a young man, an ardent young man, an earnest, ardent young man. He writes with great spirit and effect; is not seldom eloquent; and assuredly we do not like him the less that style has been but a secondary consideration with him, or, to speak more correctly, has, with the exception of some occasional fine work (chiefly in the second volume,) been no great object at all. He writes because he has something and much to say, and because he is resolved and eager to say it, not from any idle ambition of making sentences and fine writing. He has obviously long medi-tated his subject; he is master of it as a whole and in detail; he feels it intensely; it burdens him till he throws it off, or, to use a favourite phrase of the day, he has a mission to fulfil, and he applies himself vigorously to fulfil it, indifferent as to the manner.

This is so far excellent; where thought is, expression will come, and as a consequence of this absence of art, the author has attained the greatest measure of ease, vivacity and directness, without any more important sacri-fice of the essential attributes of propriety and elegance than a very idiomatic and somewhat colloquial writer will always be exposed to. But it is nevertheless true, that to this excellence is also to be ascribed an important fault

which pervades the composition of these volumes, and which
is rather to be felt on a perusal of the work, or of large
portions of it, than rendered sensible by examples. We
refer to a tendency to overdo, a certain redundance, an
accumulation of words and images, sometimes, but we will
say for the author, of ideas more often; which occurs in
the illustration and enforcement of favourite positions
and opinions, and is meant, no doubt, to impress them more
strongly on the mind of the reader, but which must only
have an unhappy contrary result, if it brings over his
composition that of the most fatal of all faults, tedious-
ness. Perhaps this fault may go farther; and in speaking
of the writer, we speak of a class of great and valuable
thinkers. Accompanying, and arising partly from the same
cause, is a certain involution and obscurity which in our
author's case sometimes, though rarely, interrupts the
general distinctness. We perceive how this and the
occasional language we speak of would disappear, if what
we read had the advantage of being orally delivered by
himself; and this, we believe, affords a clue at all
times to a great deal of defective and clouded writing.
A young author especially, or one who is new to his occupation, and who has been accustomed chiefly to render himself intelligible in discussion or spoken discourse of any
kind, when assisted by voice, by tone, by pause, by the
countenance, the gesticulation, the manner, and all that
combination of which, and not of utterance alone, speaking
is made up, and by which it is distinguished from writing,
is apt, when compelled to abandon those familiar advantages, to forget how needful it is to compensate the want
of them by the different means of perspicuity, suasion,
and power, which writing places in his hands. The present
writer we suppose to have been accustomed to pour forth,
in conversation or debate, the thoughts and emotions of a
very vigorous, fertile, and beautiful mind. He is young,
and he feels the same or a still greater anxiety to transfer to his readers his opinions in their integrity, and
with all their circumstances about them. This leads him to
needless and hurtful repetition, and to neglect sometimes,
the proper management and subordination, and what would
often be better, the total exclusion, of concomitant and
subsidiary ideas, when these crowd in for expression. In
his impetuosity and abundance, he delivers all parenthetically, or in regular procession, as may happen, with
some carelessness of transition and expression, with some
colloquial depravations, and with a tone which the best
taste does not always justify. He writes, in short, if not
what may be termed a colloquial style, yet one more
proper to the chair than to the press. It is a fault

perhaps pardonable enough, and has its own agreeableness,
and is one from which the most brilliant and profound of
living critics is by no means free....

...We have occasionally also to complain of more than
faults, of some vice of style. We do not allude now to
those villainous coinages of words by which so many incapable writers of our time do their utmost to debase our
beautiful language, nor to a rather peculiar species of
humour or pleasantry in which this author transiently indulges; for in these, if he sometimes misses, he not
seldom hits. We pass those things. What we refer to is
some slight symptom and partial outbreak of the sin of
effort. This blemish is more apparent in the opening sec-
tions of the second volume, and we notice it with the
greater regret, because what gratified us so much in the
first portion of the work was, as we have stated, a remarkable exemption from this very weakness. We wish, that,
in his third and, in some respects, most important volume,
the author would determine, at once and for good, not to
be eloquent any more.

The article with which we have some quarrel, and which
is not in keeping with the general taste of our author, is
among the tawdriest of the rhetorical wardrobe, being a
sort of accumulated and turgid period, much indebted for
its prolongation to the conjunction 'and' - in which, in
former days, a well-known writer in this city was accustomed to deliver his strained and frigid sublimities. This
miserable old garment, the worse (as most old garments
are) for the wear, is still an important article of dress
among the brood of young Wilsons and Carlyles who swarm in
the present day, and who, for wise and inscrutable purposes, are permitted to distress us, at intervals in the
magazines and in the lecture room, with their insane
emphasis and raptures, and their very overpowering sensibilities. We wish, however, that men of sense and reason
would leave it to these people, and must regret that a
writer of the manliness and vigour, the native taste, and
independent temper of our author, should have thought it
worth his while to pick it up and use it.

So much for our fault finding. As when we reprove those
we best love, we often do it more severely than we
intended, or than we would any one else, in the very
'luxury of disrespect,' we may be understood to have made
our reproof rather too loudly, but we believe it to be
true and to be important. What we owe to him of profit, of
delight, of knowledge, and of goodness, we do not care
again to say - We are, perhaps, too grateful to be very
judicious. In our own case, not only did his thoughts come
to us like manna from heaven, but they came likewise to us

in the wilderness - when in glorious autumn we found ourselves with all our friends elsewhere, 'in populous city
pent, where houses thick and sewers annoy the air,' bringing by contrast into our minds the breath of pleasant
villages and farms, the airs of the uplands and mountain
tops, the voice of the great deep, the smell of grain, of
tedded grass, of kine, each rural sight, each rural sound.
- This book which we then got for the first time, gave us
wings, opened new doors into heaven, brought the country
into the town, made the invisible seen, the distant near;
so that it happened unto us as to poor Susan, 'at the
corner of Wood Street,' when she heard, 'in the silence of
morning the song of *that* bird;' and behold! -

    'Twas a note of enchantment; what ails her? she sees
    A mountain ascending, a vision of trees;
    Bright volumes of vapour through Lothbury glide,
    And a river flows on through the midst of Cheapside.

Note

* We do not mean that our literature of art is deficient
in, much less is destitute of, many excellent treatises on
the art of painting, or the history and value of pictures,
as commodities to be bought and sold. It would be to contradict the practical tendency of the English mind in all
its multifarious doings. What we refer to, is the want of
a true philosophy, of a central idea that explains everything, and satisfies all conditions, and displays that
faculty or state of the mind which presides over the soul
of painting both in the artist and in the spectator....
There is one living writer, whom we must exempt from our
charge of ignorance and indifference as to the nature of
art; - this is that most entertaining humourist, most
vigorous writer, and most thoroughly humane man, Mr.
Thackeray, better known as Michael Angelo Titmarsh. He is
the good genius of the incomparable 'Punch;' his wit has
no malice - his mirth no folly. He is himself an artist,
and his pencil often conveys to the eye what his kindred
pen cares not or is unable to express. But we refer at
present specially to his serious, beautiful criticisms
upon the pictures in the Louvre, or his Parisian Sketch-
book, and to several notices of the London Exhibitions in
Frazer's Magazine. They are slightly done, but indicate
his knowledge, and his affection for all that is true and
good in painting.

'The Seven Lamps of Architecture'

1849

6. UNSIGNED REVIEW, 'EXAMINER'

16 June 1849, 373

The 'Examiner', a middle-class liberal weekly, exerted an influence out of proportion to its modest circulation. Until very shortly (1847) before the publication of 'The Seven Lamps' it bore the pronounced stamp of that highly principled, forceful journalist Albany Fonblanque (1793-1872). The evaluation of Ruskin's book is notable for its clarity, fairness, and balance. See Introduction, pp. 8-9.

The author of this essay belongs to a class of thinkers of whom we have still too few among us. He began by the study of art: and his range was even in that direction limited - it was the study of art in its mediæval forms. But he was insensibly led, while seeking to explain to himself the source of the pleasure derived from the contemplation of his favourite works of art, and to invent canons for expressing the merits of the artists, to compare them with the productions of other ages and climes, and thus generalise his principles. Hence his former treatise, and hence more particularly this which is before us. Possessed of a rich vein of imagination, and with a somewhat discursive turn of mind, he here pursues with eagerness all the analogies suggested by his favourite pursuit, and takes pleasure in pointing out how the maxims useful for the architect may be made available in every other department of human exertion. Combining with his other qualities, strong devotional tendencies, and that instinct of self-control which is the basis of the puritanical character, he has aimed at moralising everything - at elevating the

art of architectural construction into the discharge of a
moral duty; and at making the works of architecture enduring moral lessons.

A mind so constituted, and acting in obedience to such
impulses, necessarily generates a peculiar character in
the individual and in the results of his meditations. There
is a dreaminess about his theories, the result of the
freedom with which he habitually gives the reins to imagination; and there is a quaintness, the result of his disposition to moralise art and play with analogies. There is
an occasional tendency to generalise precipitately; to
allow imagination to usurp the throne of reason; and
unduly to indulge individual sympathies and antipathies.
But the mind that is at work is a pure and a powerful one;
and the persevering labour of years has enabled it to
evolve important truths, though they are expressed by
means of imagery and phraseology peculiar to itself. Even
this peculiarity, however, imparts a certain raciness and
freshness to hacknied themes. They assume an impressiveness to which we have not been accustomed; and in the
peculiar point of view taken throughout his book, the
writer discovers much that had escaped all notice from
others. Mr Ruskin's earnest sincerity imparts additional
value to his reflections. By following courageously the
natural bent of his genius, he has produced a work, which
though it has many defects, no one can read without advantage both to intellect and character.

By the 'seven lamps of architecture' we understand Mr
Ruskin to mean the seven fundamental and cardinal laws,
the observance of and obedience to which are indispensable
to the architect who would deserve the name. The lamps are
the lights the architect must work by. The lamp of sacrifice relates chiefly to great works of a religious or
other public character. It is the conviction that their
construction is an offering up of something which the
offerers deem precious, on the shrine of duty. The lamp of
truth is that enlightenment, moral or intellectual, which
causes the mind to reject with distaste all tawdry sub-
stitutes for real beauty, and all deceptive appearances of
a richness of material, or costly expenditure of labour,
that are beyond the means of the constructor. The lamp of
power is the sense that stedfastness and endurability are
essential elements in architectural grandeur. The lamp of
beauty is that delicate sense of the graceful which
rejects the mixture of all incoherent loveliness in form
or colour, and every ornament which is not in harmony with
the purpose and design of a building. The lamp of life is
that instinctive vitality in the architect which enables
him, even when he adopts suggestions of form and

combinations from others, to impart originality to his
work, and escape the risk of reproducing a mere lifeless
copy. The lamp of memory is that abiding impression of
historical fitness which teaches the architect the necessity of conforming to the requirements and habits of the
society amid which he lives. The lamp of obedience is the
resolution on the part of the young architect to condescend to remain long a learner before he aspires to be a
master in his art; and the avoidance of the self-pride
which leads beginners to fancy themselves superior to
rules.

As expanded and illustrated by the author's taste and
imagination, these seven cardinal principles are made to
exhaust all the requirements of the architect. The study
of 'The Seven Lamps' - for a mere perusal of it would be
unavailing - will not, indeed furnish the student with a
collection of mechanical rules to serve as a substitute
for poverty of original genius; but if the reader is an
artist in his soul, it will inspire him with the elevation
of aim, and suggest to him those clear views of what he
has to do, which cannot fail to qualify him for the highest achievements. The essay is calculated, if any mere
essay can be, to supply to the architects of the day what
they are most deficient in; and wanting which, their
architecture must of necessity continue tame and frivolous.
It inculcates throughout the necessity of preserving a
correspondence, a sympathy, between the destination of
buildings and their forms and decorations. It thus guards,
on the one hand, against profusion of tawdry, inappropriate ornament, on mere domestic structures and work-
shops; and on the other, against the silly adaptation of
ornaments suited for the religious edifices of a peculiar
faith, to structures destined for legislative debate. But
the book would be a dangerous manual for one who brings no
original thought of his own to the study of it. Imposing
and seductive from its imaginative beauty - misleading,
from the occasional subsidence of the author into mere
quaintnesses and plays upon words - it would puff the
shallow mind into coxcombry. But whoever brings to its
perusal sympathies in accordance with those of the author,
the power to winnow intellectual wheat from chaff, and
some store of acquired knowledge, will have reason to
esteem his first acquaintance with it as an epoch in the
development of his mind. And men of other intellectual
pursuits - the politician, the moralist, the divine - will
find in it ample store of instructive matter, as well as
the artist.

We may possibly hereafter subjoin a few specimens of
the author's peculiar tone and manner.

7. SAMUEL FERGUSON, FROM AN UNSIGNED REVIEW, 'DUBLIN
UNIVERSITY MAGAZINE'

July 1849, vol. 34, 1-14

Samuel Ferguson (1810-86), Irish poet and antiquarian, was
educated at Trinity College, Dublin, called to the Irish
bar in 1838 (QC 1859), and knighted for his services as
deputy-keeper of the Irish records. He wrote with some
success in the ballad form, but perhaps his most ambitious
work was 'Congal' (1872), a poem of epic length rather
than nobility. Ferguson also contributed to 'Blackwood's'
and near the end of his life was elected President of the
Royal Irish Academy. The deletions in the following
review are made where the critic strays into personal by-
ways and where he extends unduly his exegesis of each
lamp. But the criticism illustrates Ferguson's unique
apprehension of the wider implications of 'The Seven Lamps'
and of Ruskin's eminent aesthetic position. See Introduction, p. 9.

We may as well apprise the reader at once, that these are
not seven great architects, nor seven great buildings; but
the seven principles or feelings of Sacrifice, Truth,
Power, Beauty, Life, Memory, and Obedience, which Mr.
Ruskin considers the presiding influences of good architecture. The classification appears somewhat arbitrary,
and the nomenclature sufficiently fantastic. We would
rather, ourselves, that Mr. Ruskin had neither adopted a
mystical number nor a figurative terminology. We would not
feel much confidence in the invitation of the artist who
should entitle his essay the Seven Pencils of Painting, or
of the musician who set forth the principles of his art as
the Seven *Plectra* (we willingly avoid the English equivalent) of Harmony. Neither does it in the least commend
Mr. Ruskin's *Heptalampadon*, that it presents itself to us
in a mysterious binding of mediæval knots, symbolic mon-
sters, and black-letter epigraphs. A note informs us that
these mystical decorations are from the floor of San
Miniato at Florence. In San Miniato, we dare say, they are
suitable and significant; but, stamped on the cover of a
modern essay, they do not afford much inducement to penetrate beneath forms so barbaresque in search of useful
information or elegant learning. With his title and externals, however, our quarrel with Mr. Ruskin in a great
measure ceases. We remember the persuasive force and
picturesque vigour of argument which brought home his plea

for the modern painters with so much cogency to the
reason, through processes affording so much delight to the
imagination; and, recognising in the author of that book a
writer of note and consideration, we open this essay of
his on architecture, with the respect due to an original
thinker and an elegant expositor of new opinion.

Of man's works on the globe which he inhabits, the
greatest beyond measure are those effected by the husbandman. If all the structural works of mankind were brought
together in one place, they would not make, on any broad
prospect of the earth, so considerable a show as the
altered surface of one well-tilled province. But after the
husbandman, the builder is the greatest of workmen. If he
build well, he builds for both profit and delight; for
uses intellectual and moral, as well as for the purposes
of practical utility. Every excellence in his art associates itself with feeling and sentiment. Whether he raise
the towers or bastions of the fortress, or the spires and
pinnacles of the temple set apart for the worship of God,
he deals in forms and proportions, combinations, and sym-
metries which, with every purpose they subserve, speak a
poetic language of their own, intelligible, impressive,
and almost as lasting as the divine utterances of the poet
himself, dealing in the unencumbered expressions of speech.
How to build so as to attain this utterance is a more
difficult inquiry than how to compose an epic or a tragedy. For the poem is a work wholly intellectual; but the
building must first be useful, and is only collaterally
capable of this sort of expression. Hence the rarity of
essays on architectural, as compared with those on literary, taste. Of late, indeed, the peculiar theological
tendencies of England have called forth some discussions
and inquiries touching the capacity of particular architectural styles for the expression of religious sentiment;
but none of these have aimed at any comprehensive analysis
of their subject; nor do we suppose any of their authors
will dispute with Mr. Ruskin the claim to be considered
our first philosopher of the arts and chief critic of
architectural expression.

The philosophic pretensions of the essay are, as we
have said, marred by the fantastic phraseology of the
title, and by the arbitrary reduction to a mystical number
of rules and principles expounded in the text. Defects of
style also contribute to make the work less acceptable
than it ought, for its proper merit's sake, to be, among
readers of settled judgment. There are here, as in the
'Modern Painters,' many flamboyant and even a few *rococo*
passages, where outline is lost in tracery, and projection
confounded by obtrusive imagery. But if we had not the

excesses, we might want the vigour of genius; and there
are very few of these verbal excrescences which we would
not be satisfied to retain rather than lose the meaning
which they overlay.

It almost shocks us to think that we should use words
so harsh as some of these may appear, towards a writer
whose pages we cannot open without delight. Every subject
is handled with such a charming novelty; with so much
feeling, and such graceful vivacity; we encounter at every
turn opinions so judicious, and yet so original; and are
sensible that we are dealing with a mind of such perfect
candour and integrity, that it requires an effort to preserve our own equipoise, and prevent our being carried
away by the strong current of Mr. Ruskin's enthusiasm for
mediæval art.

For, although our author professes to expound only
those principles which might be exemplified in any settled
style, it is entirely from mediæval works he draws his
illustrations. He is here plainly more at home than in the
Augustan or the Grecian school. His love of the delicate,
the picturesque, and the mysterious, here gratifies itself
in congenial forms of fretwork, of irregular arcades, and
half-discovered vistas. The solemn roof, suspended from
its unseen external props, fills him with a pleasing awe;
the inlaid patterns and variegated courses and diamonds of
different-coloured masonry, delight his sense of colour;
and the venerable air of the twelfth century inspires him
with a dreamy sentiment of Anglican Catholicity, and of
Anglican progress in religion and virtue, most humane and
amiable, and blamelessly patriotic. For our part, we dis-
card sentiments and associations of the mediæval kind. We
desire light and distinctness. We wish to see the roof
over our head supported by walls or pillars evidently
adequate to the burthen. We admire stateliness, regula-
rity, and spaciousness. We wish to breathe the free air of
the *stoa*; and amid gardens and fountains, and broad balu-
straded terraces, to ponder the lessons of Greek and Roman
wisdom. We prefer the garden front of Carton to the façade
of Eaton Hall; and consider Trinity College, Dublin, a much
nobler palace than any of the Colleges of Cambridge. With
these differences of taste and mental habit, we must endeavour to do justice to Mr. Ruskin's exposition of the
excellencies of mediæval architecture, with as little
leaning towards our own prepossessions as strong opinion
will allow.

Opinion is strong on both sides. 'I,' says Mr. Ruskin,
in his preface, 'must be prepared to bear the charge of
impertinence which can hardly but attach to the writer who
assumes a dogmatical tone in speaking of an art he has

never practised. There are, however, cases in which men
feel too keenly to be silent, and, perhaps, too strongly
to be wrong: I have been forced into this impertinence,
and have suffered too much from the destruction or neglect
of the architecture I have loved, and from the erection of
that which I cannot love, to reason cautiously respecting
the modesty of my opposition to the principles which have
induced the scorn of the one, or directed the design of
the other. And I have been the less careful to modify the
confidence of my statements of principles, because, in the
midst of the opposition and uncertainty of our architectural systems, it seems to me that there is something
grateful in any *positive* opinion, though in many points
wrong, as even weeds are useful that grow on a bank of
sand.' Some allowance may therefore be made for a little
positiveness on both sides; for we own, after reading all
that Mr. Ruskin has said so persuasively, as well as positively, in favour of the Romanesque and Gothic, we remain
more attached than ever to the clear, plain, spacious, and
majestic school of art in which our youth has been educated, and with which all the remains of our country's
prosperity and splendour are associated.

But it is time that we should trim our mediæval lamps
with Mr. Ruskin; and the first which we shall take up is
the Lamp of Sacrifice. We hope it is not difference of
opinion that makes us cautious, but we feel strongly
impelled again to quarrel with this kind of nomenclature.
Sacrifice, in connexion with mediæval architecture,
suggests the idea of the expiatory offering of the altar.
We know not exactly to what extent the Anglo-Catholics of
Mr. Ruskin's school may deem this a necessary part of
their ritual; but the enunciation of the spirit of sacrifice, as being the first requisite to a complete building,
sounds at first much the same as if one were told that the
most important part of the edifice consisted in the
arrangements for celebrating mass. This, however, is a
misapprehension. Mr. Ruskin's meaning is, that in devotional and memorial architecture we should seek the light of
that spirit which offers for such work precious things,
simply because they are precious, 'not as being necessary
to the building, but as an offering, surrendering, and
sacrifice of what is, to ourselves, desirable.' 'It is a
spirit, for instance,' he proceeds, 'which, of two
marbles, equally beautiful, applicable, and durable, would
choose the more costly because it was so; and, of two
kinds of decoration, equally effective, would choose the
more elaborate, because it was so, in order that it might,
in the same compass, present more cost and more thought.'
'The question,' he says 'is between God's house (for he at

once addicts his essay to Ecclesiastical architecture),
and ours. Have we no tessellated colours on our floors?
no frescoed fancies on our roofs? no gilded furniture in
our chambers? no costly stones in our cabinets? has the
tithe of these been offered? - they are, or they ought to
be, the signs that enough has been devoted to the great
purposes of human stewardship, and that there remains to
us what we can spend in luxury; but there is a greater and
prouder luxury than this selfish one, that of bringing a
portion of such things as these into sacred service, and
presenting them as a memorial that our pleasure as well as
our toil has been hallowed by the remembrance of Him who
gave both the strength and the reward. And until this is
done, I do not see how such possessions can be retained in
happiness.'

If this spirit prevailed, our churches would, doubtless, be more sumptuous; but it may be doubted if God
would be better worshipped. It appears to us, that if a
man were about to set apart a piece of ground for building
a church, and had two plots, in other respects equally
eligible, the one waste and the other a flower-garden, he
would act more acceptably - if God regard such considerations - by devoting to the church that which was of less
use and ornament in the daily requirements of life. If the
deity to be worshipped were Capitoline Jove, or Delian
Apollo, we could understand the use and merit of decorat-
ing his fanes with objects of sensuous luxury; could conceive how the self-sacrificing spirit of the votary who
should stint himself in his ordinary comforts, in order to
procure some beautiful offering, might be counted wholesome and meritorious among the priests of that sort of
temple; but having been accustomed to read 'The sacrifice
of God is a broken spirit: a broken and contrite heart, O
God, thou wilt not despise,' we cannot accept the guidance
of Mr. Ruskin's first lamp, in seeking a way to excellence
even in church-building, with any great degree of confidence. That the buildings dedicated to the service of God
should be spacious and beautiful, no one possessed of even
natural piety will deny; but that the edifice itself
should derive any architectural excellence from this
personal zeal which might prompt the devotee to contribute
a piece of marble, or that a piece of bronze, for its
decoration, over and above the effect of the contributed
matters themselves, is a refinement too delicate for
ordinary apprehension, and quite outside the compass of
our belief. The spirit of self-sacrifice which induces the
Irish peasant to lacerate his knees in going the rounds of
the station, might as well be said to confer an architectural grace on the stone huts and altars on the summit of

Croagh Patrick. He too walks by the light of a lamp, but
it is a dark-lantern, of sacrifice. In fact, the first
principle insisted on by Mr. Ruskin is a guide rather for
the founder or endower of the edifice than for the builder
of it; and, in our judgment, adds little, if it [sic] at all,
to the illumination cast on his proper subject by the lights
which follow.

Our next principle, designated the Lamp of Truth, may,
from its name, be more readily understood. Mr. Ruskin's
enunciation of this principle consists mainly in an energetic protest against the imitation surfaces which so
generally degrade the cheap constructions of modern parsi-
mony and pretension. Nothing, indeed, can be more offensive than these mock marbles and cast-metal imitations of
stone carvings. Cast iron is, of all the substances that
can be employed, either internally or externally, in
architecture, the most unsightly. We can hardly, with
propriety, employ it in anything beyond a railing or
balcony:-

[Quotes from 'I believe' to 'real decoration', 'Works' 8:
185-6.]

If we had time to delay on a minor topic, we might
interest, and perhaps instruct, our readers, by showing
the various distinctions Mr. Ruskin takes between the
allowable arts of coloring, gilding, and inlaying surfaces, and the abuses of factitious coatings which belie
the material beneath. The subject, however, is one patent
to every eye, and however ably handled, has not sufficient
attraction to withhold us from the more refined and
original speculations with which Mr. Ruskin's next chapter
is conversant, under the title of the Lamp of Power.
We here breathe a freer air, and walk beneath a loftier
sky. The poet has laid aside his surplice and mysterious
looks, and speaks with larger utterance and franker gestures. He is now to expound the law of grandeur in construction. Taking notice, then, that the great Architect
of nature not only rounds the pillars of the forest, and
arches the vaults of the avenue, but also 'reproves the
pillars of the earth, and builds up her barren precipices
into the coldness of the clouds, and lifts her shadowy
cones of purple into the pale arch of the sky;' and that
these 'refuse not to connect themselves, in man's
thoughts, with the work of his own hands;' that 'the grey
cliff loses not its nobleness when it reminds us of some
Cyclopean waste of mural stone;' that 'the pinnacles of
the rocky promontory arrange themselves, undegraded, into
fantastic semblances of fortress towns;' and that 'even

the awful cone of the far-off mountain has a melancholy
mixed with that of its own solitude, which is cast from
the images of nameless tumuli, on white sea-shores, and of
the heaps of reedy clay, into which chambered cities melt
in their mortality:' - seeing thus that nature herself
does not disdain to accept from the works of man the sentiment of power and majesty, whence comes that sentiment,
and in what does it consist besides the material impressiveness of bulk and weight?

And, first, the ability of man to emulate the mountain
in some of its most majestic features, is less limited
than we imagine:-

[Quotes from 'The apprehension' to 'parts can destroy',
'Works' 8: 103-4.]

...But, then, again, while aiming at confounding the
spectator's eye by the number of your parts, how avoid
confusing the parts themselves? As on the façade of the
new Houses of Parliament, the eye is overpowered by the
number of the features presented to it, yet the effect is
neither that of a great whole, nor of a great partitioned,
surface; but is at once flat and broken, without the
breadth of the flatness or the boldness of the disconnec-
tion. No one will ever arrest his wherry under its espla-
nade, or pause beneath the shadow of the lime-trees of
Lambeth, to wonder at the art which 'can make the face of
a wall look infinite, and its edge against the sky like an
horizon.' His eye will rather wander to the right, where
Somerset House rises in presidential state over the subject bridge and river; or passing by the lines of pinnacles which crowd the monotonous parapet, will look
beyond the Parliament Houses, at the Abbey; but the Houses
themselves, with all their bulk, must ever be insignificant, because, vast as the expanse is, it wants projection.

This, then, is the next consideration: how, while
preserving the unity of the façade, to break it with
recesses and projections marked enough to secure that
further expression of power which is given by compelling
the eye to admit its inability to master the multitude of
the parts, while the parts themselves, from their decision
and distinctness, refuse to be overlooked. We shall here
extract the whole of one of Mr. Ruskin's sectional paragraphs, where, with poetic copiousness of illustration, he
exhibits those analogies between the aspects of life and
of art on which our enjoyment and appreciation of these
architectural effects may be said in a great measure to
depend. That there is something hyperbolical in the style,

perhaps something overcharged in the sentiment, we may not
be prepared to deny; but we cannot read it, ourselves,
without emotions of saddened pleasure; we think of the
many stirring memories that are gathered in the dark recesses of the portico and colonnades of our own Bank; of
the blood-red shadows that lie beneath the architraves of
the Madeleine; of the deep receding archway of the Villa
Pamphili:-

[Quotes from 'Of these limitations' to 'noon-day sun',
'Works' 8: 116-17.]

To prosecute the inquiry into the various expansions of
these principles indicated by our author, would exhaust
our space, perhaps unduly task our readers' attention.
Expounded by the graceful and picturesque eloquence of Mr.
Ruskin, they cause no sense of weariness; but abstracted
and condensed in the meagre indications of a review, we
doubt if they would retain any part of the attraction for
the general reader with which Mr. Ruskin has succeeded in
investing them, even to their minutest details, in his
engaging pages. We shall, therefore, here lay down Mr.
Ruskin's Lamp of Power, in hopes that we may find his
next, the Lamp of Beauty, equally luminous.
While Mr. Ruskin ascribes the effect of majesty in
building to a sympathy with the effort and trouble of
human life, the effort allying itself with the power which
can raise the mass, and the trouble finding something congenial in the gloom and majesty of the form - so that a
great building should be a kind of image of humanity - he
attributes the effect of beauty, in the secondary details
of decoration, to an imitation more or less direct of the
forms of vegetable life. We do not feel that we are here
walking under the guidance of one who takes such assured
steps as our interpreter did in his last chapter. Mr.
Ruskin does not, in fact, walk directly up to any tangible
principle, so far as we can discern, in this part of his
explanatory progress, until he comes to that of the application of colour to buildings; and here, it seems to us,
he is eminently right and original....
The Lamp of Life! What is the life of a building? Is
not all architecture the putting together, in various
forms of wall and roof, of dead materials? That these may
be made to have an effect which, by a pardonable latitude
of speech, we call expression, may be admitted; although,
indeed, we often hear of expression where the truer term
would be dumb significance. But there are not so many eyes
which have apprehended that further expression of some
buildings which goes beyond the ordinary utterance of

power and beauty, and makes the stone not only awake these
emotions in the spectator, but awake them as by the appeal
of a being having a species of life, and we had almost
said, an activity of its own. There are such buildings
from Venice to Genoa, and from Como to the seven hills of
Rome; such feelings spring up, though, to the greater
number of minds, too vaguely to be at once apprehended, in
the Place of St. Mark, or in the market-place of Verona.
We walk among buildings which not only possess a kind of
voice, but a species of gesture. How has this air of
quasi-vitality been imparted? The inquiry is a refined and
difficult one; but here again, as in investigating the
sources of the sense of power, a retrospective glance at
the great conditions of the natural world is a necessary
preparation. Life, whether animal or vegetable, conflicts
against all the tendencies of brute matter. Matter is
gravitating, chrystalising, symmetrical; life is up-
springing, flowing, and unsymmetrically expansive. No two
leaves of the forest are alike, nor no two footstalks set
at the same inclination to their branches. The wavy outline of the plant is repeated in the flowing form of the
animal. It is as if life were a fire, and all matter which
it animates agitated by a lambent flame. How, then, shall
the architect, dealing with dead stone and timber, and
coerced by the necessities of his art to affect symmetrical form and arrangement, introduce forms and characteristics so discrepant, without repulsion and disorganisa-
tion? To some extent he may do so without much difficulty.
In the horizontal divisions of a building, we admit
inequality of dimension, without question. The first,
second, and other stories of a front so divided, are never
equal. Again, the eye admits inequality of number, both
in horizontal and vertical features, with equal facility.
These are palpable importations of the class of characteristics referred to, which the builder practises daily,
from the allotment of different heights for his different
floors, to the spacing out of his odd-numbered windows,
and even of his window-panes. But in carrying out the
infusion of similar inequalities into the interspaces
between the windows, and the intercolumniations of the
pillars, of an edifice; in imparting a flowing effect to
features, the main lines of which must still be horizontal
or vertical, here lies the art - here, the delicate difficulty of the task; for all must be imparted so as to be
unobservable by any but the eye of the skilled critic,
otherwise the general effect of solidity, of symmetry, and
of repose, and with this, the essential characteristics of
strength, and of capacity for use, for shelter and protection, would be lost. How this has been done in the

instances of St. Mark's, at Venice, the Duomo of Pisa, and
the Church of San Giovanni at Pistoja, Mr. Ruskin explains
by elaborate examination and measurement. It will astonish
the reader to perceive to what intricacies of desymmetri-
sation (if we may use the word) the artists of those
buildings have resorted. We shall extract his dissection
of the façade of San Giovanni's, where, it will be observed, the element of the flowing outline (always, to a
certain extent, attainable in the arcade) is added to
those of vertical and lateral inequality, by an independent undulation of the heads of the arcade arches themselves.

[Quotes from 'The church has' to 'five or six inches',
'Works' 8: 204-6.]

...But there are still two lamps remaining, by which,
possibly, we shall see our way to less antagonistic conclusions - the Lamp of Memory, and the Lamp of Obedience.
By the former, Mr. Ruskin would guide our civic and
domestic architects into a more enduring way of building,
commemorative of families and of events, instead of the
unstable and fragile method at present in use, both in our
private residences and many of our public edifices. It is
true, no one who builds only for his own day and little
hour on the world's stage, will leave anything in this
kind of memorial to excite the sympathy or the piety of
those who come after him, or to bind the present generation, when it shall have become the past, with those which
will speedily follow and take its place. And it doubtless
contributes much to the stability of society, and to the
virtue and happiness of men, that they should be bound,
one generation to another, by transmitted institutions and
monuments; of which latter, the domestic monuments of the
halls and hearths of our ancestors are surely most condu-
cive to the perpetuation of pious and reverent feelings;
charging us, as it were, with the preservation of the
heirlooms of our race, and continually reminding us that
we are but trustees and transmitters of the noble inheritance which civilisation entails on man, of truth, freedom, and social order. Let us cite another eloquent
passage, where Mr. Ruskin handles this subject with fine
feeling, and philosophy:-

[Quotes from 'For indeed the greatest' to 'language and of
life', 'Works' 8: 233-4.]

Hence, what we do ourselves, we ought to do, if it be
worthy our enjoyment, so lastingly as to be enjoyable also

by those who will come after us, even as our worthy and
pious predecessors have done for us. Such is the tenor of
this portion of Mr. Ruskin's work, less directly suggestive of the method of attaining to that durability which
it commends, than other portions of the essay are of the
means of pursuing their particular objects, but highly
humane, refreshing, and instructive. It is more social
than architectural, more philosophical than scientific. It
neither adds to, nor detracts from, the force of the argument for mediæval revival which runs through the preceding
chapters, and against which we remain proof; but it greatly increases our admiration for the comprehensive piety
and humanity of the writer. As the ostensible object of
the work, however, is to expound the principles of architecture, as put in effectual operation in the works themselves, rather than the sentiments and feelings leading to
them in the minds of those who institute their building,
and our object in this notice is to inform our readers of
what Mr. Ruskin has achieved in the former department, we
shall not linger on what we regard rather as social ethics
than as the exposition of architectural methods, and shall
therefore proceed to the seventh and last division of Mr.
Ruskin's subject, which bears the somewhat ominous title
of the Lamp of Obedience.

Mr. Ruskin writes, in this chapter, with the saddened
tone of a patriot who perceives that his nation has
reached her culminating point, and is already tending
downward. There is a remarkable similarity in his tone and
in that of another recent writer, Mr. Fergusson, whose
work on architecture we lately noticed, in reference to
the same disheartening subject; not that we mean for a
moment to rank the two names together, but the coincidence
of opinion is the more remarkable where the pretensions of
the writers are so different. Both perceive the fact that
the point has been attained to in English society, where
the idleness of the upper classes has acquired too large
credits on the industry of the producers. It is the condition which we read of in the classics, and in the earlier
works of history, as that of national luxury. It is not
the accumulation of great wealth in the hands of a few,
but the accumulation of great wealth - that is to say, of
the right to live idly on the toil of the producer - in
the hands of a great and excessive number. The producer is
overtasked to supply so many mouths of the unproductive.
Excessive toil below begets ignorance, and lays the foundation for possible brutality. Excessive idleness above
begets folly, saps virtue, and sows the seeds of social
dissolution. Frivolous pursuits leave no adequate energy
or attention for the right cultivation of any of the

social arts. A capricious dilettantism supplies the place
of that manly and consistent appreciation of architecture
which distinguished the English nobility and gentry of the
last century. Opinion is confused, and style lost. To be
satisfied that the fact is so, one need only walk through
the gorgeous disarray of the club-houses, or pause where
the noblest site in Europe is deformed by the public
edifices of Trafalgar-square. Amid the multitude of
styles, it is impossible to predict which will be uppermost in the course of a year, or whether any one possesses
the innate vigour to take such a lead of the others as
will render it the English style of even a portion of our
century. From this confusion and distraction of the
national taste, Mr. Ruskin sees no means of extrication
but by the enforcement of some one style by law; and
indeed little hope of national or social amelioration, but
by the general inculcation of the same spirit of increased
obedience to civil and ecclesiastical authority. The
opinions of a man of so much ability are to be received
with consideration. The means unquestionably exist for
carrying out the recommendation of enforcing an established architectural style, through the schools of design
administered by the government; and unhappily so much of
our local affairs in Ireland is now under official management, that the imposition of any style, from the Chinese
to the Mexican, on Ireland, would be a matter of the
utmost facility. In fact, Mr. Ruskin's recommendation has
already here been anticipated by the Irish Board of Public
Works, who have not only selected a particular style for
public works in this country, but have adopted the very
style suggested by Mr. Ruskin. As the practical results of
that proceeding on their part are now such as enable us to
judge of it on its merits, and the results here may possibly have some influence in the further progress of Mr.
Ruskin's views in England, we propose to devote some
further attention at a future time to this important
subject.

We cannot, however, even though with a prospect of soon
returning to it, take leave of our subject or of its
illustrator, without again acknowledging our obligation to
Mr. Ruskin for the moral treat, far more valuable than any
architectural analysis, which his present essay has
afforded us. He writes with even more feeling than sentiment, and with philosophic meaning more profound than
either. Human life and destiny are his subjects far more
than any art of construction or decoration. As an essay on
the critical principles of design in building, the work
will be permanently known as containing the first systematic exposition of the beauties of barbaresque art. But

there are none of us, in however fastidious an Augustan
school we may have been educated, or however little we may
care for the *rationale* of a style which we deem unsuitable
for any purpose of present use or ornament, who will not
also recognise and prize it as the work of an interpreter
between man and nature, making us acquainted with many
unnoticed signs and tokens of the Divine love which sur-
rounds us, and while bringing our faculties of perception
into harmony with a novel and interesting class of beautiful objects, bringing our hearts and minds also into harmony with truth and virtue. Some faults there are, some
imperfections, and verbal excesses; a show of argumenta-
tive sequence somewhat ostentatious, and occasionally
assumed for passages which are not logically, nor even
analogically, consecutive; but it is a work which will
offer abundant opportunity for the exercise of the
author's maturer skill, in many future editions; and
which, we think, with some portion at least of the essay
on 'Modern Painters,' and in some form of condensation and
closer sequence of thought, may yet obtain a place among
the standard works of English literature. And when we
prophesy an admission among our standard writers for Mr.
Ruskin, we assure him we do not mean that his volumes
should rank lower than those of Burke, or that they should
be confounded in any way with the minor multitude of respectable books to which the character of standard works is
too often idly imputed by cotemporary critics.

8. J.M. CAPES, UNSIGNED REVIEW, 'RAMBLER'

July 1849, vol. 4, 193-201

John Moore Capes (1813-89) was instrumental in founding
and, for ten years, conducting the 'Rambler', a short-
lived publication primarily for Roman Catholic converts.
Newman also had some association with it and edited it
briefly in 1859. Under Capes, and others, the 'Rambler' was
fiercely controversial in its criticisms of the Catholic
Church and its priesthood. Capes's review of 'The Seven
Lamps' reveals a trenchant, aggressive pen fired with
spiritual zeal and offering a perspective on some of the
spiritual complexities of the 1840s. See Introduction,
p. 9.

Mr. Ruskin will, we trust, require no apology for the tone
of the following remarks. So plain-spoken a person will
not, we are assured, take it ill if he meets with some few
of those controversial blows which he bestows with such
hearty goodwill whenever and wherever he pleases. Nor will
he, or any of our readers, conclude, from the character of
our strictures upon his recent performance, that we
account it otherwise than a book of great ability and
interest, and well worth the study of every man who views
art as something more than a mere fashionable amusement.
If we dwell more upon its errors than its merits, it is
because the latter will commend themselves to every
thoughtful mind, while the former are often enforced with
a plausibility and an energy which will take many persons
by surprise, and captivate the fancy, while they fail to
commend themselves to the calmer and more critical judgment.

We rise, then, from the perusal of this book at a loss
whether most to admire the genius of its author or to
wonder at his folly. It has evidently been Mr. Ruskin's
misfortune to have associated with few persons who were
at all able to enter into his views, to discuss them with
him on grounds which he himself would respect, and to give
him the advice which the constitution of his mind and the
defects of his information demand. Possessing critical
talents of a very high order, a diligent observer and
investigator, and with a soul far above the trashy impostures which in the present day usurp the title of works of
art and essays on its cultivation, he yet labours under
two or three disadvantages which operate seriously to the
deterioration of his otherwise most valuable books. He has
unhappily an overweening confidence in his own theories
and feelings, and a proportionate contempt for all who
disagree with him; his studies have been a good deal
limited to works of art, books on art, and English poetry,
to the exclusion of other and more severe means for disciplining the mind and forming the taste, while on certain
topics his ignorance is as egregious as his dogmatism is
offensive; and he has adopted a peculiar style of writing,
which frequently verges on the unintelligible, through the
excessive awkwardness of its construction, and his utter
want of perception of the true genius of the English
language.

Mr. Ruskin's headlong onslaughts upon all whom he
counts his opponents are well known to those who have read
his former work on 'Modern Painters.' He is possessed with
the error that vehemence is force, and violence strength.
He thinks that people will tolerate virulence, under the
idea that it is earnestness. He writes on matters of art

as if they were questions of morals, and as if a breach of
the laws of good taste or artistic expression were a
breach of the Ten Commandments. We smile as we read his
declamations, clever and brilliant as they are, and are
surprised that any man of sense can make use of a species
of phraseology, when criticising buildings, statues, and
paintings, which would better describe the enormities of
pickpockets and housebreakers.

Mr. Ruskin's egotism is indeed a serious drawback to
the influence which his works ought to exercise on the art
of his contemporaries. We can endure the egotism of enthusiasm, but not the egotism of criticism; and Mr. Ruskin's
egotism is of the latter kind. The spirit of criticism and
philosophical investigation haunts him like a nightmare.
He is ever judicial, ever professional, ever legislative.
He is not absorbed in his subject; he absorbs his subject
into himself. We never forget him for an instant. Criticising is his nature, his element, his manifest delight.
And therefore his egotism is singularly disagreeable and
out of place. It wearies and teases us, instead of communicating to us that sort of energy and movement of
thought which a less self-conscious egotism can sometimes
infuse into a reader's mind.

Much of this intolerance and overbearing spirit doubtless arises from Mr. Ruskin's limited range of studies.
He is a man who is ever busied in working out his own
ideas by his own unaided powers, in the way of solitary
reflection, rather than in contest with other minds of
equal calibre with his own. He is not well read in philosophy, classical literature, history, or science. In
theological matters his ignorance is literally astonishing; and, like all ignorant men, he writes with an assumption of infallibility which is simply absurd. He knows
something of the imaginative, metaphorical, and pictorial
aspect of the Bible; and he has a great idea that certain
elements of morality are to be carried out with the utmost
rigour and consistency. But of religious doctrine he
apparently knows no more than the commonplace Protestants
of the day, and devoutly believes only the gospel according to Dr. Croly. It is indeed a not slightly significant
token of the shallowness of the popular religionism of our
time, that a man of Mr. Ruskin's acuteness should write a
book exalting the religious architecture of the 13th century almost to the level of a work of inspiration, and
term it pre-eminently *Christian* architecture, and at the
same time believe the Pope to be Antichrist, and gravely
propose the repeal of the Catholic Emancipation Act as
necessary to the well-being of England. There is something
so transcendently ludicrous in the notion that the Church

of Rome is *idolatrous*, and yet that the early mediæval
architecture was the result of the purest Christian faith
and feeling, that we can only suppose that Mr. Ruskin
believes that Cranmer, Luther, and Henry VIII flourished
some 700 years ago, and that Salisbury Cathedral was built
in the reign of Elizabeth. The simplicity which can identify the creed and practices of the 13th century with
those of 'English Protestantism' is so delicious, that
whatever else be Mr. Ruskin's deserts, he may at least lay
claim to the invention of something unquestionably *new*.

We are sorry to say also, that this lively, trenchant,
and brilliant writer is positively becoming tedious. Mr.
Ruskin has taken to a sort of moralising strain, and a
quaint, sermonising species of phraseology, which makes
his book sometimes read like a country parson's discourse
or a penny tract. We do not say that this is the pervading
style of his work. On the contrary, it abounds with noble
passages, forcible imagery, and a certain rude eloquence
which is highly captivating. But he is too fond of getting
up into the professorial chair, and announcing moral
truths with a grave solemnity and in professional forms of
speech, which are very far from attractive, and prejudice
us against the unquestionable originality and profoundness
of thought which he frequently displays. Now and then,
too, he seems to have caught the peculiar canting style of
the Cambridge Camden (or Ecclesiological) Society; and
elevates minute trivialities to the rank of moral enormities, talking of what is right, and wrong, and lawful,
and horrible, and immoral, and un-Christian, in a spirit
of unreality and fictitious indignation which is wholly
unworthy of a man who denounces the follies and imposi-
tions of his fellow-creatures with such unsparing severity.
Add to this, that he is far more careless than ever in the
construction of his sentences and the arrangement of his
words. He writes as most fluent people talk, with that
slovenly, disjointed, and awkward disposition of his
thoughts and expressions, which is scarcely noticed in
speaking, but on paper becomes barely intelligible. Never
was there a book which more needed pruning and polishing
than this 'Seven Lamps of Architecture'; never was there a
book which with so much that is great contained more that
is little. We pass from a superb passage of glowing eloquence to an uncouth commonplace; from a sentiment marked
by the deepest philosophy to a piece of nonsensical declamation or abuse which a child can see through.

The 'Seven Lamps of Architecture' - (why there are just
seven, and no more, we are not informed) - are, the Lamp
of *Sacrifice*, the Lamp of *Truth*, the Lamp of *Power*, the
Lamp of *Beauty*, the Lamp of *Life*, the Lamp of *Memory*, and

the Lamp of *Obedience*. On the embossed cover, however, we find seven medallions, on which are imprinted the seven Latin words, *Religio*, *Observantia*, *Auctoritas*, *Fides*, *Obedientia*, *Memoria*, *Spiritus*. Whether these latter are to be considered the same as the former seven, we are not told; nor whether those of the Latin words which do not respond to any of the English words are to be considered as so many additional lamps. We incline to the former supposition, thinking it more than probable that as Mr. Ruskin has given us a new ecclesiastical history, so he is about to favour the republic of letters with a new Latin language. Be this as it may, the book itself is concerned with those seven elements in architectural excellence, which are implied in the seven English words.

At first glance it will be seen that Mr. Ruskin has not undertaken to expound the *principles* of architectural science, in the truest sense of the word. He has not ventured upon the discussion of the ideas which lie deep at the heart of all artistic expression, or sought to define what can be accomplished by architecture as a means of expression. His essay may, however, fairly claim to be called a treatise on the principles of the *rules* of architectural art. He unfolds the spirit in which, rather than the ideas on which, the true artist will design and complete his edifice. To use terms properly applicable to a religious system, his 'lamps' are as it were the *morals* of art, and in no sense the *doctrines* of art. He thus will never succeed in making men artists, because he does not go to the root of the mischief which ruins the art of the age, and we suspect that he himself is quite unconscious that any thing more than a good *spirit* of design and workmanship is necessary to the reality of art whatsoever. If the whole race of English artists were as enthusiastic as Mr. Ruskin himself in the adoption of his views, we should see no result beyond a splendid mediocrity; a cold, meaningless, or convulsive effort to communicate to a dead body the aspect of a living being.

What we have already said, indeed, of the extraordinary delusion under which Mr. Ruskin labours with respect to the creed of the mediæval architects, is sufficient to account for his avoidance of any thing that might betray his own inability to probe the wounds of art to the bottom. His notions as to the real ideas and sentiments which the ancient architects embodied in their wonderful creations, are so vague, misty, and contradictory, that he very naturally shuns any attempt to shew his contemporaries where they ought to *begin*, if they would rival the works of their forefathers. Had he tried any thing of this kind, the inevitable result would have been that he would have

discovered that neither he nor they were agreed even in
the few positive ideas, religious, political, and domestic,
which they do possess; and that, on the whole, their creed
is a mere mass of negations, a literal *protesting* against
the intellectual, spiritual, and moral nature of other
times, with no definite faith or feeling of their own.

Mr. Ruskin's first 'Lamp' is that of *Sacrifice*. He does
not, however, very clearly define what he means by sacrifice, and a degree of confusion of thought in his illustrations and deductions is the consequence. He seems
hardly to know whether he means the principle that in
raising edifices of a religious character we should *offer*
to God whatever is best of its kind, or whether he thinks
that sacrifice means labour. Much that he says on this
branch of his subject is good, but he falls into the
commonplace error of exaggerating the universal excellence
of the works of other times, and seems to suppose that in
the 13th century every one employed 'the Flaxman of his
time,' and no one else. He tells us that 'all old work
nearly has been hard work.' This is the stale mistake of
fancying that all the buildings of antiquity were great,
strong, and enduring, because those which remain to us are
so. When will antiquarians remember that the best works
alone remain, because the inferior works have necessarily
perished? Does Mr. Ruskin suppose that London and Waterloo
Bridges, and the Nelson column, and half the deformities
of the metropolis and the provinces, will not last as long
as York Minster or Cologne Cathedral, and Sir Christopher
Wren's churches are not destined to see many a Gothic
spire and tower laid low in the dust?

The chapter on the Lamp of *Truth* contains many admirable criticisms and suggestions, with some exaggerations
and absurdities. For instance, Mr. Ruskin says that the
English nation is 'distinguished for its general uprightness and faith,' in the same sentence in which he avows
that modern English architecture has 'more of pretence,
concealment, and deceit than any other of this or of past
time.' Thus it is that Mr. Ruskin contrives to make his
views ridiculous in men's eyes. At the very moment that he
is dilating with all the vehemence of a Savonarola against
the dissociation of earnestness and truthfulness from art,
and maintaining that the hollowness of modern 'Romanist'
art is a proof of the wickedness and idolatry of Rome, he
would coolly have us believe that there is *no* connexion
between the hollowness of English Protestant art and the
hollowness of the Protestant creed. On Mr. Ruskin's own
admissions, either art has nothing to do with morals,
faith, and earnestness (in which case the present book is
the assertion of an impudent fallacy), or the wretchedness

of our modern art is the result of some deep-seated
disease in the whole mind of the nation. Perhaps, by the
way, as our author's chronology and history is not of the
most exact sort, he considers that the Emancipation Act
was the cause of the architectural abominations of Regent
Street, and the Maynooth Grant the originator of Mr.
Wilkins's design for the National Gallery.

We are sorry also to find Mr. Ruskin echoing the vulgar
cry against *cast* or *machine-cut* ornaments in iron, or any
other material. We confess that the objection so often
made to such works savours to us of the shallowest bigotry.
Mr. Ruskin, and those whom he imitates, seem to imagine
that there is a sort of magic charm in beating iron with a
hammer, and that a machine which gives to the workman's
chisel the force of a steam-engine, is something contrary
to the commandment, 'Thou shalt not steal.' Now, we are
ready to allow that cast-iron ornaments, or cast-brass, or
any thing else that is formed in a mould, which *pretends
not* to be so moulded, but to be constructed with the
hammer, or in some old-fashioned way, is an absurdity and
an imposture; and further, we are convinced that, like
other hypocrisies, it never thoroughly succeeds, but
betrays itself by a manifest inferiority and awkwardness.
But why there is an eternal impropriety in making a fender,
or a door-handle, or an iron gate for a church, by means
of a mould, or why we should regard a cast glass salt-
cellar or tumbler with a sort of moral horror, we never
could conceive. Objections to cast and machine-made ornaments on such grounds as these are a mere ridiculous
prudery and affectation, and serve only to prejudice men
of shrewd sense against any thing like a philosophy in
art, as the fantastic dream of half-insane fanatics. Let
us have cast-iron ornaments to look like what they are,
designed solely with a view to please, and not to deceive,
and no earthly reason exists why they should not have a
beauty peculiarly their own, even though their beauty be
of a different type from that which is characteristic of
iron wrought by the hand alone. There is as much genius
and truth of utterance in a bird, or a flower, or a bust,
carved in oak by Jordan's patent, as if the same result
had been produced by an unaided mallet and chisel. The
only difference is that one is produced more *easily* than
the other; and if greater facility in accomplishment is to
be accounted an evil, then the sooner we relapse at once
into barbarism the better.

In the same fantastic spirit of arbitrary selection, Mr.
Ruskin considers it '*unlawful*' to use metals as a *support* in
building. He will tolerate them as a *cement*, but as a
cement alone. Really we hardly know how to reply to such

quibbling, and such childish slavery to a cut-and-dried
set of rules. The notion that some few of the material
products of the universe are to enjoy a sort of act-of-
Parliament monopoly, and that any thing else which answers
the same purpose equally well, or even far better, is to
be for ever excluded from employment, is quite inimitable
in its way. If Mr. Ruskin had been born a savage, dwelling
in huts made of branches of trees, we can conceive his
orthodox horror at the discovery of the possibility of
making bricks, or of building houses with stone.

This theory he further enforces by one of those artificial reasonings into which men fall who dwell too much in
an intellectual solitude, and mistake their private
fancies for necessary deductions from unquestionable
premises. He says that man ought to *limit himself*, and
confine his resources within certain arbitrary bounds,
because Divine Omnipotence has restrained itself in the
construction of the physical universe, such as it is! How
like the reasoning of a publication of the Religious
Tract Society! Because Almighty God vouchsafes to employ
means to the performance of certain ends, and because
those means are not precisely those which we or Mr.
Ruskin would have chosen for the purpose, *therefore* a
poor, miserable atom like man, whose utmost efforts to
accomplish his ends are but as the devices of an infant,
is to ape the system of creative Omnipotence, and con-
ceitedly thrust away the materials which the Divine Author
of nature has placed within his reach!

On the Lamp of Power Mr. Ruskin has many excellent
reflections, with many that savour somewhat of wire-
drawing and straw-splitting, and some in which praise or
blame is awarded far more in accordance with the dictates
of arbitrary custom and chance association than on any
stable principles of art. For instance, our author will
have marble and limestone in general to be chiselled
smooth, because (as he tells us) it is easy to produce a
flat surface in marble! The following extracts, on the
other hand, strike us as containing much admirable criticism:

[Quotes from 'Let us, then, see' to 'parts can destroy',
'Works' 8: 103-4.]

The subjoined is an example of Mr. Ruskin's strength as
a writer on mere art, and of his miserably perverted
notions on the ideas which art has to embody.

[Quotes from 'Positive shade' to 'by a noonday sun',
'Works' 8: 116-17.]

Not to dwell on the palpable one-sidedness of all this as respects the power of *shadow* is painting, and its forgetfulness of the fact that, in almost every great historical picture of the greatest masters, about *two-thirds* of the whole painting is in shade, we cannot pass by Mr. Ruskin's Pagan theory on the sentiment which ought to pervade the architecture of man. Is he serious in telling us that not only domestic, social, and political architecture, but even *religious* architecture, ought to be especially impressed with the trouble and wrath of life, its sorrow and its mystery? Why, even Heathenism would often fill its temples with symbols of joy and gladness, and types of the reconciliation which it supposed to be wrought between its divinities and mankind. Is the frame of mind at which the devout Christian ought to aim, and which faith in the gospel of mercy tends to work within him, gloomy, cavern-like, and awestruck? Is a church constructed in the manner of Rembrandt's pictures a fitting habitation for a Christian soul? Truly, it speaks ill for Mr. Ruskin's theology, if this is any thing more than unmeaning flourish. He must be falling in love with dark, self-torturing Puritanism, or be oppressed with a frightful sense of the unpardonableness of human guilt, and the powerlessness of all Christian doctrine to console, which makes him thus love that which speaks only of sin, and suffering, and despair, rather than of that peace and joy, that calm repose and buoyant hope, which the religion of Jesus Christ confers on those who receive it in its true strength and purity.

In the same passion for wretchedness, Mr. Ruskin denounces every thing like an attempt to please the taste and gratify the feelings in any matter connected with railways. He hugs misery to himself with a self-sacrificing heroism of patience. Railroad travelling is with him all misery and discomfort. He says it deprives people – judging, of course, from his own experience – of that temper and discretion which are necessary to the enjoyment of beauty. He purchases his ticket with the feelings of a man who sends a prescription to the druggist's to be made up; he gets into the carriage (even a first-class one) with the wry face with which we swallow a nauseous medicine, and resigns himself to a martyrdom of anguish, until the horrible operation of locomotion is past, and he is once more sent forth to his ordinary state of being. He says that a man on a railway has 'parted with the nobler characteristics of humanity.' Henceforth we shall never see a person on the Great Western, or Birmingham, or any other line, huddled up in a corner of a carriage, dark, sour, and misanthropic in visage, and

resenting the suggestion of any agreeable thoughts as a
cruel mockery of an inward and unknown sorrow, without
thinking that we see the author of the 'Seven Lamps'
rejoicing in his woes, and oppressed with the mingled consciousness that he is moving at the rate of thirty miles
an hour, and that that wicked Papist, the Earl of Arundel
and Surrey, is a member of the Commons House of Parliament.
In common compassion to a suffering fellow-creature, we
would suggest to Mr. Ruskin, that if he were to try the
effects of 'idolatrous Romanism' upon his own mind, he
would find it quite possible to be happy even in a second
or third class railway-carriage, and to go from London to
Edinburgh with an unruffled soul.

With the chapter on the Lamp of Beauty we have serious
fault to find. Professing at the outset to assert that
those things alone are beautiful in which all will agree
with him, Mr. Ruskin proceeds to announce a theory which
is as gratuitous and unsupported as his illustrations of
his truth are inconsistent with the facts to which he
declares that he appeals. His theory is, that the forms of
all architectural beauty are to be found in nature; and
thus, with his usual reiteration of 'I believe,' 'I say,'
'I know,' 'I would,' 'I am justified,' 'I doubt not,' 'I
have no hesitation,' &c. &c., he expands his fancy:

[Quotes from 'Now, I would insist' to 'be the other',
'Works' 8: 140-3.]

Accordingly, Mr. Ruskin accounts it impossible to produce beauty with straight lines, which, as every body
knows, are very rare in natural objects. This consequence,
indeed, of his theory, is its true touchstone. Let us see,
then, wherein its fallacy consists. That it *is* fallacious,
a little ordinary recollection of the objects men do call
beautiful will shew. It condemns, for example, the Parthenon to the sentence of ugliness! In the Greek temple there
is scarcely a line to be found which is not straight,
scarcely a form which is borrowed from nature; yet who is
insensible to the exquisite *beauty* of its design, and to
the intense depth of sentiment and repose which it conveys
to the mind? In like manner, Mr. Ruskin must deny the
existence of beauty in the vast majority of Italian domestic and palatial buildings, where for every curved line
there are ten straight lines. Does he see no beauty in the
tower of Magdalen College, Oxford, where nearly every line
is straight; no beauty in Salisbury spire, in the west
front of Cologne Cathedral, or in the whole class of
Gothic exteriors, where the flowing curve is as rare, and
the straight line as general, as the curve is general and

the straight line rare in a landscape, and in all the
works of visible nature? The hollowness of this dogma,
indeed, appears in Mr. Ruskin's own illustrations of its
truth. For example, we find him uttering the following
glaring piece of misrepresentation of facts:

[Quotes from 'The next ornament' to 'deforms the stones of
it', 'Works' 8: 146.]

Now, we are not concerned to defend the beauty of the
Tudor portcullis, which is ugly and absurd enough; but, in
the name of common sense, let it be condemned with something like an adherence to truth of reasoning, and not on
the extraordinary assumption that natural reticulation is
'either of most delicate and gauzy texture, or of variously sized meshes and undulating lines.' One would think Mr.
Ruskin had passed his whole life among spiders, and such-
like unpleasant insects. Has he never seen a piece of
honeycomb?
   The faultiness of his theory is this, that he entirely
overlooks the difference between the *materials* with which
the great Author of Nature works, in the production of her
myriad forms, and those with which man is compelled to
work. He has forgotten that the animal, the vegetable, and,
in a certain sense, the mineral world also, is one bound-
less and infinitely diversified manifestation of life,
while we form and fashion objects from dead and utterly
inanimate matter. Hence it is, that, while the laws of
tenacity are the governing principles of natural forms,
the law of *gravity* is that which rules over the works of
human art with irresistible sway. The whole world of
nature, from the countenance and figure of man himself,
down to the humblest and least developed crystalline surface, are the results of life, strength, movement, and
change. They are delightful to the soul, not alone because
they often commend themselves to our natural *sense* of the
beautiful, but because of what they utter and what they
suggest, and because they are the consequences of a
spiritual and indwelling energy, which has made them what
they are.
   And being thus instinct with life, whether animal,
vegetable, or chemical, they possess certain physical
attributes which permit them to multiply their forms in so
vast a multitude of variations, that the imagination is
appalled at the thought of numbering them, and feels almost
as if it were vainly seeking to grasp the infinite. A
handful of garden-flowers, or the boughs and leaves of a
single forest-tree, present combinations of curved and
straight lines which almost defy our calculation to reckon.

And why? Because the materials of which they are formed
possess the tenacity of vitality, and are capable of being
moulded into varieties and combinations which are simply
impossible in the works of man. The moment we take the
products of creation, and employ them as materials of art,
their whole nature is radically altered. Death comes in
place of life, decay in place of change, stillness in
place of movement. We have an obstacle to overcome in
their employment, which - so to say - was comparatively
unknown to the Author of nature when they yielded themselves to his plastic hand. We cannot consult our imagination alone in devising new shapes of grace and beauty into
which to cast them. We must call in the aid of mathematical construction, and the law of gravity so as to counteract itself. We must draw lines, and smoothen surfaces, and
balance parts, and compensate for deficiency of strength,
not according to the suggestions of poetry alone, but in
subservience to the dictates of geometry. Hence arise a
thousand combinations in art which are not found in nature,
simply because they are needless. A straight line actually
becomes stronger than a curved. The eye rests with delight
on stones piled together in forms which would be utterly
detestable in a natural cave, or on a mountain height.
Proportion itself assumes a totally new aspect, and whereas it rarely exists with any rigid exactness in natural
creations, is essential to the perfection of every work
which man's ingenuity can devise. Yet the sense of *beauty*
remains. Whatever be its elements, it unquestionably is
there. We gaze upon the works we have wrought, from the
magnificent temples of Cologne or Milan, down to the puny
flower-glass upon a drawing-room table, and the very same
emotions are summoned into life in our breasts of which we
are conscious when we contemplate an Alpine range, or an
Italian vale, or an English garden. All are beautiful,
because all are expressive of truth; all express the same
ideas, suggest the same associations, strike upon the same
inward mysterious sense, and are typical of the same invisible spiritual powers and joys. Their difference lies in
the difference between the materials of which they are
fashioned, and between the wisdom and omnipotence of God
and the ingenuity and humble aspirations of man.

   As an example of what we must call the *narrowness* of
Mr. Ruskin's ideas, we give another section on this same
Lamp of Beauty, in which, as usual, he seems to mistake
his own personal feelings for those of humanity in general,
and with natural exaggeration lays down minute rules which
make the unenthusiastic man of common sense smile.

[Quotes from 'Must not beauty' to 'pastoral solitude',

'Works' 8: 161-2.]

   The whole spirit of this criticism we think false and
morbid. All the world are not like Mr. Ruskin, though he
fancies so. We do not know in what sort of a room he loves
to sit, and study, and write, and draw; but we dare say he
thinks that every other studious and reflecting man upon
earth has precisely the same feelings with himself with
respect to slovenliness, or neatness, or bareness, or
luxury of details. Why is he blind to the fact, that while
many persons are insensible to every emotion of pure
enjoyment while occupied in labour, with others it is a
joy to mingle sensations of beauty, sweetness, and repose
with the sternest and dullest toils to which man is
doomed? We do not like this passionate fondness for the
thorns and thistles with which life was cursed for the sin
of Adam. We love the spirit of Christian peace and hope to
be a ruling principle in our minds, even when busied with
the most oppressive of the labours of this life of trial.
If we have to do penance, or to mortify our senses, and
deprive ourselves of innocent enjoyments for some definite
spiritual purpose, well and good; so let it be. But when
no such objects as these are in view, we would introduce
the spirit of repose and pleasure at all times and in
every occupation, so that whatsoever be the work of our
hands, there shall be some charm for the eye ever to rest
upon, and refresh us in the midst of our toils. Thousands
and thousands of men and women are soothed and strengthened in the most repulsive of labours by the sight of a
solitary flower smiling by their side in a humble vessel
of water. Mr. Ruskin laughs at the bronze leaves on the
lamps of London Bridge, and asks who cares for them. Let
them be taken away, then, and let the old, cold, unorna-
mented bars of wood and iron, which were our grandfather's
beau ideal of a lamp-post, be substituted. In such a case
there is scarcely a passenger who would not be indignant
at the change, be offended with the hideous intruders, and
clamour for the restoration of those decorations which woo
Mr. Ruskin's regards in vain.
   As we have dwelt so long on the defects of his chapter
on beauty, we cannot forbear quoting its concluding paragraphs, which charmingly describe that exquisite tower in
Florence, which we altogether agree with Mr. Ruskin in
regarding as one of the most perfect productions of genius
to which architecture has given birth.

[Quotes from 'These characteristics' to 'following the
sheep', 'Works' 8: 187-90.]

The ideas of the two concluding chapters, on the Lamps
of Memory and Obedience, are the most artificial in Mr.
Ruskin's whole volume, though they contain some of his
most agreeable passages and most touching thoughts. The
opening of the chapter on the Lamp of Memory is especially
beautiful. We cannot, however, linger upon them, except to
point out the unsatisfactory nature of Mr. Ruskin's reflections on the creation of a new style in architecture.
He proposes the rigid enforcement of the rules of one
definite epoch of the past, which he would have studied
with all the diligence and 'obedience' with which we study
the rules of a dead language; and these rules he would
have us follow in our buildings with the same strictness
with which we strive to write Latin like Cicero, or Greek
like Xenophon. Out of this absolute obedience to one good
and practically serviceable style, he thinks that a new
style *might* naturally arise, under the pressure of certain
possible combinations of circumstances, or through the
efforts of the inward powers of genius. Whether, however,
such should be the result or no, it is his conviction that
by no other means can the production of a new species of
true architectural construction be even a possibility.

Now, with all our knowledge of Mr. Ruskin's ignorance
of history, we marvel at the obliviousness of the past
which this speculation betrays. Never yet, during the
whole progress of mankind, was a new art produced by such
a system. Never yet did any thing better result from the
method here recommended than a frigid, soulless revival-
ism. Mr. Ruskin's comparison of architectural study with
the study of a foreign language ought, indeed, to have
suggested facts to him which would have betrayed the
faultiness of his theory. No new language was ever invented by the diligent study and practice of another perfect
dead or strange tongue. New forms of architecture, and new
forms of speech, are alike the result of a *tentative* process, and not of calm and reverent study of the past
alone. In every single instance in which the history of
the creation of an architectural style is known, we find
precisely the same laws prevailing. We see a generation of
men, energetic, laborious, and full of deep emotions and
ardent aspirations, unaffectedly taking up the language or
the architectural forms and fragments which actually exist
in living operation around them, employing them boldly and
imaginatively for the accomplishment of their own purposes, combining them, modifying them, adding to them, and
developing their capacities, until at last a noble
creation is called into existence, in which the past
appears merged in the present, and the old seems to have
vanished before the new.

Such is the history of the Romanesque styles of Europe previous to the 13th century. They sprung into life at the bidding of the same voice of energy and life which fashioned the languages of Italy, France, and Spain from out of the *débris* of the ruined classical Latin. By a similar process Gothic architecture was summoned into being, and by a similar process every subsequent variation of its rules was introduced. Thus, too, was modern Italian architecture created. It was the creature of a series of *tentative* efforts to devise *something* that should be more true, more chaste, more sensible than the monstrosities of decayed Gothic, when Gothic had corrupted itself and become a caricature. Its progress was gradual, commencing with an almost total ignorance of the laws of classical architecture, and never rigidly adopting them. The stages of its growth are similar to the periods of advance in the creation of the Italian tongue; and when it had reached maturity, it was as dissimilar to the architecture of Augustus, Diocletian, or Constantine, as the language of Tasso and Boccaccio was unlike the language of Virgil or Pliny. The true parallel to Mr. Ruskin's scheme is to be found in the study of the ancient Latin by the classical zealots of Italy. They actually adopted the method here recommended. They studied and wrote with an idolatrous veneration for the rules of bygone days. But they created nothing. They amused themselves; they wrote letters and verses of faultless purity; they fancied they were speaking the voice of humanity; but their revived Latin was a mere scholar's bubble the moment it ceased to be regarded as a means for forming the taste and disciplining the mind. Their works have gone the way of all revivalisms; they are known to the studious; they exist in histories; but living man has cast them off, as he casts off the fantastic forms of a coat or a doublet when fashion calls for something new.

For ourselves, we believe that a new species of architectural art, in our present state of civilisation and knowledge, is impossible. We know the past too well to escape from thraldom to its rules. Moderate success is so easily attained, that mediocrity is our inevitable lot. We can no more create a new style of building than we can create a new language. Those who essay such a task are laughed at for their pains, and their productions are fit only to be classed with the spelling reform of the 'Phonetic News.' A man who *thinks* architecturally, thinks in the language of the old Greek, or Gothic, or Italian architects. Whatever he wants to utter, a form of architectural speech, based on well-known rules, presents itself to his thoughts, and in it he must give expression to his ideas. New rules of art, and new rules of grammar, can only spring from out of the confusion of barbarism. The very world itself was formed by its divine Creator out of a chaos. First He created a formless void, and thence educed the glorious order of the visible universe. Such, too, is the history of all human arts. A high state of civilisation and information can produce nothing that is essentially new. The old mythologists peopled the firmament of stars, and the very woods and fields, with a world of imaginative beings, not only because they possessed no pure revelation from Heaven, but because they were ignorant of the laws of astronomy and physical science. Modern unbelievers are aware that the sun is a ball of fire, at a certain measured distance from the earth, and that the planets move at so many miles per hour on their orbits; and thus they are no more inclined to invest them with the attributes of Divinity, than to see something more than human in a locomotive engine or a steam press. The inventions of imaginative genius are impossible beneath the sway of science. In the rules of the architects of the days of Pericles and of the middle ages, we see the same kind of fixed laws which we have detected in the motions of the heavenly bodies and the chemical processes of vegetation. All is open, clear, fixed and unchangeable. The ardent fire of life which moulded the piles of the Gothic cathedrals from out of the wrecks of an elder antiquity, is as impossible amongst us, as the enthusiasm of Columbus when he sought and found an unknown world. Every child now can tell its grandmother that the earth is shaped like an orange; and so too every architect's clerk knows the rules on which were built the Parthenon and the Coliseum, the abbey of the English monk and the palace of the Italian noble. We cannot be young again; with the experience of old age we become subject to its coldness and its helplessness of imagination.

We must, however, part with our author without further delay, and trust that he will not take it ill if we counsel him for the future to bestow more care on testing his theories by a larger application of them to facts, to pay more attention to history and less to his own personal feelings; and above all, to write nothing on any theological or controversial point, until he has paid some little attention to theology and controversy. He may yet become not only a very ingenious and brilliant theoriser, but a most useful writer on questions of art of every description; but if he continues much longer his present habits of thought and composition, he will end, we are convinced, in becoming simply prosy, parsonic, and dormiferous.

'Pre-Raphaelitism'

13 August 1851

9. UNSIGNED REVIEW, 'ART-JOURNAL'

November 1851, vol. 3, n.s., 285-6

Harsh as criticism of Ruskin's work often was, the reception of 'Pre-Raphaelitism' was marked by an almost uniform severity of which the following review is characteristic. See Introduction, p. 10.

However close may be the connexion between genius and that 'fine phrensy' to which poets and psychologists have declared it nearly allied, - the relationship between the conceit of it and folly is easily determined. *Extraordinary* phenomena, mental and moral, may flow from either of these sources, as the experience of all time, and most emphatically the present, testifies. Extraordinary books have been written by the author of 'Modern Painters,' about the true characteristics of which the critics have expressed very different opinions. One quality, however, is ascribed to them with a general unanimity; they are *extraordinary*. Not the least extraordinary of this author's productions is the pamphlet about 'Pre-Raphaelitism.' From which of the above-named sources its 'extraordinariness' springs, we will not, just now, decide, but hope shortly to make tolerably apparent.

Our readers are, of course, aware that a pseudo-system of art has, for some time, obtruded itself on the public, under the presumptuous name borne by our author's pamphlet, and originating with three or four, according to their chivalrous advocate, 'exceeding young men, of stubborn instincts, and positive self-trust, and with little natural perception of beauty!' To associate anything from such a source, with the name of the great Italian painter, whether in a manner expressive of concurrence or antagonism, is offensive in the highest degree. The act is presumptuous, but, perhaps, pitiable if done in all *simplicity* and sincerity. If the name is adopted, however, for sake of *éclat*, which is far from being improbable, it is a piece of empiricism, ranking with the trickery by which eager tradesmen entrap the unwary into reading illusory advertisements by prefixing to them such portentous phrases as 'Calamitous Fire,' 'The Crystal Palace,' or 'Cardinal Wiseman.'

Pre-Raphaelitism, left to its own merits, would have passed away like any other similar specimen of conceit or craft, of like origin, exciting, at most, a momentary smile in the lively, or extorting a passing sarcasm from the saturnine.

The author of 'Modern Painters' has, however, conferred a factitious importance on the 'school,' as he calls it, by taking it under his protection, and giving it the benefit of his public advocacy. He has recently issued a pamphlet with the title assumed by his juvenile *protégés*, and with little or no more just claim to it. It is a 'maundering' medley of the most incongruous ingredients, of sixty-eight pages, of which six or seven only make any mention of the professed theme. The first twenty or thereabouts are filled with a fantastic, not to say irreverent disquisition on the purpose of the Deity in decreeing labour as the lot of man, and the 'infinite misery,' caused by idle people meddling in other men's business, and others being overworked. Abortive attempts at Shandean humour alternate with seeming sanctimonious homilies. The imaginary self-communing of a man as to whether he is not 'fit to be Chancellor of the Exchequer,' or, as he 'used to be a good judge of peas, might not he do something in a small greengrocery business?' is in profane juxtaposition with the solemn admonition that 'our full energies are to be given to the soul's work – to the great fight with the dragon – the taking the kingdom of heaven by force!'

Afterwards, by an eccentric movement, our author relapses into another laudation of his old idol Turner, with which he occupies the last forty pages. This somewhat trite rhapsody might, considering how very unapparent is its connexion with Pre-Raphaelitism, surely have been omitted, and the more especially as we are promised another repetition of it in the forthcoming volume of the 'Modern Painters.' The author's declared object in putting forth his pamphlet is to contradict the alleged 'directly false statements' that have been made respecting his *protégés*' works. It affords him also an opportunity of

making an indirect claim to the supposed honour of laying,
as it were, 'eight years ago,' the foundation of a 'school
from which he hopes all things,' by advising the 'young
artists of England to go to nature, rejecting nothing,
selecting nothing, and scorning nothing.' Good advice this
in part, but not wholly so; nor is that portion which is
good of such recent date as 'eight years ago,' seeing that
it is as old as the practice of Art. The advice to reject
nothing and select nothing, we counsel the young artists
of England to *reject* altogether. A higher authority than
the author of 'Modern Painters,' says on this subject,
'The arrangement which, apparently artless, fixes the
attention on important points, the emphasis on essential
as opposed to adventitious qualities, the power of selecting expressive forms, of arresting evanescent beauties,
are all prerogatives by means of which a feeble imitation
successfully contends even with its archetype.' Rejection
and selection are not, indeed, the prerogative merely, but
the duty of the artist. Elements antagonistic to the main
sentiment are present in the most enchanting scene, and
features subversive of the prevailing character obtrude
into the fairest face. The highest truth of Art demands
the rejection of these hostile elements, and this theoretic rule is fully borne out by the practice of all the
great masters of Art. The true function and best occupation of the artist are not what the author of 'Pre-
Raphaelitism' would have us believe them, - 'to copy, line
for line, the religious and domestic sculpture on the
German, Flemish, and French cathedrals and castles,' for
archæological purposes, but to unfold the beauty and glory
of the material world, *as visible to their exalted perceptions*, and place them consciously before the eyes of
common observers; thus redeeming the senses from the low
and servile office of ministering to the mere animal
pleasures. To do this the artist must pourtray that
typical form of nature which she nowhere presents in any
single object. Where then, is it to be found? There,
where Phidias found the grand character and sublime conception of his Jupiter, and Zeuxis the fascinating loveliness of his Helen - in universal nature, over which they
looked abroad and *selected* what they found to be the
faithful and entire expression of her will, and *rejected*
all exceptions to it. The graduate's dogma, that 'no great
intellectual thing was ever done by great effort,' is not
so much untrue as absurd; it is, indeed, a contradiction
of terms. A great effort is, literally, the exertion of
great power; and the graduate himself tells us, in the
very next page to that from which we quote, that 'all the
greatest works in existence say plainly to us there has

been a great *power* here.'

Will the author of 'Modern Painters' deny that the Alexandrian geometry is a 'great intellectual thing,' and that it has been 'done by a great effort?' Or that those sublime deductions, the laws of the planetary motions, made from a twenty years' series of observations by the immortal Kepler, are intellectually 'great' and demanded 'effort?' We presume even our Oxford graduate will admit the establishment of the theory of universal gravitation, or the production of the 'Principia,' or the 'Mécanique Céleste,' or the prediction of 'Neptune,' or the composition of the 'Divina Commedia,' or of 'Paradise Lost,' falls within his category? We dissent wholly from the dictum that the artist's 'function is to convey *knowledge* to his fellow-men, of such things as cannot be taught otherwise than ocularly,' and that, 'for a long time this function remained a religious one,' whose aim was 'to impress upon the popular mind the reality of the objects of faith, and the *truth* of the histories of Scripture, by giving visible form to both.' We can understand how Art can *enforce* historical facts, but do not perceive by what means it can *authenticate* them. The subjects of Art being derived from history, must necessarily depend upon it for their own credibility. Nor has the function of the artist, in any sense, 'passed away,' but remains just what it has been from the beginning, and will remain so long as the visible creation and the human heart with its divine instincts and holy sympathies, endure. The painter is no 'idler on the earth,' but a great missionary from Heaven, sent among men to enkindle and keep alive the flame of love for all that is beautiful and glorious of the works of God. He can, too, still find his patrons as useful an occupation in contemplating even 'eternal scenes' from the Vicar of Wakefield, as in standing 'before the broken bas-relief on the southern gate of Lincoln cathedral.'

The senseless sneer at 'Royal Academy lecturings,' and the directions given by professors to students to study the works of Raphael, may be left to its own inanity. The beneficial influence of such studies is attested by the experience of ages, and has the sanction of men quite as sagacious and learned as the Oxford graduate. We have neither time nor space to expose a hundredth part of our graduate's false philosophy and shallow psychology.

'True, no meaning puzzles more than wit:' and the attempt to grasp his Protean nonsense and flagrant inconsistencies would be as embarrassing to us as wearisome to our readers. One or two specimens of these we must, however, point out.

With the view of proving that, not withstanding 'the

main principles of training,' the characteristics of an
artist's productions are necessary consequences of his
physical organisation and mental endowments, he supposes
two artists, in one of whom elaboration of detail and
meanness of general effect are due to his having 'a feeble
memory, no invention, and an excessively keen sight.' The
other owes his grandeur of effect and soft masses of true
gradation to 'a memory which nothing escapes, an invention
which never rests, and is comparatively near sighted.'
   Now, if this hypothesis is of any value in the question,
these physical and mental peculiarities in the artists,
are the *necessary* cause of the characteristic qualities of
their respective works. Yet the graduate immediately tells
us that by *modifying*! 'NO *invention*' into 'considerable
inventive powers' and bestowing upon the purblind gentleman 'the eye of an eagle,' both the characters are real.
'The first is John Everett Millais, and the second, Joseph
Mallord William Turner.' But it is obvious that these
modifications destroy the original hypothesis, and,
according to the Oxford graduate, these artists produce
their works not only *without* the conditions assumed to be
the *cause* of them, and thus not only produce effects without causes, but in spite of the presence of the most antagonistic powers; for the pictures ascribed to the *hypo-
thetical* artists are painted by the *real* ones.
   Again, near the beginning of the pamphlet, the author
ridicules - with great effort, we presume, judging, on his
own principles, from the weakness of the effect - the
modern system of teaching the Fine Arts by Royal Academy
'lecturings,' and by copying and studying the works of the
great masters, and especially those of Raphael. He further
tells us that the 'Pre-Raphaelites' have opposed themselves as a body to that kind of teaching above described;
and have, '*therefore*, called themselves Pre-Raphaelites.'
Yet, notwithstanding all this, the graduate, when writing,
near the end of his work, on representing the freedom of
the lines of nature, and commending the power and ease
manifested in the works of Leonardo da Vinci, gravely
admonishes the Pre-Raphaelites, if they 'do not understand
how this kind of power, in its highest perfection, may be
united with the most severe rendering of all *other* (!)
orders of truth, and especially of those with which they
themselves have most sympathy, let them look at —' what do
our readers suppose? - at the productions of Leonardo da
Vinci, or Michael Angelo, or Raphael, or Correggio, or
Titian, or any of those grand works which have received
the homage of civilised man for hundreds of years? - No! -
not at any of these, but at, - Oh, powers of bathos, - '*at
the drawings of John Lewis!*' And for this our author would

have his young proselytes - that promising 'school' -
abjure the first article of their creed, and denude themselves of everything that constitutes their character.

Could any inconsistency in the author of 'Modern
Painters' excite remark, we might recommend him to reconcile this advice with that given eight years ago. Excep-
tionable as that is, it is sounder than the present.
Without wishing to insinuate anything to the disparagement
of the graduate's great exemplar, we must say we prefer
nature, with all her conflictions.

Whether we regard the pamphlet as a vindication of
certain pictures from unmerited censure, or as an exposition of the leading principles of a 'school' of Art, it is
an utter failure. The attempt, indeed, to carry out the
professed object is confined to the narrow limits of a
foot-note. Here we are told the grounds on which the name
of Pre-Raphaelite is assumed, grounds for which we have
searched the productions of the 'school' in vain. 'The
Pre-Raphaelites,' says their defender, 'imitate no
pictures, they paint from nature only. But they have
opposed themselves as a body, to that kind of teaching
above described, which only began *after* Raphael's time:
and they have opposed themselves as sternly to the entire
feeling of the Renaissance schools, - a feeling compounded
of indolence, infidelity, sensuality, and shallow pride.'

This passage certainly does not justify the arrogance
involved in the assumption of the title Pre-Raphaelitism.
It is, besides, incorrect in two essential points:
Firstly, it assigns to the 'hopeful school,' as an *exclusive* characteristic, that which is not their characteristic *at all*, in any truthful sense; and, secondly, it
states, in other words, that the influence of schools
began after Raphael's time. Passing the first point for
the present, we may remark of the second that it is not
true that the teaching of schools, as described by the
graduate, 'began after Raphael's time.' There were schools
of art in Crete with scholars, at Sparta, and other
places, five hundred years before the Christian era; and
this kind of teaching has been continued from that time to
the present 'Royal Academy lecturings,' so sneered at by
our author. Polygnotus had his disciples in Art, and
Zeuxis did not disdain to copy Apollodorus.

The Pre-Raphaelites' assumption of the designation of
'school' on the ground of repudiating the teaching of
schools, is a contradiction of terms and an absurdity. The
very idea of a school involves the existence of masters
with perceptive authority, models, canons of art, and
principles of association. The hopeful school, however,
ostentatiously abjures all these, and then claims to be a

school on the ground of this very abjuration. And in this
folly they are abetted by the Oxford graduate! It might
have been supposed that the logical training the title
implies would have saved him from this inconsistency.

The antecedents of the author of 'Modern Painters'
would have led us to suppose that he must be aware that
schools of art are not founded for the purpose of making
mere copyists of other men's works, but for the dissemination of those principles on which all works of Art must be
executed. Such an enlightened critic ought to know that
studying the works of the great masters is one of the most
efficient means for teaching these principles. In this way
taste is formed and perception quickened, and the most
unpoetical mind taught to see those meanings in nature
which are hidden to all but the highly endowed few among
men. In this way Giotto's works were studied, and gave
rise to all the higher developments of Art that distinguish the Italian schools of the fourteenth, and the
greater part of the fifteenth, centuries.

A moment's glance at the mental and manual characteristics of these schools, to which we conceive the term
Pre-Raphaelite is exclusively applicable, will show us
that the *soi-disant* Pre-Raphaelites have not, indeed, the
smallest claim to the title, historic or æsthetic. Their
pictures have not one quality in common with the works of
the early Italian masters.

The true Pre-Raphaelites are distinguished by the
simplicity, the ideality, and abstract grandeur of their
conceptions, the frequently elegant forms and graceful
actions of their figures, the sweetness and serenity of
their expression, and their abstemious style of colouring.
The pseudo Pre-Raphaelites, on the contrary, are remarkable for the affectation and meanness of their conception
- their stark, starveling forms, constrained actions,
repulsive expression, and gaudy colouring.

The most prominent characteristic of the Italian
masters is their intensely spiritual expression. It is, of
course, found in the different masters in varying degrees,
but is more or less predominant in all of them. To this
emphatic exposition of their sacred theme every other
quality was made subservient, or if not susceptible of
being made so, was willingly sacrificed. This strict
subordination of the technical, enhanced, indeed, the
value of the purely intellectual part of the work, by
exhibiting it through the most refined medium, just as the
purest atmosphere and the most perfect telescope display
celestial bodies to the astronomer most clearly, without
suggesting, for a moment, their instrumentality to his
mind.

Some of these masters, especially towards the end of
the fifteenth century, united to their high expression a
more vigorous treatment. Masaccio endeavoured to impart
more than the previous dignity to the human form. He, too,
introduced a bolder relief, with a more flowing and
grander style of drapery. Benozzo elaborated his landscapes, and Ghirlandajo somewhat strengthened the heretofore pale colouring, but both maintained the pre-eminence
of expression. The same may be said of Mantagna and Pietro
Perugino.

With the Englishmen, on the other hand, expression, if
considered at all, seems quite a secondary matter. Handling and colour, in their most mechanical and meretricious
aspects, apparently absorb their whole attention. Expression, when it constitutes the subject and cannot, therefore, be wholly neglected, is overlaid by gaudy colouring
and obtrusive accessories. In their abstract theory and
guiding principles too, the Italians were quite as
opposite to the Englishmen as in their visible characteristics. The former recognise the maxims of the leading
masters, not only in the positive or demonstrative rules
of Art, so far as they were then known, but also in those
more indefinite principles which, although having a real
foundation in the nature of human emotion, are not from
their subtle and modificable characters, so susceptible of
being reduced to distinct rules, and are, therefore,
usually considered to be altogether conventional.

We have shown how Giotto impressed his own modes of
perception and feeling on all the Italian art of his time,
and indeed long after him. Some of the schools, the Paduan
for example, went so far in their obedience to these so-
called conventional rules, as to revive the study of the
ideal art of ancient Greece.

The 'exceeding young men of stubborn instincts and
positive self-trust,' look upon the lessons of the great
schools of art as folly, and scoff at the accumulated
experience of the 'old masters' as mere fatuity. Their own
sagacity is sufficient to penetrate her profoundest
mysteries, and their works show the lessons of wisdom they
derive from their self-willed study of her.

In all things, then, both manual and mental, technical
and theoretical, the *real* Pre-Raphaelites are the complete
antitheses to the pretended ones, and prove these young
men to be as ill informed as they are presumptuous in
assuming the title.

The important question, however, and that involved in
the former of the propositions above quoted, is not the
propriety of a name, so much as appropriateness of practice and truth of results. Whether the 'school' should be

designated pre-Raphaelite or post-Raphaelite, or, indeed, called a school at all, in the sense of being governed by intelligible and distinct principles, is not so necessary to be considered, as whether their works afford evidence of their having a perception of the true relation of Art to nature, and of their realising that perception in their productions. The answer to be given to this question is the complete solution of the problem. Into this question the author of 'Modern Painters' has not thought it incumbent upon him to enter. We have examined their pictures for the purpose of ascertaining their theoretical principles. All that we can find expressive of intention is ugliness of form and constrained action, combined with a laboriously niggled handling and a style of colouring in which force alone, irrespective of subject and sentiment, is obtained by the common artifice of placing the primary colours and their complementaries in immediate juxtaposition. They defend their first peculiarity by pleading that they 'dare not improve God's works.' As if the creatures of this sin-polluted world, were unchanged since they came fresh from their Maker's hand. Admitting, however, that nature were perfect and harmonious in every part, the question remains, do they study her intelligently? We believe they do not. They paint from nature as an idiot counts the strokes of a clock, as so many isolated units, without having any idea of aggregation. In the same intelligent spirit the hopeful school gives us an assemblage of dry, meagre, disjointed objects, without the smallest expression of *relation* either of sentiment or effect. They individualise strongly, but are totally devoid of the power to unite with the individuality the expression of a general whole, and thus fail to convey the spirit of their subject. Every form, near or remote, is elaborated with the same mechanical minuteness. This method of imitating Nature produces results which are wholly false; Nature unites her separate elaborations by the nicest gradation of tint, tone, and force, into one broad and grand harmony. The imitations of her by the hopeful school have none of these qualities; they all strike the eye with the same force, and, consequently, all seem to be projected on the same vertical plane. While Nature is all grace, sweetness, and simplicity, the Pre-Raphaelites' renderings are all constraint, harshness, and affectation. Thus, even regarding the aim of Art as being a servile and mechanical imitation of nature, these pictures have no pretension to the title of works of Art.

When, however, we consider what the true function of the artist is, what a grotesque and repulsive mockery do the productions of the hopeful school appear! Instead of

skilfully-conducted incident, these 'young men' give us a
microscopist's copy of some trivial accessory, and for the
pathos or the dignity of human emotion we are treated to a
childish display of glaring pigments. This is not only
false philosophy, but also depraved taste. Colour and form
are the language in which the artist expresses his
thoughts and feelings; they should, therefore, be made
subservient to this as means to an end, and never be
allowed to rise into such prominence as to become separate
qualities apart from that end. Few things injure the works
of acknowledged great masters more than this obtrusion of
mechanical qualities and secondary objects. It is a mere
truism to say that the mechanical should be subordinated
to the mental, and accessories developed in the order of
their æsthetical relation, and not in that of their mere
local contiguity, to the central idea of the work. Every
one of the pictures exhibited by the so-called Pre-
Raphaelites furnishes examples of the violation of this
rule.

Our space will not permit us to pursue this subject
further at present. We may, however, return to it at a
future opportunity.

But we cannot conclude these remarks on 'Pre-
Raphaelitism' without adverting to the tone in which it is
written. Its author professes to be exceedingly susceptible of offence at any plainness of speech used towards
him, or inadvertent disparagement of his dignity; but
seems singularly forgetful of his own requirements in his
treatment of others. He uniformly imputes the worst
motives in the strongest terms. Opinions which differ from
his, and which, if erroneous, are at most, errors of judgment, are stigmatised as 'falsehoods,' 'direct falsehoods,'
&c.; whilst 'indolence, infidelity, sensuality, and
shallow pride,' are the best sources to which he can
ascribe the actions of whole generations of men. The
author of 'Modern Painters' has written works which advance rather high pretensions to a piety of more than
ordinary purity, and even in the pamphlet under notice,
expatiates with seeming unction on 'taking the kingdom of
Heaven by force.' We should be sorry to impugn his
Christianity, but cannot refrain from suggesting a comparison of it with that of Him who admonished his
followers to do to others as they would have men do to
them; and we even venture to recommend the consideration
of how far charitable construction of motive and courteous
language are essential to the character of a gentleman.

'The Stones of Venice I'

1851

10. FROM AN UNSIGNED REVIEW, 'FRASER'S MAGAZINE'

April 1854, vol. 49, 463-78

The initial volume of 'The Stones of Venice', although
admired by Charlotte Brontë, Carlyle, and others of the
intelligentsia, was given at best a mixed critical reception. An architectural essay of authoritative dryness
whose first and last chapters, however, suggest the
grandeur of the work to come, the volume sold with dis-
couraging slowness. Most reviews were explanatory rather
than critical as is apparent from the following excerpts.

...He commences the first volume with a brief review of
Venetian history, in order that the reader may be better
able to judge of the changes which Venice underwent, both
in her art, and in her religious, social, and political
character. The former element in the well-being of the
State is made the touchstone of its greatness. All that is
great and patriotic in the public annals of Venice is
traced to a pervading feeling of domestic and individual
religion. To the same cause is attributed all that is
noble and admirable in architecture, and in art generally;
the same view being carried out into the details of the
subject, with which the author shows a minute familiarity.
  Mr. Ruskin chooses Venice as the scene of his inquiries,
not only because it contains more remains of architectural
beauty than, perhaps, any other city in Italy, but because
three elements meet there - the Roman, the Lombard, and
the Arab. The ducal palace, which contains these in nearly
equal proportions, may be regarded as the central building

137

of the world.

   True to his theory of the art of a period being the
correlative of its religion and morals, he traces the
downfall of Venetian art from the reign of Foscari, who
became doge in 1423, and 'in whose reign the first marked
signs appear in architecture of that mighty change to
which London owes St. Paul's, Rome St. Peter's, Venice and
Vicenza the edifices commonly supposed to be their noblest, and Europe in general the degradation of every art
she has since practised.' In other words, the ruin of all
noble art was caused by the same vices, the same luxury
and extravagance, the same abandonment of principle and
corruption of practice, which brought about the Reformation. 'Against the corrupted papacy arose two great divisions of adversaries, Protestants in Germany and England,
Rationalists in France and Italy; the one requiring the
purification of religion, the other its destruction. The
Protestant kept the religion, but cast aside the heresies
of Rome, and with them her arts; by which rejection he
injured his own character, cramped his intellect in
refusing to it one of its noblest exercises, and materially diminished its influence.' The Rationalist 'kept the
arts, and cast aside the religion. This rationalistic art
is commonly called the Renaissance, marked by a return to
pagan systems - not to adopt and hallow them for Christianity, but to rank itself under them as an imitator and
pupil. In painting it is headed by Giulio Romano and
Nicolo Poussin, in architecture by Sansovino and Palladio.'

   This view is worked out by Mr. Ruskin in the course of
his three volumes. As in 'Modern Painters' he exerted
himself to break down the strongholds and diminish the
reputation of Renaissance landscape painting, so in the
'Stones of Venice' he endeavours to show how all that is
bad in architecture is attributable to the Renaissance
spirit, which he considers in his third volume in detail.

   His instances are generally taken from Venice; sometimes also from Verona, and other cities of Italy; at
other times from the churches and civil edifices of England and France. It will be thought by most dispassionate
readers that our author fails to prove his point that
Gothic architecture is essentially good, Renaissance
essentially bad. How much truth there is in his remarks,
may be gathered from an impartial examination of what he
afterwards says.

   Mr. Ruskin considers architecture under two heads:
1. Construction; 2. Decoration; in one of which he tells
us we are to read the intellect of man, in the other his
affections.

   We have not space to do justice to Mr. Ruskin's remarks

on constructive architecture.

There is one remark, however, which deserves especial notice, as it refers to a principle of primary importance. In treating of 'the roof,' Mr. Ruskin takes occasion to attack a theory which finds great favour with the German critics, and many more in this country, that the pointed roof is the expression of a devotional sentiment pervading the northern Gothic. He attributes it to two natural causes; 1st, to the necessity of throwing off wet and snow, which will lodge on a flat roof; 2ndly, to the fact that rooms in a roof are comfortably habitable in the north, which are painful '*sotto piombi*' in Italy; and also that there is in wet climates a natural tendency in all men to live as high as possible, out of the damp and mist. 'These two causes, together with accessible quantities of good timber, have induced in the north a steep pitch of roof, which, when rounded or squared above a tower, became a spire or turret.' Our author is not content with blowing up this popular fallacy, but he also, as we have before intimated, demolishes the character of the northern architects in a strain that appears rather unjust, as coming from a man who claims for the Venetian architests great devotion of purpose and depth of religious feeling.

However, the practical view of the question taken in this chapter is one which will be appreciated by all who hold that 'the direct symbolisation of a sentiment is a weak motive with all men, and far more so in the practical minds of the north than among the early Christians.'

We are compelled to pass over a very valuable chapter - that on the material of ornament; but we recommend it to the reader's notice.

Having spoken of the material of ornament, Mr. Ruskin proceeds to the question of its treatment. There are, he says, two elements to be considered, - expression and arrangement; and a good effect in architecture can only be produced by the combination of both. It is a common error to suppose that ornament must be highly executed, and beautiful in itself. We are not to look upon the sculptures of the Parthenon as ornamental parts of the temple, but rather on the temple as a framework for the sculpture. Ornament would be rare, if we were to wait till we got a Phidias, a M. Angelo, or a Ghiberti. But workmen with ordinary powers of execution we can always command and out of such materials the architect will have to produce his effect. His treatment of ornament therefore, must be calculated to bring out and employ to the full the powers on which he can rely. This was done by the Egyptian and Assyrian builders; and no one can deny that they obtained

a highly effective result, perhaps the noblest that has
ever been achieved by powerful symbolism combined with
feeble execution. It is to the just union of these
opposite elements that we must look for perfection in
architectural decoration. This perfection, as Mr. Ruskin
says, can only be relative; it is better that architecture
should honestly confess its *imperfection*, than aim at perfectness more than human skill can compass. The method
which Christian art must employ is in fact the counterpart
of that which the Greek architects pursued. For if,
according to Mr. Ruskin, every man who has a soul and
hopes of salvation, has a right to find employment for
whatever artistic power he may possess; it is clear that
his employer must find such work for him as men of ordinary powers can accomplish. He must press into the service
of decorative architecture not the noblest, but the humblest forms of nature, such as the humblest workman may
imitate. These will admit of comparatively close imitation: the lowly nature of the object will prevent its
assuming any undue importance. As the ordinary sculptor
approaches the nobler objects of imitation, he must avoid
bringing his imperfect powers into competition with
nature, and his treatment must become more studiously
symbolical. The principle on which the Greek acted was, as
we know, the reverse of this. He treated all humbler
objects of imitation conventionally; and, in proportion as
he rose from these to nobler objects, his method had less
of conventionality and more of direct imitation, till in
the treatment of the human figure he approached as near to
nature as his material would admit of. Thus Phidias
employed masons to cut triglyphs, and fluted columns, and
capitals. He committed probably to his pupils the execution of metopes and friezes, himself lending a hand to the
figures of the pediments, and elaborating the chrysele-
phantine statues of the goddess of the Parthenon and the
Olympian Jove.

This system of subordination of work in proportion to
the ability of the workmen seems very reasonable, and in
the cases alluded to it was eminently successful. But it
must be remembered that Greece produced but one Phidias,
and that modern Europe is, in artistic ability, very
inferior to ancient Greece. So that we cannot reckon on
our buildings receiving such a crown of artistic decoration as those sculptures, which in their day were unsurpassed, and are now unrivalled. And it is unwise to adopt
a style which can only succeed when carried out by first
rate talent rather than one, which enables men of ordinary
powers to work successfully, and even to display originality under the guidance of an able architect. Hence, in

nine cases out of ten, it will be safer to adopt Gothic
than Renaissance architecture.

There is another reason for this preference on which
Mr. Ruskin dwells forcibly - namely, that a revival of
classic antiquity, even though eminently successful, does
not appeal to the affections of men in our times. In the
mediæval ornament there was a degree of truth, and an
imitation of natural objects, which spoke not only to the
cultivated mind, but to the rudest beholder's mind and
heart. Moreover, there was a variety which left space for
the employment of men's imaginations and powers of combining; whereas the forms which had been once approved by
classical antiquity remained stereotyped for ever; and
men of the greatest authority lent their names and
employed their learning in defence of a system, the adoption of which precluded all attempts at farther invention;
and men in general were forced to remain contented with
the forms which Sansovino and Palladio had prescribed for
them. The laws which architects laid down from an observation of Greek and Roman architectural models resemble
those which critics deduced from an examination of the
masterpieces of dramatic art; and the exclusive study of
Vitruvius and the five orders produced a school of architecture no less narrow in its views and bigoted in its
principles than the French school of dramatic poetry,
which was founded upon a rigid interpretation of Aristotle,
and the doctrine of the three unities.

Against such a school in art, in so far as it tends to
cramp the free exertion of the natural powers of man, no
one can protest too strongly. On the other hand, it must
be acknowledged that certain conditions are necessary to
all success in art; and that, when these are once ascertained, it is our duty and policy to abide by them. One of
these conditions is, moderation in the use of the means at
the artist's disposal. On this point Mr. Ruskin has some
excellent remarks, which it would be well for our architects if they would profit by. It is the privilege of
genius, he says, to employ abundance of ornament; but it
is dangerous ground to stand upon, and superabundance of
decoration may be as harmful to a building as superfluity
of wealth to its possessor.

In the last chapter of the first volume, The Vestibule,
we have an eloquent vindication of the principles of
Realism as opposed to Idealism in art. We think, however
this view may seem at first sight to be opposed to what he
says respecting symbolism, that Mr. Ruskin is, in the
main, right; and that the business of the artist is not to
improve, but to interpret nature: not to criticise, but to
select.

But we must not pass over the intent and meaning of
'the Vestibule' which is to introduce us to the scene of
our future wanderings.

Hitherto we have been in European ground, except when
we have occasionally visited Egypt and Assyria; henceforth
we are to walk up and down the streets of that 'glorious
city in the sea,' which is better known to us as the abode
of luxury than as a school of severe religious art. Yet
such is one aspect under which Mr. Ruskin is about to
present Venice to us.

He takes us with him from Padua along the banks of the
Brenta, by Dolo and Mestre, till at last we enter a
gondola, and after passing along a weary length of canal,
by the bastions of the fort of Malghera, by endless banks
of tawny grass, by the railroad bridge, and a straggling
line of low and confused brick buildings, which, but for
the many towers mingled with them, might be the suburbs of
an English town, - 'Four or five domes, pale, and
apparently at a greater distance, rise over the centre of
the line; but the object which first catches the eye is a
sullen cloud of black smoke brooding over the northern
half of it, and which issues from the belfry of a church.
It is Venice.'...

'The Stones of Venice II, III'

1853

11. THREE UNSIGNED REVIEWS, 'THE TIMES'

24 September, 1 October, 12 November 1853

Although unsigned and too early in his prose-writing career
to hazard any stylistic individuality, it is possible that
the three reviews were written by the young George
Meredith. In E.T. Cook's 'Delane of "The Times"' (New
York, 1916, pp. 186-7) occurs this passage: 'George
Meredith was among the writers whose talents were quickly
recognized by Delane, and Ruskin said of a long notice of
"The Stones of Venice" that it was "incomparably the best
critique he had ever had."' Thus a claim for Meredith is
not easily set aside. See Introduction, pp. 11-12.

RUSKIN'S 'STONES OF VENICE,' Vol. II.

In this volume Mr. Ruskin, after a preliminary visit to
Torcello, the mother city, and to Murano, the old pleasure
suburb of Venice, conducts us first over the Byzantine
buildings, with St. Mark's at their head, and then over the
Gothic buildings, crowned by the Ducal Palace. He also
discusses at great length the philosophy respectively of
the Byzantine style as it appears in Venice (for he does
not know it in its native land), and of the Gothic.
The laws of Byzantine architecture he deduces from the
principle of incrustation. Its glory is colour. It is
painting in marble, of which St. Mark's is a masterpiece.
It is brick cased with stones of price. Its superficial
nature must stand confessed. All refinements of inner
structure must be abandoned. It must be costly as jewellery; and, generally, its architect will have the liberty

of the jeweller to preserve the size of his precious stones
at the expense of perfect symmetry. But costliness and
sacrifice are essential; and the shafts which, as estimable
by the eye, are the great expression of wealth in buildings
of this kind, must be of one block, on pain of the consequences of dishonesty and deception. The impression of the
architecture must not be dependent on size; for the claim
of the several parts on attention depends on their delicacy
of design, their perfection of colour, the preciousness of
their material, and their legendary interest; so that we
must not be disappointed if, 'for the great cliff-like but-
tresses and mighty piers of the north, shooting up into in-
discernible height, we have here low walls spread before us
like the pages of a book, and shafts whose capitals we may
touch with our hand.' St. Mark's is 'less a temple wherein
to pray than itself a book of Common Prayer - a vast illuminated missal, bound with alabaster instead of parch-
ment, studded with porphyry pillars instead of jewels, and
written within and without in letters of enamel and gold.'

In a noble passage Mr. Ruskin contrasts a vast gray
cathedral of England, in its old quiet square, with St.
Mark's, approached through the alleys once thronged with
the commerce of Venice. For the description of the cathedral (which we shall never forget when we look on one) we
have not space. But we will give St. Mark's:-

[Quotes from 'There rises a vision' to 'seven hundred
years', 'Works' 10: 82-4.]

The introduction of the *sea-nymphs* is rather incongruous; and we could have dispensed with the marbles *giving us, Cleopatra-like, their bluest veins to kiss.* False
or turgid imagery is, indeed, rather a besetting sin of
this most eloquent but dangerously fluent writer. The
language and the power of discerning remote resemblances,
of which he is so great a master, sometimes master him,
and carry him beyond the boundary of the sublime into the
confines of the neighbouring kingdom. Thus, in the
present volume, we have 'the wall of ice, durable like
iron, *setting, death-like, its white teeth against us* out
of the Polar twilight;' and that in the next clause to
another simile about the 'hunger of the north wind biting
the peaks into barrenness,' - we have Venice 'writing her
history *on the scrolls of the sea surges*' - 'that beauty
which seemed to have *fixed for its throne the sands of
the hourglass as well as of the sea*' - and 'a mere
efflorescence of decay, a *stage dream*, which the first
ray of daylight must dissipate into *dust*,' Just before
the fine passage above quoted the first impression of the

symmetry of St. Mark's is most unnaturally illustrated by
saying that it is 'as if the rugged and irregular houses
that pressed together above us in the dark alley had been
struck back into sudden obedience and lovely order, and
all their rude casements and broken walls had been transformed into arches charged with goodly sculpture and
fluted shafts of delicate stone.'   And with still worse
taste the three classes of artists - Purists, Sensualists,
and Naturalists - are likened 'to men reaping wheat, of
which the Purists take the fine flour, and the Sensualists
the chaff and straw, but *the Naturalists take all home,
and make their cake of the one and their couch of the
other.*'   A little more consideration would lead Mr.
Ruskin's taste to remove these blemishes, and no injury
would be done to the freshness of his eloquence. He informs us that ten minutes before writing a particular passage in this volume he saw the occurrence which it describes. From this we infer that he writes fresh from his
impressions of the subject; which is well; but, as he may
expect his works to live, he should also correct what he
has written.

It is less on his account than on account of the imitators whom we foresee the popularity of his great passages will produce, that we enforce Lessing's just warning
respecting the pictorial power of words. By means of language we can, to any extent, depict action; and we can depict it by means of language only. The painter or sculptor
cannot depict action; they can only suggest it by the
position of the limbs and muscles, or by the expression of
the face. But language, also, has its bounds; though, of
all modes of expression, its kingdom is the widest. When
the effect of the object to be described results from the
combination of all its parts presented at once to the eye,
as in the case of a beautiful face or a beautiful landscape, language is almost powerless. It can only enumerate
the parts in succession; and the mind of the reader is unable to retain and combine the parts so as to form a whole
without an effort of attention and imagination on his part
greater in reality than that which is exercised by the
author. Thus their labour is but lost who in novels or
poems give us an inventory of the heroine's features or a
catalogue of the objects in the landscape. We do not make
a beauty out of the one or a Claude out of the other. If
we know the person or the object, we are pleased with a
description which revives the image in our minds and
quickens our perception of its beauties; but if we do not
know it we cannot imagine it from the description. The
only way to paint a landscape or a beautiful face in words
is to describe its effect upon the human mind - in a word,

its charm; as Homer paints the beauty of Helen simply by
saying that the elders of Troy when they saw her, ceased to
repine at the war which they were enduring for her sake,
while a later and inferior poet enumerates her beauties in
20 or 30 lines. So again in the case of landscapes or
buildings, or any other object which depends for its effect
on the simultaneous impression of a number of different
parts, the writer, if he cannot appeal to our experience
and memory, must give up the hope of painting, and be content with giving us the general character of the object and
its impression on the mind. A person who had not seen St.
Mark's, or a painting of it (which most people have), would
form no picture of it in his mind from Mr. Ruskin's words;
he would only have a notion of sunny beauty, and delicate
ornament, and bright colouring, contrasted with the opposite characteristics of the cathedral in the north.
Indeed, it is to produce this very notion, and not to produce a word picture in competition with the pictures of
Canaletti, that the passage is introduced; and this perfectly justifies its introduction, and the introduction of
its counterpart, the description of the English cathedral.
In the same manner Mr. Ruskin's picture of the site and
vicinity of Venice, or, as he poetically calls it, 'The
Throne,' is perfectly within the province of language, because it is not an attempt to paint a landscape as with a
brush or pencil. The principle of combination is not that
of sight, which requires the parts to be presented together, but of thought, which allows them to be presented
in succession. It is a poetical verification and development of an idea - the idea of the fitness of the spot for
the empire and the art of which it was destined to be the
seat. Let those, then, who desire to adorn their pages
with word pictures, after the manner of Mr. Ruskin, remember that his example is susceptible of a vicious imitation,
or their drafts upon the fancy of their readers will inevitably be dishonoured.

The Byzantine style is evidently the especial object of
Mr. Ruskin's affection, though he is equally just to the
merits of the Gothic. A passionate lover of colour, he
cannot but feel partiality for the only architecture which
admits of perfect and permanent chromatic decoration. But
he loves it also as the architecture of his favourite city
in her best, holiest, and noblest hour; before she became
what our imaginations always represent her - 'the revel of
the earth, the mask of Italy;' all gay without, all dark
and foul within. Mr. Ruskin believes the spirit of the
early Venetians to have been essentially, deeply, even
sternly religious, and he traces the expression of this
spirit in the first buildings erected by the fugitives of

Altinum; he bids us, if we would know how the dominion of
Venice was begun, not to estimate the wealth of her
arsenals or number of her armies, or enter into the secrets
of her councils, but to ascend the highest tier of the
stern ledges that sweep round the altar of Torcello, and
recall the forms of its exiles and the sound of their
ancient hymn. And the monuments of that high, religious
age, and of its great men, are St. Mark's and the Byzantine palaces. These are the remains - the magnificent
fragments - to exhibit which in their own strength he will
'tear away the impotent feelings of romance,' which, 'like
climbing flowers, gild but cannot save, and which in Venice
are not only incapable of protecting, but even of discerning the objects to which they ought to have been attached.'
The Venice, he tells us, of modern fiction and drama is a
thing of yesterday. No prisoner whose name is worth remembering, or whose sorrow deserved sympathy, ever crossed
that Bridge of Sighs which is the centre of the Byronic
ideal of Venice; no great merchant of Venice ever saw that
Rialto under which the traveller now passes with breath-
less interest; the statue which Byron makes Faliero address
as one of his great ancestors was erected to a soldier of
fortune 150 years after Faliero's death; and, if the mighty
Doges could now look from the decks of their galleys at the
entrance of the Grand Canal, they would not know in what
part of the world they stood. 'The remains of *their* Venice
lie hidden behind the cumbrous masses which were the delight of the nation in its dotage; hidden in many a grass-
grown court and silent pathway and lightless canal, where
the slow waves have sapped their foundations for 500 years,
and must soon prevail over them for ever.' Over the tombs
of one of these 'mighty doges' - Andrea Dandolo - in the
Church of St. Mark, Mr. Ruskin bends, with the careless,
slavish crowd of the square fresh in his mind, and the
march-notes of an Austrian regiment in his ear, and thinks
how he who lies under that canopy would have taught his
country another choice if she would have listened to him;
- 'but he and his counsels have long been forgotten by her,
and the dust lies upon his lips.'
The descriptive portions of the work consist of a conscientious and affectionate examination of details, the
interest of which is sustained, even for the non-
architectural reader, by the power of a mind which constantly educes the spirit through the body of art, and
criticizes all the works of man in the light of noble moral
sentiments, drawing sermons indeed from the mouldings of a
grass-grown and neglected stone. For to Mr. Ruskin art has
a deep moral and religious significance, both in its uses
and in its connexion with the character and condition of

the artist. Every touch is for him the thought of a human
intellect and the voice of a human heart. His general
language on this subject, if it came from another writer,
might almost be thought affected. He constantly inculcates a spirit of the deepest reverence towards the works
of the great achitects; he speaks of colour especially as
a great gift of God; he holds that the sins of Venice were
aggravated, because they were committed in the presence of
St. Mark's; he measures the spiritual degradation of the
modern Venetians by the distance between their art and
that of their forefathers at Murano; he believes the men
who designed and the men who delighted in a beautiful
archivolt to have been *wise, holy, and happy;* he rejoices
to recognize the Protestant spirit of self-reliance and
free inquiry in the characteristic freedom of Gothic architecture at its noblest epoch; he speaks of a wilful deviation from true principles in art as *corruption* and as
sin; he denounces those who love monotony in buildings
rather than variety as *luring darkness rather than light;*
he divides the different schools of art on principles at
least as much of morality as of style or taste; he distinctly speaks of the Deity as providing for different
kinds and grades of art; he calls upon us to note with
thankfulness and awe the inscrutable wisdom with which
Providence, working for a mysterious but glorious aim, prepared the sands and waters of the lagoon to give birth to
the art of Venice. But it is not so much in these direct
expressions, strong as they are, that Mr. Ruskin's religious feeling for art appears, as in the intense affection
with which he pores over the minutest details of the
words which he admires; the delight with which he discovers and reveals some almost imperceptible delicacy of
measurement or proportion, some microscopic excellence of
colouring, some happy touch of a mason's hand in a subordinate ornament. He seems to kiss the very footsteps of
that art of which he is the great expositor. And, therefore, it is with a feeling of astonishment amounting to
dismay that we suddenly come upon such a passage as the
following:-

[Quotes from 'The more I have examined' to 'felt for the
time', 'Works' 10: 124-5.]

In the two following paragraphs Mr. Ruskin seems to
limit these startling remarks to the case of religious
paintings, the indifference to which he accounts for
partly on the ground that the great religious painters and
the subjects of their pictures have been Romanist, partly
on the ground that to strong religious feeling the highest

representation of sacred subjects is unsatisfactory, while
the lowest may be invested with reality and raised to sublimity by the power of childish faith. And he turns the
reproach from the art that is scorned upon the Protestant
Christians who scorn it, by telling us 'that we refuse to
regard the painters who passed their lives in prayer, but
are perfectly ready to be taught by those who spent them
in debauchery.'

If this is all - if he means only that Protestants cannot look with unmixed feelings on paintings that represent
Roman Catholic objects of devotion - that disagreeable
associations inevitably attach in our minds to a portrait
of St. Dominic, or an Assumption of the Virgin, or the picture of a fabulous miracle - and that subjects from the
Bible, however inferior as works of art, are generally more
popular, his opinion is nothing new to us. We are ready to
add the further admission, that mediæval churches and cathedrals, being distinctly adapted to the forms of Roman
Catholic worship and the peculiarities of Roman Catholic
belief, it is difficult for Protestants to regard them as
religious buildings with unqualified satisfaction. And we
should not be scandalized to hear that this dissatisfaction was most acute in those Protestants whose religious
feelings are the strongest. We can only hope that some day
art will accommodate itself to truth. In the meantime, if
Mr. Ruskin has found that the best men among Protestants -
those, to take his own words, who are, humanly speaking,
most perfect before God - do not, in proportion to their
taste and cultivation, appreciate the pictures of great
Roman Catholic masters *as works of art,* and even, so far as
is rational or possible, as works of devotion, we can only
say that it is a question of experience, and that his experience is diametrically opposed to ours.

But if it is suggested that there is any incompatability
between a religious character and a care for art - such a
care as is implied in its full enjoyment and perfect cultivation - then, we say, it is a grave question for us all,
and especially for Mr. Ruskin, who himself cares for art
so much, and endeavours, with so much power and success,
to make the rest of the world care for it.

We apprehend that the persons on whom Mr. Ruskin's induction is grounded would appear, on examination, not only
to be remarkable for religion, but also to be men of a
peculiar, though not uncommon temperament; and that we
should find their indifference to poetry and beauty to be
more the result of their temperament than of their
religion. There are even certain views of Christianity
which, if they could be consistently followed, would
render those who hold them almost incapable not only of

enjoying or taking interest in anything, but almost of
doing their duty to society. Mr. Francis Newman, in his
'Phases of Faith,' mentions an Irish clergyman of exem-
plary piety who actually lived on the assumption that the
world was coming to an end every minute, and who was only
prevented from selling the library which was necessary to
his mental health and usefulness by the fortunate recollection that St. Paul himself had sent for his books from
Troas. Such a man would obviously care nothing for art;
but he would care nothing for literature, science, law,
civilization, or freedom either. He would be altogether
out of harmony with the world which Providence has given
him to keep, adorn, and study so long as he is in it, to
the probable detriment of his own character, - to the certain detriment of the character of his sect, if he should
happen to found one. Beauty and the sense of beauty are
from God; they are placed by Him, for high and tender purposes, in the creation and in the nature of man. And art,
as it acts powerfully on the character of men and nations,
either for good or evil, will always deserve the attention
of religious men, if they care for their kind, as well as
any other educational influence. Man cannot 'jump' this
world any more than he can jump the world to come.

But the fact is, that Mr. Ruskin should be asked to re-
consider his judgment before it is made the subject of
elaborate argument. What can he mean by saying that *there
are some who in very deed are nobler, tenderer, and further
sighted in soul than those whose heart is perfect and
right before God?* Does not this show that he has need to
settle more clearly who is the true Christian before he
pronounces that the true Christian does not care for art?
And again, he contradicts himself as to the facts. For in
one paragraph he tells us that true Christians do not care
about art, and in the next that they do care a great deal
about art of a low kind - Carlo Dolce Magdalens, with a
tear on each cheek, and black clouds with a flash of lightning by Martin, and coarse Scripture pictures by Salvator.

If it be said that Protestants, as a class, are more indifferent to art than Roman Catholics, we may point to Mr.
Ruskin himself, who is not singular among English Protestants in his love of the Italian masters, though he may be
singular in his exquisite knowledge of them. That Protestant countries have produced fewer great painters than
Roman Catholic countries is true; but the reason seems to
be principally that there are diversities of gifts among
nations as among men, and that the gifts of taste belong
to the southern, while the gifts of intellect belong most
to the northern nations. Milton is a conclusive answer to
any argument that Roman Catholics may draw from the

possession of Michael Angelo. It seems also as if art were the gift not only of particular nations, but of a particular age; at least, it has declined in Roman Catholic countries quite as much as in Protestant countries since the epoch of the Reformation. If the watchful apologists of Roman Catholicism among ourselves should pounce on Mr. Ruskin's admission as an evidence that all Protestantism is cold and fanatical, and crushes the finer and tenderer parts of human nature, they must take his observations on themselves into the bargain. 'Idolatry,' he says, 'is no encourager of the fine arts.' 'Take the vilest doll that is screwed together in a cheap toyshop; trust it to the keeping of a large family of children; let it be beaten about the house by them till it is reduced to a shapeless block; then dress it in a satin frock and declare it to have fallen from Heaven, and it will satisfactorily answer all Romanist purposes.' And, again, in palliating the *old* Mariolatry of the builders of the church at Murano, he speaks with disgust of the 'frightful doll' which now stands 'in wretchedness of rags,' and 'with rouged cheeks and painted brows,' as an evidence of the present spiritual condition alike of the worshipper and of the priest.

Nevertheless, we must make the melancholy confession that those religious distractions of Christandom, which perplex politics and education and the whole life of man, are not without their effect even upon art. It is obvious that poetry, and philosophical poetry especially, reflecting the spirit of the age, must reflect the characteristics of that spirit; and if all the controversial writings of this generation should perish, the works of its great poets would alone suffice to assure posterity that it was an age of doubt. 'There's something in this world amiss, shall be unriddled by-and-by,' is the keynote of our poetry; and the same perplexity is revealed in the paralytic or purely imitative state of all kinds of religious art. This, our misfortune, must also be our excuse when we are charged with indifference to the beautiful, - a charge which Mr. Ruskin is inclined to make in somewhat exaggerated terms - '*Carmina proveniunt animo dictata sereno*.' There is something that weighs heavier on the heart of the age than questions of architecture or painting, and which must be taken off before it will recover the freedom and originality in art, and especially in religious art, which was possessed by Dante, and by the great Gothic architects, and Raphael, and Angelico. Mr. Ruskin, as a reformer of art, will find in the spiritual and philosophical condition of his time a deeper malady than the mere prevalence of a bad style, and a stronger reason than any mere want of taste or power of

expression for our general tendency to take refuge in the
beauties of nature or in the buildings and paintings of
the past.

We have said that Mr. Ruskin is inclined to exaggerate
the want of a taste for beauty in his age. Surely he does
so, when he says that 'the rush of the arrival in the railway station is not *always* nor *to all men* an equivalent' for
the romance of travelling in the olden time. He may depend
upon it that the generation to which he preaches is not so
stiffnecked as he imagines. We are not without a desire
for beauty, if any one would show us how to attain it. We
are fully sensible, for instance, how bad an effect is produced upon us all, and especially on those who cannot
afford to change the scene, by the excessive ugliness of
our towns; and a man who would practically help us to improve them would be hailed as a general benefactor. We
most entirely sympathize with the wish to introduce some
better features into those 'miles of house, with the proper
portion of Doric portico and windows allotted to each inhabitant.' Only the remedy must be practical, and, in the
case of domestic architecture at least, it must not smell
too strongly of the *Lamp of Sacrifice*. It may be quite
true that the style of the Venetian palaces may be as convenient as it is beautiful, and that it may have the
further recommendation (scarcely appreciable by the holder
of a building lease) of lasting 15 centuries. But what
does it cost? The inhabitant of 30 feet of 'house' in
Tyburnia enjoys good-sized rooms, and such light and air as
London can afford, for a moderate proportion of his income.
Outside, his home is No. 20; but he finds comfort, and he
may find taste and variety, within; and it can scarcely be
expected that anything less cogent then a Venetian constitution will compel him to exchange his present interior for
such a portion as a man of ordinary income - to say nothing
of the poor - could afford of *the Stones of Venice*.

(To be continued.)

RUSKIN'S 'STONES OF VENICE,' Vol. II.

(Concluded from 'The Times' of Sept. 24.)

The question respecting the nature of Gothic architecture
is handled by Mr. Ruskin in a peculiar way. He declines to
regard Gothic as an historical style, and prefers to treat
of *Gothicness* as a compound idea, actually existing only in
the mind, like the Platonic archetypes, but embodied to a
greater or less degree in different buildings, which, from

their participation in it, are called Gothic. This compound idea, following the dangerous analogy of a chymical analysis, he resolves into six elements, - *Savageness, Changefulness, Naturalism, Grotesqueness, Rigidity,* and *Redundance,* - which are arranged in the order of their importance. These make up the spirit of Gothic. An element of external form is subsequently (and, we think, most discreetly, introduced - viz., the pointed roof or gable, which Mr. Ruskin regards as more essential, or, at least, more fundamental, than the pointed arch; his theory of the styles of architecture being, that they spring from the three different ways of bridging a space - either with a lintel (Greek and Egyptian), with a round arch (Romanesque), or with a gable (Gothic).

If this restriction is intended merely to give shape to a critical dissertation, it is very well; but if it is intended as a strict definition of Gothic architecture, to supersede other definitions in scientific and practical treatises, it is certainly open to objection. First, it is quite conceivable that all the moral qualities above enumerated, and the gable, should be found together in a building which, as a matter of fact and history, was not Gothic; and, secondly, while the material element is, or may be made, a matter of fact, the moral elements are and must remain a matter of fancy and individual impression. There is no reason why a person of different taste from Mr. Ruskin should not put Redundance before Rigidity, or introduce another element, such as Mystery, Reverence, or a dozen other qualities which minds of a certain character find in a cathedral, and consider an essential part of its architectural expression. And there is another difficulty. The moral qualities of a building depend on the moral qualities of the builders; and accordingly Mr. Ruskin gives a corresponding list - Rudeness, Love of Change, Love of Nature, Disturbed Imagination, Obstinacy, Generosity. It strikes us that some of these characteristics, at all events, belong to the particular age, and that it would be a hard saying to tell us that we could never hope to see a Gothic church built by any architects but such as were rude, obstinate, and of disturbed imagination.

The fact is that Mr. Ruskin has too great a faith in the virtue of analysis. Though he is very hard on Aristotle - though he invidiously compares his method with that of St. Paul (forgetting that the one was a philosopher and the other a preacher) - though (perhaps with too vivid a recollection of Oxford *cram*) he attributes to him the worst effects on the intellect of the day - he is, notwithstanding, smitten with one of his most dangerous tendencies. The attempt to enumerate exactly in their order of relative

importance the elements which make up the moral character
of Gothic architecture seems to us to be an instance of
this tendency. The same failing (for it is radically the
same) shows itself in a constant craving for classification. For example, out of the Scripture phrase '*to
worship in spirit and in truth*,' Mr. Ruskin fancies that
he gets a twofold principle of division - those who worship God *in spirit*, though not in truth, and those who
worship him *both in spirit and in truth*. The division into
worshippers of flesh and worshippers of spirit, he says,
is antecedent to all divisions into Christian and Pagan;
as though it were possible to worship God in flesh in that
sense; unless, indeed, you actually worshipped a fetish.
Again, can there be a stronger piece of Aristotelianism
than this, which is introduced in discussing the Gothic
element of *Naturalism?* -

[Quotes, with omissions, from 'Observe, then. Men are' to
'dangerous error', 'Works' 10: 217-18.]

The 'four forms of dangerous error' being, when the men
of facts despise design; when the men of design despise
facts; when the men of facts envy design; and when the men
of design envy facts.
The words which we have Italicised, and those which
immediately follow them, are, of course, a plain admission
that there is no ground for such a division at all. How
could there be? The very nature of an *imitative* art precludes the possibility of design without facts, and the
nature of *art* precludes the possibility of facts without
design. Even in a Madonna there must be the facts of the
human form. Even in a portrait there must be design in
the choice of aspect and of attitude. Mr. Ruskin has to
take a geological diagram as an instance of pure facts,
and a Turkey carpet as an instance of pure design. His own
examples ought to have taught him the futility of his
theory, since specimens of the classes into which he
divides all artists can only be found *beyond the limits of
art*, in the proper and only relevant sense of the term.
The 'four forms of dangerous error' seem also the results of a mere mechanical division of words. There is no
corresponding distinction of things. To *despise* proves to
be not to envy; and to envy proves to be not to despise.
The Dutch painters are guilty of despising design, because
they rested content with the imitation of nature; the
painters of this century are guilty of envying design, because they endeavoured to get beyond the imitation of
nature. The Greek sculptors (who come under the head of
'*pure designers*' in virtue of their admirable *imitation* of

the human form), are despisers of fact, because they disregarded the facts of lower nature. A sculptor at Bourges (who is a *pure designer,* in virtue of a spirited *imitation* of hawthorn) is an envier of facts, because he painted his hawthorn green. Mr. Ruskin's other instance of the man of facts envying design is poor Sir George Beaumont, who is accused of blinding Constable and blaspheming the work of God, because he recommended that grass should be painted brown instead of green; a recommendation which, however erroneous, must have had for its object not to make the landscape more *fanciful*, or, to use Mr. Ruskin's phrase, more *envious of design*, but to make it a better representation of the general effect of *nature*. Of course, it is very well to observe the different degrees of imitative or imaginative power in different artists, and to note any particular instances of failure arising either from servile imitation or from want of truth. But it is another thing to make a rigid division into classes, into one of which every one has to be forced by a Procrustean operation, with whatever amount of fallacy and injustice. If every painter and sculptor has, and must have in some degree, both of two qualities, as Mr. Ruskin allows, it is an obvious absurdity to classify them on the principle that the greater part of them possess only one. Such classifications must begin with philosophy and end with the grindstone. Besides, Mr. Ruskin seems to us to forget that artists are not to be judged in the abstract, but according to their subjects. He cannot tell whether an artist is too imitative or too imaginative, without knowing what he painted. If a man paints flowers he must be imitative or absurd; if he paints historical scenes, he must be imaginative or raise the dead. This seems a truism, but it is the contrary, unless we mistake, of that which is advanced by Mr. Ruskin.

Then comes another classification, grounded, it will be observed, on a direct negation of that principle of division into designers, men of fact, and men both of fact and design, which formed the foundation of the last:-

[Quotes from 'For observe, *all the three classes*' to 'leave the good', 'Works' 10: 221.]

And then the different painters are dealt round, as it were cards, upon the different classes. Raphael 'inclines to the eclectic' - that is, he inclines to belong to no class at all. Titian and Rubens are allowed to be 'transitional.' But Murillo, though he struggles hard, is brought up to the instrument of philosophical classification; and, after being held to it for a page or two, he drops into the third and worst class of pure sensualists. The *tour de force* by which this startling result is ultimately obtained is a hypercritical analysis of 'The Two Beggar Boys' in the Dulwich Gallery, wherein Mr. Ruskin lays a far greater stress than we think justice will warrant upon the facts that one of the boys is represented as feeding coarsely and without appetite, and that the foot of the lower figure is unnecessarily turned towards the spectator to exhibit the dust. Even granting the criticisms to be sound, we apprehend they will not be held sufficient to support the inference that a painter like Murillo is a vice in nature. Surely, too, it is hard to rank Teniers with men 'who delight in convulsion and disease for their own sake; who find their daily food in the disorder of nature mingled with the suffering of humanity, and who watch joyfully at the right hand of the angel of destruction.' We are the more inclined to demur at this harshness when we find that colour has a good deal to do with it; that excellence in *this* will redeem sensuality; that 'the very depth of the stoop to which the Venetian painters and Rubens sometimes condescend is a consequence of their feeling confidence in the power of their colour to keep them from falling; and that they hold on by it, as by a chain let down from heaven, with one hand, though they may sometimes seem to gather dust and ashes with the other.'

An exception might also, we conceive, be taken to Mr. Ruskin's definition of pictorial evil. He includes in it the representation of a landscape in a storm. Storm is unquestionably an evil in itself, but it does not follow that the representation of it is evil. Independently of the skill shown in the picture, it may, like the sight of the actual phenomenon, produce as its direct effect feelings of awe which partake of a religious character, and, as its indirect effect, the deeper sense of peace, - whether the peace be the succeeding calm of nature or the surrounding calm of a happy home. And be it observed that the production of these effects will depend entirely on the skill of the painter, and not at all upon his moral character, or upon his general taste in the choice of his subjects. Painting is not a moral quality, but a fine art; and a good landscape is a good landscape, whether painted by saint or sinner. That which is required to give poetry even to the highest subjects of the painter is rather sensibility than virtue. Mr. Ruskin of couse makes great play with Fra Angelico, but what does he say to the monk's next door neighbour in art, Perugino?

Let us not be misunderstood. We do not question the fact that a painter's character has an important influence on his works, or that he is responsible for his choice of

subjects, and that, whether his strong point be his outline
or his colour. Nor do we doubt the propriety or utility of
pointing out and condemning a low, gloomy, or prurient tendency, provided that the critic do not condemn circles for
not being squares and Flemish drolls for not being
Angelicos. That to which we object is the peculiar philosophy of Mr. Ruskin, who divides the whole heterogeneous
crowd of painters into three classes, upon a principle
which assumes the universal exercise of a perfectly deliberate and perfectly free moral choice, without allowing
for difference of education, religion, or opportunities,
and without considering that there are a great mass of
artists who paint from the consciousness of skill, and
select the subjects in which they are most successful without any moral purpose or intent at all. It would be almost
as rational to make a threefold division of animals, with
a horse in the centre and a camel-leopard and a rabbit in
either extreme, as a threefold division of art between
Teniers, Raphael, and Angelico.

We are the more anxious to warn Mr. Ruskin against the
errors into which he may be led by an importunate craving
for philosophic system, because we thoroughly appreciate
both his love of principles and his high moral tone; and we
wish emphatically to make this acknowledgement when we
speak with freedom of his philosophy.

While we are on the subject, however, we will notice one
or two more instances of that which appears to us to be
rather precipitate theorizing on the part of Mr. Ruskin.

The first is his doctrine of *imperfection*, from which he
appears inclined to draw some momentous consequences. Imperfection, he says, is essential not only to all noble
architecture, but to all noble art; a dogma which he advances to defend the rudeness which once made Gothic a title
of reproach. If he will review his language on this subject, he will find, we think, that he has confused together
under the term 'imperfection' two distinct things - imperfection in the sense of faultiness or failure, which there
is no need to preach to any human artist - and imperfection
in the sense of economy of finish. And the propriety of
allowing the inferior workmen to design for themselves in
the lower ornaments of a building (which is the point in
view) can hardly be connected either with the principle of
failure or of sparing finish; since, according to Mr.
Ruskin himself, the ornaments which were so executed were
both highly successful and finished to a high degree. We
observe also, that Mr. Ruskin first lays down in sweeping
terms that no great artist can aim at high finish, and
then thinks of Leonardo and the Elgin Marbles, which he has
to get rid of on what appear to us quite irrelevant grounds.

Another instance will be found in a digression on the allegorical figures of the Virtues and Vices in the arcade of the ducal palace, in which digression Mr. Ruskin disposes rather summarily of Aristotle, Plato, and Cicero, exaggerating, as we venture to think, the errors of those philosophers, and also exaggerating the amount of error respecting them in the minds of other students than himself. The special offence is the attempt to enumerate and define the Virtues and Vices. Primitive Christianity, Mr. Ruskin avers, did nothing of the kind. It knew no distinction but the broad and universal one between virtue and vice. The religious republic does not want metaphysicians. And then he comes first upon a long enumeration of separate vices by St. Paul, which he can only get over by pleading that it is unsystematic - a quality which would scarcely have redeemed Aristotle; and next upon the Beatitudes, of which he is driven to say, that they 'belong to different conditions and characters of individual men, not to abstract virtues!' Finally, he winds up by praising Dante (a *translation* of whom he prefers to the *original* of Milton) for not only enumerating, but actually graduating the vices in the most minute and technical manner, and placing in the lowest hell that particular vice of treachery which happened to be the besetting sin of his own nation, and from which he had, or supposed that he had, himself peculiarly suffered.

We cannot help observing, by the way, that, when we are required to worship Dante, and expected to find immeasurable depths of piety and wisdom in his most irrational judgments, we are provoked to ask, what sort of piety or wisdom that was which led him to pronounce judgment for God upon all mankind, and notably on his own political enemies? and whether the audacity imputed to Milton in the choice of his subject is not utterly dwarfed and eclipsed by such presumption? Dante as a poet is one thing, but Dante as a religious philosopher is another, and must be justified on grounds too narrow and humble to admit of adoration. We say this as much with reference to Mr. Carlyle and other thorough-going worshippers as to Mr. Ruskin. But, with regard to Mr. Ruskin himself, when he is inclined to exaggerate the philosophical justice of Dante, we may use an *argumentum ad hominem* of rather a pungent kind; for, as a Protestant, and one who loves truth more than authority, he would occupy a place in the lowest circle but one of Dante's Hell.

We cordially admire the moral enthusiasm of the fine homily which Mr. Ruskin gives us in defending the savageness of Gothic, on the mental evils which have arisen from setting great masses of men to mere mechanical drudgery

without interest and without exercise for the intellect.
We believe that he is quite right in saying, that the inevitable tendency of such a total want of interest in the
work by which a man lives is to throw him back entirely
upon the desire of money, and to stimulate that passion in
society to a morbid and destructive height. We must indeed make some abatement from Mr. Ruskin's language as
from that of most fervent preachers. We must give greater
importance than he does to the hours of 'fireside humanity'
into which the maker of pins or the watcher of a machine
expands when his weary and monotonous task is done. Nor
can we for a moment consent to look back to feudalism as a
condition to be practically balanced with free labour,
however mechanical. Mr. Ruskin thinks that pin-making,
and glass-bead making and the factory system are a slavery
so hideous that it would be better even 'if the lightest
word of a noble was worth men's lives, and the blood of
our vexed, husbandmen dropped in the furrows of our
fields.' He pictures to himself the state of feudalism as
one of romantic attachment between serf and lord, and considers that the hatred felt for the upper classes by the
lower to be far greater in these times of machinery than it
was in those times of **organized** brigandage and hopeless
slavery. Does he remember the history of the Jacquerie and
the rebellion of Wat Tyler, and the Peasant war in Germany?
We cannot help warning him that in the present state of the
world it may not be quite safe to trifle with these
questions.

The practical remedy which he proposes for this evil is
to leave off the use of all articles not absolutely necessary, which do not require invention; never to demand an
exact finish for its own sake, but only for some practical
or noble end; and never to encourage imitation or copying
of any kind except for the sake of preserving a record of
great works. In pursuance of these principles, be commi-
nates against glass beads and cut jewels as productions
which employ little or no intellect, and tells us that
every young lady who buys glass beads is engaged in the
slave-trade, and that every person who wears cut jewels
merely for the sake of their value is a slave-driver. But,
on the other hand, he holds that the working of the goldsmith and the various designing of grouped jewellery and
enamel work may become the subject of the most noble human
intelligence. 'Therefore,' he says, 'money spent in the
purchase of well designed plate, of precious engraved
vases, cameos, or enamels, does good to humanity; and in
work of this kind jewels may be employed to heighten its
splendour, and their cutting is then the price paid for
the attainment of a noble end, and thus perfectly allowable.'

But does not Mr. Ruskin here, and when he enjoins us
to return to the old Venetian glass, in effect condemn
the ornaments of the poor? It is only by mechanical mul-
tiplication and manufactures which require no design on the
part of the operative that the smallest object of taste or
luxury can reach the cottage. Well designed plate,
precious engraved vases, cameos, and enamels, can scarcely
find their way below the squire. It seems as unpractical
as forbidding us to live in anything but Venetian palaces
built to last for 15 centuries. We do not know how far
such a principle may lead us. There is a great amount of
merely mechanical labour employed in multiplying the
plates, and still more in the letterpress of the beautiful
volume before us, not to mention the manufacture of the
paper. 'Necessity' would be the plea' but it must be a
very stern necessity, indeed, which would justify us in
'hewing into rolling pollards the suckling branches of
human intelligence,' and 'carrying on in our own persons
a worse slave trade than that which we are endeavouring to
put down.' We need hardly add that any definition of
necessary articles will leave nine factories out of ten untouched; unless, indeed, the reformer is prepared to turn
back the stream of time and thought, and to revert to the
spinning wheel.

Until Mr. Ruskin has cleared up these difficulties, his
reform will not be in a practical shape. Nor can we think
that he will do much towards exalting manual labour or
rendering thought more healthy, by requiring all the higher
classes to learn some handicraft trade, and making the
architect work in the mason's yard, the painter grind his
own colours, and the millowner distinguish himself as the
most skilful operative among his men. Such a practice
would be a mere factitious condescension, which would tend
more to degrade than to exalt its objects. Besides, the
colour-grinder would remain a colour-grinder still. To
satisfy Mr. Ruskin's theory, he must have some part in the
picture.

Mr. Ruskin shows his independence of mind and his good
sense, in the midst of his enthusiasm, by disclaiming for
the Gothic style any peculiarly ecclesiastical character.
The church architecture of the middle ages, he says, was
merely the perfect development of the common dwellinghouse
architecture of the period.

[Quotes from 'When the painted arch' to 'everybody at the
time', 'Works' 10: 120.]

'The supposed sacredness and mystery of the ecclesiastical remains,' Mr. Ruskin says, 'has arisen from the general

debasement of all other architecture.'
     The third volume will treat of the architecture of the
Renaissance - a 'poison-tree,' of which the author's general opinion is already manifest. We shall expect some
admirable satire; but we rather tremble for the fairness
of the criticism when we are told to remark, as a most
wonderful and important proof of the self-confidence of
the Renaissance and the humility of Gothic, the fact that,
while a Gothic builder has chosen, for the sculpture of an
angle in the Ducal Palace, the Drunkenness of Noah, the
Renaissance architect has chosen, for a corresponding
angle, the Judgment of Solomon. We think it not superfluous to remind the critic of Claude and Murillo, that men
will not be reasoned or quizzed out of their admiration for
anything that is grand or beautiful, in whatever style it
may be. In art the end justifies the means, and the end is
effect. Latent beauties may be revealed and latent defects
may be exposed; the superiority of one style over another
generally may be established; but it is vain to teach mankind that they ought to see no beauty in the exterior of
St. Paul's or in the 'Paradise Lost,' because the one is
not like Cologne and the other is not like Dante; and if
prejudices, derived from the religion or philosophy of a
certain epoch, are brought to play against its art, unjust
and even absurd criticism must inevitably be the result.
     We think that, in saying this, we speak in the spirit of
the following noble passage, which we quote with pleasure.
It is a vindication of the rudeness of Gothic architecture
as the true offspring of the north, and of the name Gothic
as an expression of that fact. We have already pointed
out one metaphor as, in our opinion, a flaw:-

[Quotes from 'The charts of the world' to 'clouds that
shade them', 'Works' 10: 185-8.]

Every one will recognize in the author of this passage a
contemporary of Tennyson and Turner, and one of the consolations of an age which, unheroic in action and perplexed
in faith, has fed its sentiment on the poetical aspects of
nature and of history, and has studied them as no age ever
did before.
     We can give no adequate specimens of the detailed criti-
cisms which occupy a large portion of the book, more especially as some of the most striking require the plates
for their illustration; we can only say that they are so
written as to be perfectly intelligible to the ordinary
reader, and that they seem to us to be excellent in depth
and delicacy. Mr. Ruskin's vindication and analysis of Byzantine architecture, his theory of the deduction of all

the styles from the three modes of bridging a space, his
indication of the gable as the fundamental part and pervading form of Gothic, and several of his views as to the
expression of Gothic buildings, will probably rank as discoveries in the art. It will be seen from what we have
said that we place his philosophy below his criticism and
his morality, not because we think him incapable of philosophy or consider that which he has produced as of no
value, but because we cannot help thinking that he wants
the patience of thought requisite to preserve him from
hasty generalizations and visionary refinements, and to
render him, in this repsect, really useful to the world.
And, having said this, we will conclude by offering our
cordial thanks for a very beautiful and noble book - a
book which will do good not to art only, but to higher
things than art. We only regret that its costliness must
limit to the rich a work which, in spite of its defects,
we would gladly see as widely diffused as any that has
appeared in this generation.

RUSKIN'S 'STONES OF VENICE,' Vol. III.; THE FALL.

At the beginning of this volume Mr. Ruskin asks, what is it
that has brought architecture from the mediæval cities,
such as Rouen, Antwerp, Cologne, Nuremberg, or Venice (for
Venice is but one, and not even the richest of the class)
to the Harley-street or Baker-street of the present day?
and the answer is, It is the Renaissance.
     'Early Renaissance is the corruption of the Gothic;
Roman Renaissance is the perfectly formed style; and grotesque Renaissance is the corruption of the Renaissance
itself. First we see the features of the expiring king,
and then the Hazael who dipped the cloth in water and laid
it upon his face.'
     But here we must pause at the threshold to note that
it seems somewhat unjust to extend the name of Renaissance
to the spontaneous corruption of the Gothic style. That
corruption suggests doubt as to the inherent vitality of
the style which was seized by it; but, at all events, it
should be kept distinct and separately accounted for; the
Renaissance has sins enough of its own. It was Hazael
that stifled the dying king; but it was not Hazael that
made him sick to death.
     The decay of the Gothic showed itself in luxuriance of
ornament, not in quantity, for the best Gothic left hardly
an inch of stone unsculptured; but in *luxuriance* - in a
coarseness and violence of curve, a depth of shadow, and a
lusciousness of lines, which were the stimulants of jaded

feeling. Breaches of the cardinal virtue of temperance
they are called by Mr. Ruskin, who loves to pursue, even
to an extreme, the analogy between art and moral action.
The transition from the severe ornament to the luxurious
is illustrated by some criticisms of the usual delicacy
and beauty.

Against Gothic, thus declining, the armies of the Renaissance came up, with the names of Science and Perfection on their banners. In architecture they produced nothing but evil from the first. In sculpture and painting
they produced the greatest men that the world has ever
seen. And this difference of effect, we must again pause
to note, seems to show that 'Renaissance' does not denote
an evil principle, which invaded the hearts and minds of
men in the fifteenth century, but simply a love of classical models, which were good in one art and bad in another;
which were good in sculpture and painting, because they
were natural and free; which were bad in architecture, because they were adapted to heathern religion and a southern
sky.

The same chapter contains a curious eulogium on the
practice of *quartering* colours, which, as a natural principle, is identified with the principle of *brotherhood* in
human society and in yet higher things; a specimen of that
mystic interpretation of nature which we are inclined to
think rather confounds than strengthens our affections, and
which needs at present no stimulus, as Mr. Ruskin will see
if he will read 'Nature a Parable,' by the most learned of
the Oxford converts - a complete manual of symbolism,
wherein the priesthood is the ox, 'by labour trained to
meek celibacy,' and the laity are the ass.

In noticing the redeeming effect of inlaid marbles in
the palaces of the debased Byzantine, Mr. Ruskin takes occasion to protest with warmth and, we think, with justice,
against painted imitations of wood or marble, as preposterous in themselves and as wretched employment for the
mind of the workman, the latter being one which, so far as
we know, he has been the first to bring prominently forward, earning thereby a right to great gratitude, and to
great allowance if he should ever fall into exaggeration.
The interest and instructiveness of the natural wood or
marble - the marble telling by its veins the geological
history of its mountain - is, at least, an ingenious
argument.

The Central or Roman Renaissance was the revived architecture of classic Rome, *subsequently* modified by the study
of Greek forms. This, in its perfection as it appears in
the Casa Grimani at Venice, the Town-hall at Vicenza, St.
Peter's, St. Paul's, and Whitehall, is the true antagonist

of the Gothic school. Of its *form* Mr. Ruskin thinks it unnecessary to say much. But he falls like doomsday on its
spirit, which, according to him, consists of two elements -
Pride and *Infidelity; Pride* being subdivided into *Pride of
Science, Pride of State,* and *Pride of System;* so that we
have four mental conditions to form the subject of as many
homilies.

And here let us pause one moment. Roman and Greek
architecture, according to the author's own showing, revived through the revival of Roman and Greek literature;
a thing in itself quite independent of any of the four
evil spirits above enumerated. And the very same intellectual movement which produced this immoral school of architecture produced again, according to Mr. Ruskin's own
showing, the greatest school of painters - some of them
religious painters - that the world ever saw. Does not
this suggest that it would have been safer to treat Renaissance architecture as an historical style, however bad,
than to treat it as a compound vice? We shall see as we
go on. But, meantime, we remark that Mr. Ruskin himself
has had a little misgiving, and has felt it necessary to
provide against the difficulty by saying that Michael
Angelo and Raphael, and their compeers, were great souls,
and showed their greatness by moving freely in spite of
their plate armour. A cumbrous coat of mail indeed -
three kinds of vicious pride, and combined with infidelity!

Under Pride of Science, Mr. Ruskin, after eloquently,
but, as it seems to us, superfluously, discriminating between science and art, and the gifts of the *savant* and the
artist, proceeds to pour contempt on science as an aid to
art.

[Quotes from 'The labour of the whole' to 'did 200 years
ago', 'Works' 11: 150.]

And, again, as to the rules of art, which, by the way,
are not quite the same thing as *science* in Mr. Ruskin's
first sense:-

[Quotes from 'Nothing can be done' to 'see nothing more',
'Works' 11: 57-8.]

We do not think that, saving some fervid eloquence, we
gain more from this dissertation than the true but obvious
maxims, that an artist's knowledge ought to be kept subordinate to his art; that he ought, above all things, to be
skilled in the lore of his own profession and in the chy-
mistry of colours (which the Renaissance, as Mr. Ruskin
says, has lost); and that neither a knowledge of natural

science and anatomy, nor a knowledge of the rules of art,
without an artist's eye and hand, will go far to make a
painter. If the science of the Renaissance is pedantic and
false (and Mr. Ruskin triumphantly shows that it is false
in aerial perspective), let it be condemned for its pedantry and falsehood. There needs no newer or more recondite
reason.

Then follows a dissertation on *knowledge* in general;
with regard to the nature of which it is rather startling
to find the world labours under a gross misconception. And
yet we seem to have heard before that man's knowledge can
be nothing compared with the infinite knowledge of God, and

[Quotes from 'That the only [true] reasons' to 'taken care
of', 'Works' 11: 63.]

Nor does it strike us as a new thing to hear that men
are sometimes puffed up by knowledge, and that they are
more liable to be puffed up by the baser sorts of knowledge, such as philology, school logic, and rhetoric, than
by the grander and more liberal sciences. So, again, it
is a most true, but also a very trite remark, that our
pride ought to be corrected by the thought that we owe most
of our knowledge to others; though after all a man wins
learning by the sweat of his brow, and is not absolutely a
'beggar.' Yet this is pretty much the sum of several glowing pages in which Mr. Ruskin seems, to himself, to be rolling a mountain of fallacy off the oppressed human mind.
We must candidly say that we think the space would have
been much more profitably devoted to some practical proofs
or instances of the pedantry or false science of the
Renaissance.

In the heat of declamation assertions are thrown out
which will have to be reconsidered. It is almost wild to
say that the book of Job was meant to serve the same end
as the higher sciences in teaching men gentleness and modesty. What does Mr. Ruskin suppose to be the point of the
opening and conclusion of the book? Again, consider this
description of the revivial of learning.

[Quotes from 'They ... discovered suddenly' to 'and five
orders', 'Works' 11: 69.]

Was grammar the sole object of Politian, Erasmus,
Revetlin, and Melanchthon? Was indifference to truth the
characteristic of Luther? Did science degenerate into syl-
logism when the schoolmen gave place to Descartes and
Bacon? Is not Mr. Ruskin hastily enveloping the whole age
in the condemnation of perspective and the five orders?

Or is he not, at best, drawing most irrational conclusions from Erasmus's satirical description of a pedantic clique, which he, in common with the other great men of the age, viewed with as much contempt as we do?

Next comes *Pride of State*. Mr. Ruskin finds in the Renaissance architecture the worst character of aristocracy. 'It is coldly erudite, and offers no daily bread for the hunger of the multitude. Its architect proclaims aloud, "You cannot feel my work unless you study Vitruvius." Unlike the Gothic, it is exclusively adapted to grand and sumptuous buildings, and is better for the palace of men than for the church of God.'

[Quotes from 'It is to be noted, also' to 'in the baron's hall', 'Works' 11: 75-6.]

The last words remind us, in spite of ourselves, that the modern style, with its large windows, admitting plenty of light and air, and its perfect defences against cold, is the style not only of luxury, but also of comfort, - of actual comfort to the rich, and of possible comfort to the poor. And this is a practical consideration, a consideration which will always weigh heavily against the expectation held out by Mr. Ruskin, that by reverting to the Gothic style we may again verify the Saxon comparison of human life to a swallow flying through the hall, and see another Godfrey of Bouillon sitting in state upon a sack of straw. In all seriousness, this point of comfort and security from weather is one which in choosing a style for house architecture must not be overlooked.

'It was in Versailles, the great palace of the Renaissance, that the cry of the people at last burst forth against the tyranny of the wealthy and the proud.'

St. Paul's and Whitehall might have furnished a similar illustration. But all this, speaking in the strictest of history, proves little against the Renaissance architecture or its architects. The pride of the king and noble, and the wrongs of the serf, were not the offspring of Versailles or Whitehall. *In Gothic castles*, from every stone of which Mr. Ruskin would have drawn a moral of happiness and wisdom, was sown the wind, from which a weak and bankrupt monarch at last reaped the whirlwind. *In Gothic cathedrals,* beaming in every line with the 'Lamp of Truth,' that religion which should have made the king just and the people obedient was turned into a corruption and a lie; and if one memorable outbreak of the Revolution took place in the great court of Versailles, its bloodiest scene was enacted in the Conciergerie, its saddest in the Temple, and its most critical event was the storming of the Bastille.

Further to illustrate *the Pride of State,* the growth of pride and bad taste in sepulchral monuments is traced and exemplified in a series of specimens, beginning with some late Gothic tombs, and ending with those of the last century. And here Mr. Ruskin appears again in all his strength, though his argument against Renaissance architecture still halts, inasmuch as the pride, which he wishes to identify with the Renaissance, had already appeared in the later Gothic. The turning point appears to have been the substitution of virtues for figures of the saints and emblems of religion; and it is noted that, while the first weak man of a noble line has but *one* virtue, his successor, who was twice a fratricide, has *six.* Another fatal breach of taste was the abandonment of the recumbent and deathlike attitude, and the transformation of the corpse, first into a living man raised on his elbow, and then into an erect and attitudinizing figure. At the same time, the display of pride above the tomb was accompanied by emblems of abject terror below, both being in contrast to the mediæval feeling.

[Quotes from 'From before this rude' to 'of a dog begging', 'Works' 11: 113-14.]

Such critiques as this, from one who is a master of the subject, do their work; they do it better than all the philosophical analysis in the world. We can imagine that after reading all the philosophy of this chapter a man might remain a contumacious Vitruvian; we cannot imagine that after reading the criticism of this chapter a man could remain an advocate of heathenish and presumptuous tombs. Art, as Mr. Ruskin truly says, is a matter of sight and feeling. People might be found to deny that the exact qualities shown in Bertuccio Valier's monument were Pride of Science, Pride of State, Pride of System and Infidelity; but nobody would be found to deny that it was revolting to the feelings and hideous to the eye. Even supposing that the art of an age were more intimately connected with its morality than it really is, it seems far safest, in the first place, to criticize it *as art*; and it will be instructive afterwards to trace the connexion with the prevalent morality. The reverse process supposes a unity of thought and purpose which no age, in fact, presents; least of all, perhaps, that age which witnessed at once the Court of Leo X. and the preaching of **Luther.**

As to Pride of System, Mr. Ruskin says that he reverences law (about which he reproduces the eloquent fallacies of Hooker), but that he hates formalism and pedantic rules in art; and that he holds true inspiration to be more

essential than any rules of art at all. And in this he has
the world with him. We presume that even the Byzantine and
Gothic schools had their rules - according to Mr. Ruskin
they had some very subtle rules - and there are stong indications that the architects of those schools prized their
lore, though we may have no means of telling precisely
whether they were immorally proud of it. But the rules of
Gothic being those of a good and free style were good and
free, while those of the Renaissance, being those of a bad
and stiff style, were bad and stiff. The buildings, produced on the principles of the Freemasons, were better than
those produced on the principles of Vitruvius. That is the
essential point. If the rules about 'five orders' is an
irrational rule, sweep it away, not because it is *proud,*
but because it is *irrational.*

Moreover, it must be observed, that the pedantry of com-
mentators does not affect the merit of St. Peter's and St.
Paul's any more than it does that of the Parthenon. All
three may still be buildings of true beauty, and, when the
nonsense is cleared away, models for rational imitation.
There, no doubt, existed during the last two centuries a
tendency to pedantic criticism which extended to the other
arts, and to poetry as well as to architecture. It arose
a good deal from an exaggerated deference for the ancients,
which partook more of the nature of slavishness than pride.
Ancient literature and civilization were unquestionably
superior to those of the middle ages, and it was supposed
that the superiority extended to ancient art. It was supposed also, though most erroneously, that the critical
faculties of the Greeks and Romans were on a level with
their creative faculties, and that they who had produced
these glorious and beautiful works could best teach others
how to produce. Therefore a rule or criticism, however
peddling and irrational, of Aristotle, Longinus, Horace, or
Quintilian, was cherished as an utterance of immortal wisdom. But this servility in criticism did not hinder the
same age from being one of unexampled advance in knowledge
and rapid emancipation of the human mind. We read with astonishment such a passage as the following:-

[Quotes from 'The manner in which' to 'of fetter dance',
'Works' 11: 115.]

Now, to say nothing of the Michael Angelos, the
Raphaels, the Wrens, and the Miltons, to say nothing of the
Luthers, the Calvins, the Melanchthons, the Savanorolas,
and the Bossuets, the men who made science and philosophy a
fetter dance were such as Galileo, Kepler, Bacon, Descartes,
'noza, Pascal, and Voltaire, with their countless

descendants; and the unfettered minds with which they are
contrasted are those of the school philosophers and divines.
Let Mr. Ruskin gather all the pedantic technicalities that
he can from all the philosophers since the fifteenth century,
and a few pages of that Angelic Doctor who was the type and
the glory of his favourite epoch will absolutely swamp them
all. Talk of fetter dances and syllogisms, indeed! Why, the
first Reformers had to plead for their lives in syllogisms
regularly arranged according to the rules of *Barbara, Celarent*.

The effect of classical literature on the different
branches of art and philosophy was, in truth, too multiform to be properly described by any one general expression.
In poetry, for instance, the effect was to stifle the observation both of nature and of comman human feelings and
incidents, by setting up as models poets who were unobser-
vant of nature and who adhered to the heroic type of character and action - a double loss, which was first
thoroughly repaired by Wordsworth. In sculpture and painting the hard mediæval outline was replaced, successfully or
not, by the forms of nature. Physical philosophy owed its
being indirectly to the new and living studies which swept
away the cobwebs of the schools. And in moral philosophy
Plato arose to dispute the empire with Aristotle, and the
hoary tyranny of the Stagyrite was overthrown. How are all
these things to be brought under the same *formula* with a
taste for the architecture of classic Rome?

Here is another sweeping passage on the same subject:-

[Quotes from 'It ... acted first' to 'from being heard',
'Works' 11: 127-8.]

The Middle Ages wrote and spoke Latin instead of their
mother tongue, as well as the Renaissance, and the Renaissance was none the worse for writing and speaking it pure
and good. If Mr. Ruskin will look into any monkish writer,
he will probably find him just as anxious for classic
flowers of speech, after his fashion, as any of those pedantic Latinists who were satirized by Erasmus in his
'Ciceronianus,' and condemned by the higher spirits of the
age. As to the assertions, that an excessive passion for
rhetoric (!) and *logic* (!!) came in with the Renaissance -
that no philologist's notes on the classic poets can excite
anything but contempt - and that philology, rhetoric, and
logic (even according to Mr. Ruskin's and the mediæval misconception of logic) necessarily render those employed on
them incapable of high thoughts and noble emotions - we can
only say they fill us with astonishment. If all philologists, even in Mr. Ruskin's sense of the word, must be
dolts and brutes, what is the fate of Erasmus, Grotius,

Pearson, Niebuhr? What is the fate of Petrarch and of
Milton?

   Infidelity is the fourth and last element of the Renaissance style. But here Mr. Ruskin does not make good his
point at all, or even attempt to do so. He shows, easily
enough, that the enthusiastic study of classical literature
brought in a tide of heathen imagery in poetry, rhetoric,
and art. But he does not show, and he would not find it
very easy to show, that *Infidelity* appears on the face of
a Renaissance building, or that none but an infidel would
build in the style of the Renaissance. As to the first,
let us suppose all the decorations and emblems in a Palladian building to be Christian - a thing quite conceivable
in itself. Let us suppose all the tombs (which by the way
are more matters of sculpture than of architecture) to be
pious and inoffensive. What is there in the building itself to show that its author was an infidel? How does St.
Paul's betray the scepticism of Charles and Laud? How is
the free-thinking of the Jesuits to be gathered from the
style of the Renaissance churches with which they have
covered the face of Europe? Until we have further light on
this point, we shall decline, and gladly decline, to enter
on the tremendous question of modern infidelity with reference to a question of taste in architecture. We can only
say, first, that Mr. Ruskin appears very much to underrate
this infidelity of the Middle Ages; and, secondly, that we
envy the position of a man who can look down with such security on this weltering strife of creeds and churches,
himself standing on adamant, though, apparently, he stands
alone.

   The close of this discussion leaves us convinced that
spiritual analysis is the wrong end to begin at, especially
in the case of the most material of the arts. Again, we
say, it would have been much safer to treat the Renaissance
style and the Renaissance buildings first in the ordinary
way, allowing for their beauties and exposing their defects; and then to have traced the connexion, where it
could fairly be traced, between the character of the buildings and the character of the age. Let Mr. Ruskin consider - it is a fair test - whether he is prepared to write
a treatise showing how, by properly applying four principles, into which he has analyzed the Palladian style, an
architect may produce a first-rate Palladian building.

   The *Grotesque* Renaissance is the abyss of architectural
degradation, and exhibits the evil spirit in its most
hideous form. It is the offspring of the unscrupulous *pursuit of pleasure* which defiled the worst age of the Republic. It is especially distinguished by 'a spirit of brutal
mockery and insolent jest, which, exhausting itself in

deformed and monstrous sculpture, can sometimes be hardly
otherwise defined than as the perpetuation in stone of the
ribaldries of drunkenness.'

It first fully displays itself in the Church of Santa
Maria Formosa, the sacred scene of the 'Brides of Venice,'
and of the grand annual wedding, when there was but one
marriage day for the nobles of the whole nation, a custom
which Mr. Ruskin notes as peculiarly significant and noble,
entering at length and with great research into the history
of the 'Brides.'

The vices of the Grotesque Renaissance are illustrated
with the author's usual power. Indeed it is difficult to
see how any gross error of taste or feeling can survive his
criticism. And we should only plead for a little more
recognition of the grossness which he allows to have
existed in Gothic grotesque, when he so fervently extols
Gothic grotesque at the expense of that of the Renaissance.

He then proceeds to a long and deep discussion of the
nature of Grotesque, generally, as an element of the human
mind and character, and specially, with regard to its use
in art, dividing Grotesque, first of all, into the *Sportive*
and the *Terrible*. The pages devoted to this subject contain much glowing and lofty eloquence, and some remarks,
both critical and moral, which seem to us acute and true.
But they also contain some exaggerations both of thought
and language; they involve, if we mistake not, a confusion
between the ideas of *Humour* and *Recreation*; and they are
embarrassed, and we think marred, philosophically, by being thrown into the form of one of those rigid classifications which Mr. Ruskin, with a curious love for the formalism which he condemns, is so fond of introducing. He
here divides mankind into four classes: the men who play
wisely; who play necessarily; who play inordinately; and
who play not at all. The distinction between the first
two classes, as explained in the commentary, seems to us
really to lie in the amount of leisure and mental cultivation which their members happen to possess, a point
which surely has nothing to do with the nature of humour
or recreation in the abstract; and we feel convinced that
the whole essay might, on revision, be reduced to a simpler
and easier, and, at the same time, a more philosophical
shape. Why not examine the faculty or tendency at once and
directly in itself? It could hardly be thought rational if
a physiologist, wishing to explain the function of sight,
began by a classification of men into those who were long-
sighted, those who were short-sighted, and those whose
sight was neither long nor short, and those who could not
see at all. We firmly believe that there is much valuable
matter in this essay if its author would deliver it simply

and straightforwardly, and repress that flow of eloquence,
which, however delightful in its place, interferes very
much with the strictness and clearness of a philosophical
investigation.

We do not even feel certain that Mr. Ruskin has quite
settled the *limits* of the Grotesque. We suspect that he is
the first person who ever felt a grotesque sensation from
reading the dreams recorded in the Bible or the accessory
imagery of Ezekiel and the Apocalypse. Nor can we admit
that the retention of the four beasts as symbols of the
Evangelists is a witness in favour of the Grotesque.
Those symbols are retained because they are supposed to be
scriptural; and, if they ceased to be thought scriptural,
we apprehend they would cease to please. We have heard interpretations of them which may fairly be called grotesque,
though whether of the sportive or the terrible kind we are
hardly prepared to say.

There are two other points in this chapter, rather of an
incidental character, on which we wish to say a few words.
The first is a very plain expression of what we cannot help
thinking is an unsound view of art. It is contained in
these words:-

[Quotes from 'The novelist amuses' to 'be a jest', 'Works'
11: 156.]

Here the narrative power of the painter is actually set
above that of the writer; and this exaggeration reminds us
of Mr. Ruskin's scorn of imitative skill in a painter, and
of all that he and others are constantly saying of the infinite meaning and articulate expression of works of art;
of being *talked to* by a painter through his colours, and by
a musician through his notes; and of *reading* a great building as if it were a poem. Now, if the function of the
artist or the musician is the same as that of the narrator
or the poet, why do they put themselves to the trouble of
approaching the mind through the awkward and tedious channel of still forms and colours or inarticulate sounds?
Why do they not at once use language - the proper and
only adequate vehicle of thought? If it is so mean a
thing to please the eye by form and colour, and the ear by
melody, let them throw aside their brushes and fiddles and
take up their pen.

The second point is this: Mr. Ruskin is likely to exercise - indeed, he does exercise, great influence over the
taste of his countrymen; and he seems anxious to guide them
to Dante and to Dante's 'Inferno,' not only as a great work
of imagination, but as an embodiment of spiritual truth.
Now, the 'Inferno' is not, essentially speaking, the

creation of Dante, but of the mediæval mind; its parallels, perhaps its equals, may be found in other mediæval
books; and it embodies the peculiar belief of the Middle
Ages on a subject on which Scripture touches briefly and
in figures, and warns us away. Divine punishment (for it
is divine, though it were administered through demons) was
universally conceived in Dante's age to consist of physical tortures, the very idea of which could scarcely have
occurred to any fancy more wholesome than that of a monk.
There lies before us one of those visions in which the
narrator, after carrying us through scenes of torment
which might sicken fiends, allows these words to escape
him:- 'God is my witness, that if I saw any one, *even had
he slain all my friends and relatives,* condemned to such
tortures, I would, were it possible, *endure a temporal
death a thousand times to snatch him from them.*' There
spoke the human heart, which after all is made in the
image of God, and Mr. Ruskin will do well to ponder its
speech, and to be cautious how he represents the Divine
nature in a form which humanity cannot love.

Let us indemnify ourselves for all this criticism by
quoting one of those passages in which Mr. Ruskin appears
in the fulness of his unblemished and unquestioned power:-

[Quotes from 'How many motives' to 'on the threshing-floor
of Araunah', 'Works' 11: 163-4.]

In the concluding chapter Mr. Ruskin gathers up and enforces several detached points - the supremacy of inspiration over knowledge, the proper measure of truth in painting (with strong approval of the Pre-Raphaelites), the infinite dignity of colour, and the salutary influence of
costume. The supremacy of inspiration over knowledge he
maintains in terms which seem intended to apply generally,
but are certainly applicable only to art, if indeed they
are applicable to art, in their literal sense:-

[Quotes from 'There is not at this moment' to '"This is our
brother"', 'Works' 11: 204-5.]

Surely this doctrine, if taken at all literally, would
soon breed a sort of pedantry different indeed from that of
the learned imitator, but more offensive. What will Mr.
Ruskin say if he becomes the parent of a school which refuses to learn to draw, and trusts entirely to love and
colour?

And now comes the practical lesson of the whole work, -
to reform our architecture:-

[Quotes from 'First let us cast out' to 'court of our prison', 'Works' 11: 227.]

And then follows an eloquent exhortation to return forthwith to Gothic, as being everything that the Renaissance is not - full of life, fit for all purposes and suited to all minds, receptive of all faculties, and thoroughly Christian. Now, we say that we are convinced of the superiority of Gothic to classical architecture, especially in a northern climate and that we are all the more really and vividly convinced of it from reading this great work of Mr. Ruskin; but that we do not think he has shown cause for so sweeping and peremptory an anathema as this. He has not ventured to assert that the buildings of the best masters of the Renasissance are not beautiful, or shown us why their beauty is not the object of rational admiration. He has not even told us why we are not to admire the Place de la Concorde or the galleries at Munich. He has not accounted for the pleasure which we feel from beholding, even in juxtaposition with Gothic beauty, a grand portico or a noble dome. He has not explained why the difference between one great building of the Renaissance and another is not a true instance of originality and invention as an equal difference between two Gothic cathedrals or two Gothic grotesques. He has confined his practical criticism to bad specimens, and he has condemned those specimens, in no small degree, on the ground of bad taste in tombs and decorations which are quite separable from the architecture itself. He has drawn his definition of the style, also, from bad specimens, setting aside the good ones as abnormal, and forgetting that the measure of attainable excellence in a class or style is the highest point actually attained, and not the lowest or the mean. He has not even looked for his definition to the buildings themselves, but to the presumed mental and moral dispositions of the builders. He has thrown upon a style which is as applicable, and has been as well applied, to a hospital or gallery as to a palace, the whole odium of those selfish uses to which it was put, and to which any style would have been put, by a debauched and insolent nobility or a licentious and despotic King. He has failed to show how 'infidel' churches came to be reared by the greatest bigots and fanatics on earth, or how 'Pagan origin,' which is not fatal to the Roman Basilica, is fatal to the Roman column. Finally, he has not explained how it came to pass that great men, with the Roman and the Gothic styles both before them, chose the Roman and refused the Gothic; or why the Gothic itself changed so restlessly, and, at the dawn of knowledge and civilization, fell into decay. We say still,

the dawn of knowledge and civilization, because, if Mr.
Ruskin means explicitly to maintain, as he insinuates, the
opposite view, he must come into the field of facts, where
he will lose either his theory or his religion.

Nor is he practically satisfactory on the revival of
Gothic. It is easy to show the superiority of the streets
of Coventry over Bethnal-green; not so easy to show the
superiority of the streets of Coventry over the Boulevard.
Let it be demonstrated that with Gothic beauty in our
streets and houses we can have breadth, air, light, convenience, and health, and that we can have them at a
reasonable cost. A man must have much more highly than we
do the sense of the picturesque in uneducated men, if he
thinks it better to lodge them in a picturesque dog-kennel
than in a portion of a model lodginghouse. The dwellings
of the middle ages may exhibit 'humour' and 'rejoicing
energy,' but was not the life of those who dwelt in them
filthy, diseased, and short?

There is another weak point, and one of great significance. Say what you will of the universality of Gothic,
its great excellence was in churches; and churches are the
only buildings to which Mr. Ruskin declines immediately to
apply it. He says they 'are not the proper scenes for experiments in untried architecture.' Untried architecture!
We thought that Gothic had been tried and proved by innumerable experiments to be the only architecture in which
Christian churches could be built. The real fact is, that
without transubstantiation, sacerdotalism, and saint worship, Mr. Ruskin knows no more what to do with a new Gothic
cathedral than he does with a new Parthenon or a new
Rameseion. The single modern Gothic church which he mentions with approbation is one which, though nominally Protestant, is expressly built for the devotions of a sect
which only refuses to take the last step in Romanism because it does not choose to be merged in Rome.

The book of which we here conclude our notice is one
book which, perhaps, no other man living could have
written, and one for which the world ought to be and will
be thankful. It is in the higest degree eloquent, acute,
stimulating to thought, and fertile in suggestion. It
shows a power of practical criticism which, when fixed on
a definite object, nothing absurd or evil can withstand;
and a power of appreciation which has restored treasures
of beauty to mankind. It will, we are convinced, elevate
taste and intellect, raise the tone of moral feeling,
kindle benevolence towards men, and increase the love and
fear of God. All this we most cheerfully acknowledge: but
we must also acknowledge that it appears to us to have its
defects; to be overlaid with a philosophy which reflection

would render less technical and more sound; to run sometimes into exaggeration both of thought and language; to
be sometimes too sweeping and trenchant in its statements,
and that upon subjects which are beyond its natural scope;*
and too often to wander from its proper mark, and, in the
character of the workman, to forget the work. In the hope
that these remarks, if just, may possibly be useful, we
have been led to criticize what we would rather admire and
enjoy.

Note

* For example, on some of the great questions of politics,
finance, and education, and on Austrian Government in Italy.
The last subject Mr. Ruskin discusses in a long note, the
tone of which is quite at variance with his usual high feeling and with some of his previous expressions on the
subject.

'Modern Painters III'

1856

12. FROM AN UNSIGNED REVIEW, 'THE ECONOMIST'

1 March 1856, 226-9

Most of the review is a compendium of contents of 'Modern Painters III', but the opening and closing suggest Ruskin's position in the aesthetic world of the fifties as seen by a leading weekly of a politically liberal cast.

Mr. Ruskin's third volume of 'Modern Painters,' appearing at an interval of ten years after the second, will be hailed with interest and curiosity, if not with submissive attention, by the art-world of England. His position with regard to this art-world is strange and much to be regretted; for the study of his writings impress us deeply with the fact that he is formed to be its guide in many things, and yet the spirit in which he has constantly addressed it, and the spirit in which it has naturally retorted, show that such friendly guidance is at present out of the question, except to the few who from the first accepted him as their teacher, and have, therefore, been shielded throughout from the attacks under which their fellow-artists smart. Smart they unquestionably must, for his shaft is both aimed with too great an accuracy not to strike, and tipped with too galling a poison not to irritate. As to the wisdom of thus poisoning the truths which he so ably expounds, time might have taught him a lesson. When first he turned his thoughts to the serious study of art, he found doubtless many theories existing which had been passively received from the great lights of the last generation, but which needed only an electric shock of truth to crumble to pieces. These he attacked with all the

force that an earnest purpose, a powerful imagination, and
a clear, vigorous, and elevated style, put at his command,
but unfortunately in such a manner that, instead of crush-
ing the old prejudices, he rallied round their standard
many active supporters whose allegiance until then had been
but passive. The *reductio ad absurdum,* which proves so
powerful an argument to a audience whose choice is yet to
be made, is a dangerous weapon to wield against a man whom
you wish to convert from a system which tradition, education, and habit have endeared to him. He is, perhaps,
willing to be led, to renounce one by one his old habits as
better methods are offered to him, and to follow up fresh
ideas, if he be allowed to do it gradually, so that his
works shall not become suddenly unsuited to the taste of
his patrons and employers. (This is a primary condition to
the architect, the acceptance of whose plans depends upon
the average taste of the middle classes, whereas the
painter has generally to deal with the more unprejudiced
amateur). But to see his system reasoned to pieces till it
really does look like a hollow falsehood, and to have it
proved to him that his productions are ridiculous in-
anities, excites his indignation and arouses his combative-
ness. He naturally retorts. The critic is a madman, an
unpractical visionary, irreverent and crotchety. Now the
truth is that Ruskin is none of these. He is in possession
of a clear and penetrating mind; so penetrating, indeed,
that it sometimes destroys the confidence of his readers in
his soundness, they not being willing to believe that there
exists in any object which he discusses so much more beauty
and meaning than they would have discovered. He is undeni-
ably practical in his fundamental ideas, full of the deepest reverence for all that appears to him beautiful and
holy, and, though owning to very strong preferences, founding those preferences on reason, and fully admitting the
good that exists elsewhere, even in the works of these his
adversaries. His one fault consists, then, in expressing
too strongly his contempt of their weaknesses and errors.
His fault has both lessened and retarded his influence, but
could not destroy it, both on account of the inherent truth
and beauty of his views, and because other circumstances
tending in the same direction have since arisen and
strengthened him by their co-operation. On the mass of
English artists, however, he acts as an unacknowledged influence, instead of taking the place that was due to his
courage and powers, viz., that of an honoured and accepted
guide....
    The present volume is the only one of the three that con-
tains illustrations. The engravings are very carefully
executed, in many cases from Mr. Ruskin's own drawings.

The style is as, usual, clear, bold, and racy, though we
could wish that some passages were less high-wrought. The
author owns with pride to having submitted willingly to the
influences both of Carlyle and Helps. We can trace these
influences, and think with him that they have been salutary. Without adopting Carlyle's exaggerated and un-
English expressions, he has appropriated all that is
forcible and vivid in his peculiarities, and in the more
subdued passages we recognise a constant reader of the
'beautiful *quiet* English of Helps.' These excellencies en-
grafted on a style originally fine, have rendered Mr Ruskin
one of the first writers of our day.

13. GEORGE ELIOT, FROM AN UNSIGNED REVIEW, 'WESTMINSTER
REVIEW'

April 1856, vol. 9, n.s., 625-33

George Eliot (1819-90), before her career as a novelist,
had been a translator, writer of articles on intellectual
subjects, and reviewer of distinction. See Introduction,
p. 13.

Our table this time does not, according to the favourite
metaphor, 'groan' under the light literature of the quarter,
for the quarter has not been very productive; but, in com-
pensation, we ourselves groan under it rather more than
usual, for the harvest is principally of straw, and few
grains of precious corn remain after the winnowing. We except one book, however, which is a rich sheaf in itself,
and will serve as bread, and seed-corn too, for many days.
We mean the new volume of Mr. Ruskin's 'Modern Painters,'
to which he appropriately gives the subordinate title, 'Of
Many Things.' It may be taken up with equal pleasure
whether the reader be acquainted or not with the previous
volumes, and no special artistic culture is necessary in
order to enjoy its excellences or profit by its suggestions.
Every one who cares about nature, or poetry, or the story
of human development – every one who has a tinge of literature, or philosophy, will find something that is for him
and that will 'gravitate to him' in this volume. Since its
predecessors appeared, Mr. Ruskin has devoted ten years to
the loving study of his great subject – the principles of
art; which, like all other great subjects, carries the

student into many fields. The critic of art, as he tells
us, 'has to take *some* note of optics, geometry, geology,
botany, and anatomy; he must acquaint himself with the
works of all great artists, and with the temper and history of the times in which they lived; he must be a fair
metaphysician, and a careful observer of the phenomena of
natural scenery.' And when a writer like Mr. Ruskin
brings these varied studies to bear on one great purpose,
when he has to trace their common relation to a grand
phase of human activity, it is obvious that he will have a
great deal to say which is of interest and importance to
others besides painters. The fundamental principles of all
just thought and beautiful action or creation are the same,
and in making clear to ourselves what is best and noblest
in art, we are making clear to ourselves what is best and
noblest in morals; in learning how to estimate the artistic
products of a particular age according to the mental attitude and external life of that age, we are widening our
sympathy and deepening the basis of our tolerance and
charity.

Of course, this treatise 'Of many things' presents certain old characteristics and new paradoxes which will furnish a fresh text to antagonistic critics; but, happily for
us, and happily for our readers, who probably care more to
know what Mr. Ruskin says than what other people think he
ought to say, we are not among those who are more irritated
by his faults than charmed and subdued by his merits. When
he announces to the world in his Preface, that he is incapable of falling into an illogical deduction - that,
whatever other mistakes he may commit, he cannot possibly
draw an inconsequent conclusion, we are not indignant, but
amused, and do not in the least feel ourselves under the
necessity of picking holes in his arguments in order to
prove that he is not a logical Pope. We value a writer not
in proportion to his freedom from faults, but in proportion
to his positive excellences - to the variety of thought he
contributes and suggests, to the amount of gladdening and
energizing emotions he excites. Of what comparative importance is it that Mr. Ruskin undervalues this painter, or
overvalues the other, that he sometimes glides from a just
argument into a fallacious one, that he is a little absurd
here, and not a little arrogant there, if, with all these
collateral mistakes, he teaches truth of infinite value,
and *so* teaches it that men will listen? The truth of infinite value that he teaches is *realism* - the doctrine that
all truth and beauty are to be attained by a humble and
faithful study of nature, and not by substituting vague
forms, bred by imagination on the mists of feeling, in
place of definite, substantial reality. The thorough

acceptance of this doctrine would remould our life; and he
who teaches its application to any one department of human
activity with such power as Mr. Ruskin's, is a prophet for
his generation. It is not enough simply to teach truth;
that may be done, as we all know, to empty walls, and
within the covers of unsaleable books; we want it to be so
taught as to compel men's attention and sympathy. Very
correct singing of very fine music will avail little without a *voice* which can thrill the audience and take possession of their souls. Now, Mr. Ruskin has a voice, and one
of such power, that whatever error he may mix with his
truth, he will make more converts to that truth than less
erring advocates who are hoarse and feeble. Considered
merely as a writer, he is in the very highest rank of English stylists. The vigour and splendour of his eloquence
are not more remarkable than its precision, and the delicate truthfulness of his epithets. The fine *largo* of his
sentences reminds us more of De Quincey than of any other
writer, and his tendency to digressiveness is another and
less admirable point of resemblance to the English Opium-
eater. Yet we are not surprised to find that he does not
mention De Quincey among the favourite writers who have influenced him, for Mr. Ruskin's style is evidently due far
more to innate faculty than to modifying influences; and
though he himself thinks that his constant study of Carlyle
must have impressed itself on his language as well as his
thought, we rarely detect this. In the point of view from
which he looks at a subject, in the correctness of his descriptions, and in a certain rough flavour of humour, he
constantly reminds us of Carlyle, but in the mere tissue of
hs style, scarcely ever. But while we are dilating on Mr.
Ruskin's general characteristics, we are robbing ourselves
of the room we want for what is just now more important -
namely, telling the reader something about the contents of
the particular volume before us....
    ...With that intense interest in landscape which is a
peculiar characteristic of modern times, is associated the
'Pathetic Fallacy' - the transference to external objects
of the spectator's own emotions, as when Kingsley says of
the drowned maiden, -

They rowed her in across the rolling foam -
The *cruel, crawling foam.*

The pleasure we derive from this fallacy is legitimate
when the passion in which it originates is strong, and has
an adequate cause. But the mental condition which admits
of this fallacy is of a lower order than that in which,
while the emotions are strong, the intellect is yet strong

enough to assert its rule against them; and 'the whole
man stands in an iron glow, white hot, perhaps, but still
strong, and in nowise evaporating; even if he melts, losing none of his weight.' Thus the poets who delight in
this fallacy are chiefly of the second order - the reflective and perceptive - such as Wordsworth, Keats, and
Tennyson; while the creative poets, for example,
Shakspeare, Homer and Dante, use it sparingly.

     Next follows one of the msot delightful and suggestive
chapters in the volume, on Classical Landscape, or the way
in which the Greeks looked at external nature. Take a
specimen on the details of the Homeric landscape;-

[Quotes from 'As far as I recollect' to 'fountains in
pipes', 'Works' 5: 234-6.]

     The mediæval feeling for landscape is less utilitarian
than the Greek. Everything is pleasurable and horticul-
tural - the knights and ladies sing and make love in plea-
saunces and rose-gardens. There is a more sentimental enjoyment in external nature; but, added to this, there is a
new respect for mountains, as places where a solemn
presence is to be felt, and spiritual good obtained. As
Homer is the grand authority for Greek landscape, so is
Dante for the mediæval; and Mr. Ruskin gives an elaborate
study of the landscape in the 'Divina Commedia.' To the
love of brilliancy shown in mediæval landscape, is contrasted the love of clouds in the modern, 'so that if a
general and characteristic name were needed for modern
landscape art, none better could be found than "the service of clouds."' But here again Mr. Ruskin seeks for the
spirit of landscape first of all in literature; and he expects to surprise his readers by selecting Scott as the
typical poet, and greatest literary man of his age. He,
very justly, we think, places Creative literature such as
Scott's, above Sentimental literature, even when this is
of as high a character as in some passages of Byron or
Tennyson.

[Quotes, with omissions, from 'To invent a story' to 'self-
examining verse', 'Works' 5: 335.]

This appreciation of Scott's power puts us in such excellent humour, that we are not inclined to quarrel with Mr.
Ruskin about another judgment of his, to which we cannot
see our way, in spite of the arguments he adduces. According to him Scott was eminently *sad*, sadder than Byron.
On the other hand, he shows that this sadness did not lead
Scott into the pathetic fallacy; the bird, the brook, the

flower, and the cornfield, kept their gladsomeness for him,
notwithstanding his own melancholy. But the more we look
into Mr. Ruskin's volume, the more we want to quote or to
question; so, remembering that we have other books to tell
the reader about, we must shut this very seductive one, and
content ourselves with merely mentioning the chapters on
the Moral of Landscape, and on the Teachers of Turner,
which occupy the remaining pages; the latter preparing the
way for the special consideration of Turner, which is to
follow in the fourth volume. If the matter of this book
had arrested us less, we should, perhaps, have laid more
stress on the illustrations, some of which are very beautiful: for example, a view of the Apennines by sunset, and
a group of leaves and grasses, from the author's own
pencil.

'Modern Painters I–III'

1856

14. ELIZABETH RIGBY, FROM AN UNSIGNED REVIEW, 'QUARTERLY
REVIEW'

March 1856, vol. 98, 384-433

Elizabeth Rigby (1809-93) married Charles Eastlake in 1849;
the following year he was knighted and elected PRA. (For
his distinguished nephew see No. 39.) Known as 'Lofty
Lucy' on account of her formidable height, Lady Eastlake
had a long career as art critic, novelist, and literary
reviewer. She was first associated with a lively aesthetic
circle in Edinburgh and, after marriage, moved into a comparable society in London. Her connections with the
'Quarterly Review' were lifelong, and in December 1848 she
contributed a particularly insinuating criticism of 'Vanity
Fair' and 'Jane Eyre' in that magazine, vilifying both
Thackeray and Charlotte Brontë. Her attack on Ruskin,
whilst indicative of a conservative scepticism towards the
new and original, reflects a deep personal antagonism towards the author. See Introduction, p. 13.

There are many reasons for the popularity of Mr. Ruskin's
works. In the first place he is a thinker - a character
sufficiently rare to obtain - we do not say to deserve, for
that depends on the issue - that class of thoughtful
readers of whom a writer may be justly proud. In the next
place he is a very positive and confident thinker - also a
comparatively rare phenomenon - and any positive man or
opinion commands, at least for a time, a certain amount of
followers, for people naturally trust those who trust themselves. And, further, he is a positive and confident
thinker on a subject which is now engaging the attention of

a large class of the educated English public. But in proportion to the increasing love for art is the consciousness of ignorance about it, and in proportion to the consciousness of ignorance is the prevalence of self-distrust;
and here we arrive at a more interesting, because a more
earnest section of readers, including especially the young
and uncritical, who gratefully follow the guidance of anyone who suggests thought and lays down principle on a subject on which many can feel, but few have the power or opportunity to reason. But while the arts enjoy the advantage of being at this time a reality of the most earnest
and almost sacred kind to many, they suffer, as must always
be the case, the disadvantage of being a fashion of the
most empty and pedantic sort to many more. Here the
reasons are at once apparent which furnish Mr. Ruskin with
another class of readers more numerous than any we have
mentioned; for fashion cannot think, and must talk, and is
therefore the eager adherent of those who save the brains
and supply the tongue on the favourite topic of the day.
And, lastly, while art is now temporarily in fashion, it
must be borne in mind that strange and new doctrines on
any subject in the world are always the fashion, and this
accounts at once for the most prolific source of Mr.
Ruskin's popularity, and discloses a class of readers
larger than all the foregoing put together.

There are also many reasons why Mr. Ruskin has not been
more generally or broadly answered - we will not say more
effectually, for that he has been on particular points in
several of the monthly and weekly journals. The pure and
enthralling power excited by art over the imagination and
the emotions is supposed, and not always erroneously, to
be purchased somewhat at the expense of the prosier faculties of the mind. The lover of art, like all true lovers,
is, on that point at least, a shy and sensitive being. He
can confess his passion, but little more. Nor is art a
worship in which there is any duty to give a reason for the
faith that is in us. Taste is rightly defined by Hazlitt
as 'a sensibility to the excellences of art;' and our sensibilities to anything, from the relish for poetry to that
for an orange, are facts in ourselves, the grounds of which
we are not required to define. Why we believe in any given
thing we are bound to know, but why we feel involves no
such responsibility. A man may therefore say of art, as,
in the song, the *innamorato* of his mistress, 'I love you,
because I love you,' and yet not be thought deficient
either in enthusiasm or in understanding, but rather the
reverse. Artists themselves are seldom able to define in
words the principles which their works triumphantly exemplify. And thus it is that the lovers and followers too of

art present the anomaly of being at once the most devoted
of adherents, and yet often the least able or inclined to
fight for the cause. It is certain also that discussion
and criticism, unless of a most enlightened, and therefore
most rare, description, is more depressing than stimulating to the producers of art, while to encourage litigation
and debate among the classes who are constituted its
judges is to encourage that which most unfits them for the
privilege. Freedom of opinion, like true freedom in anything, can do art no harm, - though, from the fact that
the greatest period of art was that of the greatest religious and political thraldom, it is evident that freedom
is a condition on which it is in no way dependent, - while
all that licence which abuses the name of liberty is in-
calculably pernicious to it. This is one of the profounder
reasons why, in the economy of European civilization, art,
as a means of public education, was sent before letters,
and this is why now, and at all times, its best friends
will abstain from that war of words which is foreign to its
nature, adverse to its promotion, and incompatible with the
temper necessary for its enjoyment.

These are the reasons that may be said to apply to the
subject of art in general: as to those which especially
withhold many an answer to Mr. Ruskin, they lie chiefly in
the imagination of the persons who are otherwise admirably
qualified to controvert him. As a thinker, mechanically
considered, of the most able and elaborate class, Mr.
Ruskin is supposed to require much of that same faculty to
refute him; while, as a controversialist, of the rudest
manners, many an antagonist is deterred by the supposition
that something of the Ruskin is needed, at all events in
process, to catch a Ruskin. It would, however, be as useless to meet this writer with the same properties of
thought, as undesirable to use the mere style of argument
which he wields, and a victory so achieved would be but an
additional subject of regret. Mr. Ruskin reminds us of
the tale of the Emperor's clothes in the 'Fairy Legends'
of Andersen. Like the cunning weavers, he persuades his
readers that it is the test of their religion and morality
to see as he sees, and the delusion is kept up till some
one not more clever, but more simple, ventures to speak
the plain truth. The real way, therefore, to face Mr.
Ruskin, is not with those weapons he has selected from the
mental armoury, but with those he has left, and thus ac-
coutred the humblest adversary has nothing to fear. And
this requires us to be the more plain-spoken in the consideration of his writings, for downright and unvarnished
truth is doubly necessary in the conflict with sophistry
and irony, and doubly justified towards one who by his

treatment of others has in reality forfeited all title to
courtesy.

We must commence with a short but necessary analysis of
the author himself, before proceeding to his works. Mr.
Ruskin's own mind, judging from his writings, is an extreme exemplification of that which is pronounced - and we
do not stop to consider whether rightly or wrongly - the
defect of the present age, and to which the absence of all
greatness in the various departments of life is now-a-days
imputed. The period is declared to be one rather of brilliant intellectual talents than of great moral qualities -
those qualities which, though they cut no figure in debate,
and make no show in print, yet lead a man to prefer duty
to fame, and truth to everything. Now, Mr. Ruskin's intellectual powers are of the most brilliant description;
but there is, we deliberately aver, not one single great
moral quality in their application: on the contrary, he
appears so far more destitute than others, like himself,
more intellectually than morally gifted men, of these
higher aims, as not even to recognise the necessity for
feigning them. Where the truth of a conclusion is no object in the process of reasoning, there no restraint exists
on that activity of the thinking faculty, which can never
lead to better things than itself without a higher principle to enlighten it. Nay, there is something at once sad
and consoling in the fact that the intellect cannot even
ripen itself. Mr. Ruskin's writings have all the qualities
of premature old age - its coldness, callousness, and contraction. There is no development apparent in all he has
written. Even in his first volume, the most able, and
therefore the most favourable to himself, his overbearing
spirit has nothing of the self-excusing insolence of youth.
In his crotchety contradictions and peevish paradoxes there
is nothing of the perverse, but often charming, conflict
between the arrogance and the timidity of a juvenile
reasoner - between the high spirit and tender mouth of the
young courser in the race of thought. His contradictions
and false conclusions are from the beginning those of a
cold and hardened habit, in which no enthusiasm involun-
tarily leads astray, and no generosity instinctively leads
aright. His revilings of all that is most sacred in the
past, and his insults to all who are most sensitive in the
present, bear the stamp of proceeding rather from an un-
feeling heart than a hasty judgment; while such, necessarily, have been the vitiating effects on himself of the
unrestrained indulgence of these habits, that his latter
works, as we shall have occasion to prove, show him to
have arrived at a blind rhodomontade of reasoning and a
reckless virulence of language almost unparalleled in the

annals of literature.

It will, however, sufficiently answer all our purposes of justice, and better those of equity, to form our estimate of Mr. Ruskin's title to be considered an authority on the matters he treats, chiefly from his first volume. From this we abundantly gather those qualities by which we may define him as a writer, viz. active thought, brilliant style, wrong reasoning, false statement, and unmannerly language....

What too, we have a right to ask, have been the results of all the supposed religious and moral teaching of art upon the writer himself? Let the nature of the creed be tested by its influence on the believer. Independent of all the attacks upon painters, living or dead, which we shall presently investigate, and which may be considered the substance of his works, the mere incidental and accessory portions teem with a malice, bitterness, and uncharitableness, which is as uncalled for as it is unjustifiable. Mr. Ruskin may talk of love for trees, stones, and clouds, and profess an impious horror for those who do not represent them according to his ideas of truth, but where, throughout his writings, do we find one spark of that love for *man, woman,* or *child* which is foremost among all the precepts and the fruits of religion and morality? How comes it that the man who lives under the influence of him whom he pronounces 'the greatest landscape-painter the world has yet seen;' and further, as he owns, 'more among mountains than among men,' and therefore under nature's immediate teaching – how comes he to have formed such low and contemptuous notions of his fellow-creatures as appear directly and indirectly in every chapter he has written? Considering the little company he professes to keep, how comes it to be only of that kind as to wring from him the declaration that 'There never yet was a generation of men (savage or civilized), who, taken as a body, so woefully fulfilled the words, "having no hope and living without God in the world," as the present civilized European race:' that 'a Red Indian or Otaheitan savage has more sense of a Divine existence round him, or government over him, than the plurality of refined Londoners and Parisians'?

Again, that 'I truly believe that there never yet was idolatry of stock or stone so utterly unholy as this our idolatry of shadows;' nor can he think that 'of those who burnt incense under oaks, and poplars, and elms, it could in any wise be more justly or sternly declared, 'The wind hath bound them up in her wings, and they shall be ashamed because of their sacrifices.'

How does it happen that this man never descends from his mountains – 'the pure and holy hills' as he calls

them - without stumbling on that particular kind 'of
young lady who, rising in the middle of the day, jaded by
her last night's ball, and utterly incapable of any wholesome religious exercise, can still gaze into the dark eyes
of the Madonna di S. Sisto, or dream over the whiteness of
a crucifix, and who returns to the course of her daily life
in the full persuasion that her morning's feverishness has
atoned for her evening's folly'? Or upon that type of
'the fashionable lady who will write five or six pages in
her diary respecting the effect of such and such an ideal
upon her mind?' Or on that of 'the shallow fine lady or
fine gentleman to whom the beauty of the Apollo Belvedere
or the Venus de' Medicis is perfectly palpable' (which we
doubt), though they would have perceived none in the face
of an old weather-beaten St. Peter, or 'Grandmother Lois'?
Or, worse still, upon that rather exceptional example of
'the modern English lady, who, if she does *not* beat her
servant or her rival about the ears, it is oftener because
she is too weak or too proud than because she is of purer
mind than Homer's Juno? She will not strike them, but she
will overwork the one and slander the other without pity.'
    Are these the 'holy thoughts' which a right feeling for
art is to prompt? Is this the language of a man whose
heart and mind have been refined even by the commonest and
most legitimate influences of art? If so the world must be
weaker and wickeder even than Mr. Ruskin believes it, not
to feel it a matter of duty as well as self-interest to re-
pudiate doctrines which bear such unpalatable fruits in the
person of their especial apostle!
    Mr. Ruskin professes to have written his first two vol-
umes for the express purpose of defending Turner, which,
considering that this great painter received while living
the unfeigned and unstinted admiration of every British
artist worthy the name, and a large share of that of the
cultivated public than usually falls to the lot of artistic
genius - considering, too, that this was an admiration so
far from barren that he lived to afford to be fastidious as
to the individuals from whom he would accept commissions,
and died possessed of a larger fortune than any English
painter has ever accumulated - appears somewhat unnecessary. Neverthless, had Mr. Ruskin performed this self-
imposed task honestly and sincerely, the world would have
been indebted to him for a work of much beauty and interest, and Turner grateful even for services not needed. As
it is, however, Mr. Ruskin has taught us that there is an
admiration and love more worthy both of Turner's works and
Turner's memory, and that is one which resents the use of
his name as the pretext for the most unmannerly vituperation of all those great painters who occupy that

genealogical tree of art on which Turner's shield now
hangs proudly aloft. No enthusiasm for Turner can ever
justify, because none can ever really cause, the offensive sentiments levelled at such men as Claude, Poussin,
Canaletto, Wilson, Cuyp, Hobbema, and Ruysdael, or the
ill-disguised contempt of higher names still. If to honour
Turner it be necessary to assert of Claude that his pictures are 'the evidence of classic poison upon a weak
mind'; that he has 'the industry and intelligence of a
Sèvres china painter;' that a background city by him is
strikingly like that which Mr. Ruskin has the faint recollection of having delineated in the first page of a
spelling-book when he was four years of age! - of Poussin,
that 'distances like his are mere meaningless tricks of
clever execution, which, when once discovered, the artist
may repeat over and over again with mechanical contentment
and perfect satisfaction to himself and his superficial admirers, with no more awakening of feeling or exertion of
intellect than any tradesman has in multiplying some ornamental pattern of furniture'; - of the glorious Dutch oak-
painter, that 'one dusty roll of Turner's brush is more
truly expressive of the infinity of foliage than the niggling of Hobbema could have rendered his canvas if he had
worked on till doomsday'; - of our own Wilson, that 'his
pictures are diluted adaptations from Poussin and Claude,
without the dignity of the one or the elegance of the
other' - for he will praise those he elsewhere most abuses,
if it be at the expense of another, and then withdraw this
very praise again, as in this instance, by calling Claude's
'a foolish grace,' and Poussin's 'a dull dignity'; - if it
were necessary to speak of Rubens with an insulting apology
for 'his unfortunate want of seriousness and incapability
of true passion'; - of the great Italian masters, not excepting Titian and Paul Veronese, with a lament too absurd
to be otherwise than ludicrous for 'their blunt and
feelingless eyes and untaught imaginations'; - of all the
French, Dutch, and Flemish landscape-painters in a lump,
with a declaration that 'they passed their lives in jugglery;' that 'the deception of the senses was the first and
great end of all their art;' that 'they had neither love of
nature nor feeling of her beauty; that 'they looked at her
coldest and most commonplace effects because they were
easiest to imitate, and for her most vulgar forms because
they were most easily to be recognised by the untaught eyes
of those whom they alone could hope to please;' that 'they
did it, like the Pharisee of old, to be seen of men, and
they had their reward'; and, finally, as the climax of in-
decent contempt, that 'I conceive that the best patronage
that any modern monarch could bestow on the arts would be

to collect the whole body of them into a grand gallery and
burn it to the ground'; - if, we again say, it was necessary for the exaltation of Turner, thus ignorantly, flip-
pantly, and malignantly (and to a far greater extent than
any quotations can show) to vilify those without whom
Turner would never have been Turner, - then better were it
that the great painter's name, and even his glorious works
too, had been buried in oblivion, than raised up to notice
in such odious association. It is no slight proof of the
previous appreciation of Turner's merits, that even Mr.
Ruskin's defence of them has not been able to lower them
in public estimation. By the same rule also, indignant as
we may be that any one should be found in our times impious
enough to blacken these great benefactors - for, with the
debt of gratitude which all sound lovers of art must acknowledge, we can only so designate such an act - yet there
is no fear that Mr. Ruskin can really bay one of these
luminaries one hair's breadth out of his sphere, or that
the adherents he can agitate for Turner will be any loss
to Claude, Poussin, Wilson, and Hobbema....

In all the eloquence, therefore, with which Mr. Ruskin
has treated the subject of clouds - a chapter generally
quoted as his best - there is the unpleasant association
that his end is to mislead; and that, like an able counsel,
he increases in parade of zeal, roundabout ingenuity of invective, and simulated indignation, in proportion as he
knows his case to be unsound. Accordingly, after all this
weary length of words - this wonder, 'how little people in
general know about the sky' - this lament over 'the feebly-
developed intelligence and ill-regulated observation,' as
well as over 'the blank and feelingless eyes,' and 'untaught imaginations' of the great old masters - this playful irony, that the massive clouds of the old masters, not
excepting Titian and Paul Veronese, 'may be broad, may be
grand, may be beautiful, artistical, and in every way
desirable - I don't say it is not, I merely say it is a
concentration of every kind of falsehood' - these doubts,
whether they had any other motive for not anticipating
Turner in his skies 'beyond the extreme facility with which
acres of canvas might be covered without any troublesome
exertion of thought;' this ostentatious word-painting - a
far easier art than is generally supposed - of some of
Turner's splendid sky-effects; this needless inquiry, in
the tone of triumphant condemnation, as to whether Claude
has the same; these witticisms upon 'half-crowns,' 'ropes,'
'cauliflowers,' and 'turnips;' these lamentations over
'abuses of nature and abortions of art;' these epithets of
'childish,' 'abominable,' 'painful,' 'degrading,', 'criminal,' and 'lying' - to all this tirade, as far as regards

the not having studied the sky in the same sense as Turner,
there is the very short and simple answer, that the comparison is unfair from beginning to end; that the old
masters had different objects; and that while they often
neglected that which Turner accomplished, they accomplished
what he as often neglected. Theirs is the earth which the
husbandman tills and the miner bores - Turner's, a radiant
sphere where no such operations are possible or needed;
their skies are the beautiful, the appropriate, or, in
some of the earlier masters, only the negative accessories
to the picture - Turner's often, by the very rule of Ruskin,
the picture itself. Nay, even where his skies cannot be
called the chief object - having scarcely any objects in
them, but only serene gradation of colour, with perhaps a
few brilliant wind-swept forms overhead - yet, from the
habit of the painter's eye, the earth is equally unsubstantial; and, though exquisitely graduated in scale from distance to foreground, yet false in the position of the
scale itself.

As regards the merits of their skies, it would be useless insisting on the fact, that, as far as they go, they
are every whit as true and as beautiful as Turner's. As
Mr. Ruskin says of colour, 'one man may see yellow where
another sees blue, and yet neither can be said to see
falsely, because the colour is not in the thing, but in
the thing and them together;' so as respects the forms,
colours, and substances of clouds - proverbially rather
mutable bodies - Mr. Ruskin may see halfcrowns and ropes
where another sees what is appropriate for the scene and
the hour; for the secret of recognising what is true lies
not in the thing, but in the thing and the spectator together. While also his loss is so much our gain, we shall
be the last to combat his opinions. We know that he prefers rough seas to smooth, 'and can scarce but be angered'
as the painter who has given us the mere heave of its
placid slumber: in another part of his works, present or
future, we may find that he prefers smooth seas to rough,
for no better reason than to deride their portrayer. In
either case he has a right to his opinion, and a right also
to change his opinion. There is no law to prohibit bad
taste or absurd inconsistency, and it is against the needless offensiveness with which he expresses those tastes and
inconsistencies, and not against themselves, that we protest. When, therefore, he takes us to the National Gallery, and bids us see childishness in one great painter,
imbecility in another, and bold broad falsehood in a third,
and the fruit of our examination is to raise all three
higher than ever in our admiration and gratitude, we have
nothing to say, but to thank God who has made us like other

men - publicans included - rather than like Mr. Ruskin.
But when - as an example of their skies being 'systematically wrong' - he points to Poussin's grand picture of the
Sacrifice of Isaac, and vents a page of contempt upon it,
all based upon the assertion that the time in the picture
is 'high-noon, as it is shown by the shadows of the
figures,' - we convict him of building erroneous theories
upon a perversion of facts. We, therefore, assert that
the whole basis of his abuse of this picture falls to the
ground, for that the time is *not* high-noon. Noon shadows
are under the feet; these of Abraham and Isaac are *as long
as themselves,* being moreover shortened by the fact of their
ascending a hill. There are also shadows from tall trees
on the left slanting across the whole foreground; the time
may be, therefore, considered either late afternoon or
early morning - the latter, considering the journey before
them, most probable; these two periods of the day being in
Italy so alike, that the keeping and lighting of the picture may represent either; and as Mr. Ruskin's word and
our own here diametrically differ, the shadows themselves -
the earliest clocks known to man, and still the source and
proof of all accuracy in time - fortunately become the real
witnesses. To them, therefore, we refer the reader; and
while examining them, we should not be surprised if he
came to the conclusion that instead of their being an example of Poussin's want of veracity as a painter, they
serve rather as an example of Mr. Ruskin's want of the
most ordinary care or candour as an observer.

Altogether the vicinity of the National Gallery is in-
convenient to the stability of this writer's facts. When
he tells the reader that he 'may search through the foregrounds of Claude, from one end of Europe to another, and
not find the shadow of one leaf cast upon another,' the
magnitude of the task disposes him rather to take Mr.
Ruskin's word for the fact, than to undertake the labour
of testing it. But no such labour is wanted. The answer
is neither at Rome or Naples, nor even at Dresden or Berlin,
but in the National Gallery here in London, where, in the
picture of David at the cave of Adullam, the reader will
find, directly in the foreground, a tall large-leaved
foxglove-like plant, with certain dark appearances thrown
by one leaf upon another, as like shadows as anything
Turner or the photograph ever rendered....

One great proof, were there no other, of the falseness
of Mr. Ruskin's reasoning, is its quantity. Only on the
wrong road could so much have been said at all. As we observed before, if art be long, it is in practice not in
theory. Separate what is really to be thought and said
about art from false assumption, futile speculation,

contradictory argument, crotchety views, and romantic
rubbish, and ninety-nine hundredths of what Mr. Ruskin
writes, and one-half of what most write, will fall to the
ground. But, it may be asked, are not the precepts of common sense applicable to art as well as to everything else?
To this we readily agree; but the truth is, that all the
common sense as to diligence, sincerity of purpose, recognition of their own powers, and observation of nature,
which is so much obscured under Mr. Ruskin's jargon of
'love,' 'wisdom,' 'fear and gladness,' 'firm words, true
message, unstinted fulness and unfailing faith,' have been
said to and by painters over and over again, and, if not
realized, at all events steadily aimed at by all deserving
the name.

As regards quantity, however, it is easy to foresee that
Mr. Ruskin will always have the advantage. Nature has
given him the mechanism of thinking in a most peculiar degree. The exercise of this faculty, which is always more
or less an exertion and strain to other minds, is none to
his; and no wonder, for sophistry travels on roads where,
however much dust, there are neither stones nor tolls.
Though, therefore, the broad false principles he has laid
down may be eaily refuted, yet it may be doubted whether
any mind will have the patience to follow all the windings
of one who thinks equally without consistency and without
weariness. A man may attack iron bars, oak doors, or stone
walls, and hope with energy and perseverence to break his
way through, but to follow a thin thread, which leads him
through winding and slippery paths, and is always snapping
at an honest touch, requires a strength of nerve and tenacity of purpose which Mr. Ruskin's writings will hardly
inspire or their refutation reward.

Not that we are in the least inclined to magnify the importance of unsound ideas and absurd conclusions upon the
subject of art. Art, not being a direct moral agent at all,
can only do real harm in proportion as it can do real good -
its debasement can only be the index of a frivolous or ignorant state of society - never in any way its cause. As
regards Mr. Ruskin in particular, he will mislead no mind
and injure no career which would not have been misled or
injured equally without him. For those who have no eyes,
it matters little how entirely the pseudo moral at the end
of this chapter is purchased by the flimsy fallacy at the
beginning, while those who possess these organs to any purpose will soon forget both the one and the other. It would
have been well, therefore, for Mr. Ruskin had he erred in
nothing but what may thus be harmlessly swallowed or easily
rejected; but it is the terrible penalty of the propagators
of slander that their evil deeds should remain - for no

evil, as no good, can fall into our moral world without
fruits of which none can compute the length or the
strength; in either case, in proportion to the good or
evil, is the return or the recoil upon the author, and
upon Mr. Ruskin the recoil has begun already.

'Modern Painters IV'

1856

15. WILLIAM MICHAEL ROSSETTI, UNSIGNED REVIEW, 'SPECTATOR'

17 May 1856, 535-6

William Michael Rossetti (1828-1919) was one of the original members of the Pre-Raphaelite Brotherhood and its recorder and amanuensis. For some years he worked in the Ex-
cise Office (later to become the Inland Revenue). As the
brother of the better known Dante Gabriel Rossetti and
Christina Georgina Rossetti (as well as of Maria Francesca
Rossetti), much of the support of that remarkable household
fell upon William Michael who was art critic for the 'Spectator' (1850-60), a weekly addressed to educated liberals;
he also served in the same capacity on the 'Academy' and
'Welldone's Register' and, at Ruskin's recommendation, as
London correspondent for the American art magazine, the
'Crayon'. Ruskin and William Michael Rossetti appear to
have enjoyed an agreeable but not intimate friendship.

The fourth and penultimate volume of Mr. Ruskin's great
work is devoted, as the titlepage implies, to the illustration of mountain-nature; the beauties and lessons which
God has stamped upon it for the edification of men, the
facts which the artist has to observe in rendering it, and
in particular the mode and degree of its realization by
Turner. By those who do not lose sight of the plan of the
book in its extent and the multiplicity of its detail, it
will be remembered that this is the first section of the
inquiry into beauty and its attainment by Turner, initiated in the second volume. In the present part two broad
subdivisions are especially distinct; the first consisting
of artistic theory and speculative description of the

spiritual expression and influences of the class of
scenery under review; the second being a stern matter-of-
fact investigation of the external appearances.

Of all the volumes which Mr. Ruskin has issued, there
is probably none that exhibits his two counterbalancing
faculties of speculation and observation in a state of
such intense activity. The speculative subdivision includes the seven opening and the two concluding chapters;
which treat of what he terms the Turnerian Picturesque,
Topography, Light, and Mystery, of the Firmament and the
Dry Land, and of the Mountain Gloom and Glory. Here, besides the matter of more directly artistic bearing, peculiarly furthering the elucidation of Turner's qualities,
which the author has proposed as his central object, he
launches into Scriptural interpretation and application,
and into inquiries as to the influence of mountains upon
national character; which are apt to leave the reader,
willing as he may be to study the motions of an original
and extraordinary mind, panting a long way in the distance.
It is actually curious to thread the multitude and intri-
cacy of the topics introduced into the last two chapters.
Omitting minor points of illustration by the score, we are
led first to a consideration of the glorious and joyful
beauty of a Swiss mountain scene. Then follow the gloom
and squalor which mark the life of its inhabitants; the
spurious interest which fashionable frivolity takes in the
falsified notion of that life as presented on the stage;
the possibility of ameliorating the peasants' real condition; the element of character in mountaineers which
leads them to dwell upon objects of terror; the further
'absolute joy in ugliness' to be found, for instance, in
'the missal in the British Museum, Harl. MSS. 1892,' analyzed under five heads, and the general question pursued
into five more; and the conclusion 'that, where beauty and
wisdom of the Divine working are most manifested, there
are also manifested most clearly the terror of God's wrath
and inevitableness of His power.' Then, as we reach the
last chapter, we come to the author's statement of his own
immeasurable love and preference for the mountain lands;
the definite superiority of glory which they possess in
colour, water, trees, and clouds; the influence of mountains on religious temperament, artistic power, and literary power, with a comparison between lowland-born Bacon
and hill-born Pascal; the absence of mountain-influence
from Shakspere; his rooted adherence to what he himself saw
and knew, and the contrast in modern literature, with an
example quoted admiringly from Browning; then, once again,
the question of the possible soical elevation of the Swiss
peasantry; the tourist and railroad contractors' fast

advancing 'improvements' of the scenery; the earliest
mention of mountains in the Bible; and the meanings attached to their connexion with the deaths of Aaron and
Moses, and with the Transfiguration. Such, or rather
such tenfold multiplied, is the embarras des richesses
which the teeming brain of Mr. Ruskin accumulates round
him on this as on any other topic. No wonder if, one
after another, his readers stare, as now this, now that,
finds himself involved in some train of thought which he
had never expected, and whose conduct is as unexpected as
its occurrence.

The remaining or observative subdivision of the volume
comprises the whole of the eleven intermediate chapters.
In these, mountains are considered in their materials,
their sculpture or structure, and the resulting forms,
aiguilles, crests, precipices, banks, and stones. To the
general reader this will be the least attractive portion
of 'Modern Painters'; since, although the writer confines
himself as far as possible to his peculiar theme, the *appearances* of things, without committing himself to geologic
science or theory, the positiveness with which everything
is investigated and reasoned out is as severe as in a scientific treatise. But, if the reader's entertainment
flags, his deference for the author's immense study and
knowledge of natural phenomena, and for his consequent
judgment in art-matters, must rise proportionately. He
will find that it is not without reason, not without labour
and preparation, and experiment tested again and again,
that Ruskin claims to *know* when Nature is truthfully or un-
truthfully rendered, instead of having a mere opinion on
the subject. Indeed, the multitude of facts and observations compressed into this portion of the book alone is
fairly overwhelming, and in like degree surprising the
mastery which the author possesses over them, and the co-
herence which they assume under his ordering.

It may, however, be doubted whether the natural limits
of a work on 'Modern Painters' have not been stretched by
a large portion of the matter contained in this volume,
not only by the semi-scientific inquiries just alluded to,
but also by such discursive adjuncts as the last two chapters, of which we gave a compendium. No doubt, some
analysis of the form and the spirit of mountain scenery has
an immediate bearing on the question of Turner's or any
other artist's attainment, for we must know what there is
to represent before deciding with what amount of power it
has been represented: still, we conceive that a briefer
summary would have sufficed for the author's direct purpose, and would have better satisfied the reader who finds
his goal recede as he advances; and that the residue might

furnish forth distinct treatises, each to be read with uninterrupted interest for its own merit.

Considered as an illustrated volume, this is the most
remarkable which Mr. Ruskin has yet issued. The plates
and wood-cuts are profuse, and include numerous drawings
and etchings of mountain-form by the author, which must,
in any classification that regards other things than mere
names, remove him from the rank of amateur to that of
artist, if previous works had not effected the removal.
Mr. Ruskin, in fact, is essentially an artist. His perception of Nature has all the accuracy of a natural-born
artist of the most positive class, and his realization of
her by verbal description all the intensity and splendour
of the most imaginative. Keen sight, keen feeling, and
keen power of expression, are the qualities which go to the
making of an artist; and all these Ruskin possesses. He
adds to them a peculiarly subtile turn for theory, investigation, and exposition. This combination makes him an
unique man both among artists and writers; but if it induces him to adopt chiefly the writer's form of expression,
as capable of more fully exhibiting both faculties, it does
not obscure his possession of the artist's. Indeed, it may
almost be said that in feeling and perception he is uniformly right; it is in speculation that he becomes execp-
tional and open to challenge.

16. FROM AN UNSIGNED REVIEW, 'ECLECTIC REVIEW'

August 1856, vol. 12, n.s., 107-30

The lengthy review in the 'Eclectic Review' is largely a
summary of Ruskin's argument in 'Modern Painters IV'. However, the brief introductory excerpt is a register of
Ruskin's position as seen in a monthly magazine directed
to educated Dissenters.

It is now ten years since the first volume of 'Modern
Painters' startled the Art-loving public by its brilliant
eloquence, daring originality of thought, and want of reverence for great names, where no better reasons could be
assigned for their greatness than antiquity and general
opinion. The work then begun is now approaching its termination; four volumes have already appeared, and a fifth will
complete the series. The author has succeeded in

persuading many to embrace those views of Art which he has
himself adopted; and with reference to landscape painting
especially, has effected a reformation - almost a revolution - in the popular judgment; so that it is no longer considered absurd to compare Turner with Claude, Stanfield
with Vandevelde, Cooper with Cuyp, or Lance and Hunt with
Van Os and Van Huysum; nay, many would now be inclined to
award the palm in most of these cases to the moderns rather
than to their ancient rivals. It is no slight thing for
one not a professional artist, and still young, to have
brought about such a change in public opinion. It was a
bold undertaking to attempt the overthrow of time-honoured
beliefs and conventionalities sanctioned by the authority
and practice of many famous names. But like all great reformers, Mr. Ruskin had perfect confidence in his own resources, and the result has proved that confidence to have
been neither overweening nor misplaced. We do not indeed,
by any means approve of all that he has taught. There is
much of the husk of fancy and fallacy mingled with the
seed of truth, - much offensive self-assertion and excessive abuse of antagonists, much idol-worship, - constant
praises of humility, and as frequent displays of arrogance,
- occasional incompleteness and partiality in the consideration of a subject, and not a little twisting and perversion of the facts of nature in order to compel them to ad-
just themselves to the support of a favourite theory or
school. But in spite of this leaven of false doctrine,
how much is there of true and of wholesome teaching! - what
a precious series of observations, most carefully conducted, upon the various aspects of external nature, such
as no single observer has ever before brought together! -
what an earnestness of purpose, and what a love of beauty!
He may, indeed, have done some harm, - have led some
astray, - but he has also effected much good, and the general tendency of his teaching is in the right direction;
for it inculcates humility, the necessity of patience and
labour, and points to nature herself as the only infallible
guide; and, although the effect of this last important doctrine is, in some degree, impaired by the Turner-worship
with which Mr. Ruskin is unfortunately chargeable, yet the
very excess to which he carries this weakness is likely to
prove its own corrective; and it is not probable that many
earnest students will be content to accept of Turner as the
high priest and interpreter of nature, or submit to bow
down before a mere servant of the temple, whilst the goddess herself invites their approach and solicits their
homage.

The Fourth Volume of 'Modern Painters' is both bulkier
and more expensive than any of its predecessors, and at the

present rate of progression in size and price, we almost
tremble when we think of the fifth still to come. It is
profusely illustrated by engravings and woodcuts, chiefly
after the author's own drawings, many of which evince an
amount of technical skill, patient assiduity, and knowledge of mountain structure, that would do credit to an
accomplished professional artist. Mountain beauty is the
principal subject; and this is examined and analyzed with
the utmost care and minuteness. Neither physical nor mental toil has been spared; but the author's studies and
wanderings among the pine-clad crests, rugged glaciers,
and snowy mountains that tower above the smiling valleys of
Switzerland, have evidently been labours of love, and they
have borne abundant fruit, furnishing a mass of facts with
regard to the external aspects of mountains, whose value
to the artist can scarcely be overrated. We cannot indeed,
always agree with Mr. Ruskin in the use which he makes of
the facts thus laboriously accumulated, and some of his
conclusions we think fanciful and erroneous. But still
there are the observations themselves, affording a most
valuable and suggestive collection of materials, from
which we may draw our own inferences, without being led
away by those peculiar views which sometimes appear to warp
the judgment of our author, and dim his usual clearness of
perception; and what we conceive to be the principal merit
of the volume before us, is just its fulness and accuracy
as a record of the structure and aspects of mountain nature.
It is, in parts, beautifully written, and will add greatly
to Mr. Ruskin's fame as a word-painter, containing perhaps
the most eloquent passages he has ever composed; though
here and there we have also observed paragraphs of very
questionable taste, where he appears to have been aiming at
fine writing, and has signally failed in his attempt. Yet
upon the whole, 'the difficult air of the iced mountain
top' seems to have inspired him....

'The Political Economy of Art'

1857

17. UNSIGNED EDITORIAL, 'MANCHESTER EXAMINER AND TIMES'

14 July 1857

The two lectures comprising 'The Political Economy of Art'
delivered at Manchester on 10 and 13 July 1857 respectively
exemplify Ruskin's intrepidity in taking a markedly un-
popular message into the heart of middle-class commercial
England. His severe critic was very likely Henry Dunckley
(1823-96), sometime Baptist pastor in Salford. An out-
standing journalist who came late to his profession,
Dunckley was editor of the 'Manchester Examiner and Times'
(1855-89) and was known for a polished, vigorous style.

Mr. Ruskin has earned the reputation of an innovator in
matters of art. With the controversies which his writings
have excited it would be presumptuous for us to inter-
meddle, but we trust we have a sufficient appreciation of
his genius to be capable of offering it to our meed of
modest, but sincere homage. When he talks to us of the
Stones of Venice, of the Seven Lamps of Architecture, or of
the scenic beauty of mountains or clouds, we listen to him
with the reverence which is due to a man so deeply initiated in the speculative and practical mysteries of his
special craft. There he is strong, or, if weak, his weakness is the weakness of a giant. But Mr. Ruskin has the
adventurousness, as well as the originality and the fire,
of genius. Clad in his prophet's mantle, he roams over
heaven and earth, peering into all the corners, or knocking
down with the fist of inspired dogmatism, anything that
stands in his way. In the exercise of these prerogatives,

he said a good deal at the Athenaeum on Friday night, which
we humbly beg permission to designate as arrant nonsense.
The remark is not very complimentary, but our readers shall
determine how far it is undeserved.

'The Political Economy of Art' is the subject on which
Mr. Ruskin undertook to enlighten us. That phrase admits
of two interpretations. It may be understood as applying
either to the internal economy of art-labour, or to the
relations of art-labour, as a whole, to the industrial organisation of society. To judge from the scope of Mr.
Ruskin's lecture, he uses it in both these significations,
passing from one sphere of inquiry to the other according
to the exigencies of his theme.

Accordingly, he begins by a disquisition on law and
government in relation to the aggregate labour of the community. The welfare of a nation depends upon the right application of labour. Rightly applied, labour is amply
sufficient to supply every man with all things needful, as
well as with many pleasing objects of luxury. If a nation
or an individual misapplies labour, it is insufficient for
these ends; not otherwise. Hence 'all economy whether of
states, households, or individuals, may be defined to be
the art of managing labour.' So far we entirely concur in
his remarks. They are, as he reminds us, mere truisms;
first blush interpretations of what everybody sees to be
the natural laws of society. But how shall we secure the
right application of labour? Here Mr Ruskin enters the
field of open heresy. He replies by bidding us observe
how a farm is managed. The farmer, or farmer's wife, sees
what is necessary to be done in order to get and keep the
farm in proper trim, and bids the servants go and do it.
Hence, supposing the presiding powers to have a sufficient
stock of intelligence, we soon have a model farm. Dobbin
and his colleagues have a comfortable stable, the fields
are drained and manured, eggs and butter are brought to
market at the right season; the farmer gets rich, and his
menservants and maidservants enjoy capital dinners. Now
this, we are told, is a picture of what the nation ought to
be. The nation is a large farm; we want a head farmer, who
will tell his servants what they ought to do, and see that
they do it. Very good; but, as some would reply, there is
this essential difference between a farmer and a country,
that the farmer holds authority over his labourers, and can
direct them what to do, and turn away anyone who refuses to
work. The objection is of Mr Ruskin's own stating; how
does he meet it? He tells us this is the very difference
he wishes to see done away! The country must find a farmer,
a head steward, who shall háve all the labour in it under
his control; who shall assign to every man his task, and

make him either do it or starve. This is very candid; and
we could not do better than encourage Mr Ruskin forthwith,
at a handsome salary, to carry his theory into practice.
In return for the handsomeness of this suggestion, we
simply stipulate that, when Mr Ruskin comes to the actual
division of labour, he will be so good as to make us his
office clerks, and relegate the functions of chimney-
sweeps and nightsoilmen to less cultivated people.

All at once, however, when we least expected it, we
come across a gap in Mr Ruskin's theory. Just as we are
considering how the Queen or Lord Palmerston will get
through the onerous duties of master farmer for the nation,
he informs us that he is not prepared to place this authority in any one man, or set of men. He soon recovers from
this inconsequence, and makes it plain that, as his theory
binds him to do, he would fix the central, omniscient,
all-directing power somewhere. The French stick up for
'fraternity;' they made a mess of it because they forgot
the principle of 'paternity.' We are all brethren; who
can deny it? We confess every Sunday that we are brethren.
All that we want, therefore, is to find out our father,
who has the right to tell us what we ought to do. We supposed that most persons had a tolerably clear idea of the
'fatherhood' to which we refer, when in religious worship
we call ourselves brethren; but Mr Ruskin's conception is
more mundane. The nation represented by its laws, or its
government, is its own father, and the law-making authority ought to treat us as children, just as mamma does when
she sends Billy to school or makes Selina knit garters.
Mr Ruskin tells us that national laws have hitherto been
judicial only, but that we must make them paternal as well
as judicial. They must direct our industry and control our
occupations. Governmental interference is the only remedy
for national distress. 'The nation,' we are told, 'has a
right to claim *food* and education from the government, but
only so far as they yield to the authority of the government.' Who will help us out of this mesh of absurdity?
What is the meaning of obedience to government, in return
for which we are to get our bread and cheese? Does it
mean that we must not thwart Lord Palmerston on the Ballot,
the Divorce Bill, or in regard to China and India? Nothing
of the kind. Government is to be obeyed solely as head-
steward over the industry of the people. Every man must be
satisfied with the work allotted him to do. If Mr Ruskin
is sent to break stones, he must do it without grumbling,
and the government will repay him for his docile industry,
just as the farmer's wife regales her hard-working Molly
with buttermilk and potatoes.

Mr Ruskin's exposition of the internal economy of

art-labour explains to us how he would apply these principles within the sphere of art. The first business, of course, is to catch the artist. How is this to be done? Establish 'trial schools,' says Mr Ruskin, where the idle farmer's lad and stupid tailor's apprentice may go and show whether there is something in them. We would beg submissively to observe that the test might be applied earlier, before the sterling grains of genius become obscured. Let there be training nurseries, each presided over by a commission of artists, who would doubtless to able to tell by the mode in which the infant probationers scratch their nurses how many are likely to rival Angela or Canova in scratching marble. But when the future artist is discovered in the idle farmer's lad or stupid tailor's apprentice, what are we to do with him? Just find him a 'sufficiency of initiatory employment;' and, when he essays to draw a red lion, don't laugh at him if he fails. Blame him if he is slovenly, but praise those who strive to deserve it. This rule appears to us to be capable of wider application. Who is there that does not deserve to be blamed when slovenly, or praised when meritorious? Then, when all the artist is in full swing, we are to supply him with various kinds of work, and employ him on material which will not soon decay. But here a new difficulty besets the hapless artist. Our villainous paper makers turn out a bad article, so Mr Ruskin thinks that Government ought to take the making of paper into its own hands, indicating its excellence by a shilling stamp! But when we have got good paper, the artist may possibly be cheated into bad colours. Here the Government must step in afresh, and become colour mixers! Why not extend the principle? We want good ships, good machinery, good calico, good corn; why shouldn't Government make and grow everything? This is in logical consistency, Mr Ruskin's theory. To hear him talk, artists are the salt of the earth, the flower of creation. Provision for raising them must figure in the consolidated fund, and a secretary of state must be appointed for easels and brushes. The absurdity is too rich for comment. We leave it in its native gracefulness, to tell us what genius can become when divorced from common sense.

18. WILLIAM MOY THOMAS, UNSIGNED REVIEW, 'ATHENAEUM'

26 December 1857, 1615-17

William Moy Thomas (1828-1910), novelist, translator, and
journalist, was once private secretary to Charles Dilke,
sometime editor and proprietor of the 'Athenaeum'.
Thomas was something of an all-round journalist and contributed to such publications as the 'North British Review',
'Household Words', and 'The Economist'; he also served as
drama critic for the 'Daily News'. However, his writings
on the more profound subjects of political economy and
philosophy for the 'Athenaeum' were doubtless vital in
furthering the influence of one of the most powerful
weeklies of the high Victorian years.

Who could imagine Mr. Ruskin putting off his singing-robes
to clothe himself in a scientific suit of pauper-grey, and
sit with my Lord Brougham and Mr. M'Culloch in the school
of Adam Smith and Malthus? How should that fine imagination, those majestic rhythmical sentences, and that surprising wealth of choice and felicitous words, be tamed
down to the harsh service of such subjects as exchangeable
value, productive and unproductive labour, the nature of
money, and the duties of Government? Such a change is, indeed, hard to conceive; but if it has not been entirely accomplished - if the writer still occasionally revels in
splendid visions, and lapses into moods of thoughtful tenderness - it is in spite of himself and of his subject, for
his theme is in good faith Political Economy, and not
strictly that only which may be applied to Art; his chief
purpose to treat the artist's power, and the Art work itself, as items of the world's wealth, and to show how these
may be best evolved, produced, accumulated, and distributed. So thorough a political economist does he at one
moment become, as to present us with the hackneyed illustration of the savage, who in the origin of society,
'knows no needs but those of food, shelter, and sleep.'
and passes his time in animal repose. He picks a hole in
the logical coat of Mr. Mill on the subject of unproductive consumption; glances at the Poor Law Amendment Bill;
attacks in text and addenda the ancient fallacy that lavish
consumption benefits a nation; discusses the subject of the
currency, of 'representative property,' as he calls it; regrets that he has 'not had time to examine the various conditions of dishonest trading which have led to the late

panic in America and England'; censures the Common Council
of New York, whom he innocently classes with 'the political economists' for 'their blunt, broad, unmitigated fallacies on monetary laws'; confidently declares that 'most,
if not all,' of his own principles are 'accepted by existing authorities on the science'; and confesses, with a delightful *naïveté*, that he has' never read any author on
political economy, except Adam Smith, twenty years ago.'
A specimen of Mr. Ruskin in his new character cannot fail
to interest our readers:-

[Quotes from 'I know that no merchant' to 'gulfs of ruin',
'Works' 16: 138-9.]

This is a sober discourse; but Mr. Ruskin's idea of a
perfect economical system must be classed with Plato's
Model Republic, Sir Thomas More's Utopia, and Bishop
Berkeley's Bermudan project. Quietly setting aside the
whole question of Capital, about which so many of his
brother economists have wilfully bothered their heads, he
starts by declaring that 'a man's labour, well applied, is
always amply sufficient to provide him during his life with
all things needful for him.' So if men do not get a comfortable living, it is either because they are lazy or because their labour is not well applied; and the remedy for
this is a paternal government, which shall 'establish such
laws and authorities as may at once direct us in our occupations, protect us against our follies, and visit us in
our distresses.' In this happy state every man has an in-
alienable right to at least the equivalent of 'as much land
as he needs to feed from'; and, further, all have 'a right
to claim employment from their governours; but only so far
as they yield to the governour the direction and discipline
of their labour; and it is only (says Mr. Ruskin) so far
as they grant to the men whom they may set over them the
father's authority to check the childishnesses of natural
fancy, and direct the waywardness of national energy, that
they have a right to ask that none of their distresses should
be unrelieved, none of their weaknesses unwatched, and that
no grief, nor nakedness, nor peril, should exist for them,
against which the father's hand was not outstretched.'
All fools are to be taken care of by the wise; for what,
asks Mr. Ruskin, 'do you suppose fools were made for? That
you might tread upon them, and starve them, and get the
better of them in every possible way?' Here there shall be
government manufactories where the discipline is 'strict,'
and the 'wages steady'; gluts of commodities being prevented by the watchful care of the State; while all youths
desiring it are to be taken by the government as

apprentices, and men thrown out of work 'received at all
times.' Here pauperism, which the cruel economists, with
whom Mr. Ruskin charitably imagines himself to agree, have
treated as a kind of crime, is to be almost a virtue. The
common aversion to parochial assistance he thinks 'a singular prejudice': he would have the poor labourer take his
pension from his parish as having 'deserved well of his
parish,' which he considers as natural 'as for a man in
higher rank to take his pension from his country.' Guilds
and brotherhoods in trade, which have been steadily dying
out since the feudal baron filled up his moat, and made
gardens and fish-ponds, and which Mr. Ruskin's brother
economists (is he aware of it?) think the world now happily nearly rid of, are to live again and become real
things, all dependent on one wise, beneficent government,
where red tape is for evermore abolished; and there are
to be large staffs of officials, both central and local,
who are to fix the rate of wages, and set hungry folks to
work, make the lame and the swift, the ailing and the
strong, as one; and bring back the golden age. Here 'no
book shall be sold for less than a pound sterling' (even
Jack Cade would not have wished to have books cheap); but
the really poor, who cannot pay the pound, 'shall be supplied with the books they want for nothing.' Here, again,
there are to be 'noble groups of constellated schools'
taking separate divisions in the field of thought; and,
what is nearer to Mr. Ruskin's heart, here are to be such
seminaries for youthful artists as have never yet been
seen. With an eloquence and tender regretfulness, which
cannot have failed to enchant and carry away his hearers,
he touches upon the waste of artistic power, which he
imagines is going on among us. What inglorious Leonardo
da Vincis, Ghirlandajos, Ghibertis, Francias, or Donatellos
may be toiling among us in obscure and coarse employments,
ignorant of their inheritance of gifts divine! Who has not
indulged in the thought? The biographers of great men, as
Mr. Ruskin beautifully tells us, dwell on all the things
which helped to develope their genius, but are mostly silent on the things which might have turned them, and may
every day be turning others, from their appointed way.
Who would not gather up all these scattered germs with the
painful economy of the goldsmith, who sweeps away and
hoards the very dust of bench and floor? But how shall we
do it? Mr. Ruskin says no word upon the actual working of
such encouragement as is already given to Art-scholars here
in England. Wise men, no less anxious than he for the development of all that is glorious and good in Art, are af-
flicted with grave doubts on this subject. They see a
large production of mediocre, tricky, and marketable skill,

and suspect that we have begun at the wrong end, and that
we shall never do better until the buyers and the admirers
of pictures are educated. In the technical language of
Mr. Ruskin's new study, they think that there will be no
supply of genuine Art until there is a true demand for it.
Mr. Ruskin has no such misgivings. He admits that 'the
greater number of living artists are men who have mistaken
their vocation:' but he has no doubt that his *trial
schools* will attract the true metal. These trial schools
are to be established in every important town, and 'idle
farmer lads' and 'stupid tailors' 'prentices, who are always stitching the sleeves in the wrong way upwards,' are
to try this other trade. But why this trade only? Is it
not equally desirable that no grain of the great musician's,
the great sculptor's, the great engineer's, the great
soldier's, the great statesman's power should be stifled
for lack of nourishment? Nay, is it even good that a
latent faculty for working well in any of the manifold employments of men should be wasted? Shall we attract and
invite our youths and young men to try their hands at all
these? taking credit for the powers that we discover, and
giving no thought to the many persons we may have misled,
to the false hopes, or the false pride we may innocently
have engendered, or to all the other mischiefs, which any
man can imagine? Political economists, if Mr. Ruskin shall
wilfully keep their company, will assuredly ask him these
questions; or perhaps will say that his book is but the
dream of a man of genius, and his lectures curious, as having been delivered on a summer day in a city of plain brick
and blind windows, of factories and warehouses, of smoke
and toil. And, indeed, how could a sober Manchester
audience, even in the ennobling presence of all the accumulated treasures of our galleries of Art, listen to Mr.
Ruskin's exhortation to them to take upon themselves as a
duty, not the beautifying of English parish churches, but
the defence and preservation of the glories of the cities
of Lombardy from the barbaric hand of the 'improver,' or
the cannon balls of the Austrian, and think it anything
but a poetic vision, intended for no practical end, but
only indirectly to refine and purify the minds of those who
contemplate it. Let our readers judge:-

[Quotes from 'At Rome, the Roman' to 'streets of Verona',
'Works' 16: 66-8.]

Equally worthy of quotation is the following appeal
against the Vandalism of the world:

[Quotes from 'Fancy what we should have had' to 'chant in

the galleries', 'Works' 16: 64-5.]

These are noble passages, which may turn the laugh at Mr.
Ruskin's speculations on wealth and government into gratitude and delight. The easiest 'trial school' that could
be set up on his plan might discover in any town in this
kingdom a hundred better political economists than the
author of these lectures; but Boards of Examiners could
produce no standard whereby to test his powers.

Ruskin in the 1850s

19. FROM AN UNSIGNED ARTICLE ENTITLED JOHN RUSKIN,
'ECLECTIC MAGAZINE' (NEW YORK)

January 1854, vol. 31, 65-78

The anonymous reviewer is almost certainly Peter Bayne
(1830-96), journalist and author. The attribution is based
on striking similarities of style and content to another
evaluation by Bayne found in his 'Essays in Biography and
Criticism' (Boston, 1860), pp. 281-333, entitled Ruskin and
his Critics. Bayne was not above drawing upon one of his
own articles, modifying it slightly, and publishing it
anew. He edited the 'Edinburgh Witness' and the 'Weekly
Review'; in 1879 he published 'Letters from my Masters -
Carlyle, Tennyson, and Ruskin'. See Introduction, p. 15.

...The most important and effectual way, then, to advance
art in a nation, is to teach that nation to observe man and
nature; and in the particular art of landscape painting, he
who would advance its perfection, or promote its patronage,
must lead the artist from the studio into the field, and
teach men in general to love the face of their great mother,
and to know it when they see it.

And now to bring this to bear upon our immediate subject.
We claim for Mr. Ruskin an honor which is independent of
every conventional rule and every professional partiality -
an honor, in the accordance of which all men, whether professional or not, and however much they may differ from him
in minor points, may be freely invited to join us. We believe that the influence of the beauty of nature is always
in itself good, and we believe that it is by awakening a
love for that beauty, and leading men to mark and trace it,

that any grand advance in the public promotion and consequent perfecting of true art can occur. We therefore claim
for Mr. Ruskin, from all men, that grateful honor and admiration which are due to a great original teacher; and
from practical devotees of art an acknowledgment that,
whatever his subordinate opinions, Ruskin has devoted his
life to fill that fountain of public appreciation and support from which they all must draw. We talk with perfect
deliberation and calmness when we say, that it were utter
injustice to Mr. Ruskin, and an entire mistaking alike of
his mission to his age and his rank among distinguished
men, to judge him primarily by his agreement or disagreement with any school of art: such criticism may very fitly
follow; but we think that, ere we close, we shall make it
good, that, when first taking his dimensions and assigning
him his station, the only true and just aspect in which to
regard him is that of a great revealer and preacher of the
beautiful in nature, as nature's beauty can be seen in the
nineteenth century. We for the present restrict ourselves
to this; we intend to discuss no farther any theories of
beauty, to support or combat any dogmas of the schools; we
believe all men will bless him, be he poet, painter, or
prose writer, who opens their eyes to any gleam of beauty
which they saw not before; and we think Ruskin has read to
the men of the nineteenth century a lesson which, if they
read it aright, will lead them to discern the beauty and
glory of this universe as no generation ever did before.
And with such explanation and assertion we may be permitted
to add, that we approach our task, with whatever feelings
of self-distrust, yet with a certain confident gladness;
for we know that we are to speak of one of whom we can
speak boldly; and we pretend not to suppress that discipu-
lar enthusiasm which is needful to make us feel at all
worthily concerning Ruskin, and which, as far as we are at
present to expose its grounds, may be shared in by all men.

   Yet it were incorrect to suppose us carried away by mere
delighted admiration of Ruskin's genius, or disposed to
agree with him on all points; on the contrary, we dissent
from him in very many, and must express our decided difference on two points unconnected with art. Even respecting this last, we might have a good deal to say in the tone
of question or objection; but we must waive it all, and
shall do little more than record our disagreement with him
even on those two subjects which he has left his chosen
path to discuss.

We dissent from his conclusions on economic and ecclesiastical matters. His views on the former, expressed in
volume second of 'The Stones of Venice.' we think unsatisfactory; his pamphlet on 'Sheepfolds' we consider utterly

unworthy of him. Our space absolutely forbids our joining
issue with him on these points; but we must note one remarkable circumstance in his treatment of them, which seems
to us to be of peculiar, somewhat curious significance, and
to throw ominous conjecture on his whole success. It is
the fierce emphasis, the impatient hammering dogmatism, the
overbearing declamation and denunciation which characterize
his style in both cases, especially in the latter. There is
a problem at present agitating men and nations, struggling
for solution with a volcanic earnestness and energy, voic-
ing itself now in the six points of Chartism, now in the
vague groping and maundering of Socialism, and now in the
word 'fire' from the brow of the barricade. It may be
stated, in general terms, as the defining and settlement of
the relation between man and man as employer and employed,
in our age of the world. The greatest intellects of the
age have grappled with it, with but doubtful success. Mr.
Ruskin alleges all to be wrong in the relation referred to,
but nothing is to him simpler than the setting all right;
and so he propounds, with unfaltering decision, his specific. This specific seems to us almost totally null, and we
have thought of the matter so much as to speak somewhat
decidedly; but Mr. Ruskin is peremptory, curt, absolutely
confident. In his tractate on church affairs again, the
matter is still more palpable, and still more wonderful;
the questions discussed are, perhaps, the most difficult in
'divinity.' Mr. Ruskin expressly says, he does not teach
'divinity,' and yet he speaks with a decision and impetuosity that reminds one of a field-battery.

An extract or two will best indicate his general tone.
'I hold the resistance of the Scotch Presbyterian Church
to Episcopacy to be unscriptural, futile and schismatic.'
'The members of the Scotch Church have not a shadow of excuse for refusing Episcopacy.' 'The English Church, on
the other hand, *must* cut the term "priest" entirely out of
her prayer-book.' 'There would be then only the baptismal
question left, which is one of words rather than of things,
and might easily be settled in synod, turning the refrac-
tory clergy out of their offices, to go to Rome if they
chose.' And all this with an intimation that 'divinity' is
not what Mr. Ruskin professes to teach! The singular
point is, that on his own subject, however unfaltering his
decision, he ever maintains a certain imperial calm; in
'The Seven Lamps' there is perhaps more of haste and agi-
tation than in 'The Modern Painters;' and at any time he
may send a side-blow into some squadron of critics that
stands in his way; but as a general rule, it is of Thor's
summer heat and ethereal radiance that he reminds us,
rather than of his whitened knuckles and 'sledge-hammer'

blows. And how magnificently does he himself proclaim the
importance of moderation, and the grandeur of repose! We
think that by this argument alone, and in his own words,
Mr. Ruskin'a pamphlet on 'Sheepfolds' might be sifted and
winnowed, and almost blown away. The truth is, that Mr.
Ruskin's power in his own department is such as almost
necessarily implies the absence of nearly equal power in
any other; we may call him a man of one idea; but then it
is as we call Victoria queen of one empire.

There are three points of view in which we shall survey
Ruskin, as a revealer of the beauty of nature. We shall
first glance generally at this love, its kind and sincerity, considering, at the same time, the language in which
he gives it expression, and embodies what it has revealed
to him; we shall then consider his precise relation to
this age, as one of ripe science, when, as some men would
tell us, imagination must vanish in the full light of
knowledge, poetry die, as an antiquated lady whose tales
cease to interest, and the world be clipped into a Dutch
garden; and lastly, we shall inquire in what attitude,
while proclaiming the gospel of beauty, he stands to the
gospel of truth. We shall thus, we think, succeed in gaining a complete and correct idea of Ruskin, in those great
lineaments on which, as we say, must depend the quality
and endurance of his fame.

Ruskin's devotion to nature is intense and original; in
range, though not free from preference, it may be declared
as wide as nature; it is the love which is inborn, and independent of external influences; which is evinced not in
words of rapture alone, but in the minute knowledge which
only love can give, derived from such delighted watching
as *can* be spoken of only in words of gladness. When he
leaves a scene of beauty, his mind retains its traces, as
the calm lake retains the bank and the forest in its bosom;
he reminds us of that in Shelley:

> Like one beloved, the scene had lent
>   To the dark water's breast
> Its every leaf and lineament.

It is the memory of love, the truest and strongest of all.
This deep and genuine love of nature is a characteristic
of the noblest minds; we suspect no mind of real and complete greatness was ever destitute of it, and we know no
better test of nobleness and width of character. We consider it also almost as rare, in its higher order, as the
minds it purifies and harmonizes. Its order and degree in
the mind of Ruskin are such as to vindicate for him at once
a rank among a select and separate few of the sons of men.

We know of extremely little in English prose, and of by no
means a great deal in English poetry, which indicates so
much of that knowledge of nature which arises from obser-
vant love, as is evinced by countless separate passages in
the works of Ruskin....

By whatever test we try Ruskin's love of nature, we find
it to be true and of mighty power.

Is it narrow or partial, fixing upon certain phenomena,
and avoiding others? It is universal to an extent which
surely was never equalled by any prose writer save Richter.
Listen to his description of the sea, and you think he must
have spent his life watching the grace and the beauty of
its garlanded summer waves, and the tortured rolling of its
wintry billows; follow his eye as it ranges over the broad
fields of the sky, and you are impressed with the idea that
his days and his weeks must have been given to trace the
faintest streaks of the cirri, lying like a soft maiden's
hair along the blue,and to observe the sun touching them
with gold and 'vermilion' for his tent at eventide; of
forests, of mountains, of valleys, he can tell with the
same loving minuteness and the same poetic breadth. To
him, as to very few writers that we have ever known, his
own test can be applied with triumphant result. 'Our
purity of taste,' he says, 'is best tested by its universality; for if we can only admire this thing or that, we
may be sure that our cause for liking is of a finite and
false nature. But, if we can perceive beauty in every
thing of God's doing, we may argue that we have reached
the true perception of its universal laws.'

Is his admiration of nature acquired or assumed, and
consciously applied in order that he may be able to criticise acceptably? Such constant, passionate, all-embracing
love never was acquired; and that it grew up unconsiously
and in childhood, we have the following testimony by himself, the more satisfying that it is indirect:- 'There
was never yet the child of any promise (so far as the theoretic faculties are concerned) but awaked to the sense of
beauty with the first gleam of reason; and I suppose there
are few among those who love nature otherwise than by profession and at second-hand, who look not back to their
youngest and least-learned days as those of the most intense, superstitious, insatiable, and beatific perception
of her splendors.' He goes on to quote Wordsworth's well-
known passage respecting the impressions upon youth of
that celestial light in which nature is in early days ap-
parelled. We can well imagine the young Ruskin almost en-
tranced by the beatific vision of that light.

When we apply the test which we first mentioned - that
which refers to unity of delineation - we are led directly

to the consideration of Mr. Ruskin's style. It is one of
those styles which may be analyzed, and defined, and objected to, but never accounted for; it is a gift of expression amounting to the poetic, and reminds us sadly that
out greatest poets at present write in prose. We strongly
suspect the first and most important question for critics
in all decisions regarding style, is, whether or no it is
genuine: we think much time and pains is absolutely wasted
in pointing out faults and suggesting improvements; for,
too generally, the very characteristic selected as a fault
is the determining quality and radical beauty of all. You
will hear Ruskin charged with verbiage and bombast; and
there is no piece of nonsense thriving so well at present,
and obtruding in so many directions its lackered front, as
that which objects mannerism to such men as Macaulay, or
Carlyle, or Tennyson. If mannerism is affected, it is
prima facie, null and void; the mannerist of this order
confesses that his being is an echo or worse, and has not
heart enough, the coward, to wear his own feathers, rather
than another man's plumes. But every man of a very high
order that ever lived had a mannerism, whether of acting
or writing. He were a sapient critic who would regret that
Homer sung so much about battles, that Dante was so adaman-
tine, or that Milton never abandoned the majesty of his
port. An assumed mannerism is the worst of errors; a true
mannerism is nature's proof that, from the storehouse of
her infinitude, she has sent us another original mind.
That all men and styles have flaws, we need scarce pause
to admit; our assertion is, that the error is fatal in
criticism which considers a style otherwise than as a
whole, and is therefore apt to select that quality whose
prominence is the characteristic, and without which the
style were different, for special reprobation. Now it is
just his amazing plenitude of vocables which is the most
prominent characteristic - the mannerism - of Ruskin's
style; no man can read three of his pages without discerning that, as Foster said of Coleridge, the whole congre-
gation of English words are at his command; his memory for
words seems as natural and as wide as his sympathy for
beauty. Here, then, is a handle for a brain-racked critic;
he has deeply to regret that this able writer should be
carried away by his fatal facility: he must entreat him to
restrain his exuberance, and then no one will more gladly
recognize his excellence than the spare and spectacled
little man. Verbiage occurs when there are more words than
things, when you have strings of adjectives that signify
nothing. If a man's abundance of vocables is used by him
with precision and skill, to accuse him of verbiage is absolutely the same mistake as it would be to accuse a

painter of meretricious adornment, because he gave us ten
marvellously blended tints to express the melting of one
rainbow color into another, where a sign-painter would
have given you two strokes of yellow and red; or to accuse
a musician of indefinite redundance because his instrument
has more notes than your own piano. If the colors are
flung on indiscriminantly, the picture must be a daub,
however many its hues; if the notes make one confused
jingle, there is no harmony, however many notes there may
be; but the more colors, the better, provided they are laid
on with delicacy and power; and the greater the number of
notes, the more precious the music, if every note is made
to express some hitherto unknown tenderness or power of
feeling. Ruskin's command of words is extremely great, yet
we unhesitatingly aver that it is nowise so extraordinary
as the skill with which he can apply it. We of course do
not claim for him exemption from error; but, for ourselves,
we care not to confess that Ruskin's power of using his
words to bring out every tint and every line is to us well-
nigh inconceivable. He can make you see the sunbeams
flickering and dancing on the leaves, and the very spring
and prancing of the waves; he can paint to your eye the
wreathing of the mist, and every humor and caprice of the
sky, and you turn round and say, he is verbose and bombastic! Another piece of plausible nonsense which occasionally takes to wandering through our magazines is, that a
style should abound in substantives, and that the adjective, used abundantly, induces laxity and feebleness.
This is nonsense, because it expresses merely one phase of
truth, and, as a general rule, is false. A style where
adjectives are put in for sound, and there are few substantives round which they cling, is a body where the
bones are gristle; a style where substantives abound, in
scientific order and bareness, is a gaunt thing of skin
and bone; a style where the facts are stated clearly, and
there is plenty of them, but where every quality of beauty
- every shade of delicacy - every breath of life - is expressed by fitly-chosen adjective, is a body that has the
strength of bones, the elastic pliancy of muscle, and the
breathing beauty of life. The expression of this is its
proof. It is rendered manifest, besides, by the fact that
an original style is mainly to be known by its favorite
adjectives. You will find De Quincey throwing around certain adjectives that he loves, a charm you never imagined
them to possess; Shelley is not weak when he paints us
the really 'charmed cup'

   Of foaming, and sparkling, and murmuring wine'

Carlyle's style is not feeble for all its adjectives, because every one is alive, and speaks from the page. By
the term adjective, we of course intend to indicate all
words that qualify or define. When Carlyle speaks of a
'snow and rose-bloom maiden.' he uses as distinct an adjective as if he said lovely. Ruskin, sure enough, is not deficient in facts; it is because of the multitude of his
facts that he must multiply his adjectives; it is because
he has watched the expression of nature's infinitude, that
he finds even his marvellous command of descriptive diction
fall short. He is indeed a mighty colorist; but he draws
as well as he colors. We mean to quote one or two passages
from Mr. Ruskin's works ere we close this paper; but our
space compels us to be very sparing in our selection, and
to illustrate by each more points than one. But we invite
our readers to test the truth of our remarks by looking at,
for we can scarce say reading, the following pictures:- the
Campagna of Rome under evening light, in the preface to the
second edition of 'Modern Painters;' that passage on the
effects of light and storm among the Alps, which the reader
may be able to characterize by an epithet, but which we cannot, unless, indeed, it were *with that fulness of meaning
in which Ruskin would use it*, by the simple one, natural;
the opening paragraph to his chapter on sky-scenery; the
commencement of chapter sixth in 'The Seven Lamps of Architecture;' and at least fifty similar, if not equal, passages; after reading these, let him say which is the most
wonderful – Ruskin's command of color, or his power and
precision in laying it on. We repeat, that we do not regard
Mr. Ruskin's style as flawless, and we know well that, if
any of its qualities were grafted on the style of a different mind, distortion would be the result. But, whatever our
personal opinion of certain passages, we cannot so far
assure ourselves that such is not merely idiosyncratic preference, as to enable us to object; and we think there is
no more glaring instance of critical presumption than the
tendering of advice in the case of any such style. Whether
it is that he paints the face of nature herself, or whether
it is that he adds an imaginative glory of his own, we
think his gorgeousness equalled by his delicacy, and his
utmost exuberance governed by law.
    By every test, then, that we can devise, by continual
irresistible perception of nature's unity, by universality
of sympathy, by unconsciousness of operation, we find
Ruskin's love of nature to be true and powerful. But it is
utterly impossible to convey to any one who does not know
his works an adequate idea at once of the intensity of his
love, and the unwearying, all-tracing power of his observation. He takes you to the mountains and the clouds, to

the meadow and the lake, to the ocean and the rock; ever
and anon you exclaim, 'Yes, that is true, I have seen that,
though never so clearly until now; and I must believe that
much which I have not seen is true, both because of what I
have seen, and because, when I turn my eye from your page
to nature's, I meet with constant confirmation of your
words.' All great things are known by their rarenss either
in kind or in degree, and great men are pronounced so by
their rare qualitites; we have, therefore, no hesitation
in pronouncing Ruskin's love of nature, his power of observation, and his marvellous expression, sufficient to entitle him to be called great.

We find ourselves compelled to omit that comparison,
which we wished to have drawn, between Ruskin's love of
nature and his pictorial powers, and those of certain other
great English writers; we may just refer to the only two
who in the present day can be named along with him - Wilson
and Carlyle. We set not Ruskin on a level with these men,
on the whole, but he can well bear comparison with them
here. Wilson's 'great flashing eye' has often gleamed with
a brighter radiance as it opened on some new glory of
nature; his description of mountain scenes, and a few kindred appearances, are scarcely to be surpassed even in conception; but his range, so much wider elsewhere, is necessarily far narrower here than Ruskin's. Carlyle's love of
nature is loyal and deep; he could never have written 'Sartor Resartus,' or many passages in his other works, were it
not so; but his subject is men, and he has expressly denounced the painting of nature's face for its own expression, and that, by the way, immediately after one of the
grandest pieces of mountain scenery in English poetic prose.

But there is one point in which Ruskin leaves both
Carlyle and Wilson behind, and challenges comparison with
Richter. This we shall discover as we proceed to his
second great characteristic as a revealer of the beautiful,
and which has direct reference to the present era of the
world.

This time is scientific, as no time ever was. It is but
a very quiet metaphor now to say, that Science sets her
feet upon the world beneath us, gazes upward to the stars,
whose secrets she knows, looks around her on the known and
examined earth, from where her sons have just penetrated
the ice deemed eternally closed, to the cactus hedges and
bright-flowered fields of Southern Africa, and casts her
glance backwards over ages and epochs, to watch the fair
earth emerging from the womb of darkness and fire, to be a
home for the God-seeing creature man. There are no Isles
of the Blessed now - no Atlantis even in imagination now.
Men, it would seem, had ceased to wonder, and merely looked.

Geology tells you the forms of the mountains; meteorology
guesses at the balancing of the clouds; and the lightning
goes faster and farther, as the slave of man, than it ever
went when it dwelt alone in the thunder-cloud. The beasts
of the forest have been watched and classified; the flowers
of the field are named and known; the very rainbows that
the sun from time immemorial had wreathed in the mist and
foam of Orinoco, have been looked upon by the eye of Science. It became clear that fact and fiction were changing
their relations, and many said that imagination must decay,
and mankind fling away, in the full light of their knowledge, that mantle of poetry which had shielded them in
their ignorance. It was manifest that the old images must
be cast away one by one - that mountain waves must go with
the tales of the nursery, and the lion be probably compelled to abdicate his preëminence as a type of valor.
The problem that presented itself was simple in statement:-
Was it possible to throw the garb of poetic beauty, to
strike into poetic unity and life, the multitudinous details of science? We claim for Ruskin and another, of
whose merits we may one day speak at length, the honor of
having practically solved the problem: they have shown in
Britain what Richter showed in Germany - that there is a
power in the mind of man to make science merely a new elevation from which to gaze afresh on the beautiful. We
offer the following passages as the substantiation of the
fact:

[Quotes from 'The charts of the world' to 'that shade
them', 'Works' 10: 185-8.]

We may, in passing, remark that this passage is amply
sufficient to make good every particular of commendation
which we have bestowed upon Mr. Ruskin's style, and to expose irresistibly the glaring absurdity of applying to such
language the terms bombast or verbiage. We have bombast
when the sound far exceeds the sense, when the labor is
mountainous and the birth small, when the trumpet sounds
loud and the alms-deed is paltry; but, provided you watch
nature, you will find that your utmost effort and your
last word will be needed to paint her face, at once in the
grandeur of its expression and the definite truth of its
lines. We have verbiage, as we have already shown, when
there is an accumulation of words, and no picture formed
by their juxtaposition. There is no touch of bombast in
the description we have read, because there is no grandeur
added to the face of the world; and those glories of its
smiles or frowns, which would have struck other men into
impotent silence, are simply arrested and brought upon his

page for ever by Ruskin. To talk of verbiage is absurd,
because the vast picture is one clear indivisible whole,
and the man who cannot see it may never expect to derive
higher pleasure from poetic delineation than he receives
from a catalogue or a map. There is the revealing radiance
of a most noble imagination thrown over the whole scene,
and yet almost every word is scientifically precise; that
epithet, plumy, applied to a palm, is a picture in itself,
and no botanist could invent a more strictly correct term.

And this leads us to the grand fact which makes this
picture one actually characteristic of our century - the
union it exhibits of perfect knowledge with poetic beauty.
Every one must have read a certain number of those flights
or rides round the world which have been a favorite subject
with certain of our modern poets; and no one who has read
'Festus' can have forgotten that wild ride of the hero and
Lucifer round the world, upon the spirited horses Terror
and Darkness. But let them compare any of these with
Ruskin's picture, and say whether it is superior to the
latter, we say no in scientific truth, but in imaginative
beauty. We cannot survey that picture without, on the one
hand, knowing more than we ever did before of the actual
appearance of the world; and, on the other, having a more
intense feeling than ever before of its varied, yet symmetrical grandeur. And so it has been proved, that
nature's own beauty surpasses that which man in his ignorance of her could imagine; and yet that when man does
first reverently examine and accurately know the dwelling-
place which God has built for him, it is his kingly power
and privilege to cast over it a new mantle of uniting
beauty, woven by those sympathies and that imagination
which God has given him.

Had Ruskin lived in any former age, his fame would have
been established by his rarely wide sympathies and his
rarely powerful observation; but the nineteenth century
furnished him with a peculiar work, peculiar, at least, in
Britain, which he has accomplished in a way to make the
publication of his writings an epoch in our literature.
With the eye of Wilson and the sincerity of Carlyle, and
with a nature whose distinguishing characteristic is his
love of the beautiful in natural objects, he has a science
of which neither Wilson nor Carlyle has a trace. His works
are the vindication of his own grand principle, that
nature's loveliness can never be exhausted by science, and
show that, if the old poetry felt its inability to light
the new chambers of the world opened up by science, it was
that its torch was weak, and not that the chambers were
bare or prosaic. Science, determined of will, but with the
vision only of a miner, and a faint lamp that cast light

only on her own footsteps, indefatigably made her way into
caverned chambers unvisited before; she counted the gems
one by one, and said that they were severally more beautiful than those of which imagination had formerly dreamed.
Richter in Germany, and Ruskin, and, shall we add, Hugh
Miller, in Britain, took up boldly the torch of imagination, and entered those caverns with its irradiating
flame, and suddenly the whole kindled into one dazzling
blaze of gold veins and precious stones. But one thing now
remains: to throw over science the robe of music - to set
the knowledge of Ruskin to the melody of Shelley. This
has not yet been done; he who will do it, in the perfect
calmness of perfect power, will be the greatest poet that
ever lived. But we think we have shown that Ruskin
deserves the name of great.

We come now to the last and highest aspect of Ruskin's
character, to that all-pervading characteristic of his
writings to which most of all they owe their originality
and their worth. We no longer consider him intellectually;
we now regard his moral grandeur. The all-pervading characteristic to which we now call attention is his Christianity. Consider and understand this, and you have the key
to every thing in Ruskin's character and writings. Incapable, from earnestness and power of mind, to become a
mere collector, or admirer, or to shake away that intimation which is in the hearts of all men, but especially
in the hearts of such men as Ruskin, that he came into
this universe for some purpose, and not to grimace and sim-
per, and write honeyed or gilded twaddle, it was a necessity of his nature that he should find some sphere in which
he could work and feel as a man; all art he felt must be
flung aside, unless it could furnish him with this work.
The proclamation of the beautiful he did consider a work
worthy of a man, and he felt it was his mission to proclaim it. But he was a Christian, and, very originally,
one in deed and in truth, and not in mere name. He knew
that Christianity was simply all, or simply nothing; that
the belief that the breath of the One God is the life of
the world, and that this God is known to man by his Son,
must be a sham or futility, or must pervade every action
and feeling, professional as well as personal. From this
he starts; every consideration, metaphysical or practical,
he waives in the first instance, and looks upon nature as
David or Paul would have looked. 'Man's use and function,'
these are his words, '(and let him who will not grant me
this, follow me no farther, for this I purpose always to
assume,) are, to be the witness of the glory of God, and
advance that glory by his reasonable obedience.' It is
his first axiom, that 'God made the world;' it is his

second, that it is the beauty, as distinguished from the
utility, of nature that reveals Him; and so his mission
becomes clear to himself as that of a revealer to mankind
of that writing in which God, in nature, proclaims his
character and attributes. He disclaims proof of the being
of a God; we suppose he would say it was one of the direst
symptoms of the present age that there is so much said of
the proof of a God. In demonstration of his theory, that
the beauty of nature is the special revelation of God's
attributes, his grand argument, in general terms, is, that
in each phenomenon of that beauty there is a traceable
typifying of those attributes, and that there is no other
assignable cause for our delight, than that they tell us
of our God: his theory, we think, is confirmed by the universal instinct of humanity; for we suppose there is no
more reliable, as there is no more noble, instinct in man,
than that delighted awe with which he regards any display
of such beauty as is sublime, and that habit of connecting
such in all ages with the divine, which has clothed the
mythologies of paganism in such wonderful beauty.

When Ruskin casts his eye upon nature, he expects to see
spread over it the smile of his Father; and his duty to his
fellows he discerns to be, to lead them to unite with him
in some such apostrophic burst of admiration as the one
which, in the 'Excursion,' follows that revelation of God's
writing in the clouds, which he knows so well:-

Eternal Spirit! universal God!
Power inaccessible to human thought,
Save by degrees and steps, which Thou hast deign'd
To furnish: for this effluence of thyself,
To the infirmity of mortal sense
Vouchsafed - this local, transitory type
Of thy paternal splendors, and the pomp
Of those who fill thy courts in highest heaven,
The radiant cherubim - accept the thanks
Which we, thy humble creatures here convened,
Presume to offer; we who, from the breasts
Of the frail earth, permitted to behold
The faint reflections only of thy face,
Are yet exalted, and in soul adore!

We do not forget, in saying that Ruskin traces all
beauty in its essence to a reflection of the divine attributes, that one of the grand divisions of his system is entitled 'Vital Beauty,' and that it is defined as the felicitous fulfilment of vital functions. We begin to differ
from him, or at least to question, when we descend to matters of detail, and we imagine there is a defect in

clearness, if not in analysis, here; but we deem it unnecessary to insist upon this, or to depart from aught advanced above, since we doubt not that Ruskin would trace
vital beauty also to God, as the obscured trace of his
image, or the faint indication of his character. Thus we
find Ruskin's religion emphatically what Mr. Carlyle asserts it to be in every man, the determining point with regard to him. He considers it the glory of man to derive
enjoyment from the contemplation of that beauty which
whispers of his Creator, and, earnestly and lovingly watching nature, he endeavors to point out how each grand characteristic of nature is allied to, and unmistakably typical of, God's attributes. Disprove this to Ruskin, and he
would at once lay down his pen as a writer on art and
beauty; he would never condescend to pamper sickly tastes,
or to become a necromancer who charmed away ennui; a man's
life he must live: he must instruct and preach, or be
silent.

It is this which sheds such a hallowing light over every
work of Ruskin, and entitles him to so much higher commendation than if he were the mere propounder of some new
theory or method in art. It is this which makes his works
altogether priceless to those who love to meditate on the
ways of God to man, and the wonderful history and wonderful destiny of the human family. We know not how others
may have felt, but, for ourselves, we can honestly say,
that never, until we knew his works, could we conceive, so
fully as they revealed to us, the feelings with which Adam
in paradise, and the angels of God in heaven, look on God's
universe; we never till then saw so clearly the essentially
tainted condition of that nature, to which the excitements
of passion were so necessary to enjoyment, that the conception of any thing but ennui in Eden was impoosible; we
never until then formed so adequate an idea of the intensity of rapture with which a holy mind may gaze upon the
universe, knowing it to be wrapped in the light of God. To
indicate, though faintly, the regions of pure and beautiful
thought into which the influence of Christianity insensibly
leads Ruskin, we quote two short passages, which no one who
knows his writings will imagine to stand alone, or to be
especially beautiful. The first is on mental repose:-

[Quotes from 'But that which' to 'in the hand we hold',
'Works' 4: 116-17,]

The second is on the perpetual effect of the fall; we can
give only a mere segment of it:-

[Quotes from 'There is not any part' to 'brooding of their

kind wings', 'Works' 4: 186.]

We think we have vindicated our enthusiasm for Ruskin, and
established the fact that his powers are mighty and his
mission great. He loves nature with a love that reminds us
of Shelley, and knows her with a knowledge worthy of
Humboldt; he has shown that Poetry and Science are, after
all, sisters; and he has seen, what, alas! Shelley would
not see, that they both turn their faces upwards, that
light may fall upon them from the eye of God. With a valor
worthy of the ancient time, he has carried his faith into
every department of his character and his work; the
paganism that masks itself in the form of Christianity he
hates perfectly, and the old paganism which yet presumes
to prolong its unnatural and blasted existence, he smites
disdainfully aside; he is a Christian who has in some
measure discerned the radiance which Christianity reveals
in God's work, and who would carry its influence into every
province of human affairs. Truly it is consoling, at a
time when the eye that looks over the future is apt to grow
dim with tears, when religion, one may fear, is gradually
petrifying in the glance of Mammon, and deliberate atheism
is setting its death-cold hand upon philosophy and science,
to see this man of such vast sympathies, and such commanding powers, revealing the beautiful with such apocalyptic
powers, and yet, like John, lying humbly on the breast of
Jesus.

20. FROM AN UNSIGNED ARTICLE, 'FRASER'S MAGAZINE'

February 1854, vol. 49, 127-38

Although the plan of 'The Stones of Venice' is set out in
the concluding paragraphs of this excerpt, it will be seen
that the 'review' is essentially a discussion of Ruskin's
achievement to date from the perspective of a discerning
critic of the mid-fifties. See Introduction, p. 15.

...Perhaps the chief requisite in a writer is, a steadfast
determination to do all the good that he can, and a devotion of his best powers to the work. Without this determination, no great work ever was, or ever will be,
written. With it, combined with the feeling that the task
is worthy of great efforts, and the writer is called to it

by circumstances, much may be achieved even by inferior
powers.

It need hardly be said that - whatever may be thought
of Mr. Ruskin's temper and moderation - he possesses this
last qualification in the highest degree. Few persons have
it in their power to devote themselves as he has done for
the last ten or twelve years to the cause of art; no one
could have devoted himself more earnestly, or with a higher
conviction of the importance of the mission he was fulfill-
ing. When we also bear in mind Mr. Ruskin's high powers of
perception and imagination; the purity of his mind; his
fervent zeal for true religion and high morality; his love
of truth, and boldness in its cause; his antipathy to all
false seeming, even if it be sheltered under the wing of
authority; his knowledge of the main subject of which he
treats, and his determination to make it intelligible to
the most ignorant of his readers:- when we consider all
these qualifications in the writer, we cannot be surprised
at the position which his writings occupy, or grudge him
the pre-eminence which he holds over all writers upon art,
whom this country has produced. Mr. Ruskin's peculiarities
as a writer flow from his personal character, which shows
itself plain in the more important passages of his work.
Most of his predilections are already well known; - his
love of colour, and tendency towards symbolism in art, -
his preference of the physical sciences over scholastic
studies, as means for training and disciplining the mind, -
his admiration of Dante, Spenser, and Wordsworth, - his attention to minute points, which sometimes provokes a smile,
and makes us suspect the soundness of the writer's judgment
on points of greater interest. His method of dealing with
evidence is peculiar, and has not, so far as we know, been
noticed. He is in the habit of judging à *priori* of past
results; a habit which obliges him, in order to preserve
consistency, to allow of exceptions to the rules which he
lays down, so important, that it may be questioned whether
they are not of themselves sufficient to constitute the
rule. Mr. Ruskin defines this kind of evidence, which he
calls 'accidental,' as 'the testimony borne by particular
incidents and facts to a want of thought and feeling in
the builders, from which we conclude that their architecture must be bad.' This kind of à *priori* reasoning, based
on particular incidents, which may be misinterpreted by Mr.
Ruskin - for who can read the mind of every man in every
age? - we must be permitted to reject as a whole, and take
each case which the author brings forward into separate
consideration. It is the same kind of argument upon which
Mr. Ruskin has in a former work utterly condemned Domenichino as a painter, in spite of 'The Vision of St. Jerome,'

to which artists and amateurs still agree in assigning a
place among the noblest pictures in the world; and Greek
art generally, in spite of the Elgin marbles, which he himself allows are unsurpassed in design and execution.

Whilst we object to this kind of evidence being adduced
in support of Mr. Ruskin's opinions, we are disposed to
allow the greatest possible weight to the evidence drawn
from his own perceptive powers. Thus, when he tells us
that a thing is ugly, we have great reason to believe it
is so. Throughout the whole of the three volumes, neither
in the text nor the illustrations, can we find any exception to the general conclusion, that if any man's taste
may be relied upon as an unerring guide in art, it is Mr.
Ruskin's. Fortunately for his readers, he possesses
powers of writing fully equal to his powers of perception;
and, therefore, we may fairly reckon on his conveying to
us the same sensations which he experiences himself. It is
only when he is working out a particular theory that we
feel disposed to question his facts. In such cases we
should be unwilling to accuse him of *wilful* misrepresen-
tations even of the most trivial incidents; but we are of
opinion that he does occasionally distort facts, and must
be permitted to exercise our right of private judgment, and
add 'a grain of salt' when it appears necessary. If any
of our readers think we are at all hard upon Mr. Ruskin on
this point, we beg them to take the first volume of 'Modern
Painters' to the National Gallery, and compare the Claude
called 'The Marriage of Isaac and Rebecca' or 'Il Mulino,'
with our author's very amusing description of it; they will
thus be enabled to judge whether the above remark be true
or erroneous.

Mr. Ruskin's discussions on the philosophy of art are
full of originality and life. His analysis of the principles of Gothic architecture in vol. ii., chapter 6, is one
of the best specimens in the book. We shall recur to this
hereafter. Generally speaking, his philosophy is charac-
terized by the preponderance which he assigns to the moral
and perceptive over the intellectual and reflective faculties. In the discussion of the modes in which the Virtues
and the Vices have been severally represented (vol. ii.,
chap.8), this tendency of the author's mind fully displays
itself), - he has evidently more sympathy with poets than
with philosophers. Dante and Spenser are always right in
their delineations of the moral habits. Aristotle is always wrong: indeed, 'it is impossible to over-rate the mischief produced in former days, as well as in our own, by
the mere habit of reading Aristotle, whose system is so
false, so forced, and so confused, that the study of it at
our universities is quite enough to occasion the utter want

of accurate habits of thought, which so often disgraces men
otherwise well educated.' Yet Dante, the 'central man' -
i.e., the greatest poet and philosopher, of all the world,'
as Mr. Ruskin calls him, speaks of Aristotle as *Il gran
maestro di color, che sanno.* Which is the true view, that
of our author, or that of the great poet whom he regards as
the prophet and teacher of mediæval Europe? The two are,
indeed, hard to reconcile; but not more so than some of the
philosophical doctrines which occur in different parts of
the 'Stones of Venice,' and Mr. Ruskin's other works. For
instance, in 'Modern Painters' he states that the sublime is
not distinct from the beautiful. In the 'Stones of Venice'
he treats of the two as distinct from each other, - a doctrine which is more in accordance with the use of language,
and with the common feeling on the subject. On the whole,
we are inclined to think that Mr. Ruskin's claims to be
thought a philosopher are very slight, as he is deficient
in calmness and consistency; but that his love of all that
is beautiful in nature, and his sympathy with poets and
artists, in their aims to represent whatever is noble,
pure, and elevated, enable him to enter fully into the
heart and soul of poetry, and every branch of art; whilst
his powers of writing, joined to his half-intuitive, half-
acquired, knowledge, qualify him to stand forth as the
interpreter between the world of artists and his countrymen. The ground upon which he has taken his stand has
been occupied by Mr. Hazlitt alone of English critics; and
it is so broad and extensive a field, that it affords room
for as many as will take a similar line, and interpret the
works of man's hand by the manifestation of human thought
which they contain. He is far from arrogating to himself
the exclusive privilege of judging wisely of works of art;
on the contrary, he regards the æsthetic faculties as inherent in almost all men, and only requiring exercise. In
the body of his work he says to his readers, 'Come, and let
us reason together,' and not 'Come, and learn of me;' and
this modesty is the more remarkable as his acquantance with
the details of portions of his subject exceeds that of any
living man, and therefore qualifies him to speak with
authority. On the other hand, he has been accused, with
much show of reason, of dogmatism, and of condemning in
this place what he praises in that, on precisely the same
grounds. Thus, he is evidently possessed by a fixed idea
that the Venetian architects were devout men, and that
their devotion was expressed in their buildings; whilst he
will not allow our own cathedrals to have been built by any
but worldly men, who had no thoughts of heaven, but a vague
notion of keeping out of hell, by erecting costly places of
worship. Again, he praises the irregularity of the windows

in the Ducal Palace as showing 'true greatness of mind,'
whilst he condemns the middle arch of the west front of
Peterborough Cathedral being narrower than the others, as
a piece of 'destructive absurdity.' Truly, dogmatism is
dangerous to an honest and thoughtful man, as he is sure
to convict himself of inconsistencies. Let Mr. Ruskin be
content to leave it to people who depend upon others' eyes
and others' brains, and who fear to quit the beaten track
of respectable authorities.

Another objection that has been made to Mr. Ruskin's
writings is, that they exhibit too much self-consciousness
on the part of the writer. This is a venal fault in an insignificant writer, or even in a writer of Mr. Ruskin's
ability, when he is dealing with light subjects. Nay, in
some cases it is amusing, as showing a naïve simplicity of
character; as in the childish pleasure which the author
took in the accidental resemblance between his own name and
that of the architect who pleaded for the maintenance of
the ancient fabric of the Ducal Palace. In other cases it
is not inconsistent with true dignity of character, as in
the instance where Mr. Ruskin declares that he is not the
enemy, but the friend, of true architects.

If I could obtain the public ear, and the principles I
have advocated were carried into general practice, porphyry and serpentine would be given them instead of
limestone and brick; instead of tavern and shop fronts,
they would have to build goodly churches and noble
dwelling-houses; and for every stunted Grecian and
stucco Romanism, in which they are now forced to shape
their palsied thoughts, and to whose crumbling plagi-
arisms they must trust their doubtful fame, they would
be asked to raise whole streets of bold, and rich, and
living architecture, with the certainty in their hearts
of doing what was honourable to themselves, and good
for all men.

Mr. Ruskin writes here as an enthusiast, and passes out
of himself; and he therefore commands, if not our belief,
at least our sympathy. This is not the case in passages
which are, unhappily, too numerous; where he returns to
himself – to what he has before said, or to what has been
said of him. One instance of the former kind is his recurrence, with avowed satisfaction, to an expression which
occurs in the first volume. 'The Renaissance frosts came,
and all perished.' The poet Wordsworth used sometimes to
try our patience by telling us how he came by an idea; but
he never went beyond this, to the extent of telling us
what a good idea it was, and he had no notion he was so

clever. References to newspaper or other criticisms are
frequently in the appendices. For a specimen of one, in
which a feeling of self exhibits itself under the most
peevish and undignified aspect, we may refer to the third
volume of folio illustrations, letterpress to plate 12,
where Mr. Ruskin says, in answer to a mistaken *Tu quoque*'
of a newspaper critic, who hanged Calendario as a counterpart to the transportation of Leopardo, the architect of
the Vendramin's tomb:- 'Thus I have the trouble of gathering facts, and putting them in their true light, merely
that English reviewers may run their pens through them,
and blot them back into unintelligibility.' It is with
real pain that we see such exhibitions of infirmity of
temper in a writer of such great powers. But, it may be
asked, where is an instance to be found of an author who
forgets himself, and thinks only of his subject? Alas,
it must be confessed, there are very few to be found in
Christian times. Dante's great poem is full of allusions
to himself; yet, no one can find fault with the person
who tells us of a vision, which he has seen, if he describe his own sensations, or allude to the circumstances
of his life. The poets of the Elizabethan era were far
from being self oblivious. They had always a very distinct
sense of their existence, and of their prospects of getting
on at court. Spenser, in the Preface to the 'Faerie Queen,'
addresses Queen Elizabeth as a goddess; and Shakespeare, in
the most imaginative of his plays, 'Midsummer Night's
Dream,' takes occasion to compliment the 'Virgin Queen.'
Act ii., sc. 1,

Yet marked I where the bolt of Cupid fell.

And Cranmer's speech, at the close of 'Henry VIII.,' is
couched in less mistakable language. Neither does Milton
lose himself in his subject. Where shall we look? Where
but to old Homer, and Æschylus, and Sophocles, and Plato,
and Thucydides, who stand conspicuous for the pure light
in which they exhibit the actions and thoughts of men, a
light which as little resembles the self-created atmosphere
of modern writers, as the sky of Greece resembles the sky
of London, as yet unpurified by Lord Palmerston. If Mr.
Ruskin would study these heathen writers more carefully, he
would learn at least one lesson, how to make the most of
his subject without bringing in himself. If he would do
so, his pages would not lose in interest, whilst they would
gain in dignity.
Another failing of our author is one which was glaringly
apparent in 'Modern Painters,' and which diminishes the
pleasure with which we read his last production, namely, -

conceit: an apparent belief that he is qualified to instruct the world, on all subjects. Now if we allow Mr. Ruskin's superior knowledge and taste in matters of art, that is all he has a right to require. He cannot expect that we should listen to him on subjects with which he is slightly acquainted. Yet if he were not possessed with the idea that he was competent to teach all men all things, he would have spared us a great deal of extraneous matter, which serves no purpose but that of swelling the bulk of his book....

We believe that, on many points, Mr. Ruskin is the victim of self-deception. He inveighs in several parts of his work against systematizing, and makes 'the pride of system' one of the causes of corruption in architecture. It is curious that, with his professed scorn of systematizing, he should indulge in it to so great an extent. Any one who runs his eyes over 'Modern Painters,' the 'Seven Lamps of Architecture,' or the 'Stones of Venice,' will see that the author arranges and tickets everything. According to him, the cry which arises from our manufacturing population is to be answered and met by the observance of *three* rules. The civil laws of our country have just *two* objects. Gothic architecture is composed of *six* moral elements: the Renaissance architecture of *two* exceedingly immoral elements – the first of the two is divided into *three* parts. Men who take recreation are of *four* kinds, one kind being those who play not at all. These are only a few instances taken from the 'Stones of Venice'; but they are sufficient to show the writer's habit.

So, too, of rhetoric, Mr. Ruskin professes a sovereign contempt:-

The study of rhetoric (he says) is exclusively one for men who desire to deceive or be deceived; he who has the truth at his heart need never fear the want of persuasion on his tongue, or, if he fear, it is because the base rhetoric of dishonesty keeps the truth from being heard.

Yet he commonly employs some of its least creditable artifices. Every one knows how much a description of an object depends upon the choice of epithets. Take the instance of the Doge Vendramin's tomb, which is considered the chef d'œuvre of Renaissance sculpture. Mr. Ruskin says, 'the subject of its chiselmanship consists of fat-limbed boys sprawling on dolphins, dolphins incapable of swimming, and dragged along the sea by expanded pocket-handkerchiefs.' Had this been a Gothic tomb we should have had a very different, though perhaps a less amusing

description. The case of the Chigi Claude, 'il Mulino,'
already quoted from 'Modern Painters,' is no less to the
point.

Some of the lighter qualifications in a writer Mr.
Ruskin possesses in a high degree; his fancy is inexhaus-
tible, his wit at times very diverting, nor is he destitute
of genuine humour. This is a point which he appreciates in
his own countrymen, a circumstance which deserves our
notice, as he does not regard with favourable aspect either
the times or the country in which his lot has been cast.

His love for symbolism has been alluded to before, and
instances of it must be familiar to all his readers.
Whether symbolism be inseparable from *religion*, as Mr.
Ruskin seems to think, or not, we cannot doubt of its being
an important element in *art*. Indeed, it is impossible to
conceive of the highest ends of art being attained by entire realisation. We cordially agree with our author in
'wishing back in the menagerie' the hairy and well-
whiskered lions that a Renaissance sculptor placed on the
steps of the west front of the cathedral at Genoa. We are
aware that symbolism is often carried to an extravagant
pitch; and we are far from asserting that Mr. Ruskin always
keeps within the bounds of moderation in this respect; but,
as critics are never wanting to point out such trans-
gressions, and to give a ludicrous turn to what is in itself noble, we shall abstain from any similar remark,
thinking, with Mr. Ruskin, that 'it is difficult to calcu-
late the harm' that jesters do, by 'destroying the reverence' for things that are important and true; and that
'we do infinite mischief by exposing weakness to eyes
which cannot comprehend greatness.'

It is only when our author ceases to be intelligible
that we feel disposed to quarrel with him, and to complain
that, whereas we want connected thoughts, he gives us words
and sentences, which, taken by themselves - like the masses
of colour in Turner's later pictures - are very striking,
but which transcend our utmost endeavours to extract any
sense out of them. In the following extract we believe
that Mr. Ruskin is desirous of proving that those persons
are mistaken who think the Venetian character is fairly represented by the Venentian carnival, or by those globes of
coloured glass which lie about in our drawing-rooms. But
it is difficult to trace the connexion between the simple
thought and the highly coloured language.

[Quotes from 'That mighty landscape' to 'painted upon the
cloud', 'Works' 10: 178-9.]

We do not question the eloquence of this passage, but

we would plead the weakness of human faculties of comprehension, and request that Mr. Ruskin, when he wants to
leave a truth impressed upon his readers' minds, should reduce it to a less transcendental shape, and prove it by
less ambiguous language.

This brings us to the consideration of Mr.Ruskin's style,or
the expression of those faculties and habits of mind which we
have endeavoured to trace, as gathered from his writings.
It is common to hear him spoken of as a great master
of language. Let us see how far this epithet is justified.
It would be absurd to speak of his style as we should of
Milton's, or Addison's, or Walter Savage Landor's, or
Macaulay's, or that of any other great writer of English
prose, because it exhibits every kind of variety, according, it would appear, to the humour in which the writer is.
Sometimes it is clear, concise, and suited to the conveying
of instruction. At other times it is misty, verbose, and
tending to obliterate whatever ideas the reader may happen
to possess, without giving him any new ones. However much
we owe in other respects to Mr. Ruskin, he does not do well
in encouraging by his example a great fault of our day, -
much talking. Men commonly talk more than they think, and
far more than they act; their fine theories and good intentions evaporate in many words, and they imagine they have
done a great deal when they have talked a great deal.
Speech is silver, but silence is golden. It is a good
thing to know when to cease writing, as well as when to
write, and Mr. Ruskin does not always put in practice this
knowledge, till he has drawn out his arguments to such a
length that they become weak. They would be much strengthened if he would prune their luxuriant tendrils, sending
back their pith into the main branches of his discourse.
In the best parts of the 'Stones of Venice' the language is
full of thought, and faithfully and adequately expresses
the ideas intended to be conveyed. In other parts there is
an apparent attempt to make language perform two functions,
- that of conveying thought and that of impressing the mind
with its own power. This attempt shows itself in luxuriant
periods, in redundancy of epithets, and especially in the
use of alliteration. It is not too much to say that in
some passages the sense seems completely lost sight of, the
writer's clearness of perception being dazzled, as that of
his readers must be, by the brilliancy of the language
which he employs. Thus he talks of Venice as 'a city which
was to write her history on the white scrolls of the sea
surges, and to word it in their thunder, and to gather and
give forth in world-wide pulsation the glory of the West
and East, from the burning heart of her fortitude and splendour.' This passage may be very taking to people who are

caught with the sound of words; but there is very little
definite meaning in it. One great characteristic of the sea
is, that it retains no impression on its waves, and tells no
history of the past. It is a great pity that Mr. Ruskin
should give way to faults which any one can see, and which
he would not venture to defend. Some of his criticisms on
the style of authors are among the best that we remember
to have seen; and we need seek for no severer condemnation
of the vices which mar the excellence of his style than
that which his own pages furnish. It remains to be seen
whether he will submit to be judged as he has judged
others. On his candour and fairness of mind in this respect depends his position as a truly great writer of English prose.

Mr. Ruskin's eloquence and power of description are well
known. The reputation which his earlier works won for him
for these rare qualities has not suffered by the appearance
of the 'Stones of Venice.' Rather, we should say, he has
surpassed expectation in the vivid and gorgeous descriptions of Venice in his second volume, and in the thoughtful
and eloquent passages which occur at the beginning and end
of his first, and here and there in his third volume. One
of the most striking among many striking passages is the
following description of the struggle between the old Faith
and the new at the Reformation:-

[Quotes from 'Here was at last' to 'against each other',
'Works' 10: 123-4.]

We shall have occasion hereafter to make some remarks on
the view that Mr. Ruskin takes of the Reformation. Here we
are only viewing him as a writer of English prose, and surely no
one will deny to the above passage the praise due to vivid imagination, and a vigour and beauty of expression unsurpassed, almost unequalled, in the English language. Among the most vivid
and truthful of our author's descriptions is that of the English
Cathedral, vol. ii. ch. 4. Its quiet tone forms a striking
contast to the gorgeous description of St. Mark's Place
which follows, and which recalls forcibly to our mind some
of Turner's pictures. There is the same fulness of imagination, the same 'confusion of delight,' conveyed in language which by its beauty and indistinctness reminds us of
the colours and of the handling of the great painter.

The eloquence which pervades this noble description is
sustained throughout a great portion of the second volume.
The interior of St. Mark's, the Ducal Palace, in fact all
the principal features of Venice, are described by Mr.
Ruskin as no pen has ever painted them before. His genius
enables him to penetrate to the very heart and soul of

nature and of art, whilst his imagination lends reality to
the forms, which rise up before his mind, and claim to be
represented in words that may move the hearts of men. As
a specimen of a passage where vigour of imagination and
descriptive power are combined to present a series of pictures to the mind's eye, we should select the bird's-eye
panorama of the earth's surface. It is well when these excellencies are combined by our author, without redundance.
That is a fault to which he is prone. He does not know
when to leave a subject, when to act on the precept *'manum
de tabulâ.'* If he would furnish, in his own writings, a
practical illustration of the excellent principles laid
down in the concluding chapter of his third volume, his
words would have more weight, and he would not be accused
of 'riding his hobby to death,' a trite way of expressing
what we must allow to be the fact, that Mr. Ruskin is sometimes carried away by his enthusiasm, beyond the bounds of
truth and common sense. His peculiar charm, as a writer,
lies quite as much in what he suggests as what he proves to
his readers. In some of his least prominent remarks lie
the germs of noble thoughts, which take deep root in the
mind, and bear fruit afterwards. We should remember this,
and let our censure be tempered with gratitude.

Mr. Ruskin has a tendency to excess not only in quantity, but in quality. In other words, he is much given to
exaggeration. This is but the outward expression of that
vehement and impatient spirit which, as we said before, is
often found in great reformers. Our author occasionally
resembles the Turkish artillerymen, who, on a recent occasion, as we are informed, after expending their ammunition
with good effect on the Russian army, flung bullets in the
faces of the Cossack horsemen, who charged up to the mouths
of their guns. Such, for instance, is the following petu-
lant denunciation of the window in the side of the arch,
under the Wellington-statue, next St. George's Hospital:-
'The richness upon the ornament is a mere patch and erup-
tion upon the wall, and one hardly knows whether to be most
irritated at the affectation of severity in the rest, or at
the vain luxuriance of the dissolute parallelogram.'

But the gleaning of the first and second volume is, in
respect of exaggeration, nothing in comparison with the harvest of the third. For, in that volume, the author goes
forth in the true spirit of an orthodox Jew, to break down
all the symbols of idolatrous worship, with axe and hammer.
He has to humble the pride of Renaissance architecture, and
he is not careful by what means this is to be accomplished.
What wonder if like 'vaulting ambition,' he should sometimes 'o'erleap himself and fall on the other?'

Yet as something is to be learned from the errors of

earnest and zealous men, who go beyond the truth, so we
may extract from Mr. Ruskin's extravagance, sound and
wholesome doctrine. Although we may reasonably think that
he outsteps the mark, in denouncing Pride of Science, Pride
of State, and especially Pride of System, under which head
he tells us that 'there is not a side chapel in any Gothic
cathedral, but it has fifty orders, the worst of them
better than the best of the Greek ones, and all new; and a
single inventive human soul could create 1000 orders in an
hour.' (16¾ per minute!) yet it will be found that there
is much good corn under the overwhelming heap of chaff,
which, in this volume, is piled up to gigantic proportions;
and it will be our endeavour, in dealing with the matter of
the book, briefly to set this forth.

Another fault which Mr. Ruskin has is love of digression. As we have above intimated that he is more of an
artist and poet than of a philosopher, it is not to be wondered at, if we should assert him to be deficient in 'the
logical and sequential faculties,' which, he justly says,
are the heritage of the man whom God intends for a student.
To many persons the charm of Mr. Ruskin's book will not be
diminished by the author's rambling propensities; but to
serious men, who like to see the subject taken in hand
fairly worked out, the frequent interruptions in the thread
of the argument cannot but be a source of dissatisfaction
and regret. Much of the matter, especially in vol. iii.,
is wholly irrelevant to the subject, and only introduced
to illustrate some favourite theory of the author. We are
constantly hurried away from the streets of Venice, to
listen to discussions on education, and on various religious and social questions of the day, on which Mr.
Ruskin has opinions - as who has not? And, as reading is,
after all, a mechanical process, we are called upon to exercise more attention, and work our eyes for a longer time
than, we humbly submit, the author has a right to demand;
to say nothing of our judgment being held so long in sus-
pense, that, without a memory like that of Mr. Macaulay,
or clearness of head like that of Lord Lyndhurst, it is
very difficult to connect the head with the tail of an argument. We shall presently consider some of the points
upon which Mr. Ruskin diverges from his main channel. It
is now time that we should pass on to the general drift
and purport of the work.

The three volumes of the 'Stones of Venice' contain -

1. A record of the present and former beauty of Venice
(descriptive and historical).

2. Instruction in the principles of architecture (demonstrative and exegetical).

3. An inquiry into the nature of the three kinds of

architecture found at Venice, joined with an attack on
Renaissance (critical and polemical).

4. Denunciations of various real or imaginary evils of
the day (polemical and discursive).

With respect to the first of these heads, it need
scarcely be said, that any attempt made to save from oblivion the records of Venetian power before the sea waves
have destroyed them, deserves our acknowledgments. The
greater the powers employed in the work, the more lively
must be our feelings of gratitude: and therefore, all persons who, from associations connected with the historic
past, or their own experience of Venice in the nineteenth
century, feel interest in a city which once occupied so
large a space in the eyes of Europe, and is now so beautiful in the decay of her splendour:- the historian, the
poet, the artist, the moralist, - all must feel deeply
grateful to Mr. Ruskin for the pictures of Venetian heroism, Venetian devotion, Venetian power, and Venetian pride,
that his pen has drawn, and for the specimens of the far-
famed architecture of the Queen of the Adriatic, which his
taste has selected, and his pencil delineated.

On the second head we will quote Mr. Ruskin's own words,
showing both what he has attempted, and the reason which
induced him to do so; and we are bound, in justice to the
author and to our own feelings, to express our cordial sympathy with the object of this part of his work, which is,
to lay down a law, based on such principles as shall be intelligible to every one, according to which the merits of
architectural works shall be judged. He may well say, 'I
believe that most of my readers will at once admit the
value of a criterion of right and wrong, in so practical
and costly an art as architecture; and will be apt rather
to doubt the possibility of its attainment than dispute its
usefulness if attained.' How great a necessity there was
for such an attempt is very well shown by a quotation Mr.
Ruskin gives from an architectural review, which says of
St. Mark's:-

'Mr. Ruskin thinks it a very beautiful building: we
think it a very ugly building.' I was not surprised at
the difference of opinion, but at the theory being considered so completely a subject of opinion. My opponents
is painting always assume that there is such a thing as
a law of right, and that I do not understand it; but my
architectural adversaries appeal to no law, they simply
set their opinion against mine; *and indeed there is no
law at present* to which they or I can appeal. I set myself, therefore, to establish such a law, in full belief
that men are intended, without difficulty, and by use of

their general common sense, to know good things from
bad; and that it is only because they will not be at
the pains required for the discernment, that the world
is so widely encumbered with forgeries and basenesses.

The greater part of the first volume is taken up with an
analysis of the principal features of constructive and
decorative architecture; to use Mr. Ruskin's words, 'he has
endeavoured to arrange those foundations of criticism on
which he is to rest in his account of Venetian architecture.' To persons already conversant with the principles
of architecture, it may appear at first sight unnecessary
for the author to go into such elementary matters; but he
professes to write for the instruction of those who never
thought of architecture before; and, truly, a most excellent grammar of the art does this volume present. It is
all the better for general readers, in that it is free
from technicalities. It assumes nothing, and gives the
rationale of everything. A strong love of systematizing
runs through the whole: the plan of the work is simple, and
the carrying out conscientious and good. Some of the illustrations will appear fanciful: but, whenever they are
not drawn from man's work, they are from God's work; and
this, however unusual it may be in treating of architecture, will hardly be thought a fault. Nay, we think Mr.
Ruskin deserves our thanks for pointing out a few of
those instances where the hand of God has given to natural
objects a grandeur, or a grace and delicacy, of which art
can only be a humble imitator.
Having established certain principles of criticism,
equally applicable to all architecture, our author proceeds to apply them to the styles prevalent at Venice, Byzantine, Gothic, and Renaissance. His method is at once
historical, critical, and explanatory. He traces the
origin, the progress, and decline of each style; he inves-
tigates the principles upon which their excellences and
short-comings, or faults, severally depend: and he explains
his meaning throughout by references to examples, and by
illustrations taken from his own drawings.
For the complete view taken of the subject, and for the
able and conscientious way in which the details are carried
out, Mr. Ruskin deserves the thanks of the antiquary, the
man of taste, and the student of architecture. The first
of these may well feel grateful for the record which Mr.
Ruskin has preserved of that style of architecture - Byzantine - which is associated with our earliest traditions of
Christian art. The man of refined taste has reason to hail
with satisfaction the completion of a work in which so true
a perception of what is beautiful in art is combined with

knowledge so accurate, and illustrated by engravings, the
execution of which is for the most part delicate and
beautiful, conveying a very favourable impression of the
original drawings. These are, doubtless, better represented in the folio illustrations, which give on a larger
scale some of the details of the architecture of Venice
to which Mr. Ruskin especially refers. Three volumes
have already appeared, and it is to be regretted that this
work, owing to the expense of publication, should be for
the present abandoned. Lastly, the student of architecture
will find the principles which are laid down in the first
volume applied in the second and third, to the three styles
of architecture above mentioned. He will thus learn the
value of what he has been taught, and will be induced to
make a similar application of the knowledge he has acquired.

Combined with criticism on Byzantine, Gothic and Renaissance architecture, we have a good deal of skirmishing
against debased forms of the two latter, terminating in a
grand attack against Renaissance. For this attack Mr.
Ruskin has, it must be owned, sufficient cause. Whatever
good the revival of the study of Gothic architecture may
have done to our churches, it has not been applied to our
streets. Our author appeals to the common sense as well as
to the taste of his countrymen, in favour of a style which
is much more in accordance with Northern tastes than the
imported architecture of Greece and Italy. He exhorts them
to use their own eyes, and not to be led captives by con-
ventionalism; to exercise in domestic architecture the same
judgment which they have already employed - to an insufficient extent it must be owned - in church architecture;
and not to deny themselves the natural sense of enjoyment
which buildings of picturesque and convenient structure -
of however small dimensions they may be - convey to the eye
of the beholder.

The fourth divison can hardly be looked upon as coming
within the scheme of the book. Some of the points upon
which Mr. Ruskin diverges from his subject would find their
place within a work written upon 'The principles and
present condition of the Fine Arts;' such as the philosophy
of art; the relation of science to art; the influence of
the study of anatomy, aërial perspective, &c. Others,
such as the pursuit of knowledge, national education, the
effects of the Reformation, &c., deserve no place either
in the 'Stones of Venice,' or in any work of which the
avowed subject is art. Mr. Ruskin's ambition to reform all
the evils of the day, as well as those with which he is
most conversant, leads him to outstep the natural boun-
daries of his subject, just as Mr. Cobden was led away,
after his great financial and commercial scheme had been

carried, to indulge in prophecies relating to the political state of Europe, which the events of a few months
proved to be nugatory. Mr. Ruskin - who avows himself a
free-trader - should take warning by the example of the
man to whose exertions we mainly owe Free-trade, the principle of which is not 'unrestricted competition' (as Mr.
Disraeli would tell him), with all the world in *every
article* - but only in those branches of *mental* as well as
manual industry, in which our habits of thought and application enable us to compete with advantage.

   As many of these subjects are - although not connected
with architecture - of great importance and interest, we
shall reserve them for future consideration. At present
we must content ourselves with having examined Mr. Ruskin's
characteristics as a man and a writer, as gathered from his
works, and with having given a sketch of the general plan
of the 'Stones of Venice.'

21. HENRY FOTHERGILL CHORLEY, FROM AN UNSIGNED REVIEW,
'EDINBURGH REVIEW'

April 1856, vol. 103, 535-57

Henry Fothergill Chorley (1808-72) was primarily a music
critic for the 'Athenaeum' and 'The Times'. He also tried
his hand at the novel, verse, drama, and various libretti.
Chorley's 'Autobiography, Memoir and Letters' (ed.
H.G. Hewlett) appeared in 1873. See Introduction, p. 15.

It has been noted by physicians that such epidemics as
plague, or falling sickness, or nervous distemperature, on
every new recurrence, seize hold of some class or susceptible persons not attacked by them when disease last
made its round; but, during one visitation the malady will
be more fatal than during another, by reason of this very
change in the victims of the infection. The remark holds
good if applied to literature. Convulsions there must be,
so long as the Poet's imagination is liable to disorders,
- so long as the Professor's brain is accessible to vanity.
But when the convulsionary spirit passes from those who
create to those who teach, the malady assumes its most
malignant form, and engenders evils which it may take a
century to eradicate. A 'Werter,' a 'Nouvelle Héloïse,'
or any other morbid romance, does its immediate work of

harm by exciting the passions; but its influence may at
any moment be superseded by some such simple and healthy
writer as Scott - more able than Goethe or Rousseau to
enthral millions, without quickening a single unwholesome
appetite. Longer-lived may be the influence of the pulpit,
when fanaticism by way of faith, and dogmatism in place of
research, are recommended by theatrical gestures and declamatory periods. False taste in poetry or in art is bad;
but false deduction in history and false doctrine in criticism, are the worst of all. So far as Painting is concerned, we seem to be passing through such a period of
false and superficial pedantry under the disguise of
superior attainments and infallible authority. The right
of imagination to confound terms and of self-will to fling
out new definitions has been asserted with a rhapsodical
fluency which has taken modest persons by storm. They have
been stunned into submission while the teacher of principles has maintained that a series of contradictory paradoxes comprised the one saving consistency which is to re-
generate Art. They have been bidden to prove their
humility by a total surrender of the functions of memory.
But the frenzy has reached - possibly has passed - its
crisis; and Mr. Ruskin must forgive us if we deal with his
vaticinations as if they were amenable to the laws of common sense, and proceed to examine some of his claims to be
a master in Israel.

This third volume of 'Modern Painters,' if viewed in
context with its writer's former works, shows the extent
to which excessive pretensions and imperfect acquirements
have bewildered and corrupted a mind rich in ingenious
knowledge of detail, and gifted with rhetorical powers
which ought, if better guided, to have done service to the
study and philosophy of Art. If we examine how far, in
Mr. Ruskin's writings, desire for display has superseded
the love of truth, the task is entered on, not because it
is agreeable, but because it is seasonable. After having
made a fame, by hanging on to the skirts of a famous
artist - after deluding those craving for novelty into the
belief that a dashing style must imply precious discoveries - after having met the humour of the time, by
preaching the religion of architecture with a freedom in
the use of sacred names and sacred things from which a more
reverential man would have shrunk - after having served as
an eloquent though too flattering guide to the treasures
of Venice, - after having enriched the citizens of this
Scottish metropolis with receipts how to amend the architecture of our city by patching Palladian squares, streets,
and crescents with Gothic windows, balconies, and pinnacles, - after having lectured to decorators on the beauty

and virtue of painting illegible letters on signboards and
shop-fronts, - the wisdom of Mr. Ruskin has of late begun
to cry in the streets. He attempts to erect the most extravagant paradoxes into new canons of taste; and the
virulence of his personality is only exceeded by the eccentricity of his judgment. He now periodically enters the
exhibition-room as an overseer, summoning gallery-loungers
to stand and deliver their sympathies, - calling on bad
painters to tremble, - and assailing those whom he dislikes
with menaces and insults. Thus in the third edition of his
Royal Acadamy *vade mecum* for 1855, after having referred to
a former vituperation of a picture by Mr. Roberts, -

'I have great personal regard for Mr. Roberts,' says our
Oracle, 'but it may be well to state at once, that whenever
I blame a painting, I do so as gently as is consistent with
just explanation of its *principal* defects. I never say half
of what I could say in its disfavour; and it will hereafter
be found, that when once I have felt it my duty to attack a
picture, the worst policy which the friends of the artist
can possibly adopt will be to defend it.'

Absurd and impertinent as this language is, especially
when addressed to artists who do not owe their fame to Mr.
Ruskin's favour, it is worth while to inquire what right
he has to use it. It may be conceded that few English
writers have devoted themselves to the literature of Art,
who have been more richly gifted by nature than Mr. Ruskin.
He has that warmth of admiration which is eminently quickening to the spirits of colder pilgrims; he has that
brightness of imagination which enables him to seize what
is subtle in intention, and to comprehend what is noble in
design. He commands an expressive style - fluent, versatile, and sonorous in no common degree. He can allow for
the varying relations which exist betwixt art and society.
Mr. Ruskin, too, has wrought industriously, travelled far,
seen much, collected largely. These are precious attributes and qualifications; yet rarely has the value of
such gifts been more completely neutralised than in the
case of the author of 'Modern Painters.' Rarely has
vanity, so overweening in stature, so unblushing in front,
so magisterial in language, risen up between a writer and
his public. That the praise of others has encouraged this
tone proves the weakness of the apostle, as much as the
credulity of his auditory. There is much of folly and of
fashion in all similar epidemics of admiration; but there
is something, also, more generous than mere folly. The
persons of quality who swooned and fainted on the pulpit-
stair at Hatton Garden while Irving held forth during what
Dr. Chalmers called 'his exhausting services,' must not
bear the whole blame of Irving's aberrations and

eccentricities.   There lurked in the preacher's mind -
there must lurk in the minds of all belonging to the
school to which he belonged, and to which Mr. Ruskin belongs, including Poets, Critics, or Social Reformers - a
morbid avidity for immediate effect, for immediate recognition, for immediate adulation, which becomes absolutely
poisonous, - and poisonous to none more than to the Professors or Preachers themselves, since it destroys in them
not only the will, but even the power of being truthful.

It is necessary - to avoid the imputation of unjust
severity - to recapitulate some facts of our author's past
career. Mr. Ruskin, after having made himself favourably
known as a writer of fugitive verse, was tempted into his
first emission of prose in the hope, he says, 'of compelling the English public to do honour to an English painter
of genius,' who had not received his just dues. There
may be generosity in such a case of officious advocacy, if
the advocate does not, by way of advertising his own
tropes and metaphors, take up a cause which stands in no
need of it. But, strange as it may seem to Mr. Ruskin,
Turner had his English appreciators and his English public
previous to the year 1843. There were persons who delighted not in Turner's oil paintings only, but in his
drawings, which our author eulogises with such commendable
warmth.... There was no cruel neglect of Turner before Mr.
Ruskin rose to protect him; there was much toleration for
his visions and eccentricities. This was extended to him
long before Turner had a champion; and although Turner
may owe something to so fervent a disciple as Mr. Ruskin,
Mr. Ruskin owes a great deal more to the celebrity he had
contrived to borrow from so great an artist as Turner.

After this fashion has been the progress of Mr. Ruskin
as a writer on Art. His next device was to transfer to
the newest eccentricity of the day - that of what are
called the Pre-Raphaelites - the devotion he had hitherto
paid to a Painter who was not only their superior but their
opposite. But the real direction and consequence of such
efforts cannot be for ever disguised by the most adroit
master of rhapsody, let him be ever so able to amuse his
readers, and to keep them from thinking. When the excitement of novelty has subsided, even the most stupid of
those who have been commanded to believe will find a spirit
of inquiry stir, and the faculties of comparison awaken.
And thus students of Painting will not, because it is Mr.
Ruskin's pleasure, receive Turner's scenic effects, and
the finish of the Pre-Raphaelites as the growth of the same
tree, as illustrations of the same system. They will not
consent to denounce all Greek architecture as base, dis-
gusting, utterly to be scouted from earth, with all its

dependencies and descendants, when they recollect that it
was on Greek forms that the mediaeval builders based their
edifices, and from Greek fragments and materials that they
drew their first examples of decoration. They will ask how
far it is just that a censor, who in some cases adduces
every exception as an example, every blemish as a beauty,
and every irregularity as a sign of enterprise, in others
shall denounce the smallest deficiencies as damnatory of
those who exhibit them. - They may inquire, for instance,
how an arbiter of taste, who finds the festoon and garland
decorations of the Palladian architecture abominable because
they are not natural, can delight in the pillars supporting
porches and resting on the backs of couchant animals, which
flank so many a mediaeval door-way. Nor will honest persons
rest till they have endeavoured to ascertain how far all
these contradictory prejudices can be reconciled; how far
they are based on a burning desire to surprise and to over-
rule - how far on the love of Truth - how far on the knowledge of it. We have no doubt as to the result of such inquiries. The strange assumption and inaccuracy of Mr. Ruskin as an oracle of Art will become clearly evident even to
those who recognise his industry in collecting detail, his
ingenuity in finding a reason for everything that it suits
his whim to invent, and the poetry of language with which
he embellishes what he attempts to describe.

But all who desire to be taught have a right to claim
from those who profess to teach them, besides the name of
Truth, something of its nature - truth in research - truth
in definition - truth in reasoning - truth in interpretation. That these things go far to make up truth in belief, few of those who are the most profoundly impressed
with mortal fallibility will dispute. Hence, in proportion as the cry of Truth is raised by the empiric to
justify paradox, to excuse license, to accredit insolence,
in so much is the wrong done cruel. But the offence is
common, and profitable. The most unscrupulous persons are
the noisiest in assuring mankind of their scrupulosity.
Who are so hypocritical as those whose lips overflow with
the profession of sincerity? Who are so inexact as the
dogmatists, who *not* having satisfied themselves by warrant-
able means, choose that no subsequent inquirer shall be
able to ascertain on what *data* they rest their conclusions? No one has ever exposed his claims to truthfulness to a sterner examination than Mr. Ruskin; since rarely
has the serviceable cry been raised more loudly than by
him, whether to authenticate the examples he has collected,
to recommend the principles he expounds, or to praise the
artists whom he delights to honour - 'He will not' (he
says) 'put forth an example of Raphael's tree-work without

having copied the trees leaf for leaf.' He will not defend the irregularities on the *façade* of Pisa Cathedral,
without having precisely counted the arches in each arcade.
He does not specify merely the coloured marbles which har-
moniously encrust a Murano achivolt, but he calls attention to the very spots in some of the fragments. The
speciousness of such professed accuracy is calculated to
inspire confidence and to discourage all counter-
examination. Yet those who rely on Mr. Ruskin's precision
of detail will receive severe shocks when they come to
test it precisely....

Here is a second passage concerning truth in Art, by
aid of which anything may be rejected, or everything
accepted, according as the truth-lover is in a critical or
credulous humour.

'There are some truths,' says Mr. Ruskin, 'easily obtained, which give a deceptive resemblance to nature:
others, only to be obtained with difficulty, which cause
no deception, but give inner and deep resemblance.'

The convenience of this theory of inner and deep resemblance need scarcely be pointed out, since it invests the
seer with full power to pierce where others cannot enter,
- to decide where simpler observers doubt, - to assume or
lay aside authority in proportion as his tendencies are
peaceful or warlike.

Many more such elastic definitions of truth will be
found under the section Sincerity, in the chapter On the
Real Nature of Greatness of Style, by a skilfil application of which the most glaring infidelity might receive
canonisation, and the deepest ignorance pass for wisdom.
Having recommended them to the attention of those who
imagine that language was given for the purpose of clear
expression and not of concealment, - let us proceeed to
illustrate Mr. Ruskin's appreciation of truthfulness in
performance, as exhibited by his favourites among the
painters. Such truth, it will be remembered, is claimed
by him as the crown of glory for those minute finishers
who have banded together by similarities of humour into
the school called Pre-Raphaelite. To hear these persons
extolled for their literal veracity has always amazed us,
even while recollecting the lengths to which advocacy
will go in favour of a theory, and the courage with which
a sophist can prove affectation to be simplicity and simplicity affectation, should he take up the defence of the
attack of *della Cruscanism*. The energy and minuteness
with which the Pre-Raphelilte brotherhood have mastered
and recorded certain individual details, has not yet
taught them truth in arrangement, truth in form, truth in
colour, let Mr. Ruskin declare the reverse as loudly as he
will....

Another example of self-contradiction we shall give,
even more emphatic than these amazing theories of clean-
ness and uncleanness, since it refers to a branch of art
at which Mr. Ruskin has laboured unceasingly, - especially
since it has pleased him to advocate the Pre-Raphaelites,
because of their affinity to the monkish missal painters
in their love of gay colours. In this third volume of
'Modern Painters' he denounces our times as sad, though
the sadness is 'noble sadness,' as compared with the times
of old, when the monks were such brave colourists. This
sadness, he says, we moderns evince by our love of grave,
and melancholy, and mixed hues, - of bad greys, dirty ash
colours, and the like. What, then, are we to make of such
a definition of good colour as the following? -

> The fact is, that, of all God's gifts to the sight of
> man, colour is the holiest, the most divine, the most
> solemn. We cannot speak rashly of gay colour and sad
> colour, *for colour cannot at once be good and gay.*

It would seem impossible to exceed these examples of
childish inconsistency; but Mr. Ruskin enables us to do
so....
Closely akin to this arrogance, which enables the lecturer to define as he pleases, in order that he may defend
what he pleases, is the abuse of interpretation, as applied by him to what others have said or done. Incorrect-
ness of observation, incoherence of system, are but (as it
were) two leaves of the trefoil. To adopt Mr. Ruskin's
own jargon - 'by stern anatomical law' the third leaf must
be injustice in imputation; and this has been rarely if
ever carried further than in this series of books. Let us
illustrate Mr. Ruskin's real power of dealing with great
works of art by his appreciation of Raphael; - for we can
discover nothing more decisive of his true value as a
critic....
In point of fact, Mr. Ruskin appears to us to be utterly incapable of comprehending either the greatness of
conception or the refinement and ingenuity of execution,
which mark the highest productions of the great painters.
His mind is so unfortunately constituted that he analyses
to the last excess what is intended to produce effect as a
whole, though he generalises in the same sweeping and extravagant manner when he is dealing with particulars. Let
us take, for example, his observations on that admirable
and affecting work of Raphael, the 'Charge to Peter,'
which even in the gallery of the cartoons is conspicuous
above all its fellows for sublime and supernatural effect.
Mr. Ruskin's description of that solemn scene amounts to

this, that a couple of fishermen are tumbling over their
nets on the beach of the Sea of Galilee, and that the
others join them in the presence of Our Lord and 'eat their
broiled fish as he bids.'

[Quotes from 'And then to Peter' to 'head of Greek philosophers', 'Works' 5: 81-2.]

As this is Mr. Ruskin's verdict on one of the finest
works of Raphael, we are content to leave the worth of his
writings to be weighed against the worth of that picture.
That one or the other deserves the charge of 'infinite
monstrosity and hypocrisy' we have no doubt; but that one
is *not* the work of Raphael. In the absence of any higher
or better feelings in Mr. Ruskin, a little humility might
have spared us the pain of quoting a passage which is an
outrage on the public taste; but to all such feelings it
would be vain in this case to appeal....
Nor is it only the painters denounced by Mr. Ruskin, on
whom he turns the 'lamp' of his imputation and interpretation - he is still more weighty, still more marvellous,
still more unerring, when he tells us how the poets whom
he worships made their poems, - entering into the chambers
of imagery belonging to the mighty dead, instructing us why
they left what they did leave there untouched, - and what
we are to think of all they have given us. In these chapters Mr. Ruskin has attempted to apply to literary criticism the principles which have led him to such unexpected
conclusions in examining the works of the great painters;
and we suspect that if the whole truth were told he is of
opinion that as the art of landscape-painting began
with the late Mr. Turner, so the art of fine writing began
with Mr. Carlyle and himself, for he respectfully informs
us that Mr. Carlyle is above all men the 'guide, philosopher, and friend,' of the author of these disquisitions.
When, however, he asserts that all minute observation and
relish of the aspects of Nature, such as bear on landscape
painting, is a modern invention (which he assumes, with a
simple patronage of Dante, Homer, Shakspeare, that is edifying), he goes too far, in reasoning from his own particular habits to the general tastes and tendencies of
thoughtful and poetical men....
As a last illustration of the spirit in which this book
'of many things' ['Modern Painters III'] is written, - of
the truth which may be expected from its author, - of the
soundness of his judgment as a critic, - and of his self-
respect as a collector diligent in qualifying himself for
his task, - let us advert to his dealings with what may be
called the collateral branches of his subject. Mr. Ruskin

treats of the relations of Art with civilisation and society, and its reflection in literature, in the 16th and 17th
chapters of this third volume, - those devoted to Modern
Landscape, and to the Moral of Landscape. That one who has
fathomed the secrets of the ancient authors should also be
able anew to judge and appraise the moderns, can be no
mystery or cause of suprise. That a lecturer on Art, who
points out the uselessness of all lecturing to the artist,
who would have the student fling to the winds all such
academical discoveries as perspective and *chiaro scuro,*
who delivers his testimony in favour of bright colours,
which can only reach their perfection when the colourist
is in a state of savagery, - should also hold peculiar
ideas in morals, and politics, and civilisation, was but
to be expected. These 'Latter-day Prophets' deal with no
question by halves. Thus we find Mr. Ruskin launching off
into the old diatribe against modern inventions and modern
society, with a huge disdain of fact and possibility. The
progress of the human intellect (a divine gift entrusted
to Man for Man's improvement) is denounced, as a cheating
and feverish delusion; and our author declares that the
highest faculties of the human creature should be devoted
uninterruptedly to watch the corn grow or the blossoms set,
- to 'draw hard breath over ploughshare and spade.' Long
before this new school of believers in barbarism sprung
up, the sceptics, tired of all established religions, were
in the habit of expressing their discontent by satirising
every sign of progress and civilisation. Long before Mr.
Ruskin began to rhapsodise in favour of his stripes of
primitive scarlet and blue, the painted savage was set up
by many a French *bel esprit* and *philosophe* as a living example of wisdom, experience, and virtue, deserving the
worship of rational and educated creatures. To denounce
what never can be undoune, to preach what never can be
done, is one of the most stale resources of the fanatic;
but it denotes a mind unsettled in its convictions, unstable in its principles, and falling from paradox to paradox into the abyss of scepticism and infidelity. For, as
if resolute to destroy all such respect for his sincerity,
as may linger in some corner of the hearts of those who
have been enchanted by sonorous periods and bold assertions, in the seventeenth and eighteenth chapters of this
Third Volume, Mr. Ruskin does his best to discredit all
minute observation of Nature as a humour characteristic of
modern times, as false, morbid, and belonging to a time of
unbelief and to a race of blasphemers!
    Few essays by a man in whom trust has been reposed, and
in whom genius must be recognised, are more amazing than
Mr. Ruskin's lucubrations on the authors whom he refers to

as having written concerning Nature, or than his classification of those among whom the passion for Nature was intense or subordinate. Walter Scott we are told was sor-
rowful, sceptical as an author, 'inherently and consistently sad;' a politician whose 'love of liberty was at
the root of all his Jacobite tendencies in politics; a man
who believed in "destiny"' (which Mr. Ruskin defines to be
'not a matter of faith at all, but of sight'). But the
love of Nature was *intense* in Anne Radclyffe (whose moon
that rose twice in the same night has been a stock joke
for these twenty years past); it is intense in M. Eugene
Sue, who is credited with having produced a beautiful pastoral scene in 'Les Mystères de Paris' having *Fleur de
Marie* for its shepherdess; - whereas in Milton, despite of
his 'L'Allegro,' despite of his 'Lycidas,' despite of his
'Paradise Lost,' the love of Nature is described as
'*subordinate.*'

We shall not follow Mr. Ruskin through the pages of
æsthetic auto-biography by which he has illustrated the
'Moral of Landscape,' from the day when this infant
prodigy was taken by his nurse to the brow of Friar's Crag
on Derwentwater, to the time when Scott's Monastery became
his favourite book, and he lived 'with a general presence
of White Lady everywhere.' These particulars will no doubt
be of permanent interest to those who may hereafter examine the life of so remarkable an individual. Nor can we
charge ourselves with an analysis of the political rhapsody
which terminates this volume, though we are told in Mr.
Ruskin's finest language, that 'the helmed and sworded
skeleton that rakes with its white fingers the sands of the
Black Sea beach into grave heap after grave heap, washed by
everlasting surf of tears, has been to our countrymen an
angel of other things than agony': and that 'the scarlet of
the blood which has sealed this covenant will be poured
along the clouds of a new Aurora, glorious in that eastern
heaven; for every sob of wreck-fed breaker round those
Pontic precipices, the floods shall clap their hands
between the guarded mounts of the Prince Angel.' To these
elevated regions it is impossible for us to pursue Mr.
Ruskin, and as for the 'guarded mounts of the Prince Angel'
we have not a conception where they are, unless this singular expression conveys an allusion to St. Michael's Mount,
which is now turned into a prison or a madhouse.

We have already bestowed on this volume more space than
its merits deserve, but its gross and glaring extravagancies and defects constitute a strong claim to notice.
It is the worst book of a bad series of books, mischievous
to art, mischievous to literature, but mischievous above
all to those young and eager minds, animated by the love

of art and of literature, which may mistake this declamatory trash for substantial or stimulating food. We are the less disposed to acquit Mr. Ruskin because he is not altogether without faculties which might have made him a useful and an elegant writer. His style, when it is not too inflated, is generally perspicuous and sometimes forcible: his perceptions are acute; he is not devoid of industry or even of taste. But all these qualities are perverted and destroyed by the entire absence of masculine judgment, by the failure of the logical faculty, and by a strange propensity to mistake the illusions of his own fancy or his own vanity for the laws of reality and the principles of truth.

22. EDWARD BRUCE HAMLEY, AN UNSIGNED SATIRICAL ARTICLE, MR. DUSKY'S OPINIONS ON ART, 'BLACKWOOD'S MAGAZINE'

July 1858, vol. 84, 122-6

Edward Bruce Hamley (1824-93) was a distinguished soldier and military writer. He served in the Crimea throughout that war, taught at Sandhurst (subsequently becoming Commandant), and occupied numerous posts in the army at home and abroad. Hamley became a Lieutenant-General in 1882, was knighted, and in 1885 was elected Conservative MP for Birkenhead. He also wrote several novels and contributed many articles on various subjects to 'Blackwood's'. Hamley's career exemplifies that admirable Victorian admixture of markedly responsible activity in one direction and sustained interests in other, different spheres of endeavour. See Introduction, p. 15.

MR. DUSKY'S OPINIONS ON ART

I am a blessed Glendoveer;
'Tis mine to speak, and yours to hear.
Rejected Addresses.

It is quite clear that the Glendoveer of the above couplet was commissioned to deliver to the world a divine message about Art. I argue thus on account of the air of absolute and uncompromising authority with which he announces the conditions of his teaching, Art being a subject on which

two opinions ought not to be permitted. To the culpable neglect with which this high commissioner from the Court of
Nature was probably treated by the vain and self-sufficient
artists of the time, is chiefly to be attributed the lamentable state of Art in general, and Painting in particular, up
to eight or ten years ago, when I took up the subject.
Since then I am happy to observe that all artists gifted
with any degree of talent, and all the public possessing
the slightest measure of judgment or reflection, have
followed the paths I have so clearly indicated. Of course,
as very few artists possess any talent whatever, and the
great body of the public is, and must long continue to be,
utterly deficient in the qualities I have mentioned, both
the authors of fine works and those who patronise and admire them must expect to remain in a minority conspicu-
ously small. But let them be comforted: for as in the
stillness and splendour of a summer's evening, when the
golden torrents rushing from their fountains in the west,
bathe the sky up to the zenith, where commences that pale
green which heralds the approach of twilight, the chirp-
ings of a few grasshoppers resound shrilly amid the glit-
tering grass, while whole armies of sensual caterpillars,
mutely feeding on leaf and flower, crawl unheeded; so, by
perpetual self-assertion, and utter contempt of all antagonistic sentiment, may the prophets of Art and their
disciples secure to themselves, even among the undiscern-
ing, a share of attention immeasurably greater than their
mere numbers or consideration would entitle them to claim.

Without affecting any diffidence which in me would be
transparent pretence, or any misgivings as to any opinion
I have ever delivered, yet I find it necessary to be
cautious in wielding, as I annually do, the trenchant
weapon of irresponsible criticism, lest, in its whirlwind
evolutions, it might haply lop a limb from some humble but
trusty follower. It grieved me much to find that a single
word of censure uttered by me some years ago, and which,
though perfectly just, was too keen and searching for the
sensitive nature of the artist whose work I was criticising, had the effect of causing him to abandon painting as
a profession, and to revert to his original calling of an
oil-and-colour man, in which I hear he is realising a
moderate competence. Excellent, therefore, as it is to
have a giant's strength, it will be easily understood how
cautious I must be in the exercise of the perilous gift;
and when I refrain from noticing a picture in which I find
nothing to praise, it is either because I am unwilling
utterly to crush and destroy a painstaking though erring
artist, or else because, the painter being a personal
friend, I prefer gently correcting him in the privacy of

social converse to publicly gibbeting him. By these remarks I wish to guard against the imputation of hesitating
in, or shrinking from, the formation of decided opinion on
the merits of any picture that ever was painted, which I
am always ready to accomplish at the shortest notice, my
conclusions being generally directly opposite to those
which would be arrived at by most other persons, or, in
other words, by those less confident than myself in their
own infallibility.

The first thing that strikes me, in the work of the
present year, is, that though all other seasons and times
of the day are reproduced in land-scape (except the pitch
dark of a winter's night, which it would be difficult for
any one, in the present state of art, to place satisfactorily on canvas), yet that particular state of the atmosphere which exists in the month of August from about five
minutes before two to about twenty minutes after, when the
sun's sultry and lavish splendour is tinged with some fore-
boding of his decline, and when Nature is, as it were,
taking her siesta, is nowhere sought to be conveyed. I
thought, on first looking at a small picture in the east
room of the Acadamy, that this hiatus had been filled up;
but, on further study, I perceived that the picture in
question had been painted rather earlier (about five-an-
twenty minutes before two is the time I should assign to
it), and is therefore deficient in many of the chief characteristics of the remarkable period I allude to. How
comes it, too, that, amid all the rendering of grass and
flowers, there is not a single dandelion – a flower which
has often given to me, no less than to Wordsworth,
'thoughts that do often lie too deep for tears;' nor a
group of toadstools, which can give interest to a foreground else bald and barren; nor, among the minute studies
of insects, a daddy-long-legs, swaying delightedly across
the path, and dancing to inaudible music, as the mid-day
zephyr waves the slender fabric of his gossamer home. I
am surprised, too, to find (so far as my survey had enabled me to note) that there are nowhere any frogs, though
every artist who painted out of doors in the first warm
days of spring must have heard their choral music from the
neighbouring ditches. The old heralds, speaking of the
manner of the frog's holding his head, talk of the pride
and dignity, or, as they phrase it, 'the lording' of frogs,
and gave them a place in heraldry; and their ideas are
generally valuable to artists, and worth studying, both
for their literal exactness and their allegorical significance. Let us have some frogs next year.

No. 18 – 'A Man Washing his Hands' (J. Prig). A step
in the right direction. The painting of the nail-brush,

showing where friction has worn away and channelled the
bristles in the middle, is especially good. But how comes
it that, the nail-brush having been evidently made use of,
the water in the basin is still pellucid, with no soap apparent, either superficially or in solution? This over-
sight I should not have expected in so clever an artist.
Even granting clearness to the water, the pattern of the
bottom of the basin visible through it is of a different
character from the exterior of the vessel, which is not
the case in any specimen of that particular delf which
has come under my notice.

No. 24. – This is directly imitative both of Titian and
George Cruikshank, with Smith's handling, and a good deal
of Brown's manner.

No. 29. – As I told the artist last year, he is deficient
in fulness of form and looseness of texture. He should,
therefore, for some years, paint nothing but mops of
various colours (without the handles), which would give him
wooliness and rotundity. On the other hand, the painter
of No. 32 has too much of these qualities, with too little
firmness in his darks; and I should recommend him, as a
counteracting influence, to study only blocks of coal – not
the common coal (which is too dull), but the kennel or
candle coal – a perseverance in which practice he will find
attended by the happiest results.

'The Nativity' – This is nearly perfect. The infant,
which at first appears to be wearing a broad-brimmed straw-
hat, is distinguished by a peculiar halo, in which there
is no trace of servile imitation of those absured pretenders known as the old masters. Thoughtless and superficial observers have objected to the angel holding the
lantern, as an office inconsistent with the dignity of the
angelic nature; saying, too, that the act has some offici-
ousness, since the lantern might have been placed on the
ground or hung on a nail. For my own part, I consider the
idea eminently happy, and if one of the other angels had
been represented as snuffing the candle with her fingers,
my admiration would have been complete.

No. 40. – The sky is weak and heavy, the distance too
hazy, the middle distance absurd, and the fore-ground like
a cartload of bricks ready for use. However, on the whole,
I consider this the leading picture of the year.

No. 501. – I was nearly overlooking this picture, which
at first sight seemed unworthy of notice, when a second
glance showed me what I conceive to be the print of a man's
shoe in the dust of the high-road in the corner of the foreground. This little incident gives poetry to the whole
composition, and is quite equal to the memorable invention
of Defoe, when he makes Robinson Crusoe discover the print

of a foot in the sand. The shoe, a hobnailed one, evidently belongs to the owner of the little white-walled
cottage in the middle distance, the smoke from whose chim-
ney curls bluely upward against a sky which has in itself
nothing remarkable, but which the late J.M.W. Turner would
have filled with magnificent cloud-forms of grandest outline and miraculous colour. One feels at once that the
wearer of that shoe was one of our conscripts, fighting
our battles against the barren swamp and the dull clod,
and that, toilworn and careworn, he passed, in his vic-
torious march, up that dusty road, to the domestic haven
where rest, if not glory, awaited him.

> There were his young barbarians all at play;
> There was their Saxon mother - he their sire,
> Sweating to make a rich man's holiday.

It reconciles me in great measure to the inequalities of
the gifts of fortune, and to the necessity that almost
seems to exist for a class which takes on itself the manual
labour of the world, when I consider that we derive from
thence the elements of purest pathos in art.

No. 520. 'Venus and Adonis' (D. Corum, R.A.) - The
great charm for me in this picture is the total absence of
all sensual imagination in its treatment. The goddess,
purified from all taint of earth-born passion, with the
immortal light of divine friendship beaming in her lustrous eyes, invites the reluctant youth to seat himself
beside her on the glowing couch of amaranths and aspho-
dels (with some gentianella and one or two ragged robins
skilfully introduced), which have sprung responsively to
the pressure of her roseate feet; while, in the distance,
the fatal boar is seen whetting against the trunk of a
blackthorn in full blossom the remorseless tusks which
are shortly to be imbrued in the stream of the boy's
young life. A similar purity of thought distinguishes the
'Susannah and the Elders,' by the same artist, and quite
marks a new epoch in art. The Elders, grave men of most
reverend appearance, approach the beautiful woman in her
bath, evidently for the purpose of studying the flowing
outline of her form and the delicate articulations of her
joints (the ankles are especially well drawn). Lovers of
exalted art, they come, with words of courteous greeting
on their lips, to study in leisure and privacy the combinations of lines and gradations of flesh-colour with
which Nature in her most perfect efforts delights to
exercise the reasoning powers of man; while the matron,
'clothed only in chastity,' calmly awaits their coming.
The 'Satyrs and Nymphs Dancing,' by the same hand, is

equally removed from the gross impurity which the subject
would have derived from the licentious Poussin, and the
hideous immorality of a modern quadrille. 'Potiphar's
Wife' is another illustrious instance of the power of Mr.
D. Corum to give new life to old subjects. The wife of
the great Egyptian noble holds in her hand a roll of
papyrus covered with specimens of early Egyptian art, to
which she seeks to direct Joseph's attention (by the by,
the style of these drawings, especially the man in profile
with two eyes, belongs to the time of the later Pharaohs,
and not to the pre-Mosaic period); but without success,
for the youth, in whose countenance the struggle between
curiosity and bashfulness is exhibited in a very remarkable
manner, turns resolutely away from his kind instructress.
Altogether the treatment of the whole of these works reminds me strongly of the manner of Fra Puritano.
　　No. 603. - I formerly had some slight hopes of this
artist, and consequently bestowed on him a word or two of
advice. But as he seems systematically to defy every principle I have ever laid down, and obstinately to ignore
every opinion I have ever enunciated, his whole method has
of course become hopelessly and irredeemably vile, and his
works are in painting what ribaldry is in literature.
　　No. 650. - This artist had better go without delay to
Venice. He will find in one of the vaults of one of the
churches there (I forget which) a picture without a name,
but which I know to be an indubitable Paul Veronese. The
whole composition is fine; but I would particularly note
the third hair from the top in the right whisker of the
cat in the corner, the painting of which is very precious.
This he should study in a reverential spirit, and I will
answer for the result.
　　'The Dead Stonebreaker.' - On nothing have I ever insisted more strongly than on the absolute necessity of
painting altogether in the open air, with all the accessories of the scene that are to be transferred to the canvas actually present; and here I am happy to see an illustration of the good effect of following my advice. I have
no doubt that this picture was painted strictly under
these conditions. Ribald critics may perhaps object that,
as atmospheres of that extreme purpleness (as if mulberry-
juice were substituted for the ordinary vehicle) are very
rare, and that as the mere work of the picture must have
occupied several weeks, these infrequent opportunities must
have extended over a great length of time, during which the
deceased stonebreaker would have become a skeleton, while
the weasel could scarcely be expected to remain so long
looking at the body. Nevertheless I adhere entirely to my
opinion; and I am thus reminded of one particular count

of the heavy indictment I formerly brought against that
perverter of nature and imposter in art, Claude Lorraine.
I pointed out that in a picture of his in the National
Gallery, the shadows of two different objects are falling
in opposite directions; and this I noted as a blemish, or
rather one amid a mass of blemishes. I now perceive that
this was owing to the fact that, for once, Claude was
honestly studying from nature out of doors; and being absorbed in his miserable work (for the absorption of the
artist in his efforts by no means depends on their value),
he did not perceive that the sun, which was on his left
hand when he began to paint in the morning, had gone
round to his right before he left off, and consequently
threw the shadows in the opposite direction. This is the
only occasion on which I have ever found it necessary to
alter an opinion I had once expressed; and I freely admit
that what I formerly censured I now consider the sole
merit to be found in this painter's numerous works, and he
is entitled to so much posthumous fame as my approval in
this solitary instance can confer.

No. 902. - A fine example of what may be called the
botanico-geologico-astronomico style of art. Here the
primeval masses of the old red sandstone, the granite
boulders, which, ere they became fixed for ever, hissed
in fierce fusion round the sweltering materials of the
chaotic globe, the grey slate, the gneiss, the feldspar,
and the gypsum, lend their multiform variety of outline to
the harmonious forms of the foreground; while, in the
coalstrata of the extreme distance, methinks I can descry
the faint impress of ferns and other vegetable deposits.
Note the fossil tooth of the mastodon in the centre as
particularly precious, finely relieved as it is against
the leatherly texture of the wing of the pterodactyle.
These superb combinations of the dædal forms of the earth
are clothed in lavish magnificence with all known and possible specimens of herbaceous life, from the stupendous
Wellingtonia to the small celandine of our native fields;
while over all are set the sentinel stars, Orion and the
Pleiades, which shed over the dawn of creation the same
sweet influences that still gild its decline. The natural-
ist may study this picture with profit, only second to that
derivable from a knowledge of the works of the late J.M.W.
Turner, as expounded by myself. Still there are some
natural features not to be found in European landscape, of
which I lament the absence. I should therefore recommend
the artist to spend the summer on the top of the Peter Bott
Mountain, while he may get a suitable foreground in the
rich autumnal splendours of the trackless South American
forests; and may, on his return, paint in the less important

details from the Botanical Gardens in the Regent's Park.
I wish him a pleasant trip, a stout heart, walking-stick,
and pair of shoes.

'Red-deer,' by Landseer, - I have already told Mademois-
elle Rosa Bonheur, that as she has not yet satisfactorily
proved to me that she can paint a man's face, it is a delusion to suppose that she paints horses; they are merely
trotting bodies of horses; so I tell Landseer, that as he
has never (that I am aware of) painted a porcupine, it is
a popular fallacy to suppose that he can paint red-deer.
He merely paints their horns, hoofs, and hides.

I have now given the public all that it is necessary
for them to know, and more than they can appreciate, of my
decisions on the Art of this year. The above pictures are
all that I have had leisure to look at. Still, the mere
fact of my not having seen them, would not prevent me from
criticising all the rest, if it were expedient or necessary. On the whole, I consider the works of this year decidedly in advance of those of the last, as that was of
its predecessor, which I attribute to my annual critiques;
and I doubt not that, after diligent study of this little
brochure, considerable progress will be manifested next
summer.

'Modern Painters V'

1860

23. UNSIGNED REVIEW, 'ILLUSTRATED LONDON NEWS'

22 September 1860, vol. 37, 282

'Earnestly domestic', the 'Illustrated London News', which
enjoyed at this time a healthy circulation among the prosperous middle classes as a family publication, is mock-
ingly hostile towards Ruskin and his work. The review,
however, whilst tainted with an embarrassing anti-
intellectualism, is pertinent in its suggestions of the
writer's relationship to his public.

We are so grateful for the announcement that the ponderous
volume before us completes this long-protracted work that
we are little disposed to quarrel with the author for the
delay which has occurred in its production. Mr. Ruskin,
however, is conscious of his apparent dilatoriness himself, and thinks it necessary to say something by way of
apology. 'The disproportion between the length of time
occupied in the preparation of this volume,' he says, 'and
the slightness of the apparent result is so vexatious to
me, and must seem so strange to the reader that he will
perhaps bear with my stating some of the matters which
have employed or interrupted me between 1855 and 1860.'
We need not go into the details of these multifarious
interruptions and onerous occupations, the relation of
which is thus introduced. We quote the sentence merely as
an illustration of a peculiarity we have through a long
course of observation remarked in Mr. Ruskin, and which
seems to be the ruling principle of all his performances -
namely, a bold repudiation of all logical restraint, and
which is equally observable in the construction of a

sentence as in the treatment of an argument. It must be
obvious to all who know the meaning of words that Mr.
Ruskin intends the very converse of what he states, and
that, so far from his apprehending the existence of 'disproportion between the length of time occupied in the preparation of this volume and the *slightness* of the apparent
result,' he means a 'disproportion, &c.,' and the *bulk* or
importance of the result - for the word 'apparent,' as it
seems to us, may be dispensed with.

Nevertheless, the result, 'the apparent result,' has at
length been given to the world, and the duty devolves upon
us now for the fifth time to investigate the mysteries of
Ruskinism, and to attempt to follow it in its rather erratic progress. Let us not pretend to underrate the importance of the subject. There is no denying the fact,
Ruskinism is an institution, and Mr. Ruskin one of the marvels of the age. He is marvellous in himself - marvellous
as regards his influence in the so-called world of taste;
whilst the inference to be inevitably drawn as to the intellectual capacity of the latter is most marvellous of all.
Yet there is nothing extraordinary or incredible in the
affair when we come to consider other marvels which are going
on around us. Mr. Ruskin, in his way, is not unworthy of his
generation - a generation which has invented clairvoyance,
spirit-rapping, and Mormonism, which builds a costly taber-
nacle for a Spurgeon, and which accepts a Roebuck as the im-
personation of wisdom and patriotism, and a Bright as the
embodiment and measure of the statesmanlike capacity of the
country.

Nor let any inference be drawn from all this that we look
upon Mr. Ruskin as an imposter - *vulgo,* a humbug. On the
contrary, we believe him to be perfectly sincere - sincere
in his high estimation of himself and in his contempt for
the opinion of all the rest of the world; sincere in his
conviction that nobody knows anything about art, be it
more or less, but himself, and that his mission is to give
the law upon the subject to all comers; and - a prerogative
inherent in law-giving - that he has a right to change his
own opinions and the opinions of all who follow him as
often and as capriciously as he thinks proper. We believe,
also, that his numerous readers and disciples - not so numerous, we apprehend as they once were - put implicit faith
in him, accept reverently all that he vouchsafes to communicate to them, and none the less so because, too generally, what he propounds is wrapped in a flood and mist of
words, which ordinary perceptions cannot hope to pierce,
and enforced by arguments which successfully baffle all
known rules of logical treatment. One thing, at least,
may be said of Mr. Ruskin, his teachings, and his

disciples, which, if not altogether satisfactory as regards results actually attained, is encouraging, as indicating ground to work upon for the future. The avidity
with which his voluminous effusions have been received
indicates a strong desire on the part of the public to
know something about art; and, if the deference which has
been paid to his dicta but proves how very much such
education is still wanted amongst us, there is consolation, at least, in the reflection that the taste and
aptitude for it exist, which may one day, in proper hands,
be satisfactorily cultivated and turned to profitable
account.

From what we have said above it may be judged that,
looking upon Mr. Ruskin as a sincere and conscientious
man, we believe that he has done all that he has done to
the best of his ability, and in the firm conviction that
he was rendering a great service to his fellow-men. Indeed, he assures us that the work before us, which he has
been seventeen years completing, 'has not been written for
fame, or for money, or for conscience' sake, but of necessity.' He wrote because he could not help it; he was impelled by an irresistible impulse which left him no moral
control over his actions. 'I knew not,' he says, 'how
little or how much might come of the business, or whether
I was fit for it.' The *cacoethes scribendi* was on him,
and he wrote whatever came uppermost, not knowing exactly
what it meant or what it was worth; and what he wrote was
printed, not because any publisher could be found to pay
him for it in the usual way, but because he could himself
afford to stand the risk of the printer's bill. To proceed further with Mr. Ruskin's account of himself and his
qualifications for the task which 'necessity' thus thrust
upon him. He tells us:-

The first volume was the expansion of a reply to a
magazine article, and was not begun because I then
thought myself qualified to write a systematic treatise
on Art, but because I at least knew, and knew it to be
demonstrable, that Turner was right and true, and that
his critics were wrong, false, and base.

Rather strong language, this; but let it pass. Suffice
it that 'An Oxford Graduate,' fresh from his humanities,
first discovered, he 'at least knew,' the transcendent
merits of Turner, heretofore basely denied or under-
estimated by the critics, and came prepared to defend them
against all the world. Unfortunately, in this bold champion's view of the case, to establish the merit of Turner
it became necessary to deny merit in any of the great

landscape-painters - Claude, Salvator Rosa, Poussin, Cuyp, Berghem, &c. - who had preceded him; and this, regardless of consequences, he at once proceeded to do, heaping ridicule plentifully upon them and all who could see anything to admire in them. Nor in thus running counter to the mass of hitherto received opinions did he restrict himself to landscape-painters. The greatest names of the greatest age in historical painting - names held in reverence by men of education and mature judgment in all succeeding ages, Leonardo da Vinci, Michael Angelo, Raphael, Correggio, Titian - were all pulled down from their pedestals, their pretensions rudely scrutinised - denied with ribald jokes or coarse revilings, whilst one or two 'modern painters' - Holman Hunt, Millais, &c. by name - who had been fortunate enough to come to the exact level of the great reformer's comprehension, were pointed to as worthy of engrossing the world's admiration and praise.

Did it never occur to Mr. Ruskin, when he ventured thus to assume the power of judgment over the whole range or art, that the task he undertook was one which called for an amount of education, besides natural endowments, which should have qualified the possessor, if he thought proper, 'to write a systematic treatise on art;' and that when, 'having engaged seriously' in this matter, he, 'before writing the second volume,' went 'to study in Italy,' he went a little too late? With astonishing complacency, however, he admits that in the course of this and subsequent visits to Italy (always 'to study') he found occasion to reject or modify many of the opinions he had previously expressed very strongly in print. He tells us, for instance, that before this course of study he 'had chiefly delighted in northern art, beginning, when a mere boy, with Rubens and Rembrandt,' which is about as rational as it would be to talk of Italian art headed by Guido and Carol Maratti. This profound and comprehensive northern inspiration, however, did not prevail long; for, as he next tells us, 'the strong reaction from the influence of Rubens threw me at first too far under that of Angelico and Raphael, and, which was the worst harm that came of the Rubens influence, blinded me long to the deepest qualities of Venetian art, which the reader may see by expressions occurring not only in the second, but even in the third and fourth volumes, I thought, however powerful, yet partly luxurious and sensual, until I was led into the final inquiries above related.' And again:- 'The reader will, perhaps, on this ground forgive the strong expressions of admiration for Rubens, which to my great regret, occur in the first volume.' And even so late as the winter of 1858, 'with much consternation but more delight, I found that I

had never got to the root of the moral powers of the
Venetians, and that they needed still another and a very
stern course of study. There was nothing for it but to
give up the book for that year. The winter was spent
mainly in trying to get at the mind of Titian - not a
light winter's task, of which the issue being in many ways
very unexpected to me (the reader will find it partly told
towards the close of this volume) necessitated my going in
the spring to Berlin,' &c.

And so he went on learning and unlearning, receiving
impressions one day to be discarded the next, and with a
complacency which is really nothing short of marvellous,
promulgating each newly-accepted impression to the public
as a discovery of incalculable value and undoubted authen-
ticity. And now, at the close of this strange proceeding,
when he calmly surveys the patchwork and discordant re-
siduum, he pronounces it none the worse for its incongruous
character:-

> These oscillations of temper and progressions of dis-
> covery, extending over a period of seventeen years,
> ought not to diminish the reader's confidence in the
> book. Let him be assured of this, that unless impor-
> tant changes are occurring in his opinions continually
> all his life long, not one of those opinions can be on
> any questionable subject true. All true opinions are
> living, and show their life by being capable of nour-
> ishment, therefore of change. But their change is
> that of the tree - not of the cloud.

What is meant by the 'cloud' allegory the author does
not explain, nor do we pretend to understand, but the
'tree' figure is thus dimly elaborated:-

> So that as the work changed like a tree, it was also
> rooted like a tree - not where it would, but where need
> was; on which, if any fruit grew such as you like you
> are welcome to gather it without thanks, and so far as
> it is poor or bitter, it will be your justice to refuse
> it without reviling.

All which we humbly submit to be arrant nonsense. A tree
is known by its fruit, and you cannot gather sweet fruit
and bitter fruit, true fruit and false fruit, from the same
stem. The changes which take place at successive periods
in the life of a tree are those naturally incidental to
growth and progress, and are never inconsistent with themselves or with 'tree truth.' On the other hand, the
changes in Mr. Ruskin have been those incidental to a

person of ignorant conceit, venturing without guide or instructor upon unknown paths, where he is arrested at every turn by novel appearances or suggestions, the true import of which, instrinsically and relatively with others, he has not the capacity justly to appreciate, and which sway his unprepared judgment alternately into each extreme of error. Having perhaps, some lurking misgivings as to the balance which may one day be struck between the true and the false, the bitter and the sweet, in his writings, Mr. Ruskin says:- 'Had I wished for future fame, I should have written one volume, not five;' which we would venture to amend by suggesting that, leaving future fame alone, had he cared to escape present and enduring obloquy and ridicule, he would have written none at all, or at least would have deferred publishing until he had got up his subject in some form of consistency and completeness. In an economical point of view he has also his doubts; for 'in this wealth-producing country seventeen years' labour could hardly have been invested with less chance of equivalent return,' and a little further on, 'It seems to me, and seemed always probable, that I might have done much more good in some other way.' The last suggestion we are inclined to acquiesce in. And, after all, there is comfort - negative comfort - even in the maxim 'ne sutor ultra crepidam;' and if Mr. Ruskin has wasted seventeen of the best years of his life in a pursuit for which he was wholly unqualified, there is no reason why he may not yet make up for lost time by industrious application to some vocation for which he may be gifted with capacity.

The preceding observations have reference to general ideas suggested by the author's preface: in a concluding article we shall notice some of the points in the text of this volume.

24. LOAMMI GOODENOW WARE, FROM AN UNSIGNED REVIEW, 'CHRISTIAN EXAMINER' (BOSTON, MASS.)

January 1861, vol. 70, 29-48

Loammi Goodenow Ware (1827-91) was educated at Boston Latin School, Harvard College, and Harvard Divinity School. Ordained in 1854, he was an assistant to Edward Everett Hale with the Christian Unity Society, an association of working men and women in Boston. He was involved in numerous educational and philanthropical ventures and for a time was

pastor of the First Congregational Society (Church) in
Burlington, Vermont. He contributed several articles (including another on Ruskin) to the 'Christian Examiner' and
was known as a man of the highest character deeply versed
in art, poetry, literature and drama. An early example
of literary-artistic criticism in America, the review
merits attention for its sympathetic, if over-defensive,
position towards not only the final volume of 'Modern
Painters' but a considerably larger corpus of Ruskin's
work.

It was a memorable excitement which waited on the publication of the first volume of 'Modern Painters by a Graduate of Oxford.' There was good promise in it, which is
nowadays plainly in its fulfilment. Among the elements in
the interest aroused, these were obvious, - curiosity as
to the unknown author, admiration of that wonderful style
which at once took its place with the noblest expressions
of English letters, and equal admiration of strong thought
and fine imagination, and of precious material drawn from
generous learning and large acquaintance with literature,
from careful study and love both of nature and art, and
from scientific knowledge. And deeper sympathy, too, was
given to the earnest humanity and religiousness of the
writer. But, to intensify the interest into excitement,
there were, beside these elements, on the one hand eager
reception of, and on the other quick opposition to, strange
general views of art, put forth with great boldness, in
connection with particular criticism, quite unorthodox,
of certain old masters, and a hearty assertion of the
claims of Turner to the highest artistic rank. The excitement became controversy, and the controversy strife. For
here was, to some denial of the gods; to others, a pulling
down of idols. Here, in one regard, was the bolstering up
a pretender, and, in the other, a rightful apotheosis.
Extremists in the contest still hold Mr. Ruskin as a de-
ceiver in art, or as an infallible guide. Platonists and
Aristotelians were never at wider variance. Realists and
Nominalists, after their day's easy fashion, dealt more
finishing blows with fist or dagger, but were not more in
earnest than the contestants for and against 'Modern
Painters,' in skirmishes of table-talks and battle of quarterlies and magazines.
The present review will not assume the fanaticism of
either party. It confesses, still, its sympathy with the

over-enthusiastic defenders, rather than with the ultra-
illiberal offenders. For, in this fifth volume, as in the
preceeding four, we have found more that is enjoyable,
helpful, and inspiring, than in any other work of art, so
that we place it on the library shelf and in the mind's
corner with the choice and friendly few. And we hope to
give here some poor expression to our rich feeling of
honor to the man, and of admiration of his work.

At the outset, therefore, we must notice, with regret,
that the one journal devoted to the well-being of art in
this country reviews this new volume with a foolish flippancy more disreputable than stupid attack. We have a
right to expect better things of it, since it puts upon
its title-page, as expressing its purpose, that direction
of Paul, to think on things true, honest, pure, lovely,
and of good report. The appearance of such a book-notice
is a direct disclaimer of the noble legend, which at once
commits it to the largest toleration, and holds up to it
the loftiest of aims. By such writing is neither advanced
what is 'true, honest, just, pure, and lovely' in art, nor
the 'good report' of artists. Its spirit is adverse to
real 'virtue' in the work, and to worthy 'praise' of the
worker. It bears no mark of having thought 'on these
things.'

Whether the quality of work done by Mr. Ruskin in these
last seventeen years be regarded, or its quality, or its
effect, it is the ample vindication of the free expenditure of the best part of his life. Certainly, it is no
small result. Beside five volumes of 'Modern
Painters,' there are three of 'The Stones of Venice,' and
some six or eight smaller ones upon special art-topics,
not to number the 'Academy' pamphlets and infrequent
papers for the reviews. This is a larger contribution to
the literature of art than that of any other English
writer, save, perhaps, the compilers of books of reference.
And in all, the author takes to himself the command to
honest painstaking, obedience to which he so often enforces
upon artists, as a great part at once of their duty and of
their success and fame. Now, if work is of that divine
quality that genius can be defined as but the imperial
capacity for working, for doing where other men are idle,
then Ruskin may rest his claim to the high attribute simply
upon this sum and substance of his diligence. But the
quality fits the quantity. And in this the justice of the
claim most appears. For there meet here in rare combination and striking exercise those fine intellectual and
moral powers, whose memorable possession and use by great
poets and by all higher æsthetic and spiritual teachers,
we call, as by peculiar right, genius. The effect, too,

though hindered by prejudice and tradition, now bears
some good proportion to the amount done, and responds not
faintly to the nobleness of spirit which dictated, and to
the greatness of the powers which have carried the work
through. Genius, besides, has its own way at last, though
late. And it needs little prophetic skill to foretell that
the result will be a wider and better appreciation of art,
exactly commensurate with the large and good service to art
so faithfully rendered.

In an attempt to assign the rightful place to 'Modern
Painters' in our art-literature, a brief review will not be
amiss of what has been done for art in English and American
letters. This for comparison's sake. Then we purpose some
consideration, necessarily brief and incomplete, of intrinsic qualities and essential merits in the book....

We therefore leave the historical contrast, to take in
hand some closer investigation of the merits of 'Modern
Painters,' Yet we are sensible that, in any unfolding of
the special argument from nicer regard of this work, we
can follow only a little way along the line of it, which
draws quicker sight and keener apprehension so far and so
finely. Indeed, the argument will be, in the main, a
gathering up of some of the reasons of our admiration.
For little is learned in the *nil admirari* school. And we
hold it the more profitable, as it is the pleasanter
criticism, to select some from the many admirable features
which are essential, than to linger over the few, not so
admirable, which are by the way and partial, which damage
the illustration more than hurt the substance, being defects of form, not vices of the spirit.

In brief, we accept wholly the writer's own showing in
respect to his book. 'From its first syllable to the
last,' he says, 'it declares the perfectness and eternal
beauty of the work of God, and tests all work of man by
concurrence with or subjection to that;.....not written
either for fame, or for money, or for conscience' sake,
but of necessity,.....rooted like a tree, therefore, not
where it would, but where need was; on which if any fruit
grow such as you can like, you are welcome to gather it
without thanks; and so far as it is poor or bitter, it
will be your justice to refuse it without reviling.'
Still the wonder returns, that, where unequalled power
seconded an attempt of such worth to art, there should not
have been appreciation so quick and welcome so generous as
to make it needless that the writer should thus explain
himself. We could not account for the 'reviling' of
review-tirades, did we not know that the completer the
treatment of a subject, the more partial may be the criticism; and the more radical the reform intended, the blinder

and ruder is apt to be the opposition. The controversy is
to be interpreted in Ruskin's favor. Had he done less, or
worse, or with smaller promise of influence, no such stir
would have been raised about him.

To begin with the most external merit, - that of style
is allowed on all hands....

The rich flow of the style, which is the most obvious
quality of it, represents the most obvious quality of the
writer's genius, its affluence. The very valuable and complete indices which appear in the last volume prove at a
glance the close proportion in the work of large faculty
and earnestness with large design and full accomplishment.
If some one gifted with Carlyle's power of mental and moral
portraiture shall, by and by, attempt an intellectual and
spiritual likeness of Ruskin, and it chances to be as
faithful as the great essayist's picture of Luther, the
truth of it will appear in the prominence given to this
affluence of vigorous and various ability. This will be
the pervading expression, the general look of the picture,
from which the expressiveness of particular features, the
lines of thought, the traces of emotion, the tokens of
sentiment, the marks of imagination, may be caught in
detail.

Sometimes this affluent, many-sided ability seems
hardly managed deftly and successfully. The stream is not
'without o'erflowing, full.' There is trouble in guiding
it, some splash and confusion in the direction of it.
The very abundance causes turbulent eddying and wild swirl
of side-currents, not good for calm passage and happy voy-
aging. Therefore, in this last volume we have had the impression of incompleteness and incoherence of parts, a
certain indecisiveness and hurry of action, and failure of
full attainment. As if in an embarrassment of riches the
writer chose what seemed most important, but by necessity
left many things fit to the harmonious conduct and symmetry of his work. Perhaps nothing beside this should be
expected. Certainly, complaint is most ungracious that great
and full benefit is not made better and larger. There are
over-critical people who would quarrel with the favors of
the very gods. If Pegasus were sent to their door, all
saddled for them, they would be sure to look the gift-horse
in the mouth. It is best to be content with what signal
ability, let alone genius, does in its own way and
direction. It is modest and profitable to keep a teachable
temper before masterly adaptedness and special preparation.

Save for a final and express assertion of Turner's rank
among the highest, - the design proposed, from the first,
as a prime object, - the closing volume, though the end of
the publication, is no more the conclusion of 'Modern

Painters' than the fourth, or the second. It is a work of
conclusions, rather than a conclusion. It is not wound up
with a last page or last chapter of definite and confined
statement. The eloquent chapters, in this last volume, on
Greek Sculpture and Venetian Art, are conclusive on those
themes, but no more conclusive on the work than the memorable metaphysics of the second volume....

Now we should think it precisely on this affluence and
variety of his gifts that Ruskin's claim most rests to
special honor from the class of artists. Yet their vote
of golden opinions and good words is refused on this account. This is the very ground on which his peculiar place
as a teacher is disputed, and the proper rank of 'Modern
Painters' is denied. The opinion is not uncommon that he
is too eloquent to be a safe guide, that his poetic feeling persuades him away from practical views, that his enthusiasm affects his precision, and that all the seductive
qualities which put him so high in literature, are, in
proportion to their eminent power and combination, hind-
rances to reasonable counsel and profitable instruction
in art. Fine writer, poet, philosopher, political economist, literary critic, - call him which of these you will,
or all of them, but not a wise adviser or good teacher in
the one purpose of his book, and of his life also. It is
a mistake. For he who gives right impulse to the artist's
head and heart is a wiser counsellor and better instructor
than he who systematizes rules for his hand. He who sets
forth, after such fashion that it cannot but be felt, the
great intellectual and spiritual forces which work in and
for true art, does more in the cause of art than the definer of processes or the adviser of manipulations [sic].
In which has Ruskin done most for the great profession and
its professors, - in the Two Paths, or in the Elements of
Drawing? The narrow conceit of those priding themselves
on being 'practical' men has been often exposed. But much
remains to be learned about the difference between the
meanly and the nobly practical.

'Modern Painters' is nobly practical. It proceeds upon
the conviction, and is fairly judged only by the belief,
that, the better stored and cultured the artist's mind,
the better artist he will be, supposing his innate bias
towards art....

It may serve our purpose to follow out a little more in
detail Mr. Ruskin's relation and benefit to the artist-
craft. It will further our present suggestion of those
merits in 'Modern Painters,' on which depend our admiration
of it, and our claim for it of the first place in English
art-literature. The failure justly to appreciate it
arises, however, from much the same reason in general

readers as in the artist-class. Only they have the advantage of coming to it without professional and technical
prepossessions, which are the hardest of all for a teacher
to fight against, and for the pupil to rid himself of and
leave his mind clear and generous. The misapprehension
arises from mistaking the intention, and from judging by
some portion, not by the whole.

The intention is mistaken. That intention, we mean,
which is not so much meditated in the deliberate purpose
of the writer, as spontaneous in the character of his mind
or the quality of his genius. It is to be borne in mind
that 'Modern Painters' is not a strict system of art-
precept and practice, where principles and rules all hang
together and the parts are closed up with obvious coher-
ence. It is not an art-philosophy, if, as terms go,
exactness of form and closeness of method are conditions.
Yet it does deserve that name, we claim, if philosophy be
an aspiration rather than an acquisition; love of wisdom,
for so the root of the word intends, more than attainment
of wisdom. Its author is, however, no philosopher in the
sense of a system-maker and definer of metaphysical
niceties. His power is in his perceptions, so fresh and
so fine. And in these vivid and truthful perceptions, his
work bears close relation and imports great benefit to the
class of artists; likewise, to all students and lovers of
art and nature....

The work ['Modern Painters'] is also wrongfully judged
by portions of it, not as a whole; - an injustice equal to
mistaking the intention of it. Some persons seem never to
get over the shock an unlucky writer gives their prejudices or affections. The early severities against Claude,
Salvator, and the Dutch masters still rankle. And how can
the unhallowed handling of Raphael's sacred cartoons be
forgiven? A sturdy defiance, at the outset, of convention
and tradition, in æsthetics, morals, or religion, is the
unpardonable offence....

We press the claim of 'Modern Painters' to be studied
in its wholeness, judged by the spirit and scope of it,
and esteemed for its fine impulse to what is best in mind
and heart. We, however, by no means claim that its
solution of certain particular questions and its dictum on
special matters concerning art must be at once received,
or that they will finally be accepted. Their settlement
rests, in the main, not upon those popular grounds of
æsthetics and morals from which the general reader draws
his reasons, but upon arguments and issues of proper artistic pertinency....

It is, at last, not the extent of the view reported to
us that moves our admiration and praise, but a sense of

the height climbed to secure that breadth, the reflection
what a summit is reached to command that view. The affluence and variety of the power at work are at first the
striking things; - and we take delight in the attractions
of the style, where dignity and clearness are constant
and beauty ever recurs, - in the wealth of manifold illustration, the treasures of observation and learning, the
reach of reasoning and conclusion, the calm assurance and
fervid passion, the wise comprehension, subtile thought,
gentle sentiment, and high imaginings. But more than the
amplitude and varied range, the quality of the power engaged is the essential condition of the regard we feel
and the claim we press. This, unregarded at first, in
such unstinted bestowal, holds at last our admiration, and
chastens transient and confused excitement over the work
into a justified appreciation of it, and lasting, quiet
plasure in it.

Its intrinsic quality of spiritual insight is the prime
characteristic of 'Modern Painters,' which makes it supreme
in the literature of art. Not that this does not appear
in other works. Lord Lindsay's, Mrs. Jameson's, M. Rio's,
Mr. Norton's, are distinguished for it. But here it is at
once more subtile and more full. In its early search, it
did not seem quite catholic. But, in the progress of the
book, and notably in the fifth volume, all suspicion of
asceticism is cleared, and the inseeing faculty found to
inquire broadly as well as to look keenly, both wisely discursive and finely scrutinizing, tolerant and delicate.

Therefore, the religiousness of true art has been all
along asserted. The corollary has been drawn, too, that
labor in art is worthy, as it is pious service, reverential
and thoughtful. The sacredness of the art-calling is urged
as the interpretation of the perfection of God's works, and
all purpose and all work persistently depreciated which is
not religious by humility and faithfulness, when it cannot
be so by height of sentiment and grandeur of imagination.
Good service this to artists and the friends of art; -
from which it is no deduction that certain Pre-Raphaelites
misuse it like fanatics and pedants, claiming to follow in
the strait way of its direction, when they walk in the narrowness of their own vanity and slender powers. And let
it be confessed that it greatly enhances that service, and
proves how good it is, that, under its encouragement, if
not by its suggestion or inspiration, have appeared the
noblest expressions our day can show of romantic and sacred
art, - in Millais's 'Huguenot,' and Holman Hunt's 'Finding
of Jesus in the Temple.' Much less is it any deduction
from its credit or worth, that some have not the wit or the
virtue to see or receive it, and so deny that any service
is rendered.

There is nothing in letters or in life more impressive than to observe how surely he who deals with profound principles and lofty ideas is influential in many directions beside the one to which his affection or his will is consciously pointing. Their relations are infinite, and while he works by their inspiration to one end, he works also to many ends. He labors in numerous interests beside the special one to whose furthering or defence he brings their great authority to bear. He has truly 'builded wiser than he knew.' His edification is larger than appeared in his plan. This is the fine impression which remains upon closing the volume in which Mr. Ruskin ends his seventeen years' work. He is a true preacher of the Word. His service is not to artists only and students of art. Men and women, unlettered in and unconcerned with the fine arts, are encouraged and helped by him in the art of life. Among whose workers are few Angelicos and Angelos, - angelical, indeed, in their divine sending and inspired ministration. But in it each is to do what he can; great imaginations and inventions falling to few, but faithfulness, with its discoveries and exploits, denied to none; sublime frescos of Paradises and Judgments not to be achieved by every one, but something ever to be caught of the beauty which blooms by all way-sides, and in the sunshine of every day.

Now, when this review is of necessity come near its close, the matter is just touched which promises richest development. A high place has been assigned to 'Modern Painters,' because we are confident that to admire here is only to be just, and to pay great honor is only to give a small part of the due. But the best argument for its right to such a place must thus remain suggested here, and not followed out.

It is memorable - for justice' sake and for praise - what the writer asserts to have been his object: 'To declare the perfectness and eternal beauty of the work of God.' It is no after-thought of the last preface, but the fore-thought of his mind and the fore-speech of his attempt. That, the whole work, through all the volumes of it, proves. Will it be thought, then, a strain at a figure to call it a true 'Magnificat'? But who has not felt the language of it rise into music, and heard at intervals along its lines the absolute rhythm of a sacred lyric? It is so intrinsically, more than figuratively, - 'Magnificat anima ejus Dominum.' A drawing of Angelico's 'Ancilla Domini' fronts the opening page of the last volume. To our fancy, it is rightly placed there, typical of the office and service of the book. For, as she sits there in her glorified humility and gracious aspect, herself the sweet

prelude to her song, the hymn seems rising to her lips:
'My soul doth magnify the Lord.'

To the author, the picture may mean simply that art is
the handmaid of the Lord and the servitor of religion.
Sure, that is the high rank and office of art. By that its
works and its servants, in all its forms, of painting,
sculpture, architecture, music, or of life and action, are
all to be tried, and proved worthy or unworthy according
as they approach or recede from that rank, accept or scout
that office. And when the book appears which shall make
that truth plainer and more convincing than this, now so
incompletely reviewed, then 'Modern Painters' will take a
second place in the literature of art.

'Unto this Last'

1860

Only once or twice before in his stormy career could it
be said that Ruskin encountered such ferocious and widely
hostile criticism as was visited upon him with the appearance in monthly parts of 'Unto this Last' in the 'Cornhill
Magazine' (August-November 1860). The anonymous review
in the 'Saturday Review', a powerful weekly of considerable appeal to the educated, conservative mind is, with
only a touch of exaggeration, characteristic of many
contemporary publications. For a fuller account of the
background to, and reception of, 'Unto this Last' and
other economic writings by Ruskin, see Introduction,
pp. 16-17.

Very delicate questions sometimes arise as to the point
at which folly becomes so glaring as to be harmless, and
the difficulty of deciding whether, in any particular case,
it ought to be so considered is increased by the reflection
that the capacity which men, and still more women, possess
for being affected by absurdity is almost unbounded, and
hardly conceivable. This is especially the case with
tawdry and half-picturesque folly; and perhaps the noxious
power of absolute nonsense is at its maximum when it is
dashed with a sort of milk-and-water asceticism, which
affects, by the help of a profusion of texts, to be pious
as well as silly. These considerations induce us, not without considerable doubts whether good indignation is not
wasted on a worthless object, to return to the subject of
Mr. Ruskin's papers on Political Economy in the 'Cornhill

Magazine.' That Mr. Ruskin should consider Ricardo inaccurate, and look upon Mr. John Mill as inconsistent -
that he should suppose that the Devil fell because he believed in political economy - that he should drag quotations
from Zechariah and the Proverbs into the midst of declamatory accounts of exchange and profit which he occasionally
describes as definitions - that he should conclude his
speculations with a maudlin exhortation to all mankind to
wear sackcloth and ashes, and to 'go forth weeping' - is
what might have been expected from his former career. But
his former career contains, unhappily, the lesson that
this sort of writing is popular. People like, for some
strange reason, to see a man degrade himself; and there
are few forms of self-degradation which are more flattering
to mankind than the abjuration by a really able man - and
where he has only to talk and to describe, and not to
think, Mr. Ruskin undoubtedly is that - of the duty of
moral continence and self-respect. If a man of any sort
of mark will condescend to go about weeping and howling
quoting texts with a voice choked with tears, insulting his
country and reproaching his neighbours with the querulous
female virulence, he may obtain a certain sort of worship.
There will be people who admire his insolence, the little
airs of coquetry which he constantly gives himself, like
a flirt who has ceased to be pretty, and, above all, the
slightly refined Spurgeonism of his religion. So long as
Mr. Ruskin confined himself to art, he had a subject on
which the presence of a high degree of sensibility and
descriptive power would atone for the want of more vigorous
qualities; but it is intolerable that a man whose best performances are deformed by constant eruptions of windy hysterics should be able to avail himself of the pages of one
of our most popular periodicals for the purpose of pouring
out feminine nonsense, in language which women would have
far too much self-respect to employ, upon so grave a subject as political economy. The 'Cornhill Magazine,' properly enough, mixes with the lighter matter to which much
of its popularity is owing discussions on subjects of
serious interest. They should be, and they generally are,
handled in the grave and quiet tone which educated men and
women ought to employ in their communications with each
other; and it is to be regretted that such a journal should
admit such tirades upon such a subject. It is not becoming
that such a man should be allowed the use of such a pulpit
for the purpose of delivering spasmodic rants against political economy. The world may have been mistaken in looking
upon Adam Smith, Mr. Ricardo, and Mr. Mill as some of the
clearest and most useful thinkers that England ever produced, but they are, at any rate, entitled to better

treatment than, like Sydney Smith's dean, to be preached
to death by a mad governess.

It is an act of condescension to argue at all with a
man who can only write in a scream. But, without attempting to disentangle the maze of empty sophisms which Mr.
Ruskin has been revelling in for some months past, we may
give a few instances of his utter incompetency to have an
opinion at all upon so difficult a subject as the one
which he handles. The quality of his mind appears in the
following remark. Mr. Mill observes - 'The word 'value,'
when used without adjunct, always means, in political
economy, value in exchange;' 'so that,' adds Mr. Ruskin,
'if two ships cannot exchange their rudders, their rudders
are, in politico economical language, of no value to
either.' One of Mr. Ruskin's curious delusions is that he
is witty, and another that he is pre-eminently logical. Any
one who will take the trouble of looking at the passage in
which this quotation from Mr. Mill occurs will obtain at a
glance an estimate of the silly and flippant puerility of
mind which underlies his brilliant language. We may observe that the sentence is absurd on the face of it.
Stated fairly, Mr. Ruskin's illustration would run thus: -
'If a ship's rudder could not be exchanged, it would have
no value in exchange - which is (as it ought to be if the
political economists are right) an identical proposition.
As worded by Mr. Ruskin, it is an attempt to fix an absurdity on another man by uttering one himself. He omits the
obvious possibility that the masters of the ships, instead
of exchanging their rudders, might sell them elsewhere. In
another place, Mr. Ruskin again attacks Mr. Mill for stating - what most persons who have studied the subject consider quite an indisputable truth - that a demand for commodities is not a demand for labour, but (which is a very
different thing) for the results of labour, and that
labour is supported and employed by the capital expended
in setting it to work, and not by the demand of purchasers
for its produce. Mr. Ruskin attempts to controvert this
assertion, and he does so in a manner which shows that he
does not understand the position which he attacks. Mr.
Mill's example is the case of a man who spends money in
laying out a pleasure-ground instead of buying velvet.
In the first case, he says, he creates a demand for labour,
but not in the second. Upon this, Mr. Ruskin interpolates
into his paper the ungrammatical and spasmodic observation
- 'Error, colossal as well as strange' (a remark which
would not even be good French); and he observes in a note
- 'The consumer of the velvet pays the weaver with his own
funds as much as he pays the gardener.' 'The velvet is as
much produced by the consumer's capital, though he does

not pay for it till six months after production, as the
grass is produced by his capital.' If this were true, Mr.
Mill would be right by Mr. Ruskin's own confession, for
his position is that, whoever produces the velvet, it is
produced by *capital*, and not by the price paid for it
after it is made. Mr. Ruskin does not understand Mr. Mill
well enough to be able even to contradict him consistently. But in point of fact it is not true, unless the
man who uses the velvet engaged and pays the labourers
who make it - a case expressly referred to by Mr. Mill.
The obvious test is this: If there were capital, but no
demand, velvet or anything else could be made; if, on
the other hand, there were the greatest possible demand
(as in the case of a famine) but no capital, the velvet or
corn could not be made. Upon this Mr. Mill observes -
'So that the capital cannot be dispensed with - the purchasers can.' This remark is altogether beyond Mr. Ruskin,
who accordingly makes it the peg on which to hang one of
the little jokes which a strange delusion leads him to
believe to be amusing. 'I do not know if Mr. Mill's conclusion has yet been reduced to practice in the City on
any large scale.' This is just the sort of observation
which would draw from a certain kind of young lady the
graceful compliment,'Oh, Mr. Ruskin, you are so satirical.'
Perhaps the culminating point of Mr. Ruskin's impudence is
to be found in his attack on Ricardo, who is probably one
of the most accurate of English thinkers and writers.
'Ricardo,' he says, '*with his usual inaccuracy*, defines
what he calls "the natural rate of wages," as "that which
will maintain the labourer." Maintain him, yes, but
how?... First as to length of life. Out of a given number
of fed persons how many are to be old, how many young?...
Will you arrange their maintenance so as to kill them
early, or so as to enable them to live out a natural life?
Which does Mr. Ricardo mean to be their natural state,
and to which state belongs the natural rate of wages?' Mr.
Ruskin, with his usual inaccuracy, omitted to observe that
Ricardo answered these questions in the very passage which
he pretends to quote. What Ricardo said is this - 'The
natural price of labour is that price which is necessary to
enable the labourers, one with another, to subsist and to
perpetuate their race, without either increase or diminution. The power of the labourer to support himself and
the family which may be necessary to keep up the number of
labourers does not depend upon the quality of money which
he may receive for wages, but on the quantity of food,
necessaries, and conveniences *become essential to him from
habit,* which that money will purchase.' Impudence cannot
go far beyond this. Mr. Ricardo specifies the number to be

supported, and the degree of comfort in which they are to
be supported - namely, that which has become essential to
them from habit - and Mr. Ruskin accuses him of inaccuracy
for having omitted to do so.

We will add only one other illustration of the utter
imbecility of Mr. Ruskin's reasoning powers. His papers
are one long attack upon political economy. He charges it
with promoting every sort of meanness and avarice, and
with being negligent of, if not opposed to, every moral
virtue. We will put a precisely parallel case. In whatever sense political economy is opposed to charity, to
philanthropy, and to self-denial, medicine is also opposed to them. It is just as true to say that medicine
exhorts men to be cowards, as to say that politcal economy
exhorts them to grind the faces of the poor. Suppose a
physician were to say, as he might with perfect truth, If
you go and visit that poor woman who is lying ill of scarlet fever, you will very possibly catch it yourself; if you
get in the way of the shot and shell which are flying about
those Chinese forts, you will be maimed, and perhaps killed;
if you will go on nursing your husband, you will ruin your
constitution; if you do not give up your profession, you
will very probably shorten your life. Would any one say
that his science was false, or that he was advising cow-
ardice and selfishness? On the contrary, he would be telling the truth and doing his duty; and it would be for those
whom he advised to do theirs, as the circumstances of the
case might require. The case of the political economist is
precisely the same. He says to a landlord, The principles
of rent are so and so - you can get so much for your cottages. But he does not advise him to get all he can. He
says to the employer of labour, The natural rate of wages
is so and so - you can, if you please, obtain labourers
for so much, and you can starve them into taking it. But
he does not advise him to do so. Suppose a landlord were
to say, 'The labourers on my estate having been radically
demoralized by the old Poor-law, and having from ignorance,
extravagance, and vice, been reduced to a state of extreme
misery and want, I have it in my power, as political
economy shows, to obtain their services for 7s. a week,
whereas they now receive 9s. This is what I could do if I
pleased. I should gain by it 2s. a week per head in wages.
On the other hand, I should perpetuate beggary and misery,
and should be surrounded by wretched slaves instead of
free Englishmen. I will, therefore, pay them wages on
which they can live. I will improve their homes. I will
establish schools. I will try to raise their notions of
comfort, and to increase their powers of work. Thus they
will have more and better labour to sell and I more to buy;

they will become more and more independent, and I shall be
at once better served, and a happier and better man, and
I think all this worth much more than the immediate sacrifice of wages.' Surely this is straightforward, and consistent both with political economy and with social duty.
Whether the writings of Ricardo and Mr. Mill, with their
vigorous logic and manly simplicity of style, would conduce to such a tone of feeling more than Mr. Ruskin's intolerable twaddle about Ixion, Demas, Dante, and Ezekiel's
vision of the wheels, is a question which people will determine according to their preference for strong exercise
on the one hand, or hysterics on the other.

    There is another side to Mr. Ruskin's theories which is
to us even more repulsive than his attacks on political
economy and the great writers who have investigated it.
The way in which he writes of the relations of the rich and
poor is worse than ridiculous. It is positively wicked,
for it can produce amongst the poor nothing else than
bitter and causeless hatred, base ingratitude, and a vile,
servile temper of mind, the contemplation of which can excite nothing but indignant disgust. The following are the
passages to which we refer:-

[Quotes from 'It is proposed' to 'holy perfect, and pure',
'Works' 17: 106-7; and from 'And if on due' to 'weary are at
rest', 'Works' 17: 114.]

    Putting these two passages together, what do we learn
from them? That the rich are responsible for all the sins
of the poor - that they are wicked tyrants who 'refuse not
only food to the poor, but salvation' - and that, in consequence, they ought to go forth mourning in sackcloth and
ashes, and to live on bread and water till every labourer
in the country is in perfect comfort. Whether Mr. Ruskin
practises his own doctrine - whether he wears sackcloth,
and 'goes weeping forth, bearing precious seed' - are
questions which greatly concern his own sincerity, though
they are not very important to the public; but though his
evidence is worthless against others, it is good against
himself. He is a man of property - he therefore, by his
own confession, has refused the poor not food only, but
salvation. If he has ever enjoyed anything beyond mere
necessaries - if he has ever lived in a good house, kept a
carriage, worn good clothes, bought expensive books, made
expensive journeys, indulged expensive tastes - he must,
by his own statement, be cruel and ignorant; and if he continues to do so for the future, he is a hypocrite as well.
One of the duties which he prescribes to the rich he has
certainly fulfilled. 'The light of the eyes can only be

through tears,' and he is a perfect paragon of blubbering.
He whines and snivels about England and the poor like the
Jews who howl before the wall of Jerusalem. However this
may be, he has certainly put together, in the passages we
have extracted, such a heap of calumnies and insults
against all classes of English society as few writers can
match. The poor, it seems, are mere slaves, and irresponsible slaves. They are vicious and degraded, and it is
all the fault of the rich. Was there ever such an idol-
ator of wealth as this denouncer of riches? The notion
of the poor praying to the rich for leave to be good, is
one which could only have occurred to a sentimental philanthropist. If Mr. Ruskin's words are not as idle as
they are false, he must mean to say that the poor have no
will, no conscience, and no responsibility; that if a
labourer gets drunk and beats his wife it is the fault of
the squire, the parson, and the attorney; that if a servant steals his master's property it is the fault of his
master for being rich, and that the poor depend upon the
rich not only for their food, but for their salvation.

To state such absurdities is to refute them, but poor
men would do well to consider that what Mr. Ruskin says is
only the broad statement of a popular fallacy which often
lurks under philanthropic phrases. They can lay their sufferings at the door of the rich only by laying their freedom there also. Free agents may sin, and reasonable beings
may suffer, but it is possible to sink beneath sin and suffering by becoming a thing instead of a person. They would
also do well to consider carefully the concluding paragraph of their kind patron's advice. Luxury is at present
a sin - 'the light of the eye can only be through tears.'
This applies to the prosperous mechanic as well as to the
rich merchant, for no sharp line deivides them. The frugal
and skilful labourer has no more right to dress well or
to carry a watch than Mr. Ruskin himself. If a mechanic
abjures spirits and puts off his marriage till he has got
a good stock of clothes, some shelves of books, substantial
furniture, and the means of hiring a maid-of-all-work, he
is little better than one of the wicked. If he can furnish
a few rooms and let lodgings, he is next door to a capi-
talist; and if he eats meat more than once a week he is on
the high road to perdition. It is simply awful to think,
too, how he neglects the great duty of crying. The wretch
has been known to go to the play when he ought to have been
weeping between the workhouse and the hospital, and he
sometimes allows himself to be pleased with his wife's new
gown though he has a drunken neighbour whose wardrobe is at
the pawnbroker's.

To English feelings the most revolting part of Mr.

Ruskin's performance is his gross calumny on the nation to
which he belongs. Ours is not a country to cry about.
Philanthropic gentlemen are infinitely too ready with their
pity. It is simply false and absurd to assert that a man
who is industrious and sober - and how the rich prevent the
poor from being either utterly passes our understanding -
cannot, as a rule, get a living here. On the contrary,
there is no old country in the world in which he can do
this so easily. With prudence, and self-command, and a
moderate amount of manual skill, almost any one can both
live and marry; and what do men wish for beyond this? Do
they wish some paternal despotism to coddle and dandle
them, to protect them against their own faults by depriv-
ing them of their free will, and to convert them into emas-
culate animals, for fear that some of them may be unhappy
men? The English people are far too sturdy for such
wretched crutches and leading-strings as these. Indeed,
they have had enough of them. The old Poor-Law, which per-
petuated the pauperism originated by the monasteries, was
framed upon the sort of half-understood notions of paternal government which Mr. Ruskin would wish to revive, and
its traces still remain, both in our laws and our villages.
The absurd law of Settlement still disgraces the one, and
a considerable degree of servility and misery lingers in
the other. If any one wishes to see the difference between
the social effects of the application of the principles of
political economy and those of merely instinctive charity,
let him compare Lincolnshire, the East Riding of Yorkshire,
and that part of the Scotch lowlands which is scientifically cultivated, with the south and west of England. The
difference between the man who earns eighteen shillings a
week under the one system and the man who earns nine shillings under the other will give him some notion of the comparative value of the philanthropy of Mr. Ruskin and that
of Mr. Mill.

26. UNSIGNED REVIEW, 'LLOYD'S WEEKLY NEWSPAPER'

18 November 1860, 9

The editor of 'Lloyd's Weekly Newspaper' at the time of the
review was Blanchard Jerrold (1826-84), son of the wit,
radical journalist, and playwright, Douglas Jerrold (1803-
57). Douglas Jerrold himself edited the journal until his
death when he was succeeded by his son. Blanchard Jerrold,

biographer and playwright as well as journalist, inherited
many of his father's antipathies towards *laissez-faire* economics, and it is very likely he was Ruskin's champion
against the onslaught of the 'Saturday Review' (see No. 25).
'Lloyd's' was in the best tradition of both father and son
in its appeal to lower-middle-class readers of liberal per-
suasions; it is estimated that its circulation in the early
sixties was well over 150,000 per week.

There is a class of writers that despises, or affects to
despise, the man who exhibits heart in addition to logic,
in his treatment of subjects that fall within the scope of
his pen. The 'Saturday Review' office is the head-quarters
of this class. Readers by the thousand are to be found by
critics at once hard-headed and heartless, because there
are thousands of men who delight in mischief. Mr. Ruskin
has enjoyed a great popularity during many years. His
noble English has stirred the pulse of his countrymen. He
has brought a fine imagination and a cultivated mind to the
art-criticisms with which he has enriched the literature of
his time. He has helped largely to cultivate the taste of
his generation. He has become, in short, a popular writer;
and by making himself popular, he has made himself the
enemy of the 'Saturday Review.' He shares the enmity of
this 'Review' - it may be some consolation to remember -
with Dickens and with his present editor. He is savagely
hounded from paragraph to paragraph, down columns where a
kindly word or hearty expression of good will has never appeared. He may bear, then, to be hunted in his turn - when
much nobler prey has been uncarted [sic].
    He is told that his exhortations are maudlin. His popu-
larity is based on the fact that 'people like, for some
strange reason, to see a man degrade himself.' He has ab-
jured 'the duty of moral continence and self-respect;' -
and therefore he is popular. He is allowed 'the presence
of a high degree of sensibility and descriptive power' in
his art writings; but these gifts are only atonements for
his 'want of more vigorous qualities.' His performances
are 'deformed by constant eruptions of windy hysterics.'
Mr. Thackeray is rated for having allowed such a writer to
discourse from the Cornhill pulpit. Having offered Mr.
Ruskin these hard hits - the writer pauses, and appears to
ask whether the gentleman has had enough. Then a second
round opens. It is condescension in the critic (it would
be amusing to discover who is this gracious dignitary
whose affability stoops even to Mr. Ruskin) - it is a condescension in the critic 'to argue at all with a man who
can only write in a scream.' Mr. Affable means, we presume,

'can write only in a scream.' Mr. Ruskin has a delusion
that he is witty - if the critic himself have this delusion, we trust his friends will not lose sight of him.

We are supporters of Mr. Ruskin's attacks upon political economy. We see errors enough in his views, but we
shall not therefore throw a slang dictionary at his head.
Mr. Ruskin has a claim upon our respect, as much for his
thorough and courageous honesty as for his genius.

But it is in the latter part of the 'Saturday Review's'
article on Mr. Ruskin's 'intolerable twaddle,' that we
approach the reason why he is placed in the Southampton-
street pillory. Mr. Ruskin pleads the cause of the poor,
and of the duties owed by the rich to the poor. These
passages we quote at length, because they come direct from
the depth of the writer's heart; and because it is against
the man who can give to the world this fine outburst of a
noble nature that the 'Saturday' critic throws his stale
eggs:-

[Quotations identical to those on p. 278.]

This passage stirs, in the mind of the 'Saturday'
critic, 'indignant disgust.' Disgust at what? At the call
which bids the rich and powerful be more mindful of the
souls and bodies of the poor? At the suggestion that by
such care as we ourselves have received, we may make them
continent and sober as ourselves? At the declaration that
meat is not all that is kept back from the poor - but that
wisdom and virtue are held back?
The critic endeavours to reduce Mr. Ruskin's appeal to
the absurd. Mr. Ruskin is asked whether he practices his
own doctrine; whether, pending the advent of the labourers'
perfect comfort, he wears sackcloth and tastes only bread
and water? If not, the 'Saturday' critic dubs him hypocrite, ignoramus. This reasoning has been again brought
against men who preach Christian doctrine; for let the
critic remember, Mr. Ruskin, in these passages which excite
his disgust, preaches pure Christianity. He says, give, and
largely, to the poor; not only from your tables, but of
your knowledge. Does the reviewer pretend to be a Christian, or simply a logician, with no more heart than suf-
fices to the life of an oyster?
Be it especially observed that Mr. Ruskin does not say
- as his critic coolly asserts - that the poor have no will,
no conscience, and no responsibility. He simply asserts
that the poor, like the rich, have their dispositions by
inheritance or by education; and he reminds the rich that
by better education than the poor now receive they may be
made continent and sober, wise and dispassionate, as their

rich and highly cultivated neighbours. Then saith the
critic, the poor 'can lay their sufferings at the door of
the rich only by laying their freedom there also.' Who
asks them - who implores them to fall upon their bellies
at the rich man's doors, and show the napes of their necks
to him? Not Mr. Ruskin. It is the rich man who is be-
sought to come forth and teach and help the poor - not
with meat alone, forsooth! but to lift him from the earth
and place him erect beside himself - giving him equal nobility, by affording him all the knowledge that he has to
give. By giving knowledge and help to the poor, shall we
debase and enslave them? Why, knowledge will bring them
power to stand on their own ground, and maintain their
independence.

Is it not rather the belief of the 'Saturday' critic in
the great power that the raising up and educating of the
poor would give them - a power which the scoffing pedant
fears - that lashes the storm of his indignation? Every
man who aspires, in these days, to do good to his fellow
creatures, is dubbed a philanthropist by the 'Saturday
Review,' only that he may be accused of cant or hypocrisy.
Mr. Ruskin is a hypocrite because he eats meat daily, while
he calls aloud to the rich to show the light of knowledge
to the poor. It would appear that 'Saturday' reviewers
enter upon their duties with the same spirit in which a
player enters a skittle ground. The honours are to him
who scores the greatest number of dead men.

27. UNSIGNED REVIEW, 'PRESS'

28 June 1862, 617

Termed by Lord Blake 'an organ for progressive Toryism,'
the 'Press' had Disraeli as its proprietor from 1853 to
1858. Its reasonableness towards Ruskin provides a welcome
calm amid so much abuse.

These essays ['Unto this Last'], on their first appearance
in the 'Cornhill Magazine,' were so copiously abused by all
the adherents of those opinions, which are rather apparently than really opposed to Mr. Ruskin, that we fancy the
public has hardly been allowed a fair chance of understanding them. There is much in these essays, and we believe
that Mr. Ruskin himself would be the first to admit it,

which requires expansion; and which, in consequence of the
extreme brevity with which it is stated, carries with it an
appearance of confusion with which we doubt if it be fairly
chargeable. But with the backbone of Mr. Ruskin's theory,
with the plain and courageous argument which gives it its
distinctive character, we feel confident that the world
must agree more and more nearly every day. There may be
very many points of detail with which Mr. Ruskin is in-
competent to deal; he may misunderstand the particular conditions of special branches of industry; but we say again
that we believe him to be insisting upon a general principle, which is not only sound in itself, but which is so
simple that he who runs might read it, if only the laws of
commerce had been made the subject of as much refined
study as the laws of jurisprudence, government or warfare.

In order to understand the scope of these essays
thoroughly the reader must place before his mind at the
outset a distinction which Mr. Ruskin only draws out gradually, and as it were indeed almost accidentally; and that
is the distinction between mercantile economy and political
economy. If we choose to call by the former name what is
commonly known under the latter, we shall have nothing to
fear from Mr. Ruskin. There *is* a science, he would admit,
of individual wealth-getting: but that is not political
economy. It is not the best economy for the whole πολις.
The accumulation of large fortunes in the hands of individuals has never yet been thought a national blessing by
the disciples of any school whatsoever. Yet this is the
end to which the lessons of pseudo-political economy (*i.e.*
mercantile economy) are always tending. Far better than
the wealth of the country should be distributed over a
wider surface, and through more numerous gradations. And
how to accomplish this distribution is, according to Mr.
Ruskin, to be learnt from true political economy. Even
economists of the school of Mill would regret in the abstract the disappearance of the old class of yeomen, middle
class substantial tradesmen, *et hoc genus omne:* but they
say it is inevitable; that the progress of civilisation,
and of the knowledge of the true laws of wealth, necessi-
tates their extinction. Now, this is just what Mr. Ruskin
flatly denies. So far from necessitating their extinction,
true political economy from his point of view involves
their preservation. And this opinion, whether right or
wrong, is not left by Mr. Ruskin on a purely sentimental
basis, but is deduced from first principles by a chain of
reasoning in which we at least have been able to detect no
flaw. It is not equality that Mr. Ruskin is aiming at; he
disclaims it, *totidem verbis,* fifty thousand times over
for the benefit of those persons who are too obtuse to see

that his theory is plainly opposed to it. It is a more
nicely graduated inequality at which he aims. He is
neither a communist nor utilitarian. Nobody would laugh
more heartily at the ridiculous fallacy of communism. Nobody frowns more sternly at the Oriental arrangement of
labour which makes one millionaire the lord over a thousand serfs, instead of adjusting the relations between
labour and capital on the model of English society, which
is formed of an infinitesimal number of layers, reaching
from the highest to the lowest.

Having separated political economy or the science of
national wellbeing from mercanitle economy or the science
of individual money-getting, and having found that the
latter, like slave-labour in America, however profitable
for a time, must ultimately overwhelm its upholders, we
may examine with advantage Mr. Ruskin's views of the real
political economy. We have not space just now to draw
these out at full length; but by referring to his idea of
the merchant *qua* a citizen, our readers will perhaps be
enabled to make out the rest for themselves. Mr. Ruskin
certainly has reason on his side when he says, that it is
just because this view of commerce has not hitherto been
adopted, that the commercial life has always been held in
less honour than any other life. Commerce, in the utilitarian sense of the word, is not in fact a 'liberal' profession; but pursued on the principles of Mr. Ruskin, it
would at once become so.

Mr. Ruskin's theory on the subject of payment is the
least conclusive portion of his book. His theory is that
the bad workman should be paid at the same rate as the
good workman, if employed; but that he ought not to be employed, and that so we should gradually drive bad labour
out of the market. But the answer to this assertion which
naturally rises to one's lips is, that you would be more
likely to deteriorate good labour than to destroy bad. If
the better workman found he got no more than the worse, he
would sink to the level of the other, through despair or
his superiority doing him any good. Mr. Ruskin, we suppose, would say, that if he has enough, he ought not to be
discontented because an inferior man gets as much. Perhaps
not. But till we can alter human nature, a man so placed
always will be discontented. We could wish, therefore,
that Mr. Ruskin had gone into this question a little more
carefully; for though we have every inclination to think
well of him, we cannot quite accept this particular
proposition.

28. UNSIGNED REVIEW, 'WESTMINSTER REVIEW'

October 1862, vol. 22, n.s., 530-2

The reception of 'Unto this Last' by the 'Westminster Review' is in keeping with the general tenor of criticism afforded that work when it appeared in book form. See Introduction, pp. 16-17.

Mr. Ruskin, in his preface to 'Unto this Last,' has given a fresh instance of that exaggerated affection we are all apt to bestow upon our weakest and most helpless offspring. The attention he again claims for the papers he published in the 'Cornhill Magazine,' will result in a fresh estimate of his powers, and a more correct verdict on his pretensions to the character of a public teacher, which he so unhesitatingly puts forth. His unquestionable love of nature, and his equally unquestionable power of expression, if, indeed, *copia verborum* be not the juster epithet, gave to his writings on painting and the fine arts a popularity which nothing but the general absence of settled principles of taste in the public mind could have rendered possible. When he had nothing but a vague way of thinking, and a set of artificial judgments to contend with, he could display his swashing blow with effect, and his own incoherences passed muster among those of his adversaries, because they were associated with so much that was fresh, original, and strongly felt. In the absence of science his rhetoric prevailed over the arbitrary dicta of schools of criticism from which any animating principle had long since departed. The public, weary of a worship which was carried on in a language almost unintelligible to them, gave a ready ear to the destroyer of idols they had ceased to reverence. Pre-Raffaelitism was welcomed as a fresh start on a road where all had confessedly lost their way; the stumblings and uncertain gait of the new school were excused on account of the resolute effort made to walk without supports. The necessity of a fresh return to Nature in Art was as evident as the absence of definite purpose in those who had resolved to adopt that course. Their practices were accepted with patience, in the hope that from the originality of the experiment principles of true art would ultimately be evolved. That Mr. Ruskin cleared the ground for these experiments, and rendered more easy the first steps of those who were endeavouring to form a new school of taste, is abundantly acknowledged; but only the absence of any well-grounded principles could have made such a success

possible, or justified the reputation which he has reaped
from his polemics. A reputation, however, which was acquired in a combat with shadows, cannot be expected to
maintain itself when its possessor is so far deluded by it
as to enter on a similar conflict with the more substantial
realities of an established science.

The attack made by Mr. Ruskin on the principles of political economy at once displays not only the weaknesses of
his intellect and the utterly unscientific turn of his
mind, but also a want of power in seizing upon the real
questions at issue between him and his opponents, that is
something marvellous in itself. A rigorously inductive
body of doctrine is not to be destroyed and scattered to
the four winds of heaven by the most energetic declaimer,
even though he patch his motley with the apocalyptic
spangles. Accustomed to contend only with popular notions,
he thinks it sufficient if he attacks equally vulgar conclusions drawn from a misunderstood science. He is so far
from having taken the trouble to understand the real doctrines of his adversaries, and is so utterly ignorant of
the scope and limitations of their science, that we are
sure his rhapsodies are read simply in deference to his
name alone; we have no doubt about the fate which would
have attended these letters had they been signed Smith or
Jones. In the confused *mêlée* of his former conflicts,
loud shouting and confident assertion had stood him in
such good stead that his first concern is to bring an
equal confusion into the fresh subject he has taken in
hand. When he defines wealth as life, and political economy as the science of consumption, he at once shows that
he has no concern with those he chooses to call his adversaries, and that no true issue can be joined where
such misconceptions are paraded as discoveries shamefully
neglected by economists. Political economy and common
sense alike agree to call commodities wealth, and economists profess only to investigate the laws which have
regulated and do regulate their production. Economists
have no direct concern with what ought to regulate either
consumption or production. They are as well aware as Mr.
Ruskin that the second great commandment is as little regarded by mankind as when it was first spoken; ethical inquiries form no part of their science, except in that important sense in which economists show the only ground on
which ethical progress can be hoped for. It is quite useless and beside the mark to indulge in rhetorical descriptions of the high majesty of man's moral nature, or to
expatiate on his lofty prerogatives and spiritual possi-
bilities; these things are only attainable when lower re-
quisitions have been complied with. Our animal wants must

be supplied before our peculiarly human ones can make
themselves regarded; the stomach will always take prece-
dence of the head and heart; our material existence must
be first secured before our spiritual needs can be felt,
much less attended to. Mr. Ruskin ought to be the last
to forget that even our sense of the highest natural
beauties is incompatible with a situation of peril in
which they may offer themselves to our notice. Political
economy is the science of the laws of the production of
the material bases alone of our existence; whenever these
laws involve any determinate relation between man and man,
they cease to be purely economical ones, and are determined by conditions with which political economy, as such,
has no concern, and to which its conclusions are as subject as men themselves. In such cases, the science is
merely declaratory, and publishes its doctrines subject to
those well-known conditions. Its duty is discharged when
these relations are fully pointed out, and indeed, the
full insight into whatever is to be deplored in them is due
exclusively to the investigations of economists.

It may be questioned whether Mr. Ruskin's extension of
the sphere of political economy to include politics, education, and police, be the result of ignorance or wilful
misrepresentation, but as a quibble of the kind would alone
make room for the remarks he had to deliver, it is of
little importance to trace it to its origin. The whole
argument of his book rests upon the fallacy that the State
should constitute itself into a temporal Providence watching over and controlling all its members. However Mr.
Ruskin may disclaim socialist tendencies, this assumption
is of the very essence of those theories on which he verb-
ally turns his back, only to reproduce them in a dress of
his own. The principle of competition which is the *bête
noire* of all enthusiastic reformers, is simply the salt of
the earth; by it only are men educated to the height of
their powers, and their wants supplied with a delicacy of
adjustment unattainable by any human intellect without its
aid. The whole creation is but a harmony of conflicting
claims, and every step onwards is but a new compromise.
It is useless to complain of the shallow presumption with
which Mr. Ruskin accuses men like Ricardo and Mill of having misunderstood the scope and tendency of their doctrines. This is sufficiently shown by the very title of
his book. Does he forget who it was who said, 'I will give
unto this last even as unto you?' The levity which feels
itself not out of place in adopting the words of the Master
of the Vineyard is not likely to be reached by any remarks
of ours. Our ultimate rewards and punishments will no doubt
be as little in accordance with the judgment passed on us

by our fellows, as the penny given to the labourer of the
eleventh hour appeared to his brother husbandmen.

But there is another order of considerations which we
would strongly recommend to Mr. Ruskin. Does he not think
that the same Master still has his eye upon his labourers,
and that he as much educates them by the hard consequences
of their own conduct, as rewards them when deserving. If
he thinks a milder discipline would have been more benevo-
lent, his next controversy will be the natural outcome of
his constitutional irreverence.

'Essays on Political Economy'

1862-3

29. FROM AN UNSIGNED REVIEW, 'LONDON REVIEW'

11 October 1862, 317-18

The 'Essays on Political Economy' were published quarterly in 'Fraser's Magazine' commencing in June 1862, and the following excerpt is from a criticism of the second, or September, essay; but, more significantly, it reflects in relatively gentle terms what many contemporary journals felt about Ruskin's excursions into political economy. The short-lived 'London Review' (1860-9) was under the editorship of that most prolific journalist, song-writer, and very minor poet, Charles Mackay (1814-89), at the time of this review. The paper was of a liberal bent and directed to middle and upper-middle-class readers; but it had difficulty competing with the more respected journals of the day, including the 'Athenaeum', and at the end of the decade was incorporated into the 'Examiner'. Ruskin's 'Essays on Political Economy', in substantially different form, were republished a decade later, in 1872, as 'Munera Pulveris', with a remarkably modest fanfare.

Mr. Ruskin continues to distress his friends and to delight his detractors. In the September number of 'Fraser's Magazine' he published a second part of the 'Essays on Political Economy' which are to form a sequel to his papers in the 'Cornhill.' More painful reading it would be difficult to discover in the literature of the day. Whether we consider the importance of the subject or the obligations under which Mr. Ruskin has laid his contemporaries, his utter inability to grapple with his task is

290

most grievous, and demands exposure. Had an inferior man
made the attempt, we might have passed by the failure in
silence; had the subject itself been of less importance,
we might have pardoned in Mr. Ruskin his harmless fooling;
but when a writer of great power, and, on some themes, of
so much authority, uses his power so as to lead the unthinking mass astray on matters in which all are more or
less practically interested, it is criminal to remain
silent.

Mr. Ruskin's task, briefly stated, is the reconciliation of political economy and Christian morality; the
importance of that task can scarcely be overrated. The
apparent antagonism between economic science and the
teaching of the Gospel has struck many minds of late years;
it has seemed to them that the problem which has perplexed
all ages of the world has in these latter days become more
dark and insoluble. Thinkers for countless generations had
asked themselves how evil could co-exist with the Divine
goodness; how could the misery and injustice of the world
be reconciled with the belief in a perfectly just Ruler;
but, inexplicable as they had often confessed the question
to be, they had always believed that misery and injustice
were abnormal - that they were irregularities and depar-
tures from the order which appeared to them to be the true
idea of the government of the world: it was impossible to
deny that Lazarus was found at the doorway of an un-
righteous Dives, but they refused to look upon that as his
proper position. Political economy, however, seemed to
approve of the disorders of social life; the inequalities
of work and reward which had before been deplored were
declared by the new science to be the proper results of
the laws of social action; want and pain might be found
sometimes caused by selfishness, but selfishness was the
mainspring of man's work, and upon it society was built.
Students to whom political economy presented this aspect
were perplexed at its apparent opposition to the maxims
which had formerly been held in veneration, and they asked
themselves whether they had rightly understood the new
science, and, if so, must they reject it or their earlier
lessons. Many have attempted to solve the difficulty; it
was met by Archbishop Whately, in the first lectures which
he delivered, now many years ago, as Professor of Political Economy at Oxford; but the Archbishop's lectures do
not appear to have quieted inquirers: in almost the last
number of the 'National Review' a writer discussed the
problem, without, however, convincing us that he had
accomplished its solution. In France, the writings of
Frederick Bastiat are largely occupied with the same
question; nor has any writer known to us dealt with it so

satisfactorily. More recently, however, M. Cherbulioz has
re-opened the inquiry, so far testifying that he, at least,
looks on no previous answer as complete.

This is the labour which Mr. Ruskin has undertaken. In
the eloquent but rhapsodical papers published in the
'Cornhill Magazine,' he uttered anew the oft-heard plaint
over a dislocated society; but, to the lamentations of his
predecessors, he added a charge against political economists that the method of their science directly tended to
the encouragement of disorder and injustice. Their fundamental maxims were false; their reasoning was inaccurate;
their results base and detestable. It remained for Mr.
Ruskin to unfold the principles of a true political economy, which should put to silence and to shame the disciples of Adam Smith, Ricardo, and Mill. In the pages of
'Fraser' this true political economy is expounded. Mr.
Ruskin's best friends must have received with dismay the
announcement of his self-imposed task. Great as his
abilities undoubtedly are, their power lay in an entirely
different direction. So subtle a critic had not probably
appeared since the time of Coleridge. He was unrivalled in
the somewhat feminine faculty of entering into the
thoughts of others. He could expound the half-unconscious
intentions of poets and painters. Add to this subtlety an
intense love and minute observation of nature, and a
purity and generosity of spirit without which both his
sympathy for nature and the works of genius would have
been impossible, and then set forth his thoughts in a pomp
of magnificent words, and we cannot be surprised that Mr.
Ruskin captivated many readers. Yet even as a critic there
were limitations to his faculty, whilst in the indescribable power which marks a creative thinker, he was altogether deficient. He has told us, with characteristic candour, that for a long time he misunderstood the power of
the Venetian school, and in particular he had failed to
appreciate the 'equal eye' with which Titian surveyed the
world. With the special circumstances of modern life he
was unable to grapple. From steam-engines and cotton-mills,
railroads and steamers, he recoiled; they might be used,
but beauty could never be associated with them. It never
seems to have struck him that the man of genius must
subdue these machines to himself, and, indeed, that it is
his especial privilege neither to flee from them nor to be
enslaved by them. The water-mills which countless painters
have delighted to sketch, the windmills which Turner so
often drew, must at one time have appeared to feminine
thinkers as base mechanical contrivances, degrading the
rushing stream or the untameable air, and supplanting the
time-honoured labour of women grinding at the mill; nay,

this latter simplest form of converting grain into flour
was itself once a new machine, putting aside the still
older and simpler machine of two stones, between which the
husbandman by manual labour pounded his grain. No one
could hope that a thinker of Mr. Ruskin's quality could
master the phenomena of social life; it was inevitable
that he should take refuge in sentimentalism from the
apparent injustice of society. Those who knew the man, and
had sympathised with his admiration of genius and his exposure of pretence; those who felt that they had been
instructed by his criticism, and had become his debtors
for an increased love of nature, must have been foremost
to regret his ill-advised efforts.

But as we have said, it is because Mr. Ruskin is a man
of authority, and the subject he meddles with is most
important, that every effort should be made to stop him.
A half-delirious man, however highly gifted, cannot be
allowed to move about unchecked with a lighted candle in a
powder magazine. Some years ago, a writer for whom Mr.
Ruskin has a great and deserved respect, wrote of the very
question which Mr. Ruskin discusses:- 'It must be taken
out of the hands of absurd, windy persons, and put into
the hands of wise, laborious, modest, and valiant men.'
Mr. Ruskin has, in his last contribution to 'Fraser,' recommended the book from which this extract is taken, as
containing all that need be said on his subject; but the
same book teaches different lessons to different men, and
another part of it so exactly expresses our feelings towards Mr. Ruskin's political economy, that we may be pardoned for asking his consideration of it:-

Catch your no man, - alas! have you not caught the
terriblest Tartar in the world! Perhaps all the
terribler, the quieter and gentler he looks. For the
mischief that one blockhead, that every blockhead does,
in a world so feracious, teeming with endless results
as ours, no ciphering will sum up. The quack bootmaker
is considerable; as corn-cutters can testify, and desperate men reduced to buckskin and list-shoes. But the
quack priest, quack high-priest, the quack king! Why do
not all just citizens rush, half-frantic, to stop him,
as they would a conflagration? Surely a just citizen *is*
admonished by God and his own soul, by all silent and
articulate voices of this universe, to do what in *him*
lies towards relief of this poor blockhead-quack, and
of a world that groans under him. Run swiftly; relieve
him, - were it even by extinguishing him! For all
things have grown so old, tinder-dry, combustible; and
he is more ruinous than conflagration. Sweep him *down*,

at least; keep him strictly within the hearth; he will
then cease to be conflagration; he will then become
useful, more or less, as culinary fire. Fire is the
best of servants; but what a master! This poor blockhead, too, is born for uses: why, elevating him to
mastership, will you make a conflagration, a parish-
curse or world-curse of him?

It is not pleasant to have to apply this language to
any man, but Mr. Ruskin is so pertinacious an offender,
and the occasion is so pressing, that we cannot think Mr.
Carlyle's language one whit too harsh.

Mr. Ruskin's last paper cannot be said to present much
novelty of error, but his previous blunders are reproduced
with amusing good faith. His former paper having consisted,
he tells us, of little more than definitions, he has in
this expanded and illustrated the given definitions so as
to avoid confusion in their use. The aim is good, but un-
luckily in no way attained in Mr. Ruskin's article; his
practice appears to be to define a term, and then incon-
tinently to forget the meaning he has attributed to it;
with a show of elaborate precision in the outset, there is
the loosest possible use of language in the sequel. Indeed,
it seems doubtful whether Mr. Ruskin knows what a definition means; certainly he has a very vague method of arriv-
ing at one. Take, for instance, the term wealth; a writer
on political economy may adopt two ways of expressing its
meaning, according as he is using the synthetic or
analytic method of developing the science; in the one case
he will, at the outset, tell us what he wishes to be
understood by the term, and although he may not be at
liberty to attribute to it a meaning wholly different from
those commonly associated with it, yet we may say, as a
rule, that we are bound to accept his definition, and can
only require that he should be consistent in his use of
the word; this is, of course, the method used by Euclid in
his 'Elements of Geometry.' According to the second method
he must determine, by examination of several examples of
things usually called wealth, the common qualities which
are expressed by giving them that generic name. Mr. Ruskin
uses the synthetic method; he started in his former paper
with a definition of wealth as consisting of things useful
in themselves, but in his last article he surprises us by
proceeding not simply to illustrate his meaning, but to
prove the accuracy of his definition; he devotes three or
four pages to an exposition of the errors other writers
commit in using the word wealth in a sense different from
his own; we might expose the blunders he commits in these
three or four pages, but it would be idle to comment on

errors in the conduct of reasoning which is vicious in its
inception; had its course been unexceptionable, he would
at the conclusion have only arrived at the point from
which he started, viz., that his definition of wealth was
not that generally put forth by political economists.

It is impossible to pass over Mr.Ruskin's sins in forgetting his own definitions. When we last discussed his
pretensions as an economist we pointed out that, after
carefully distinguishing between wealth and riches, -
wealth being an absolute and riches a relative term, - he
proceeded to use the two words without any reference to
the distinction between them. This blunder and others of a
similar character are found in the present number of
'Fraser.' Thus, we find him discussing the question of the
effect on the condition of a nation caused by a diminution
of its numbers, whilst its stock of useful things remains
unchanged, or, as he puts it, 'Given the store - is the
nation enriched by diminution of its numbers?' It is impossible, at the outset, to tell whether Mr. Ruskin is
about to inquire whether the nation is enriched or whether
it is made wealthier, and in his discussion of the question we are led to believe, at one time, that he is engaged on the one, and at another time that he is attacking
the other problem....

We do not intend to enter upon the fallacies of Mr.
Ruskin's currency notions; they are very, very old; they
have been exposed time after time, but will probably re-
appear as long as 'absurd, windy persons' attempt the work
of 'wise, laborious, modest, and valiant men.' Mr. Ruskin,
however, we must again repeat, has gifts which have done
the world some service, and might again be useful if
rightly employed: his present occupation awakens regret
rather than anger. It was said some months ago that a
great writer had retired from London in sick despondency;
the belief had seized him to which all men are at times
subject, that his life had been spent in vain toil; all
that he had said might be comprised in one sentence, and
that sentence had not been believed. In weariness, if not
in despair, he sought, in the austerity of mountain solitude, relief from the frivolity and inanity of human life.
No generous mind could have heard the announcement without
sympathy or without a desire to assure the sad thinker
that he had underrated his usefulness; many could have
confessed that they were indebted to him for help in keeping their tastes healthy, their vision clear, their minds
pure. But the consolations which might be addressed to the
author of 'Modern Painters,' must be denied to the economist. Men perplexed with the phenomena of life find in
these latter lessons confusion instead of comfort, hindrance instead of help, and for delight distraction.

'Sesame and Lilies'

1865

30. ANTHONY TROLLOPE, SIGNED REVIEW 'FORTNIGHTLY REVIEW'

15 July 1865, vol. 1, 633-5

Anthony Trollope (1815-82) at the time of this review was
still a civil servant attached to the Post Office and had
also made his name as the author of the Barset novels and
other writings. Trollope was much involved in the launching of the 'Fortnightly Review' and later edited 'St
Paul's Magazine'. His 'mixed' review of 'Sesame and Lilies'
(to which a third lecture, one of Ruskin's finest, The
Mystery of Life and its Arts, was added in 1871) is, by
comparison with many other contemporary evaluations by
well-known journals, relatively generous. See Introduction,
p. 17.

This work is the publication in a little volume of two
lectures by Mr. Ruskin, the first treating Of Kings'
Treasuries, and the second Of Queens' Gardens. To those
who are conversant with Mr. Ruskin's writings, it need
hardly be told that no national exchequer holds the kings'
treasuries of which speech is here made, and that the
queens' gardens in question lie round neither Buckingham
Palace nor Windsor Castle. The kings' treasuries are those
treasuries of knowledge which are found stored in well-
chosen libraries for the edification of men; and the first
lecture, applying to them, is called 'Sesame,' because Mr.
Ruskin would wish to see the doors of such libraries
thrown open somewhat wider than they at present stand. His
second lecture, of queens' gardens, is called 'Lilies,'
and in that it is his purpose to instruct women generally
as to their early preparation for life, and subsequent

duties while living.

Mr. Ruskin is well known to us as an art-critic, and as one who has written to us on Art in language so beautiful, and with words so powerful, that he has carried men and women away with him in crowds, even before he has convinced their judgments or made intelligible to them the laws which he has inculcated. He has been as the fiddler in the tale, who, when he fiddled, made all men and women dance, even though they were men and women by nature very little given to such exercise. But the fiddler was thus powerful because he understood the art of fiddling. Had he dropped his bow, and got into a pulpit that he might preach, we may doubt whether by his preaching he would have held the crowds whom his music had collected. To a fiddler so foolishly ambitious, *Ne sutor ultra crepidam* would have been the advice given by all his friends. It seems that the same advice is needed in this case. Mr. Ruskin had become a musician very potent, - powerful to charm as well as to teach. We danced, and were delighted that we could dance to such music. But now he has become ashamed of his violin, and tells us that his old skill was a thing of nought. He will leave talking to us of the beauties of art and nature, of the stones of Venice, and the wild flowers of Switzerland, and will preach to us out of a high pulpit on political economy and the degradation of men and the duties of women! He goes out of his way in his lecture on Kings' Treasuries to read a passage from a work of his own, in which he tells the world how unjust wars are maintained and how just wars should be maintained. That, he says, is the only book worthy of the name of a book which he has written. But the world of English readers, whose approbation of Mr. Ruskin as an art-critic has alone made it possible for him to obtain a hearing as a political economist, will not agree with him. They will still recognise him as a great musician, but they will not accord to him the praise of a great preacher.

Mr. Ruskin, in these preachings of his, has become essentially Carlylesque. He tells us that that which we have taken for our own 'judgment' is 'mere sham prejudice, and drifted, helpless, entangled weed of castaway thought;' that 'most men's minds are indeed little better than rough heath wilderness, neglected and stubborn, partly barren, partly overgrown with pestilent brakes and venomous wind-sown herbage of evil surmise;' and then, further on, in the same lecture, that 'what we call our British Constitution has fallen dropsical of late.' And in the second lecture, that 'this is to me quite the most amazing among the phenomena of humanity.' Now it is, I think, felt by most English readers that teaching such as this comes well

from Mr. Carlyle, although it sometimes comes in language
overstrained and with deeper denunciation of existing
Englishmen than existing Englishmen altogether deserve.
Mr. Carlyle has for many years been denouncing sham workmen and sham heroes, and using all the powers of his eloquence to produce true work, and, if such may be forthcoming, true heroism also. He has been recognised by us as
a preacher, and almost as a prophet, and if in the enthusiasm of his wrath he has allowed himself to be carried
away by the ever-increasing strength of his own convictions, we are ready to pardon the abuse he showers upon us,
on account of the good that we know that he has done to us.
We have sat at his feet and have been instructed. We have
listened to his words, and, as we have heard them, have
made some inward resolution that they should guide us. But
I doubt whether many men will receive Carlylesque denunciations from Mr. Ruskin with any good to their souls. He
produces them, indeed, with the grace of poetic expression
and the strength of well-arranged, vigorous words; but
they do not contain that innate, conspicuous wisdom which
alone can make such preachings efficacious.

He first advises men to read, and tells them that they
should read attentively. This in itself is very well, and
an excellent treatise on reading might probably be given
by a man so well instructed as Mr. Ruskin. But when he
attempts to define the way in which the general reader
should read, he mounts so high into the clouds, that what
he says, - if it were not altogether so cloudy as to be
meaningless and inoperative, - would quench all reading
rather than encourage it. Young or old, boys or girls, we
should have our Greek alphabets, and get good dictionaries
in Saxon, German, French, Latin, and Greek, in order that
we may trace out the real meaning of the words which we
read! After this, he is carried away by his wrath against
the nation, and tells us that, after all, we are not good
enough to read. 'My friend, I do not know why any of us
should talk about reading. We want some sharper discipline!'
'We have despised literature,' Mr. Ruskin says, and this
he proves by asserting that men will give more for a large
turbot than for a book; - but cheap literature he does not
like; and he tells us that we are 'filthy,' because we all
thumb the same books from circulating libraries! He says
that we have despised Science, and this he proves by showing that the Government has haggled at buying a collection
of fossils for £700, as though the science of a nation
depended on the propensities or means of the existing
Chancellor of the Exchequer! He says that we have despised
Art, and proves it by asserting that if all the Titians in
Europe were to be made into sandbags to-morrow at the

Austrian forts, it would not trouble us as much as the
chance of a brace or two of game the less in our game
bags! This assertion, which is simply an assertion, I may
leave to the judgment of those who know aught of the
market value of a Titian in England at the present day. He
says that we have despised Nature, and proves it by showing that we, - (not we English, but we mankind, I presume,) - have put a railroad bridge over the fall of
Schaffhausen, and by asserting that there is not a quiet
valley in England which we have not filled with bellowing
fire! He tells us also of the consuming white leprosy of
new hotels! That such a man should write on Art may be
well, but that he should preach to us either on morals or
political economy is hardly to be borne. We have despised
compassion, he tells us, and this he proves by a story
from the 'Daily Telegraph' of lamentable destitution in
London, corrected by another story from the 'Morning Post,'
of equally lamentable Parisian luxury; - as though want
and debauchery were evils of which large cities could rid
themselves by efforts of compassion! If men were not
sinful, if we were gods on the earth, then, indeed-! But
we hardly want a lecture from Mr. Ruskin to tell us this.
   Throughout his second lecture, which is of Queens'
Gardens, the spirit and the tone are much the same. The
words are often arranged with surpassing beauty, with such
a charm of exquisite verbal music that the reader, - as
was no doubt the hearer also, - is often tempted to forget
that they have no definite tendency, and that nothing is
to be learned from them by any woman living or about to
live. Again, he rebukes his hearers for the coal-furnaces
of their country. He is speaking of England, and says, -
'The whole country is but a little garden, not more than
enough for your children to run on the lawns of, if you
would let them *all* run there. And this little garden you
will turn into furnace-grounds, and fill with heaps of
cinders, if you can!' Then, with less of absurdity, but
hardly with more of reason, he speaks of the natural
beauties of Snowdon and Holyhead, telling us that such
hills, such bays, and blue inlets would have been always
loved among the Greeks. 'That Snowdon is your Parnassus;
but where are its Muses? That Holyhead Mountain is your
island of Ægina; but where is its temple to Minerva?' And
this he says because a statement as to a Welsh school
gives a very deplorable account of its scholars! Then he
goes on: - 'Oh ye women of England! from the Princess of
that Wales to the simplest of you, do not think your own
children can be brought into their true fold of rest while
these are scattered on the hills as sheep having no shep-
herd. And do not think your daughters can be trained to

the truth of their own human beauty, while the pleasant
places which God made at once for their school-room and
their play-ground, lie desolate and defiled. You cannot
baptize them rightly in those inch-deep fonts of yours,
unless you baptize them also in the sweet waters which the
Great Lawgiver strikes forth for ever from the rocks of
your native land, - waters which a Pagan would have worshipped in their purity, and you worship only with pollu-
tion?' Now the meaning of this, if you bolt the bran from
the discourse, is simply nothing; - there will be found no
flour left good for making bread for any woman. It is to
be lamented that Welsh children should be uneducated, and
we all hope that our revised system of national instruction will effectually cure such gross ignorance as Mr.
Ruskin describes. But English women are not polluted by
this ignorance. The causes and excuses for this ignorance
are far to seek and difficult to handle, and cannot be now
discussed here; but the manner and style and language, by
means of which Mr. Ruskin mingles the subject with Snowdon
and Parnassus, with Holyhead and Ægina, and with the
general duties of women in England, are simply rodomontade.

The line in literature which seems to belong to Mr.
Ruskin, partly from the nature of the man, and partly from
the special training which he has undergone, is very high,
and has become perhaps higher in his hands than it ever
was in the hands of any of his predecessors. He has given
to us wonderful words on Art, which have had all the
exactness of prose and almost all the grace of poetry. He
has numbered his readers by tens of thousands, all of whom
have seen with clearer eyes, and judged of Art with a
truer judgment, because of his teaching. Had it not been
so, this change of his, this desire to preach sermons
instead of making music with his bow, would be matter of
small moment to us. As it is, it is much to be hoped that
he will return to that work which he can do better than
any of his compeers.

31. JOHN DE CAPEL WISE, UNSIGNED REVIEW, 'WESTMINSTER
REVIEW'

October 1865, vol. 28, n.s., 574-6

John de Capel Wise (1831-90) was a Shakespearean critic
and frequent contributor to the 'Westminster Review'. That
Wise was a friend of Ruskin and his father may account for

the restrained and defensive tone of the criticism.

...Mr. Ruskin has lately been stoned by the critics. They
have flung enough stones at him to build his monument, and
enough mud to cement it together. Doubtless, his book is
very provoking to some minds. In his logic he draws too
large conclusions from too small premises, and in his
political economy draws them from none at all. Then he is
transcendental, carries himself on his own shoulders,
jumps down his own throat, eats the wind, and drinks the
clouds. Sometimes, however, it is the duty of the critic
to leave the faults alone, and dwell only on what is valuable and explain what is likely to be misunderstood. And
this book especially demands such criticism. Everybody has
enjoyed their joke at it, but nobody brought a grain of
sympathy. Even the passage printed in red ink, which has
produced such peals of laughter, is really not quite meaningless. Just as in the Libro d'Oro, and the Libri Vitæ
of the Catholic Church, men's noble actions and deeds of
charity were chronicled in letters of gold and silver, to
typify their nobleness, so, we suppose, did Mr. Ruskin by
his rubric intend to typify the sins that are scarlet.
Nonsense there is enough in the book, but Mr. Ruskin's
nonsense is sometimes more valuable than his critics'
sense.

Its great value, however, is in the tone of its feeling,
pitched often far too high, and most difficult to be
understood by a certain class of minds; and yet it is not
at all difficult to be understood by those who have
suffered from the flippancy and hardness of the day. When
Mr. Ruskin speaks of our national taste, or rather distaste, of art, and says that if 'we heard that all the
Titians in Europe were made sandbags to-morrow on the
Austrian forts, it would not trouble us so much as the
chance of a brace or two of game less in our own bags in a
day's shooting', he is only stating in an exaggerated form
what many at times of exasperation have felt. We ourselves
know a country squire, who hangs a magnificent Reynolds
in a dark corner of his gunroom. Remonstrance with him is
useless: he prefers the copies of Frith which panel his
drawing-room walls. Again, what Mr. Ruskin says about our
apathy concerning science has some truth. We ourselves
have been nearly taken up as a poacher for watching the
habits of birds, and hunted down like a thief by keepers
for venturing upon some grouse-moors in search of the site
of a British fort. Still such cases are exceptional. Besides, it is to be hoped that even the most unenlightened
British squire may some day learn the difference between

Reynolds and Frith. Mr. Ruskin's fault is that he too
often magnifies the exception into the rule. Besides, it
is not good to dwell on what is base. Let us rather rejoice at the little light which is dawning, than repine at
the great darkness which is so feebly yet so surely melting. Still, Mr. Ruskin's strictures upon the national hard-
heartedness and the national lust for money are needed. Any
one who has lived for the last four years, that is to say,
during the space of the American civil war, in one of our
large manufacturing towns, and has heard, as we have heard,
Southern brutalities applauded by men and slavery upheld
by women, will not say that Mr. Ruskin has overcoloured one
line or overcharged one sentence. Utopianism is at times
good for us, if it be only to lift us out of our usual
atmosphere of prudence and pence. And we can sympathize
with, though we feel how purely utopian for the present
they are, his visions of a kingdom where only the great and
good shall be kings, and where the sword shall be beaten
into the ploughshare, and men shall cease to stab one
another, and revel in a scientific murder, which is now
dignified by the name of war. Others, beside Mr. Ruskin,
have set themselves to bring about the millennium of peace,
– peace which is so often more chivalrous than war, – but
they have all paid the penalty of being too far in advance
of their day; and Mr. Ruskin's eloquent sentences will,
equally with the plain words of Cobden, fall upon deaf
ears. However, he is not wholly impracticable, wholly
utopian, and we feel real pleasure in quoting a passage
where delicate fancy serves to brighten and illustrate one
at least of the duties which every English lady can perform:-

[Quotes, with slight omission, from 'Have you ever considered' to 'flower of promise', 'Works' 18: 141-3.]

'The Crown of Wild Olive'

1866

32. UNSIGNED REVIEW, 'SATURDAY REVIEW'

2 June 1866, 659-60

The anonymous critic of the 'Saturday Review' is even more
vitriolic than at the time of 'Unto this Last' (see pp.
273 ff.). 'The Crown of Wild Olive' was fashioned from
three lectures and, although received adversely by most of
the significant major journals, went into three editions
within the first year of publication. It is permissible to
hazard that the book sold well because of the superb
second lecture, Traffic, one of Ruskin's most metaphori-
cally successful pronouncements upon *laissez-faire* economics. Subsequently, in 1873, a fourth lecture, The Future
of England, was added to the book which sold with some
vigour through the later decades of the century. See
Introduction, p. 17.

Why does not Mr. Ruskin publish an Encyclical, setting
forth, in eighty or eighty thousand distinct propositions
about which there can be no mistake, the particular views
and practices of the time which he holds to be so
infinitely abominable and accursed? Here is the third
volume which he has published within some nine or ten
months, full as its two predecessors were of declamation
against things in general, so rambling and so windy that
the most ingenious and painstaking reader is forced to
confess his inability to fathom the depths of the author's
meaning. The solitary conviction which the credulous disciple can get to carry away from Mr. Ruskin's vague inter-
minable Jeremiads is that we are all the perversest
generation of men that ever encumbered the earth, given up

to sordid evil and pitiful selfishness, and marching off
straight to hell as fast as our feet can carry us. The
vile band may, according to our teacher, be divided into
two vile companies. First, there are those who believe
that the Bible is the word of God, and that there is another life after this is ended. Secondly, there are others
who feel that with death everything comes to a close as
far as the individual is concerned, and that he will have
no part nor lot in anything that may be done in heaven or
upon earth after his heart has ceased to beat. But though
there is this divergence in theory, the two companies go
tramping on to the same goal, grinding the faces of the
poor with the same busy intrepidity, stamping out happiness and life with the same brutal confidence in the law
of supply and demand, and insensible in just the same
degree to all beauty and simplicity and true honour. This
seems to be the substance, only very temperately expressed,
of what Mr. Ruskin has to say about his contemporaries.
The professed Christian and the secret Unbeliever are a
meet pair, *Arcades ambo*, blackguards both. If we look
through the book for precise and apposite illustrations of
so hateful a state of things, we cannot find any. Distinct
and intelligible instances of our corruption there are
none. We search in vain for palpable statements of the
points at which modern English civilization breaks down,
and of the ideas which should be introduced to strengthen
and amend them. In the midst of the uproar of this wild
shrieking, we hear no clear and articulate suggestion such
as a simple man might either realize or act upon. Let Mr.
Ruskin tell us plainly what functions in the body politic
are disordered, and how. We do not ask him to prescribe
specific remedies, but the least that any Jeremiah can do
is to hint, in a general but intelligible way, how we can
raise ourselves from the miry and foul slough into which
some demon has contrived to plunge us. Eloquence is the
noblest of gifts, when wholesome robust ideas lie at the
bottom of it. If a man has anything to say, the more
forcible, elevated, and impressive his language, the more
valuable is his service. But if we find that he has really
nothing at all to say which his hearers can grasp in their
minds or get fruit of, then his three-page sentences about
wild olives and crystals and mountains and junipers and
agates are as wearisome and offensive as the pretentious
paraphernalia of any other form of public charlatanry. It
would be preposterous to demand of every writer that he
should confine himself to bald, bleak categorical statements of what he thinks and what he wishes. But we have a
right to ask that when anybody is drawing up a capital
indictment against the generation to which he belongs,

what he says should be at least capable of being reduced,
if necessary, to this strict and intelligible form.

The one single piece of tangible opinion in these two
hundred pages of uproarious reviling is that, 'of all the
ungentlemanly habits into which you can fall, the vilest
is betting, or interesting yourselves in the issues of
betting. It unites nearly every condition of folly and
vice,' and so on. To call betting the 'vilest' habit, when
one thinks of the consequences of drunkenness, or of a
vice still worse because it entails the maintenance of a
whole caste of vicious persons, is in Mr. Ruskin's usually
rash manner; but, though a most absurd exaggeration, this
is unimpeachably good advice to give to Woolwich cadets.
Still this is but a sorry morsel of bread to such an
immense quantity of sack. And even while we are clutching
this bit of solid stuff, we are dragged away into the
waters of unfathomable nonsense by the assertion that all
the war in Europe is the fault of women. 'The real final
reason for all the poverty, misery, and rage of battle
throughout Europe, is simply that you women, however good,
however religious, however self-sacrificing for those whom
you love, are too selfish and thoughtless to take pains
for any creature out of your own immediate circles.' This
may be true, but if it is, how on earth are we to infer
from it that 'if the usual course of war, instead of un-
roofing peasants' houses and ravaging peasants' fields,
merely broke the china upon your own drawing-room tables,
no war in civilized countries would last a week'? And then
a line or two further on, 'Let every lady in the upper
classes of civilized Europe simply vow that while any
cruel war proceeds, she will wear *black* - a mute's black -
with no jewel, no ornament, no excuse for, no evasion into
prettiness. I tell you again, no war would last a week.'
If this is a mystical riddle, we give it up. If it is
meant seriously, let us examine what it can possibly be
intended to convey. First, who is to decide what war is
cruel, and what is not? In a general way, every war is
cruel, because its miseries fall mostly on absolutely
guiltless people. But what war of our own time has taken
place which all the ladies in the upper classes would
agree in calling an especially cruel war? French and
English ladies thought the war against Denmark cruel, but
German ladies did not think so at all. French, English,
and German ladies mostly thought the war against Poland
cruel, but the Russians did not. If Mr. Ruskin means that
when all the ladies of all nations agree that any war in
Europe is cruel, war would be impossible, he might as well
have said that if the sky were to fall we should catch
larks. Does he mean, then, that if all French and English

ladies had only put on deep mourning, the German troops
would have withdrawn from Schleswig-Holstein before the
end of the week? or that, if all the ladies in Europe had
put on mourning, Grant and Sherman would have instantly
left the South to itself? 'I tell you,' says Mr. Ruskin,
'that at whatever moment you choose to put a period to
war, you could do it with less trouble than you take any
day to go out to dinner.' That is, by simply ordering home
a black gown and black bonnet and shawl. This incredible
stuff reminds one of Mr. Ruskin's wish in a former work,
that 'there were a true order of chivalry instituted for
our English youth of certain ranks, in which both boy and
girl should receive at a given age their knighthood and
ladyhood by true title, attainable only be certain probation and trial both of character and accomplishment, and
to be forfeited on conviction by their peers of any dis-
honourable act.' That is, you will make Tommy and Jenny
truthful and high-minded by making them wear a coloured
ribbon and a medal, and styling them Sir Tommy and the
Lady Jenny. Virtue in the one case, and Peace in the other,
are each to come of a costume and a childish trick.
Besides, what talk is this, of war being in the hands of
one sex? Is not war the outcome of a certain state of
moral ideas, and how is it likely that, by the time women
have arrived at more elevated ideas, men will have remained where they are, only to be governed by their more
enlightened mates? Surely, if women advance beyond war as
the arbiter of differences, men may hope to advance with
at least equal paces.

It must not be supposed that Mr. Ruskin is a hater of
war. On the contrary, in his search through history he has
'found, in brief, that all great nations learned their
truth of word and strength of thought in war; that they
were nourished in war, and wasted by peace; taught by war,
and deceived by peace; trained by war, and betrayed by
peace; in a word, that they were born in war, and expired
in peace.' Of course, this must be taken with qualifications. Mr. Ruskin only means righteous war, and war
chivalrously conducted; and he objects, so we take it, to
all cannons and forts, and everything else which interferes with personal prowess. And he has rather queer views
about what has commonly been held the most essentially
military national character the world has ever seen:-
'However truly the Roman might say of himself that he was
born of Mars, and suckled by the wolf, he was nevertheless
at least more of a farmer than a soldier.' Apart from this,
which Mr. Ruskin quite satisfactorily establishes in less
than half a page, what can he mean by saying that all
great nations have been nourished in war, and wasted by

peace? If he means that they have acquired a political
existence by war, it was scarcely worth saying. If he
means much more than this, it is hardly worth arguing. The
Dutch Republic, for instance, was born of war, but the
valour and tenacity by which they won their independence
the Netherlanders had formed in trade. It was the burghers,
the men who followed those ignoble and treacherous pursuits for which Mr. Ruskin has such a grand disdain, whom
the bloody legions of Philip were unable to crush. The
stubborn virtue which was exhibited in the trench and in
the field had been first nourished at the loom and in the
shop and the warehouse. The American Republic, again, was
not trained into greatness by war. The men by whom the War
of Independence was waged against England had got the germ
of all the vigour which conducted the war to a fair issue
at the plough, and in trade, and in the sordid pursuits of
peace. It would certainly be very unfair to read all past
history with the eyes of the last fanatic who has joined
the Peace Society. War is not incompatible with the existence of heroic qualities, and to a man who is content to
dream of war as a game of chivalrous jousting where fine
gentlemen tilt at one another, fighting may seem a better
trade than weaving or working in iron or employing mill-
hands. War may develop a set of virtues which may grow
attenuated in peace, and a really great warrior is a
character whom the world may well delight to honour. But
that war is the seed-ground of all virtues, and that peace
is only a soil for tares and choking weeds, seems to us
about as inverted a view as a man professedly in his
senses could well take. We pardon the little boy or the
silly schoolgirl who thinks the blusterous grenadier in
his bearskin the finest fellow in the world. But what is
to be said of a grown-up author who talks as if the fighting character were the best in the world, and the peaceful
character the stupidest and worst; as if every swaggering
ruffian who in old days made it his business to murder men
and violate women, and burn and rob towns, was teaching
himself and his country 'truth of word and strength of
thought,' while every man who builds a great cotton mill
and gives good wages to hundreds of people who would
otherwise have been famishing in picturesque hovels is a
sleek cozening knave who is undoing his country? Besides,
if war is such a fine thing, what did Mr. Ruskin mean in
his last book by talking savagely about the middle ages
'when it had become the principal amusement and most admired art of Christian men to cut one another's throats
and burn one another's towns?' According to his present
opinion, the admiration bestowed upon the art was just.
These Christian men were nourishing virtues which only

pestilent peace could destroy. They were teaching, while
modern peace only deceives. They were training, while the
men of peace have only betrayed. 'The exercises of war
were with the Roman,' says Mr. Ruskin, 'practical, not
poetical.' We should like to know how many of the wars
which have cursed and devasted the face of Europe since
the time of Charlemagne have been poetical and not practical. And we should like to know, in plain unadorned English, what Mr. Ruskin simply and practically means when he
says - 'Gentlemen, I tell you solemnly that the day is
coming when the soldiers of England must be her tutors,
and the captains of her army captains also of her mind.'
Does it really mean that we are to go on the Continent of
Europe, and trail the national paletot, with a defiant
invitation to France or Prussia to tread on it? and that,
in so acting, we shall be doing a wise, virtuous, and
Christian thing? How, for example, would the tribulations
and pinchings of the labouring classes, which Mr. Ruskin
so constantly bewails as the crying evil of the time, as
we all do, be mended by an operation which would instantly
cramp trade and lessen the resources of those who give
employment to these very classes? War might be a fine
thing for bracing up the moral character of the rich, but
it would make the present hardships of the poor seem
happiness in comparison with what they would then have to
endure. The war in America may possibly have developed new
virtues in Northerners or Southerners, or both; but a
loud-talking friend of labour should be the last person to
forget the horrors which this charming and efficacious
medicine inflicted on the workmen of Lancashire.

But it is sheer waste of time to examine the violent
paradoxes by which Mr. Ruskin - sometimes roystering,
sometimes maudlin, at no time reasonable - attempts to
convict the age, which at all events, he should never
forget, has had the merit of producing its Ruskin, of so
many villanies and impostures. Every man who reflects at
all upon the state of things around him admits that the
present form of English civilization, like every other,
has its peculiar dangers and its peculiar vices. The enormous expansion of industrial activity, the prime characteristic of the epoch on which we have entered, tends, if
unchecked, to make men think too much of labour and production and accumulation as ends in themselves, and to
blunt those sensibilities, interests, and aspirations
which bring into play the finer qualities of human nature,
and give a gracious beauty to human life which is what
makes it most worth having. It may be granted that people
are apt to think too much of production and too little of
the manner of consumption, too much of accumulating and

too little of imparting, too much of the possession of
wealth and too little of its most beneficent uses. But how,
in the name of all that is reasonable and just, is this
tendency to vulgarity of thought and selfishness of feeling amended by an invitation to us to go and cut throats
and pillage towns and lay waste fields, 'poetically' or
otherwise? And it may be granted that there is too much of
a general inclination to hug ourselves for our wealth and
industry and peacefulness. But is this likely to be
corrected by showering upon us a promiscuous and wild
abuse which everybody who heard Mr. Ruskin at Camberwell
and Bradford and Woolwich must have felt to be profoundly
unjust and one-sided? The delicate Socratic irony of which
Mr. Arnold is so excellent a master may do something to
open our eyes to our national weaknesses. But the arrogant
injustice of Mr. Ruskin excites a natural reaction, and
the people who might have been wholesomely affected by a
substantially just remonstrance against the too sordid
leanings of the modern spirit, however sternly and
scornfully it might have been worded, are simply disgusted
by a long string of egregious exaggerations put into fine
sentences. Nothing can be further from our desire than to
pipe an accompaniment to the song of self-gratulation
which members of Parliament and newspaper writers are for
ever singing in the public ear, or else we might dwell on
a contrast between England in 1866 and England in 1766, or
England in 1666. But the stock of happiness is still low
enough, and too low. The prevalent ideas are susceptible
of almost immeasurable elevation, the prevalent practices
of an almost indescribably closer approximation to even a
commonplace ideal. The only comfort is that so many men
are found in all orders of activity - in theology, in
legislation, in pure thought, in the fine arts - zealously
doing something to exalt the character of knowledge, and
to promote its wider diffusion. A member of Parliament who
gets a Bill passed for the regulation of Irish dogs, or a
vestryman who agitates for the compulsory cleansing of
cesspools in Little Pedlington, is doing better work in
his day and generation than the author of all Mr. Ruskin's
wordy and unjust declamations and random onslaughts
directed indiscriminately against the worst and the best
features in modern English life.

33. ANTHONY TROLLOPE, SIGNED REVIEW, 'FORTNIGHTLY REVIEW'

15 June 1866, vol. 5, 381-4

In comparison with his criticism of 'Sesame and Lilies'
(see No. 30) Trollope shows a hardening of approach towards Ruskin's social-prophetical work. The review is
clearly at one with other major publications. See Introduction, p. 17.

These three lectures were delivered by Mr. Ruskin, the
first before the Working Men's Institute at Camberwell,
the second in the Town Hall at Bradford, - on which
occasion the lecturer seems to have been invited to
Bradford to give a little advice as to the architecture of
a projected new Exchange, - and the third at the Royal
Academy at Woolwich. But though they were thus given by
the lecturer to separate audiences, they were, as he tells
us, prepared not without reference to each other; and,
they are called by the somewhat fantastic name of 'The
Crown of Wild Olive,' because it is hoped that some may
learn from them how to win for themselves 'the crown of
all content; no proud one! no jewelled circlet flaming
through heaven above the height of the unmerited throne;
only some few leaves of wild olive, cool to the tired brow
through a few years of peace.' Now if Mr. Ruskin can by
his lectures teach men and women, either young soldiers at
Woolwich, or merchants with their wives at Bradford, or
working men at Camberwell, to win for themselves the inestimable treasure of a clear conscience, - which I presume to be the Crown of Wild Olive intended, - I for one
should certainly not be inclined to quarrel with him because his language is fantastic. Fantastic as it is, it is
always beautiful. Even when his words most offend the
judgment, they would gratify the ear if one could allow
the ear to receive them without exercise of the judgment.
But when the conviction is forced upon the reader that no
human being can learn anything from such teaching, indeed
that there is no lesson taught whatsoever, that the words
are words and words only, then the absurdity of the names
chosen, the Crown of Wild Olive, Sesame and Lilies, and
the like, becomes an additional offence.

 To analyse Mr. Ruskin's intellect from his published
works is more than I will undertake to do. But I will
assert on his behalf, - and I think that readers of modern
English will agree with me almost without exception, -
that he is possessed of a wondrous power of teaching men

to use their eyes. It is not only that he has written
charmingly on painting, on architecture, and on scenery,
but that he has absolutely taught men to see and appreciate the beauty of pictures, to understand the lines and
forms of buildings; and to feel the charms of Nature's
loveliness out of doors, who were before dead or half dead
to these things. He has given almost a new delight in
existence, certainly a much extended delight, to many men
and women, and has done this by conveying to us, in
language of almost unsurpassed eloquence, lessons taught
to himself by perfected taste and accurate eyesight. In
speaking of Mr. Ruskin's early work I would wish to do so
with all the enthusiasm of ungrudging admiration. Such
work as this he has now abandoned, and he has taken to
teach other lessons, - lessons of political economy,
lessons of what I may call general conduct, - to be, in
short, a prophet among men; one qualified by sure
instincts of right and wrong to denounce the evil of the
present day, and to bid men turn themselves to better
things.* I venture to assert also, - and I think I shall
have the agreement of all who have read Mr. Ruskin's
latter works as to the justice of my assertion, - that he
has taught no man or woman any useful lesson as to general
conduct in life. He may tell us that avarice is bad, and
that justice is good, and in so saying he will say what is
true. But we knew that before, and, though useful lessons
may probably still be taught to all of us on these head-
ings, such lessons to be useful must have in them something that shall be new, some words that shall be especially persuasive, or something at least of strength. But
Mr. Ruskin, in teaching these old lessons, not only is
neither new nor persuasive nor strong; but, moreover, he
accompanies them always by special doctrines of his own
which rob them of all their old value. He tells us in his
preface to these lectures of a certain gin palace at
Croydon, before which he saw certain iron-rails to which
he objects. The gin palace, is perhaps, bad altogether, -
and we will presume, for the sake of Mr. Ruskin's argument,
that the rails are bad also. Then Mr. Ruskin goes on to
tell us how the work employed in making these rails could
have been better employed in cleaning certain dirty pools
at Carshalton. We will skip the absurdity of assuming that
a certain amount of labour, if not employed on these rails,
could then have been employed on the pools, - and will go
on to his description of the work itself, - the work of
producing the rails; 'work,' he calls it, 'partly cramped
and deadly in the mine; partly fierce and exhaustive in
the furnace; partly foolish and sedentary, of ill-taught
students making bad designs.' The reader at once perceives,

- becomes unconsciously aware even if he is an absolutely
unthinking reader, - that the author is here denouncing,
not only these unfortunate rails, but all working in mines,
all working at furnaces, and all attempts of sedentary
students to make designs for iron-rails, let those iron-
rails be used for what purpose they may. And the reader,
- even our most unthinking reader, - knows that mines and
iron furnaces are essentially necessary, that they have
been given by God as blessings, that the world without
them could not be the world which God has intended, - and
he rejects such prophesying as this. The gaze of the
denouncer who denounces like this has not been sufficiently intense to discover truth.

There is hardly a page in the little book under notice
by which the same feeling of false teaching is not produced. In the first lecture on Work, Mr. Ruskin speaks of
justice. He intends to inculcate justice on the labouring
men of Camberwell, and to do this takes the mode, - always
taken by the prophets, old and modern, inspired and un-
inspired, from Isaiah to Carlyle, - of denouncing. He denounces the injustice of his hearers, and he does this by
drawing a picture. A working man goes out on a Sunday with
his little boy, and the little boy has a nice hat with a
feather. They come to a very dirty little boy sweeping a
crossing, and they give him a penny. Then Justice says to
the working man, why shouldn't that little boy have a
feather as well as your little boy? The working man re-
joins that Justice is foolish here, as the feather would
be inappropriate for the work of sweeping. But Justice has
her answer for this: 'Then why don't you, every other
Sunday, leave your child to sweep the crossing, and take
the little sweeper to church in a hat and feather.' The
working man replies that everybody should be kept in the
place that Providence has assigned to him. And then Mr.
Ruskin comes forward with his 'Oh, my friends!' and knocks
the working man over. Providence, Mr. Ruskin says, had
nothing to do with this unfair partition. You have done
it. You have been cruel to the sweep, and, therefore, if
you are just, you will give him his share of the hat and
feather. Here is a lesson as taught by Mr. Ruskin, and by
such a lesson I say that no human being will be instructed,
or even so much as misled. The most unthinking of hearers
or of readers will know that the boy in the hat has got
his feather because his father has earned it for him, -
honestly or dishonestly does not matter to the argument, -
and that the gist of Mr. Ruskin's teaching is simply a
denunciation of all property whatsoever. But yet Mr.
Ruskin does not mean to denounce property.

In the second lecture, called Traffic, Mr. Ruskin

begins by telling the people of Bradford that he can give them no assistance whatsoever in the matter of architecture. And hereon, speaking on a subject which he understands, he says a word or two which are probably true enough. 'Now pardon me for telling you frankly you cannot have good architecture merely by asking people's advice on occasion.' But being then at Bradford, and having to lecture, and declining to lecture on architecture appropriate for a Bradford Exchange, Mr. Ruskin takes again to prophetical denunciation, and preaches against the goddess of Getting On. 'Pallas and the Madonna,' he says, 'were supposed to be all the world's Pallas and all the world's Madonna. They could teach all men, and they could comfort all men. But look strictly into the nature of the power of your goddess of Getting On, and you will find that she is the goddess, not of everybody's Getting On, but only of somebody's Getting On. This is a vital or rather deathful distinction. Examine it in your own ideal of the state of national life which this goddess is to evoke and maintain.' Now the unthinking hearer or the unthinking reader of whom I have before spoken will probably have but a hazy idea of the godhead of Pallas, and, perhaps, not a very clear idea of what Mr. Ruskin means by his allusion to the beneficence of the Madonna. But unless he be too hazy to receive any meaning at all from Mr. Ruskin's words, he will comprehend that the goddess Pallas and that which Mr. Ruskin calls the goddess of Getting On are called goddesses in two perfectly different senses. A man who cares much for eating is said to make his belly his god. But no one will think it wise to lecture to such a man and tell him that his belly can't bring him to heaven. Though he makes his belly his god, he does not make it his god in that sense. Mr. Ruskin is permitted to talk of the goddess of Getting On because he delights in fantastic language, and uses it with unusual effect. But he is scarcely honest when he takes advantage of his own imagery, and speaks of the spirit of getting on in the world, - which of course is, in every case, the individual ambition of a single mind, - as the goddess which is to evoke and maintain national life. All this was denunciation as from a prophet; but it is denunciation which can have no effect.

Mr. Ruskin permits himself to attempt to prove any idea which occurs to him, but seems to give himself no time to examine his own proofs. In his lecture on War, he tells the young men at Woolwich that all art has been produced by war. To most men this will appear to be a paradox; but I will not argue here as to the assertion itself. I will only allude to two of the instances brought up by Mr. Ruskin from among nations to prove his assertion. The Romans were deficient in art. So Mr. Ruskin says, and so doubtless they were. But the Romans are generally supposed by most readers of history to have been of all people the most warlike. By no means. 'I believe, paradoxical as it may seem to you,' says Mr. Ruskin, 'that however truly the Roman might say of himself that he was born of Mars, and suckled by the wolf, he was, nevertheless, at heart, more of a farmer than a soldier.' Then he goes on to say, truly enough perhaps, that of all people the Venetians were the greatest in art. And he calls Venice 'the city which gave to history the most intense type of soldiership yet seen among men; the city whose armies were led in their assault by their king, led through it to victory by their king, and so led though that king of theirs was blind and in the extremity of old age.' Now in this matter the English world will take as truth from Mr. Ruskin the statements that the Romans were deficient in art, and that the Venetians excelled in art; and the English world will add its knowledge from other sources, that the Romans were a people specially addicted to war, and the Venetians a people specially addicted to commerce.

But Mr. Ruskin allows himself to be so carried away by his own eloquence that he will state and prove anything. He is telling the lads at Woolwich that they should not be careless or indolent. This is good advice, - though, as given in a lecture, not likely to be of much use. Then he says that many a giddy and thoughtless boy has become a good bishop or a good lawyer, but none such has become a good general. 'I challenge you in all history to find a record of a good soldier who was not grave and earnest in his youth.' What was Clive in his youth? What was Marlborough? Are we not told that Alexander got drunk? Was not Cæsar in debt? Of course military lads should be steady, - as should other lads. Let Mr. Ruskin so tell them, if he thinks he can do them good by such precepts. But these special statements, - statements which are intended to convey very remarkable tidings as to individual facts, - should at any rate be correct. It would be very odd, if it were the case, that no boy, not grave and earnest in his youth, had ever become a good soldier; - and the fact would be very much against the military profession. Nevertheless, if it be so, let us know it. But if it be not so, why startle the Woolwich lads with the narrative of so wonderful a phenomenon? Mr. Ruskin, as he spoke the words, no doubt thought they were correct. He thinks such things without ground for thinking them. Mr. Ruskin's fault is, that he has seemed to himself to discover truth; but that in doing so he has neither used reason, nor, as yet, that 'intense gaze' of which the author speaks whom I have above quoted, and which with prophets stands in lieu of reason.

Note

* I will borrow a few words, in a foot-note, from the
author of 'Ecce Homo.' 'Now this mode of communicating and
receiving truth,' he says, and he is speaking, of the mode
in use with the Eastern prophets of old, 'is not repugnant
to the Western nations. From the time of Pythagoras and
Heraclitus to the time of Carlyle and Mazzini, men have
risen at intervals in the West who have seemed to themselves to discover truth, not so much by a process of
reasoning, as by an intense gaze, and who have announced
their conclusions in the voice of a herald, using the name
of God, and giving no reason.' This describes accurately
what Carlyle has done, - and readers of Carlyle's words
have felt the presence of the prophet. It describes as
accurately what Mr. Ruskin is attempting; but there comes
home to the listener no faith. The preacher is not recognised to be a prophet. The words are not found to have
inspiration.

'The Queen of the Air'

1869

34. FROM AN UNSIGNED REVIEW, 'WESTMINSTER REVIEW'

October 1869, vol. 36, n.s., 663-6

It is almost a certainty that the criticism was written by
that remarkable bluestocking and intellectual, Emilia
Pattison (née Strong), later to be the second wife of the
gifted if notorious Sir Charles Dilke. She was an art
critic of ability and a friendly antagonist of Ruskin over
some years. Her remarks upon 'The Queen of the Air'
deserve attention for their awareness of Ruskin's grasp of
the significance of the mythic. Other reviews tend,
rightly, to recognize this, too, and to emphasize the
first lecture as the subsequent parts of the book - dis-
paragingly spoken of by Ruskin himself as 'desultory memo-
randa' - lose their shape and direction. See Introduction,
p. 18.

...That notable compiler of other people's thoughts has
lately published a volume which, although not in the main
directed upon art matters, yet has at such matters certain
side glances of which we may be allowed to take notice
here. The book consists of three parts: one headed Athena
in the Air, the next Athena in the Earth, and the third
Athena in the Heart. The first part was in the main
delivered in the form of a lecture in March of the present
year; the second part is a study supplementary to the
first; the third a loosely stitched collection of notes,
partly from former numbers of the 'Art Journal,' and of
fragments of other lectures. With the mythological aim,
which is also the principal aim of Mr. Ruskin's work, we
have strictly nothing to do; yet we should like to pause

and point out how fruitful and suggestive, how finely and
subtly imaginative, Mr. Ruskin's treatment of this part of
the subject is - at any rate in the first lecture. Sub-
tracting what we think too great a readiness to attribute
to the Hellenie intellect divination of modern discoveries,
and pre-occupation with modern perplexities, we are
inclined to call this the most brilliant and successful
piece of interpretation to which any set of Hellenic myths
have been subjected in England since the discoveries of
philologists have set interpreters on the right road. And
it is done in the author's very best manner, with a lavish
and delightful exercise of that power which he has of
fixing in melodious periods the most evanescent, and to
other men indescribable operations of nature, her subtlest
and most fugitive lovelinesses. There is another part of
the book with which we have nothing to do either, and with
which we are very glad to have nothing to do - the part in
which the author insists on the doctrine of control, or
Law, and denounces liberty, or rather that which he understands by the name of liberty. The two chief passages
referring specifically to art both occur in the last and
loosely-connected chapter headed Athena Ergane, or Athena
in the Heart. The first of them is an expression of
opinions on the relation of art to morality, directly or
nearly directly, contrary to those which were ventured on
the same subject in a recent number of this Review.

[Quotes from 'Great Art is' to 'so is the maker of it',
'Works' 19: 389-90.]

One would be glad to hold an opinion so plausible and
so tempting as this is, especially when it comes enforced
by the cogent eloquence of a writer of genius; but it is
an opinion which closer examination to us seems only to
render more untenable. The thing is surely not quite so
simple as this. Can one not conceive some Socratic ques-
tioner applying his elenchus here: '*A virtuous man builds
beautifully*. Very well. But what do you understand by a
virtuous man? Do you mean a virtuous soldier, a virtuous
citizen, a virtuous husband, a virtuous father, or only a
virtuous builder? *As the made thing is good or bad, so is
the maker of it*. Very well indeed. But in what way must
the maker of the good thing be good? Must he be a good
statesman, a good actor, a good runner, a good blacksmith,
or only good as the maker of that particular thing?' To
the former question Mr. Ruskin would have to reply, that
to build beautifully the builder must possess all those
other virtues, and in addition to them the natural gift
and acquired art of building. To the latter we must not

make him reply (as Plato, by-the-bye, would have been apt
to make a subject of the elenchus reply) that the good
maker must also be a good statesman, actor, runner, blacksmith, but only that the good maker must also be morally
good - that is, that he must have justice, right conduct,
honesty, gentleness, and the like. That is precisely the
point that lacks proving. To us the experience of the past
(witness the commonplaces about the aberrations and vices
of genius) seems to assert that a man may do a particular
thing excellently well, and yet be in other respects
nearly a worthless man....

Ruskin in the 1860s

35. WILLIAM MICHAEL ROSSETTI, SIGNED ESSAY, RUSKIN AS A
WRITER ON ART, 'BROADWAY'

March 1869, 48-59

This comprehensive estimate by Rossetti (see headnote to
No. 15) of Ruskin's influence is also noted in the Introduction, p. 18.

For some sixteen years, fresh in the memory of many of us,
or from 1844 to 1860, there was a great influence or impulse in fine art active, which has since then become inactive. It has left off, or at least intermitted, and
lives now in reminiscence or tradition, still glowing
enough certainly in that way, rather than in present force.
This influence was Ruskin and Ruskinism.
    To a person who traced contemporaneously the birth,
growth, and culmination, of Ruskinian influence in art,
who observed how eagerly the master's utterances were
awaited, and how keenly discussed, it seems strange that
the time should be already come when he neither speaks out
nor is listened for on questions of art; when his is no
longer the paramount voice giving many subordinates their
cue, and many opponents their occasion - the voice to
uplift, establish, depress, excite, and exasperate. Such
is the case, however. Mr. Ruskin, yet in the prime of life,
and in masterly possession of all his splendid powers, has
now, as compared with what was the normal condition of
things but recently and for years together, few direct
adherents in the art-world, and not many antagonists. A
Japanese of a year ago might have said that Ruskin has
ceased to be the Tycoon of art-theory, and has become, to

some extent, its Mikado. His sway is now, to a considerable extent, remote, abstruse, and ceremonial. He no longer wields the practical powers of government, but remains a great unfamiliar abstraction of sovereignty. When the idea of authority has to be invoked, he is there for the purpose: but, when people want immediate instructions as to what they are to do next, it is not to him that they recur.

Of various causes which have conduced to this result, two are extremely obvious. Mr. Ruskin has for years past almost wholly ceased to write or lecture about art, nor is he so actively engaged as he once was in the practical direction of the studies of beginners, although his own personal addiction to artistic pursuits is understood to be more systematic and diligent than ever. He is said to have abandoned the field of art-literature, partly because of the concern it caused him to see, rampant and noxious everywhere, now audacious 'restoration,' and now sordid neglect, of the works which formed his subject-matter and his delight - a restoration and a neglect which equally find their outlet in demolition. Thus seceding, Mr. Ruskin is necessarily removed from the casualties and controversies of the day. Art continues passing through incessantly new phases and *nuances*, and of these he says nothing. The disquisitions of permanent application in his books remain there not more congruous to the present times than to any other; the matter of more directly temporary bearing was written to meet the needs of those years, and not of these; and when these years ask for guidance or interpretation, they find no response from Mr. Ruskin.

The second of the two causes to which we adverted is that Mr. Ruskin has, to a certain extent, already won the day. His theories have been embodied in practice which meets with popular acceptance. Thus ceasing to need reinforcement for proselytizing purposes, the theories cease also to be much ventilated or discussed: they have partly passed out of the stage of debate into that of ratification. This reason why Mr. Ruskin does not influence the daily ebb and flow of art so much as he used to do is of course a very satisfactory one to his admirers, and (one may suppose) to himself. It applies to such questions as the merits of Turner, or of Claude, Domenichino, or Tintoret; the claim of the Præraphaelite movement in painting to calm and respectful attention; the suitableness of Gothic architecture for revived use, whether ecclesiastic or secular. It cannot certainly be said that Mr. Ruskin has conquered absolutely in all these matters. True connoisseurs (I am thinking more particularly of connoisseurs who are themselves practical artists) are still to be found who resist the witching of Turner, and

pronounce him a man of fallacious and harmful, though
exalted, genius. The claims of Præraphaelitism are not -
and now will probably never be - admitted to the extent
which Mr. Ruskin asserted for them, and it may be that he
himself is disappointed in the outcome of the movement.
The Gothic architecture practised at the present day, even
by the best architects, is no doubt far from satisfying
his aspirations. Yet, with whatever deductions, he has
carried his point on all these and some other questions:
the result is partly such as he summoned it to be, and it
confesses his regulating hand.

Let us glance at some of the principal matters discussed
by Mr. Ruskin in his various books about fine art, and
thus gain some degree of collateral insight into the conditions of the discussion, as they stood before and after
his engaging in it. We will take six such principal
matters - 1. Turner; 2. Landscape; 3. Præraphaelitism;
4. Architecture; 5. Art Education; 6. The Theory of Art.

1. *Turner*. - Few readers, one may hope, will need to be
informed that Mr. Ruskin began his preëminent career* as a
writer on art by publishing in 1844 the first volume of
his 'Modern Painters,' which eventually extended to five
volumes; and that the direct main object of this book, in
its inception, was to demonstrate the great superiority of
Turner to all other landscape painters. The author was at
that time known simply as 'A Graduate of Oxford.' The
first volume concerned itself with the comparison between
Turner and others so far only as positive truth of representation is involved; and it is a sign of the obtuseness,
levity, or uncandour, of critics with pen or tongue, that
to this day fragments of assertion made by the author in
this fragmentary comparison will be cited as proofs that
he assigns only a totality of merit to Turner, and only a
totality of demerit to other famous landscapists, such as
Claude, Salvator, Canaletto, or Gaspar Poussin. The subsequent volumes of 'Modern Painters' continued the same
'great remonstrance'; but overlaid that with so much
theoretic and so much more discursive matter that the
reader, on rising from a perusal of the entire work, finds
that his impression of Turner as a whole, as interpreted
by Ruskin, is scarcely so defined as his impression, consequent upon the first volume, of Turner as a painter of
actual truths. However this may be, the influence of
Ruskin with regard to opinion on that artist has been
immense and triumphant. When he began writing, the name of
Turner was bespattered with ridicule - the froth of mere
witlings and pretenders at criticism for the most part. It
is true that his lofty genius and great performances had
been cordially recognized years before either the ridicule

got the ascendant, or Ruskin began writing - recognized
both by many brother artists, by a number of patrons, and,
to some considerable extent, by the general public also.
But it is not the less true that Ruskin took up the
defence at a critical moment; turned the tables on the
mockers; established the grounds of Turner's fame (not
without due confession of many faults on his part), and
the terms of comparison between him and other landscape
painters; raised the entire subject, by his lofty treatment of it, into a more elevated region; and definitely
set up Turner as one of the Englishmen from whose genius
and achievements the very summits of what this country can
do are to be measured. Probably, before Ruskin, no one had
ventured to affirm and argue out the extreme superiority
of Turner to all previous and contemporary landscapists in
general height of performance, in the sum of his gifts, in
almost all the greater and many of the subordinate excellences of a painter. Since he began to write, this has,
with very many people well and ill qualified to judge (and
I will claim my place at least among the latter), become a
sort of point of faith, comparable to that of Raphael
being the greatest of painters, or of the supremacy of
Titian in colour, or of Greece in sculpture. That there
are authoritative gainsayers I have already admitted: but
the impetus and the basis which Ruskin has given to the
enthusiastic opinion seem destined to survive all sorts of
shocks. And this is one of the extremely rare instances in
which it may be said that an extended knowledge of the
natural materials wherewith the painter had to deal, and
the powers proper to an ardent, eloquent, and poetic
master of writing, have had, on a question of fine art, a
legitimate influence greater than any which a professional
critic, however discerning and experienced, could well
have commanded. Turner will descend enhaloed to posterity
by dint of his own intrinsic greatness; but the halo will
be all the brighter while the name of Ruskin continues to
be associated with his, and while the splendid words in
which the prose-poet celebrates the painter live in pro-
tracted memory.

2. *Landscape.* - The services of Mr. Ruskin to Landscape
Art in general are, to a great extent, involved in his
services to Turner. He undertook to show what it was that
Turner had to paint, and why his result in painting was
better than that of anybody else; and, in showing this, he
necessarily went over most of the whole field of landscape
scenery, and much of that of landscape painting. No writer,
if we except the greatest poets, has done more than Mr.
Ruskin to excite in his readers the passion for natural
landscape, and for many of its constituent aspects and

details; while none at all, probably, has done so much to
analyse, define, and summarize, our knowledge and perceptions on these matters. The admirable study on the antique
and the modern feeling for landscape, and many a glorious
page on mountain beauty, or on the clouds or the sea,
attest this. His general discussion as to the ultimate
value of landscape art is also, with little doubt, the
best treatment that the subject has ever received. One
main conclusion (if I may attempt to put it in my own en-
feebling words) is this. Landscape Art has to represent
the richness and multiplicity of Nature, as well as her
simpler and more retiring aspects; for this purpose, the
most intense truth has to be preserved. But the criterion
of truth is more perfectly in the imaginative than in any
other mind. Nature, whether simple or complex, is always
too various and overwhelming for precise reproduction: the
business of the painter, therefore, is to represent truth
- truth of all kinds, and whole of truth - by a culling of
particulars which will be cognizable by art, and appreciable by the sympathetic spectator. Landscape Art has to
present to the eye and mind such a selection of truths,
and such a form of them, as can be apprehended with a
greater enjoyment of those truths, and deepened reverence
to the God of Nature. It elicits, in the artist, truthful
perception and imaginative construing; in the spectator,
a clearer, because a more compendious, sense of natural
beauty and wonderfulness.

I heard lately from one of our most distinguished landscape painters, a remark which impressed me: That, whereas
a figure painter may, in his youth, master his main
subject-matter, the human figure, no landscape painter
could well be expected to master *his* subject-matter,
scenery, before the age of forty, or consequently to be at
his best earlier than that age: the number and difference
of the things to be learned off being so enormous. The
landscapist must learn the normal and abnormal phenomena
of skies, atmosphere, seas, rivers, rocks, plains, vegetation, and no end of things besides. The figure painter
might be disposed to contest this comparative estimate;
but there certainly seems to be something in it, and perhaps the confutation, if carefully analyzed, would be
found to rest rather on the greater dignity of figure over
landscape painting than on its greater or equal difficulty
and research. Mr. Ruskin has gone in investigation, and to
some extent in practice, through the arduous processes
referred to by the artist in question; and had attained a
great measure of mastery in them at a period of his
literary career when the predicated standard age of forty
was yet distant indeed from him. Even an unsympathetic

mind must reverence the amount of knowledge which Mr.
Ruskin has collected on the facts and aspects of Nature,
and the spirit in which he uses this knowledge. In these
matters he is and must remain a teacher of teachers, an
expounder to expounders, and a poetizer among those who
feel or write poetically.

It is remarkable that, notwithstanding the example of
Turner, the acceptance which Mr. Ruskin's books met with
for several years together, and the new path struck out in
Landscape Art by Præraphaelitism, that branch of art
should be on the decline among us. Possibly I ought not to
have said *notwithstanding*, but *because of*. A second Turner
was assuredly not to be expected; and it may be that the
colossal example overshadowed and depressed succeeding
painters, that the Præraphaelitic requirements pestered
them with particulars, and even that the atmosphere of
thought and sentiment induced by Ruskin was a forcing
atmosphere, more like a hot-house than the liberal open
air. There was certainly a kind of fashion or dilettante
furore in Ruskinism at its height, and that could only be
unhealthy so far as it extended. For this, however, we
need not blame Mr. Ruskin; at any rate, not nearly so much
as some gangs of worshippers, of one sort or another, bent
with deadly determination upon repeating shibboleths, and
sitting with foolish faces of praise.

3. *Præraphaelitism*. – Mr. Ruskin is popularly known as
the champion of Turner, and the prompter, as well as
champion, of Præraphaelitism. In this there is a considerable mistake.

Præraphaelitism began in total independence and virtual
ignorance of Mr. Ruskin's writings. Three students of the
Royal Academy, Holman Hunt, Millais, and Dante Rossetti,
with whom the sculptor Woolner and two or three other
young men cooperated, began Præraphaelitism, so far as
direction of thought and study and practice are concerned,
in 1848, and exhibited their first consequent productions
in 1849. The works of Mr. Ruskin published by that time
were the first volume of 'Modern Painters' and the 'Seven
Lamps of Architecture.' I am safe in saying that probably
not one of the artists referred to, and certainly not one
of the three leading painters, had at that time read
twenty pages of these books; and, even had they read the
whole, they would have found little to their purpose
beyond some general intellectual or sympathetic incitement.
Præraphaelitism was a practice of certain artists, and
not a theory of Mr. Ruskin or any other critic. In 1849
the Præraphaelite pictures were received with marked
approbation by the ordinary organs of public opinion – the
real significance and stubbornness of the movement not

being understood: Mr. Ruskin made no sign. In 1850 the
Præraphaelite pictures were received with a storm of abuse
and contumely, a clearer inkling of their purport having
been obtained; still Mr. Ruskin made no sign. In 1851 the
vituperation gathered fresh fury: then Mr. Ruskin came
forward in vindication. Personally unknown as he still was
to all the leaders of the Præraphaelite school, he was
naturally looked upon by them as a generous and important
ally; but it would be as much a mistake to suppose that
they placed themselves under his patronage, or acted out
his precepts, as to attribute to his influence the first
beginnings of the movement. As fresh recruits - some of
them of real distinction, many others an element only of
weakness - joined the rapidly winning Præraphaelite band,
it must no doubt be true that several of these inspired
themselves not less out of Ruskin's theories than out of
the practice of Millais and the others; but this again has
nothing to do with the origin of the school.

Ruskin, however, threw himself vigorously into the
movement, thought it out for himself, and preached it for
himself - not invariably in the precise line that the
practical artistic leaders would have indicated or pursued:
and, as in the case of Turner, he produced a marked effect.
There are people in plenty in England who look with acid
dislike or blank stolidity upon anything new in aspect -
not having facility of mind enough to take it as it is
meant, or to project themselves into the feeling which
they would entertain regarding this matter were it only a
trifle more familiar; but who, as soon as they can be persuaded that the antipathetic externals cover a world of
sentiment, something 'too deep for words,' are charmed to
apply that all-opening key, and to find out that they
'know all about it.' This was to a considerable extent the
case with the Ruskinian oracles upon Præraphaelitism, and
their reception by the public. After Ruskin had had so
much to say, and so practically and profoundly, about the
subject, many people, among those who profess a taste or
a sentiment, were compelled to pique themselves upon
seeing with his eyes. Nothing short of a pet parson could
compete with a Præraphaelite picture. Of course I am
speaking here of the meaner levels of Ruskin's influence
on this question; the effect he produced upon persons in
society educated enough to perceive that they ought to
form *some* opinion concerning Præraphaelitism, and that
Ruskin's was refined and elevated guidance, but not
sufficiently advanced or discerning to see through his
expositions into the heart of the thing itself. Such
persons are always influential: they give the tone, and
put into the current small change of society the bullion

or bank-stock of the intellectual capitalists.

Mr. Ruskin, in his pamphlet entitled 'Præraphaelitism,' observed that the Præraphaelite painters had done what he, in the first volume of 'Modern Painters,' had asserted that young artists ought to do - namely, to study nature, 'rejecting nothing, selecting nothing.' This has always appeared to me an unfortunate and misleading phrase; it may have been implicitly - but not, I fancy, explicitly - rectified in some other of Mr. Ruskin's many utterances concerning Præraphaelitism. I can understand a student who, by way of practice, might set himself to copy whatever he saw before him, 'selecting nothing'; but as soon as that student develops into an artist, and undertakes to invent or compose his own subjects, the non-selecting process appears to me simply impossible, - and, in the degree that it is possible, stupid and wrong. In point of fact, this was not the process pursued by the Præraphaelites. Their ideal rather was (to repeat a curt definition I have given elsewhere) direct and entire truth in conception and in art, so far as the limitations of conception by art allow of such truth. This recognizes, what was and is eminently true, that the Præraphaelite movement in the minds of its founders aimed at being a reform in the conception and calibre of subjects, quite as much as a reform in the realizing representation of objects. The young artists felt indignant, firstly, at the dulness or frivolity with which the living men then in repute in the British School chose or treated their subjects; and secondly, at the sloppy, perfunctory, and feelingless way in which they represented the appearances of nature. Præraphaelitism was a protest against both degradations, in the order of their importance; and, of the two, the former was certainly the more important, at least in the eyes of these reformers. The movement ran its course; effected, improved, chastised, and developed much; and at last has practically come to an end without producing such lofty and permanent results as Mr. Ruskin and others had augured of it. Perhaps the secret of this half-success is that *saeva indignatio* cannot be in the long run the basis or the bond of a school of art. The time comes when the common impulse, and the pertinacious adherence to a principle of work, wane before the mounting individuality of each several painter in the sect; each finds that he has something of his own to work out, dissimilar from the faculties of his colleagues, and not compatible with rigid observance of a dogma, or strenuous reiteration of a protest; and finally each starts off on his separate tack. This will all the earlier and the surelier be the case with the artists concerned, if they are men of innate gift and

vigorous personality; and this was the case with the leading Præraphaelites. At the present day one could hardly
name a trio of painters more trenchantly distinguished one
from the other in the obvious (they always were so in the
essential) qualities of their work than that first Præraphaelite trio - Holman Hunt, Millais, and Dante Rossetti.
Madox Brown, Wallis, Arthur Hughes, Windus, Brett, Boyce,
William Davis, and other painters mixed up with the Præraphaelite movement, are in like manner diverse. Others,
again, to whom the name of Præraphaelites has sometimes
been given - Burne Jones, for instance, and even Whistler
- were never properly so describable in the sense which
the name bore originally: they respond to entirely different motive powers and lodestars in art.

4. *Architecture*. - Amid the many volumes and the multitude of pages that Mr. Ruskin has given to architecture,
the positions laid down are so numerous, varied, and extensive, that one may perhaps fail, in a summary notice
like the present, to state the deepest gist of them. I
think, however, that the following three principles will
be found to cover a great deal of his ground: he has, at
any rate, given them special prominence, and the most eloquent and potent advocacy:-

I. Architecture is Decoration; or (to be a trifle less
oracular), in any building which deserves the name of
architecture, the architectural element of it is the
decorative element.

II. The best decoration, and therefore the best architecture, are consistent with truth of structure, material,
and application, and consistent with nothing else.

III. The other arts of form find their proper place as
auxiliaries to architecture. Architecture, therefore,
links and harmonizes all the arts: its crown and glory is
cheerful and duly subordinated co-operation. True architecture is the integer of true art, and is, at the same
time, true brotherliness. It is Human Fellowship manifested in the form of the Beauty of Art.

Of these principles none can be called positively new,
if we understand the word 'new' in the sense that the
thought which has thus fructified in one mind had never
germinated in any other; but they have all received from
Ruskin a freshness, a power, and an extension, which no
one had given them in modern times, and which they sadly
lacked at the precise period when he began writing. The
second of the three principles - the one which concerns
truth and use in architecture - is less than the two
others the special property of Mr. Ruskin: Pugin had,
before him, preached it with equal enthusiasm, and not
without much awakening effect on the public mind. Pugin

also preceded Ruskin in the strenuous, and possibly even
somewhat too exclusive, advocacy of Gothic architecture as
the right form of construction to be recurred to at the
present day. His was a case, however, in which practice
did not entirely recommend precept. Pugin preached,
practised, and perhaps, to some extent, discouraged;
Ruskin only preached, with still greater eloquence, and
with the advantage of the preparation secured by his pre-
cursor; and, working along with other agencies of the time,
he produced a very decided and wide-spread effect. Let us
hope that his deposit of architectural thought will prove
to be an investment at *compound interest*: as yet it has
elicited or fostered much effort and talent, and a whole
hell of good intentions, but not in answerable proportion
what can rightly be called eminently good buildings.

The first of the three Ruskinian principles, that
'Architecture is Decoration,' is the most startling; the
third, that 'Architecture is Co-operation, exhibiting
itself as Art or Beauty,' is the most pregnant, the
loftiest abstract, and the most deeply practical. We remit
it to the meditation of the present, and to advancing and
perfecting realization in the future. As to 'Architecture
is Decoration,' that laconism ruffled many minds in its
time; but, the more people thought it over, the more they
found it was not far from the truth. I do, indeed (with
every deference), think that it excludes too absolutely
from the province of architecture the quality of proportion of masses, and their arrangement. Of course, Mr.
Ruskin is the first to recognize the excellence of that
quality: only he implies that it is a part of mere building, not of architecture - that it belongs to the constructive brain, not necessarily to the artistic. Mr.
Ruskin's mind is markedly a distinguishing and defining
one, and perhaps the reservation which he makes as to proportion or arrangement of masses will eventually be
accepted as the right one, and the axiom 'Architecture is
Decoration' as not only near to the truth, but true altogether. Meanwhile the counter-plea might very briefly and
faultily be set down thus. Building is *capable* of being so
treated as to become Fine Art, *i.e.* architecture. In any
work which partakes of fine art, the great test whereby to
recognize that fine art is the influence of the work upon
the imagination, the feelings, and the sense of beauty. A
building which has proportion and arrangement, even without decoration, does impress the imagination, or the
feelings, or the sense of beauty, or all three. But a
building *may* be architectural or artistic: therefore, when
I see a particular building which does thus respond to a
test of fine art, I conclude that building *is* artistic.

With these few remarks I must leave Ruskin's position
in relation to Architecture, for to enter into detail -
into the particular views he has expressed regarding
Classic, Gothic, and Renaissance Architecture; Northern
and Southern Gothic; the sequence of beautiful architecture
out of the most primitive rudiments of common sense in
building; the need of adopting one common national style,
and working forward from that, instead of beating about
after an 'Architecture of the Future' - to do even a little
of this would be an unending task.

5. *Art Education*. - Mr. Ruskin has written some books
for the special guidance of beginners in drawing, and he
conducted in person, for some years, one of the drawing-
classes at the Working Men's College. I believe also that
his labours in the way of correspondence and advice have
been great. He has generously held himself at the beck of
all sorts of people to whom he could, or fancied he could,
do some service in the way of art-training, or who fancied
he could do it to them.

The point which chiefly distinguishes his teaching on
art with a view to direct practical instruction from his
general investigations on the same subject is that the
former has in great part been addressed to persons who are
to learn something of drawing, but without any attempt to
become accomplished or professional artists. The principal
educational work, 'The Elements of Drawing,' is of this
kind: it sets forth a scheme of study suitable to the
classes of the Working Men's College, but not professing
to be necessarily or equally available for the students of
the Royal Academy. So again, when Mr. Ruskin engaged in an
attempt to promote a re-development of the illuminating
process, he started from the assumption that the persons
to be incited to action were those who had a gift of
invention, and of simple outline-drawing and colour, without any such knowledge or power of art as would qualify
them to venture the painting of pictures. This distinction
has to be borne in mind, because it affects the nature of
the instructions which the teacher lays down as most needful for his pupils to act upon. One thing may be the
essential for a student who is an artist, and another for
a student who is not. The former has to train himself for
a certain range of achievements; the latter for a certain
other and very subordinate range. Allowing for this, the
point upon which Mr. Ruskin particularly insists at start-
ing - that his learners should not address themselves to
drawing outlines first, and then filling them in with
shadows and demi-tints, but should, from the beginning,
contemplate any and every object as such or such a field
of lights and of shadows and demi-tints, to be expressed

accordingly in the transcript - seems well selected. See everything as it is, and show it as you see it, not only to the same result, but by following out in representation the same process as in perception - such is the rule. It was adapted for producing, and did in fact produce at the Working Men's College, really noticeable results in the way of sympathetic observation and consequent exact and delicate accuracy of object drawing. To say that it neglects a structural study of form, and would thwart the range of perceptions termed æsthetic, and their rightful result an artistic ideal, is presumably a true remark: but it is not properly an objection to Mr. Ruskin's teaching, because he was providing for draughtsmen who are not artists, while the counter-plea in question has the artists for its clients. Mr. Ruskin has continually been called dogmatic, pragmatic, arrogant, and so on; and no doubt passages supporting this estimate of his mental constitution may be cited from his books. Yet, like many another man obnoxious to the same charges, he is, from another point of view, eminently modest - *i.e.*, he is as ready to confess his insufficiency when he knows it as to assert his knowledge and the fruits of it when he is conscious to himself of these. Thus he has always, I believe, disclaimed any pretension to lay down a detailed plan of study for artists aiming at the higher attainments of art; and has implied that such a plan can be adequately laid down only by artists who have themselves realized those attainments. The man who produces works of art of a noble ideal is the man to tell others how he produced them, and how they also - if indeed the faculty is in them - may work towards the like result.

6. *The Theory of Art*. - If my picking-out of points of doctrine or opinion enforced by Ruskin has been partial and inadequate hitherto, it will necessarily be still more so now that I come to the largest and most inclusive speculations of all. Paring down and diluting as I may, I present to the reader the following as some sort of abstract of what Ruskin has imparted as his general Theory of Art.

An artist of the greatest class is a sort of reflex deity - a subordinated creator. That the critical mind should legislate for the divine, the uncreative for the creative, is obviously absurd: therefore, in all that a true critic says about art, he confesses the inferiority of his function, and the supremacy of those greatest men, either tacitly by laying down no rules at all concerning them, or empirically by tracing out from their work what the noblest qualities of art actually are. These the critic classifies and elucidates, not assuming to benefit

artists of the creative order, but either to assist outsiders in understanding them, or to urge on, towards the
highest things of which they are capable, other artists of
a less exalted but still sincere and right-minded class.
Thus, if the critic dilates but little upon the foremost
works of creative art, which are generally such as deal
with human emotion, passion, and action, it is not to be
inferred that he is necessarily cold to their grandeur -
his reticence may proceed from his feeling that the faculty
of creation or inspiration in these works does not admit
of much verbal analysis. Or if he points out in such works
now this and now that passage of profound thought, with
ends subtly and from afar provided for by their appropriate
means, he does not imply that the thing was vamped up,
piece by piece, by processes of long-drawn self-consciousness and ingenious dovetailing; rather that, produced as
it was by the power of creative imagination, it is found
to yield to a critical scrutiny these and legion of other
materials of thought and truth, thus expressible by the
critical vocabulary. Those highest qualities of art, if
hardly definable, are in a still stronger sense incommunicable: some few men are born gifted to develop them; the
others never will develop them, and need not cudgel their
brains for them in the attempt.

The highest art, therefore - imaginative or creative
art - cannot be imparted: but the sources of true and
beautiful art can be ascertained and studied. Art is
properly the expression of man's delight in God's work:
every noble element of art has its basis in, and corresponds to, some divine attribute. God's work cannot be
improved. To investigate it, to retrace it patiently,
faithfully, and affectionately, according to the immeasurably diminished scale of glory and of gift which pertains
to man; to re-exhibit it in all humility and docility of
spirit, but still as passed through the one inevitable
medium, the faculty and the delighting contemplation and
interpretation of man - this is the true function of Fine
Art.

How shall man penetrate into and understand the work of
God, and the Divine attributes as embodied in that work,
and re-exhibit them with fidelity and with beauty? By
having a faithful and beautiful mind and soul, vibrating
to the Divine effluence, conscious of the Divine manifestation. The highest artist must be a man of the highest:
the work is not to be done on other terms. The stupid will
apprehend and present stupidity; the frivolous, frivolity;
and the gross, grossness. The pure will apprehend and
present purity; the majestic, majesty; the strong, power;
the beautiful-minded, beauty. Simple and zealous study of

visible nature is the way to produce a sincere artist; the
like, combined with a rapt contemplation of the abstract
qualities (or, in other words, Divine attributes) which
have moulded and taken form in visible nature, is the way
to produce an exalted artist; and both these, with the
imaginative or creative gift, innate and unlearnable, is
the way to produce a supreme artist. The supreme artist
has a kind of short-hand process for attaining his results:
he often finds it possible, and even indispensable, to
exhibit the highest truths by penetrating through their
husk to their core, through the many particulars to the
one reunited impression, - by re-casting, rather than representing the obvious fact. The imaginative mind, which
has to be the medium through which nature converts itself
into art, is sometimes more a crucible than a filter. But
it is still Truth which such a mind and such an artist
exhibit at the last - no conceited 'improvement' or idle
fancy of his own - truth of the centre if not of the cir-
cumference.

The foregoing, if it summarizes incompletely, does not
(I believe) falsify the general views concerning art pro-
pounded by Mr. Ruskin. Those views will be found to be
much more extended and unsectarian than many hostile or
hurried critics have said, and numbers of other people
imagine.

The most intelligent and vigorous critique that I know
upon Ruskin - in many respects a masterly performance - is
a French one, forming a small volume, 'L'Esthétique
Anglaise, Etude sur M. John Ruskin par J. Milsand' (Paris,
1864). The writer admires and sympathizes with the English
theorist to a great extent, but on the whole he writes in
opposition. He conceives that Mr. Ruskin insists far too
strongly upon the value of the abstract ideas of human
intellect, and the moral sentiments of the conscience, for
the purposes of fine art. Similar objections, and also the
objection of a want of interest in the art which deals
with humanity, have frequently been raised in English
reviews, and not often in so fair, respectful, or discerning a spirit. Yet I apprehend that these objections are
considerably overstated by the French critic, as well as
the English ones. Let us examine the question a little.

It is true that Ruskin has written many more pages
about landscape art than about the imaginative art of
passion and character; about truth than about invention;
and he has spoken and argued much concerning the ideas
and the knowledge expressed in pictures, and the moral
truths which ought to be congenial to the artist's mind,
and implied in his productions. But, in acknowledging this,
we must remember also that he says from the first that

imaginative or creative art is so great and incommunicable
a thing as to be available not at all for direct devolu-
tion by way of teaching, and not much even for analysis
and exposition. These things, therefore, are left apart to
some extent, not as less important, but as important in an
incommensurable degree; and the writer has bestowed his
chief attention upon landscape art, partly, no doubt,
through his intense sympathies in that direction, and the
particular subject-matter of his longest book; but partly
also because it is a more debateable and proveable sphere
of work. As to the relative claims of truth and invention,
it would be a mistake to say that Ruskin slights the
latter in favour of the former. He asserts both with energetic persistence; and moreover he identifies the two to a
very great extent, affirming that the most powerful invention is also the deepest truth. There is some colour for
demurring to this treatment of the subject, on the ground
that, by a sort of verbal shuffle, it intermixes two
things really very distinct; but the man who says that
truth is supreme, and that invention is truth, cannot
rightly be said to undervalue invention. As to the question
of the morality of the artist and his art, there is a
great deal to be said, and much latitude for misapprehension. We must understand first what is meant by morality
in this connexion. Does it mean a strict conformity in
conduct to the professed standard of the 'respectable,'
and chiefly of the respectable of our present time? or
does it rather mean an inner sense of uprightness, dignity,
honour, benevolence, energy, and virtuous self-respect,
which may indeed be at times belied in the conduct at the
incentive of passion or of interest, but which is still
genuine as a sentiment, and as a regulator of the main
course of life? If we attach this latter signification to
the term, and reject any identification of morality with
prudence, I think we need not doubt that most of the great
artists have so far been moral men in life and in art; and
indeed that a character formed of the opposite elements -
as falsity, meanness, dishonour, malignity, indolence, and
vicious abandonment - would soon come to the end of its
tether in artistic productiveness.

There remains the objection that Ruskin 'insists far
too strongly upon the value of the abstract ideas of human
intellect for the purposes of fine art,' or upon 'the
ideas and the knowledge expressed in pictures.' In this
there is a show of truth: yet not less true is the directly
opposite allegation - that Ruskin, preëminently among
critics, upholds the value of art based upon direct and
spontaneous perceptions; that he exalts simple good painting or carving above fine-drawn intellectualisms in art;

and that he entertains a dislike, almost amounting to a prejudice, against such a school as the modern German, which takes systematic intentions in thought and in work as its inspiration. The explanation of these semi-conflicting, though not exactly contrary, sides to the Ruskinian theories and disquisitions, is to be sought, I think, not so much in his speculative opinions about art as in the constitution of his own mind. His mind is at once remarkably intense and remarkably minute, and in the highest degree conscientious besides. The result of his intensity and minuteness is that, in analysing the contents of a work of art, he is impelled to discern and enforce a number of minor or individual points; and the result of his conscientiousness is that he cannot rest without assigning a motive and a significance to all of these. His sense of responsibility masters him, and he refuses to allow to chance its natural and adequate share in the productions of mind. But, as I have before said, even in over-elaborating this side of his critical labour, he does not exactly imply that every element of thought which he finds in the work of art was separately and distinctively present to the artist's own consciousness at the moment of production; rather that the work is one of imagination, of perception, or of thought, long familiarized and assimilated, which on analysis, is found to reveal these constituents, and to be endowed with these virtues.

To this frame of mind in Mr. Ruskin there is no doubt a weaker as well as a stronger side. He allows his thought to meander too much, and to pursue the objects of its study into too many bye-ways and tortuosities. To which it may be added that these excursions of mind are continually guided and companioned by that quality which is so easily summed up in the one word sentimentalism. His sentiment is real, deep, full of beauty, brimmed with suggestiveness, an opener of many hearts with many keys: but it is not, I think, to be denied that an infusion of the 'sentimental' often tinges, and sometimes avails even to taint it.

Whatever his blemishes, Ruskin stands forth as a deep-thinking theorist, a deep-seeing critic and investigator, a splendid and unique writer, and an altogether exalted personality. The arts are the richer for his enthusiasm and his studies; and the literature of art - and one may even say the English language - the poorer for his having at last vacated the large place which he filled in that department of writing.

Note

* 'Began,' practically speaking, not literally; for some
traces of Mr. Ruskin as a writer sympathetic with art are
to be found years before the appearance of the first
volume of 'Modern Painters.'

36. JUSTIN McCARTHY, FROM 'PORTRAITS OF THE SIXTIES'

London, 1903, 274-88

Justin McCarthy (1830-1903) was an Irish politician, journalist, novelist, historian, and lecturer. Although he was
an MP of Liberal convictions, McCarthy's real bent was
literature. Some of his novels achieved transient popularity, but his 'History of Our Own Times' is his most
significant piece of writing. His consideration of Ruskin's
position in the sixties is of particular concern because
of its long perspective and broad coverage.

John Ruskin was one of the great intellectual forces of
the Sixties. His influence was in its way as strong, far-
reaching, and penetrating as that of Carlyle, Dickens, or
Tennyson. But there always seemed to be this pecularity
about Ruskin's dominion over his public - it was the power
of an intellectual influence merely and not of a man. The
general public never saw anything of the living Ruskin. He
seldom, if ever, attended a public meeting, or was a guest
at public banquets; he never unveiled any memorial statue
and delivered a discourse thereon; he was never, so far as
I can remember, seen in the boxes or the stalls on the
first night of some great theatrical performance. I can
remember one time, when the British Association or the
Social Science Association - I am not certain now which it
was of these two learned bodies - was holding its annual
session, and we were all delighted by the announcement
that a paper was to be read by Mr. Ruskin. I was among the
eagerly expectant audience, but I was doomed like all the
rest to disappointment, for Mr. Ruskin did not present
himself to the meeting, and his paper was read for him in
his absence....
    Sometimes Ruskin ventured outside his own spheres of
thought and opinion, and set much indignation going by
undertaking to lay down the law on subjects concerning

which he had no claim to be recognised as an authority. In
1862 he wrote four essays for the 'Cornhill Magazine,'
which were entitled 'Unto this Last,' and were afterwards
republished in a volume. These essays dealt with subjects
some of which were beyond the range of Ruskin's familiar
studies, and they provoked much criticism from writers who
refused to acknowledge his right of dictatorship outside
the realms of art. One irreverent critic ventured to be
facetious and declared that the very title of the work
embodied a motto which ought to have been a warning to
Ruskin, inasmuch as the proper work of his life was to
mend art, and that 'Unto this Last' he had better stick....

It is no part of my task to attempt an exposition of
the triumphs Ruskin accomplished in his own especial
fields and of the new era he opened in the world's appreciation of English art. A more thoroughly disinterested
man never worked in the cause of artistic education. The
generosity of his endowments to institutions which were
helping to promote that cause, was only limited by the
extent of his personal resources. His brilliant, imaginative poetic style called up hosts of imitators among
literary men and women who professed no craftsmanship in
pictorial art, and for a time there was a style of
Ruskinese just as there was a style of Carlylese, and a
style fashioned after that of Dickens or of Thackeray. No
imitation proved to be more than a mere imitation, and
Ruskin stands, and is ever likely to stand, alone. We have
now completely passed through the era of controversy; we
judge of Ruskin by his greatest triumphs and accept him as
one of the best literary exponents of true art whom the
world has ever known. But one should have lived during the
Sixties and many of the years following in order to understand what a battle-call to controversy was always sounded
when Ruskin sent forth any proclamation of his creed on
this or that subject of possible debate. I know whole sets
of men and women whose most eager and animated conversation was founded on some doctrine laid down by Ruskin, and
who debated each question with as much earnestness and
vehemence as men commonly display when they are fighting
over again in private life the battles of party politics.
There was something thoroughly healthy in the animation of
literary and artistic discussion thus created in a public
which up to that time had not concerned itself overmuch
with the principles and doctrines of high art. In other
countries more especially consecrated to artistic culture
such a condition of public feeling would not have been
new, but it was new to England of Ruskin's early fame, and
the breath of that artistic awakening has suffused our
atmosphere down to the present day. I think it is not too

much to say that the English public in general had never
taken art seriously and earnestly until Ruskin began to
write, and that his influence has never faded since and
shows no signs of fading.

But I am again brought back to the fact that all this
time Ruskin was to the great mass of the public only an
influence and not a living personality. Among a large
circle of friends in those far-off days I knew very few
who had any close personal acquaintance with the great
teacher and could tell me what he had been saying or doing
last week, when he was likely to come up to London from
his home in the Lake country, and where there might be a
chance of seeing him when he did come within the range of
our streets. The influence exercised by Ruskin was in my
opinion even more distinctly original than that of Carlyle.
I am not suggesting a comparison of the value of the two
influences, but merely considering the relative independence of either inspiration. It cannot be questioned that
Carlyle's way of thinking was much guided by German
thought. There are passages in 'Sartor Resartus' which may
almost be called translations from Jean Paul Richter. We
can easily understand that this was not a conscious adoption by Carlyle of ideas from the German writer, but
merely came from the fact that Richter's ideas had settled
into his mind and become part of it. The influence of
Goethe and of Schiller may be recognised through most of
Carlyle's writings at one period of his literary career.
But Ruskin's ideas are all his own as his style is, and
the shadow of no other thinker seems to have come between
him and the page on which he wrote. When he avowedly
adopts and expounds the theories of other men he always
does this in his own way, and manifests his own individuality even in his interpretation. His influence, so long
as he kept it within the range of subjects he had made his
own, was always of the healthiest and purest order. The
keen artistic controversies which he set going had something inspiriting and elevating in them. We, the commonplace mortals, were ever so much the better for being
taken now and then out of the ordinary topics, political
and social, the Stock Exchange, the Income Tax, and the
odds at the Derby, and drawn into partizanship with one
side or the other in some dispute on the true principles
and the best methods of the painter's art. So far as the
truest lessons and the highest practice of art are concerned, it may be said without hesitation that Ruskin left
England much better than he found it, and that his best
influence, to adopt Grattan's words, 'shall not die with
the prophet, but survive him.'...

'Lectures on Art'

1870

37. UNSIGNED REVIEW, 'SATURDAY REVIEW'

30 July 1870, 143-5

Ruskin's old adversary (see No. 25) is here perhaps less hostile in language - although not in tone - than before. See Introduction, pp. 18-19.

The establishment of Professorships of Fine Art at the old Universities is one of the occurrences, often in themselves apparently of very trifling importance, which mark a stage in the advancement of the national mind. The public has long been familiar with the idea of a drawing-master in a school; every school has a drawing-master of some sort, and therefore it seems consistent that Oxford and Cambridge should have their drawing-masters too. The difference is that, when Oxford and Cambridge have Professors of Fine Art, an idea is conveyed to the public mind that there is something seriously worth learning to be professed on that subject - an idea which the body of drawing-masters, though numerous, has hitherto scarcely succeeded in conveying. No one will deny that the English public, or at least the more refined portion of it, takes an interest in art, but then the interest that it has taken has not hitherto been of a very elevated kind. Suppose, for instance, that an average English gentleman, whether graduate or undergraduate of a University, finds himself in the presence of a picture; he will experience, no doubt, certain feelings of pleasure on seeing an expressive face, or a fine horse or dog, clearly set before him, but it is almost a certainty that the artistic aims and qualities of the performance, if it has any, will be a sealed book to

him. If this is so with regard to painting, it is so still
more decidedly in the case of sculpture. A thousand non-
professional Englishmen can read Homer in the original for
one who can really read and enjoy the Elgin marbles. It
may be answered that knowledge of this kind cannot be of
much importance, because so many truly great men have done
without it. We have the best of evidence that some of the
greatest statesmen and commanders, and even poets, lived
and achieved greatness in perfect ignorance of fine art;
and many an undergraduate of to-day might consider himself
supremely fortunate if he could look forward to so bright
a career as theirs. It is true that the knowledge of art
is not a necessity, but this kind of argument may be used
with equal force against some of the favourite studies of
our fathers, especially their philological studies. On the
other hand, we cannot consider the knowledge of so profound a matter as art in the light of a mere ornament. We
take the truth to be that although a man may be an excellent patriot and a good Christian without either art or
erudition, still he cannot have a really catholic mind so
long as any one of the great provinces of the human
intellect is absolutely closed against him. If Wordsworth
had understood men of science better, and if Scott had
understood painters better, these men of genius would have
approached more nearly to universality, and it was a point
of superiority in Thackeray to understand the aims of fine
art as he did. The purpose of a liberal education ought to
be to make a gentleman understand at least what the various
arts and sciences are. It is not possible that he should
know them in detail as specialists know them, but it is
quite possible for him to know the aim and spirit of those
who have laboured in these particular fields. Men of
special culture are in these days better able to explain
the drift and purport of their sciences than ever they
were before. It is astonishing in how few pages a thorough
modern botanist will convey to a pupil a correct notion of
what botany is, and in the same way a Professor of Fine
Art ought to be able to teach him what painting and en-
graving are. At present the fine arts in this country are
all but universally misunderstood, simply because there is
no general apprehension of the five or six fundamental
ideas on which the whole edifice rests.

We were therefore sincerely glad to know that at last
these matters were to be authoritatively explained at the
Universities, and also, for some reasons, that Mr. Ruskin
should have accepted the Professorship at Oxford. It is a
post which ought to suit him thoroughly, and of which
there can be no doubt that he will discharge the duties
with the utmost conscientiousness. A few years ago we

might have hailed his appointment less unreservedly, because at that time his influence on art in England was
sufficiently considerable to be dangerous. In these days
we trust that undergraduates, though they will learn much
from a master in many respects so distinguished and so
competent, will scarcely take him for the infallible prophet that enthusiastic young people of both sexes believed
him to be in the good old pre-Raffaellite times. Mr. Ruskin
is still occasionally tempted to talk as if he continued
to believe in his own little papacy, but the chair of Fine
Art is neither so ancient nor so august as that of St.
Peter, and the best plan for the future seems to be to
leave infallibility and anathemas to the other venerable
gentleman over the water, and simply accept the position
of a teacher respected for his accomplishments, and
beloved for his kindly nature, though good-humouredly
laughed at for his eccentricities. There is an expression,
however, on the very first page of the Inaugural Lecture
which seems to imply that the Professor looks back somewhat wistfully to the old prophetical days. 'It has
chanced to me of late,' he says, 'to be so little
acquainted either with pride, or hope, that I can scarcely
recover so much as I now need of the one for strength, and
of the other for foresight.' Certainly Mr. Ruskin cannot
any longer indulge in the pride of an intellectual auto-
cracy, or in the hopes of a successful founder of a new
artistic religion, but we think he may fairly be both
proud and hopeful yet. No other writer on art is either so
extensively read or so willingly listened to; and, not
withstanding the decline of his influence over practical
work (now scarcely traceable), we may safely hazard the
prediction that what is best in his books will live.

What most lessened his influence was the spreading
power of the French school, a school which now sits central
in the world, and visibly affects art-production in every
nation where paint is laid on canvas. The work of the
French painters was done in perfect independence of
Ruskinism, of which they had never heard, and which, when
some faint echo of it did finally reach their ears through
M. Milsand, seemed to them merely a bit of British eccentricity unworthy of serious attention. The younger English
painters observed this, and discovered that it was possible
to be successful in art, and to lead all Europe, without
knowing anything of Ruskinism. In a word, when the foreign
movement began on the decline of the pre-Raffaellite movement, the conviction spread amongst our younger men that
Ruskinism was superfluous, and after that time it has had
little to do with English art-practice. Again, it was
found that Mr. Ruskin's criticism was not ratified by the

most cultivated European opinion. To take a special instance, one amongst many, his eulogy of Mr. Wallis's
'Chatterton' - 'faultless and wonderful; a most noble
example of the great school.' The picture was exhibited at
Manchester in 1857, and afterwards in Paris, where the
French painters saw it and found it wonderful indeed, but
in quite another sense.

The truth is that Mr. Ruskin was believed to be the
leader of an art movement which in fact he only accompanied, and when the painters turned in another direction,
and he no longer kept up the appearance of leadership, it
became apparent that there had existed an illusion on the
subject. So with reference to the fame of Turner, people
who read 'Modern Painters,' and knew nothing of the
previous history of English art, fancied that Turner's
merits had been discovered by Mr. Ruskin; but a simple
comparison of dates proves that Turner's merits were very
handsomely recognised before Mr. Ruskin was born.
Constable, in 1813, said that Turner had 'a wonderful
range of mind,' and thought it an honour to sit next him
at dinner; whilst Constable's friend, Fisher, writing in
the same year, calls Turner's 'Frost' 'a picture of pictures.' Mr. Ruskin was born in 1819, at which date Turner
had been admitted to the honours of the Academy for fully
eighteen years. A child born in 1873 would stand chronologically in something like the same position relatively
to the fame of Leighton that Mr. Ruskin occupied relatively to that of Turner. When the first volume of 'Modern
Painters was published, in 1843, Turner was the richest
and most successful landscape-painter in the world. The
labour of fifty years had interested a large public in the
painter and his works, and they were ready to listen to
any one who had ability enough to explain them eloquently.
With the absorbing egotism of men of genius, Mr. Ruskin
made himself the representative of the whole body of
Turner's admirers, and said so much, and said it so well,
that it became scarcely possible to write anything favourable about Turner without seeming to plagiarize from him.
After that the younger English artists began the pre-
Raffaellite movement, and when it had attracted public
attention and proved its strength, Mr. Ruskin did for it
exactly what he had done for Turner. He gave full literary
expression to ideas already expressed by the artists on
canvas, and in a word made himself the public orator of
the most important artistic movement of the day. But a
rôle of this kind could not be permanently sustained. The
very earnestness and honesty of the writer made it impossible for him to proclaim the movement which succeeded to
pre-Raffaelitism as he had proclaimed pre-Raffaellitism

itself. After having announced in 1856 that the battle was
completely and confessedly won by the Pre-Raffaellite
party, that animosity had changed into emulation, astonishment into sympathy, and that a true and consistent school
of art was at last established in the Royal Academy of
England, after having announced the finality of the movement in these terms, it was not possible for Mr. Ruskin to
become also the orator of the foreign movement which
originated in the study of Continental work at the Paris
Exhibition of 1855, and in the foreign education of the
painters who were students in the succeeding years. Mr.
Ruskin shortly afterwards abandoned the leadership which
he had assumed, and of late years has written several
volumes on other matters than art. The influence that he
once exercised was due to his hearty sympathy with what
certain English artists had done, or were then doing, and
to a power of language which made the expression of that
sympathy efficacious. The criticism of the eighteenth
century had been left far behind by the painters themselves; the public wanted a more modern writer. Ruskin was
thoroughly modern, as modern as the living painters; so he
was listened to with eagerness. But the power he had was
that of a representative man. So long as he and the artists
marched in the same direction he seemed powerful; when
they changed their direction he was left like a trumpeter
without an army. His reputation has suffered a good deal
since in consequence of certain wild theories of his about
political economy and other matters, which have already
been commented upon in this journal.

If Mr. Ruskin's fame had been based upon his eloquence
alone the world would already have outlived it. But behind
the eloquent exponent of modern artistic innovations there
was a patient student, one of the most patient students in
England, and it is in this quality that Mr. Ruskin still
commands our most sincere respect - a respect which we
hope will be fully shared by every undergraduate who
listens to him. He has the true student-spirit, and is
therefore, so far, admirably qualified for teaching. In
this he differs notably from all common writers on art,
and even from all ordinary painters. The common critic
never studies in any serious sense at all; he merely goes
to picture-exhibitions, and writes down his impressions
afterwards; the ordinary artist becomes absorbed in
picture-manufacture, and ceases to acquire fresh truth.
Mr. Ruskin's steady persistence in study has made his
position a substantial one, and given him a firm hold on
the esteem of all who work in the same temper. We forgive
him all his eccentricities for this - for the quantity of
downright hard work that he has gone through, and still

imposes upon himself. No one is more widely removed from
fashionable amateurship. And as Mr. Ruskin complains that
he has not much hope left, let us suggest that he may
still have the noble hope of doing a great work in Oxford.
If he succeeds in making the unprofessional study of art
accepted and recognised as a real discipline, he will have
rendered a better service to his age than if he had bound
down all our painters to pre-Raffaellitism, and reduced
the market-value of all Claudes and Vandeveldes in Europe.

These lectures begin the great task well. But why con-
fuse the students with new and eccentric classifications?
Why attempt changes in the use of language which no single
teacher can ever prevail upon a nation to adopt? The
reader who has not seen these lectures will be amazed to
hear that Mr. Ruskin now classifies Holbein and Albert
Dürer as painters of the Greek school. This is so far-
fetched, so oblivious of important characteristics, so
contrary to all received ideas, to ideas received by all
men of the highest culture and experience in art, that the
attempt to make such a classification prevail is utterly
hopeless and useless. And if attempts of this kind are
useless they are injurious, because they create confusion.
Imagine the effect on an audience of European artists who
have studied Greek work all their lives, if they were told
that we had a critic in England who said that Holbein and
Dürer were artists of the Greek school! What would they
think of our critic, what would they think if they were
told further that this doctrine was professed in the chair
of Fine Art in the University of Oxford? And if we went
into detail, and said that our teacher affirmed the Gothic
school to be always cheerful, and the Greek to be always
oppressed by the shadow of death, what would they think of
him then?

The process by which Mr. Ruskin arrives at this amazing
conclusion is so round-about that it would take an article
to explain it. We may, however, attempt an abstract.
1. The Greeks worshipped light in Apollo and Athena, and
had terribly sombre conceptions of spiritual darkness.
2. Through their intense love of light, darkness was
particularly apparent to them. 3. Albert Dürer saw what
was spiritually dark and melancholy; *ergo*, he was an
artist of the Greek school. Further, all the chiaro-
scurists are of the Greek school, so that Rembrandt is
pre-eminently Greek. On the other hand, the Egyptians are
of the Gothic school, so are the Chinese, &c. We need not
be at the trouble of refuting so wild a theory as this,
but it is worth mentioning because it lets us see the
working of Mr. Ruskin's mind – first, in its almost
sublime contempt for everybody else; and, secondly, in its

curious processes of induction and generalization. Because
the Greeks worshipped Apollo and liked light, therefore
they were really very melancholy; Dürer is melancholy,
therefore Dürer is of the Greek school. Mr. Ruskin told us
long ago that he was an infallible reasoner; but what if
any ordinary mortal, not infallible, had put forth such a
piece of reasoning as this?

The Oxford undergraduates are also taught to divide all
art generally into the schools of crystal and the schools
of clay. Now, though it is true that we have adopted the
poetical title of the Crystal Palace for the glass-house
at Sydenham, it is improbable that Oxford undergraduates,
however poetical, will talk to each other habitually about
the crystal schools of fine art. Egyptian and Chinese work
is of the school of crystal, but Corregio and Turner are
of the school of clay. These things may astonish us, but
the more we are amazed the happier Mr. Ruskin feels. He
delights in shocking our ignorant and weak minds, and is
never better pleased that when we betray by word or look
that he has succeeded. By this time, however, we are like
an electric eel which the operator has thoroughly
exhausted. The brass saddles have been so often laid upon
our backs, and we have so often given off the electricity
of amazement, that we really have no more left.

Seriously, the only safe ground for Mr. Ruskin is the
study of natural fact. He can teach this; he can at least
teach the main facts about natural landscape, about the
sky and the earth and vegetation, so far as these concern
artists. We have no evidence that he has any knowledge of
animal form. As a theorist he is too wild to be relied
upon, and though his sentiment is nearly always tender and
kindly, it is often morbid. For instance, in the lecture
on the Relation of Art to Religion, we have the following:-

And do we dream that by carving fonts and lifting
pillars in His honour who cuts the way of the rivers
amongst the rocks, and at whose reproof the pillars of
the earth are astonished, we shall obtain pardon for
the dishonour done to the hills and streams by which
He has appointed our dwelling-place; - for the infection of their sweet air with poison; - for the burning
up of their tender grass and flowers with fire, &c.

This is a perfect specimen of the kind of sentiment in
which Mr. Ruskin so frequently indulges. How is a manu-
facturer who builds a mill by a stream-side to obtain the
Divine pardon for the injury he has done to the grass and
flowers - the tender grass and flowers? Not by building a
church; and if not, how then? A grave question, truly, for

all who erect mills and foundries.

Casting aside the sentiment and generalizations in the book as superfluous, we come at last to the main matter, how Mr. Ruskin intends to teach drawing at Oxford. He insists upon 'absolute accuracy of delineation' - a good provisional doctrine to preach to very young students, though they will find out later that true art, as distinguished from simple copyism of nature, is never accurate. We are sorry to find that Mr. Ruskin shares the vulgar conception that the best painting is that which is most like a mirror. He quotes Leonardo to the same effect. It was natural that in the naïveté of Leonardo's times a painter should believe, as the uncritical public believes still, that the best art is that which is most lavishly imitative; but cultivated European criticism has long since recognised the fact that all personal expression, all that in one word constitutes *art*, necessarily involves deviation from accuracy. This is so well understood on the Continent now that even in his studies, if a pupil is servilely and photographically accurate, without artistic feeling and selection, such accuracy is considered a proof that he is naturally unfitted for the pursuit of the fine arts. There have been passages in Mr. Ruskin's writings which seemed to indicate that his views were wider and more mature. Such a doctrine as this belongs to the infancy of criticism.

We had hoped to trouble our readers no more with Mr. Ruskin's denunciations of the age, but they occur in the midst of the most practical counsel. Thus, the undergraduates are told that they are to draw lines first, and then fill in spaces with flat colour, after that they will advance to animal forms and to the patterns and colour-designs on animals - which is all very rational indeed. But the next minute the *idée fixe* asserts itself and the undergraduates are informed that they 'live in an age of base conceit and baser servility - an age whose intellect is chiefly formed by pillage and occupied in desecration, one day mimicking, the next destroying, the works of all the noble persons who made its intellectual or art-life possible to it - an age without honest confidence enough in itself to carve a cherry-stone with an original fancy, but with insolence enough to abolish the solar system, if it were allowed to meddle with it.' So it is all through the volume - a little practical sense, perfectly sane as it seems, then a wild flight, alternately. The first conditions of a school of art in England are the use of water-power instead of steam, and absolute refusal or banishment of unnecessary igneous force:-

> And until you do this, be it soon or late, things will
> continue in that triumphant state to which your mecha-
> nism has brought them; - that though England is
> deafened with spinning-wheels her people have not
> clothes - though she is black with digging of fuel,
> they die of cold - and though she has sold her soul for
> gain, they die of hunger.

The simple answer to this nonsense is that the population
of England is better clothed, better housed, and better
fed that it has been at any former period of the national
history, and that this improvement is chiefly attributable
to steam. Without steam manufactures the poor could not
use linen and cotton as freely as they do, and all woven
fabrics would be much less accessible for them. The distress which does exist is not attributable to the steam
engine, or the use of fire, but to the habits of improvi-
dence which unhappily prevail in this country, to vice of
various kinds especially drunkenness, and to inevitable
misfortune.

38. STOPFORD BROOKE, SIGNED ESSAY, RUSKIN'S LECTURES ON
ART, 'MACMILLAN'S MAGAZINE'

October 1870, vol. 22, 423-34

Stopford Brooke (1830-1912) was born in Ireland, educated
at Trinity College, Dublin, and ordained in the Church of
England in 1857. Although he was chaplain in ordinary to
the queen for several years, Brooke was more critic than
cleric and, in 1880, withdrew from the Church for reasons
concerning dogma. He subsequently embraced Unitarianism.
His interests in art and literature were considerable, and
he stands an important critic in the nineteenth century.
He wrote on many literary figures including Shakespeare,
Tennyson, and Browning; and he was a recognized authority
on the history of English Literature.

There are few men of our time who have been more largely
praised or more bitterly attacked than Mr. Ruskin. There
are none who have deserved more praise or more resolutely
challenged attack. He has been so lavish in his approbation of certain artists and schools of art, that he has

raised against them a cloud of opponents. He has been so
unsparing in blame of certain others, so curiously inventive of terms of reproach, so audacious in his tilting
against received opinions, and so felicitous sometimes in
his hits, that he has forced into combination against him
a number of determined foes. Of all men he should be the
last to object to criticism, for his own sword seldom
seeks the scabbard. And on the whole, though he professes
with a certain archness a desire for peace, nothing gives
him so much pleasure, or brings out his intellect so well,
as war, when it is on a subject with which he is acquainted. He will run on, giving birth to paradox after paradox
in an apparently gloomy manner, choosing for very wilful-
ness the obscurity of the Pythoness, as long as his
listeners sit rapt and receptive at his feet. But the
moment one of them, seeing that the paradoxes are becoming
intolerable, starts up and meets them with a blunt contradiction, and declares war, Mr. Ruskin becomes radiant with
good humour, his intellect becomes incisive, and he rushes
to the fight with joy. Nothing is worse for him than worship; and if he had had less of it, he would have done the
State more service. Half of his morbid and hopeless writing comes directly of this – that he has not been of late
sufficiently excited by respectful opposition to feel
happy.

It may be said that he has had plenty of opposition of
late, but it is not the sort which makes a man draw his
sword with pride. Since he has devoted himself to economical and political subjects, the criticism he has met has
been a criticism of laughter from his enemies and of
dismay from his friends. It has been felt impossible to go
seriously into battle against him, for his army of
opinions are such stuff as dreams are made of, and their
little life is rounded with a sleep. Throw upon them a
clear light, and they disperse –

The earth hath bubbles, as the water has,
And these are of them. Whither have they vanished?

We cannot say with Macbeth, 'Would they had stayed,'
but when we look back on the extraordinary series of proposals for regenerating the country, and remember the
criminal classes set to draw canal boats under the lash,
and the poor dressed all in one sad-coloured costume, and
other things of this character, we may follow with
Banquo's words,

Were such things here as we do speak about?
Or have we eaten on the insane root

Which takes the reason prisoner?

In this way he has brought upon himself the loss of the
impulse he derives from respectful and vigorous war. He
has left the Delectable mountains where he fed his sheep,
and gone back to the valley of the shadow of death. There,
impressed with the withered image of Carlylism, which
having surrendered hope sits now like giant Pope shaking
its hands at the pilgrims of the world, and unable to do
more than mutter curses at Liberalism, and invoke the help
of the aristocracy to sanctify and redeem the people:
enthralled by this phantom of a past glory, he had found
it almost impossible to go on drawing, with the peace
necessary for an artist, the tombs of Verona, or to note
down the fleeting loveliness of a sunset cloud. While the
poor were perishing for want of fresh water and decent
houses, he seemed to himself, we conjecture, to be like
Nero, fiddling while Rome was burning. So he abandoned his
own sphere - in which, whatever may be his faults, he was
supreme by genius - to follow, *haud passibus aquis*, in the
track of our Jeremiah, whose style is open to the same
charge which Mr. Arnold makes so pathetically against the
Jewish prophet. But the prophetic cry does not suit the
gentler temper of Mr. Ruskin. With all his efforts we are
thankful to say that he cannot arrive at making the uncouth noise which Carlyle made, and the uncouthness of
which gave what he said more than half its force. He is
too tender-hearted to curse heartily, and he cannot bear,
like his prototype, to pour forth torrents of blame without proposing remedies for evils. But the remedies Ruskin
has proposed are unpractical at this time and in this
country, owing to his ignorance of the state of the poor.
No man is less fitted to understand their true position.
He is too sensitive to beauty, to cleanliness, to quietude,
not to exaggerate the apparent misery of a life passed in
the midst of ugliness, dirt, and noise. He thinks all the
poor feel these things nearly as much as he does, and he
cannot conceive, as we see from these lectures, that they
should endure to live. We should suppose that he has never
lived among them, nor seen how things among them are
seasoned by custom. Those who have gone from room to room
in the courts which Ruskin thinks so unendurable, know
that there is, on the whole, as much happiness among them
as there is among the upper classes; that there is more
self-sacrifice, more of the peace of hard work, more good
humour, more faithfulness to others in misfortune, more
every-day righteousness. Their chief evils are drunkenness, which has only lately vanished from among the upper
classes; the torrent of alms which has been poured upon

them, and which has drowned their independence and postponed their learning the lesson of prudence as opposed to their reckless extravagance. Their main wants are a really active sanitary board, directed by gentlemen in the cities and provinces, who will see that the common work is done with common honesty; and education, especially education in physical science. The commonest training in the first principles of physiology and chemistry, given accurately, will soon produce that state of active anger at their condition, and determination to have it rectified, which no State interference can give them, and which State interference sends to sleep. True, Ruskin advocates this kind of education, and has advocated it well; but he has done it as part of an elaborate system of direction by the State and by the upper classes, - direction which would be as evil to its victims as Romish direction is to the moral force of its patients. No nation has ever been saved by foreign help: the poor can never be saved by the action of the rich, only by their native exertion, and everything that Ruskin says on the subject, in these Lectures and elsewhere, is open to this most grave objection, that it takes away from the people the education which is gained by personal mistakes and personal conquest of mistakes.

Owing to these two things then, - ignorance of the real state of the poor, and the vicious idea of interference from above with the poor, - the remedies which Ruskin proposes are unpractical. At the same time many of his hints, divorced from their principles, are valuable, and we cannot doubt the earnestness and charity with which he speaks, nor refrain from loving him, though we disagree with him. But with the want of practical knowledge has come exaggeration, and with exaggeration disproportioned remedies; and the world, listening to the recital of woes rendered unreal by the violence of the denunciations, and still more unreal by the proposals for their abolition, has lent its ear to Mr. Ruskin for a transient hour, and smiled and gone on its way, and he, having expended so much force for nought, and meeting no real opposition, has slid into melancholy, and from thence into despair.

Moreover, the treatment of such subjects at all, at least their direct treatment, was a great mistake on his part, the error of mistaking his calling. He has been given great powers, as great as those bestowed on any man in this century. He has read the book of nature with unwearied diligence and conscientious observation. He is in every sense a student. But he is far more, in that he is a man of genius; for he can not only see rightly (see the outline beneath the fulfilment), but he can express with passion which is sufficiently tempered to be intense, and

with copiousness sufficiently charged with fact to be
interesting, that which he has seen in the natural world.
It is not too much to say that for many of us whose deepest
pleasure is in the beauty of the world, he has tripled our
power of pleasure. And it has been done, not as the Poet
does it by developing intensity of feeling, but by appealing to feeling through the revelation of fact, and by the
exquisite delight which we feel he takes in the discovery
and the beauty of the fact, and by the charm of the vehicle
through which he tells his story. Nobody before him took
the trouble to tell us what mountains were like, for the
descriptions of the geologist bear the same relation to
the actual mountains that the detail of the skeleton bears
to the living man. Nobody before him made the aspect of
the sky, morning, noon, and evening, familiar as a household word, nor led us to look on clouds and all their
beauty as as much objects of daily observation and delight
as the ways of our children or the face of those we love.
No one before him took us by the brooks of water and upon
the sea, and made every ripple of the one and every wave-
form of the other a recognized pleasure. Wordsworth gave
us much help, but he taught us to feel more than to observe and understand. But Ruskin has taught us to observe
and understand, not as the scientific man does for the
ends of science, but for the ends of *delight* received from
the perception of truth, and no more faithful and splendid
work has ever been done. One would say that this observer
of the vaster aspects of nature for the end of Art, would
be likely to fail in seeing the loveliness of the infinitely little, of the 'beetle panoplied in gems and gold,'
of the 'daisy's shadow on the naked stone,' of the opening
of a sheaf of buds, of the fairy wilderness of an inch or
two of meadow. But neither here has he failed, and the
reader of Mr. Ruskin's books may lie on his face in a
field for half an hour, or watch the water of a stream
eddying round a mossy trunk, and not only feel unremitting
pleasure in what he sees, as Keats or Wordsworth would
make him feel, but know why he feels his pleasure, add to
his stock of artistic fact, and gain additional power of
knowing beauty. All our hours of recreation have been
blessed through him.

The same delicate sensitiveness to beauty combined with
acute critical perception of minuter points of excellence
has been applied by him to poetry. Since Coleridge we
have had no finer work done on the Poets. It is a pity
that his criticisms on Dante, Shakespeare, Scott, Wordsworth, Keats, and others, are not collected out of his
volumes and published separately. A book of this kind
would be of infinitely more value than the useless

'Selections from Ruskin;' a book which irritates one, even more than selections usually do, and has given an entirely false impression of his work to that luckless personage, the general reader.

The work which he has done on Pictures has been equally good of the same kind. He was perfectly capable of explaining their technical excellence, but he did not choose to write for artists, and we are glad that he laid this sort of work aside. For, however good it might be for special students, it gave no help to the public, and only led certain would-be connoisseurs to prate about morbidezza and chiar'oscuro, and bold handling and a hundred other things, which in their mouths were little better than cant. We have been delivered by Mr. Ruskin from the technicalities of ignorant persons. He has led us more than all others to look for the conception of a picture, and to study the way in which the artist carried out that conception. He has taught us to compare it with the facts of nature which we are capable of observing, and to judge it partly from the artist's reverence for truth. We can now, having a certain method, enjoy the thing done with a great deal of delight, without knowing how it is done. Of course the enjoyment is not so great as his who can not only appreciate the ideas but also the mode of work; but it is something, and the smattering we had before of artistic phrase was worth nothing. Those who have time and inclination can go further, but the many who cannot, have now a real pleasure; they can give a reason why they like a picture instead of talking nonsense. Of course the dilettante Pharisees are angry, but that only increases the general thankfulness of the public.

Mr. Ruskin has not only shown us how to go to work. He has a rare power of seeing into the central thought of a picture, and his wide knowledge of the aspects of nature enables him to pronounce upon truth of representation. He has performed this labour notably on Turner and Tintoret. Turner's phrase, that 'he sees meanings in my pictures which I did not mean,' is the exact truth; and Shakespeare would no doubt have said the same had he read Schlegel. He has revealed the genius of Turner to the world by comparing Turner with Nature; and those who have spent hour after hour in the enchanted rooms of the Ducal Palace, or wandered day after day through the sombre galleries of the Scuola San Rocco, know what he has done for Tintoret. It has been said that the world appreciated Turner before Ruskin spoke. A few persons and the artists did (no one ever imagined that the artists did not heartily acknowledge his genius), but artists have not the gift of speech, nor, with an exception or two, such as Eastlake, the faculty of criticism, and we have only found out at last from their biographies what they thought. It is absurd to quote their isolated sayings as a proof that the public understood and valued Turner before Ruskin wrote. Artists say that they pointed out Tintoret to Ruskin, but why did not they point him out to the world? The public wish to be taught, and the artists are silent. We expect it is that they have not much to say. They know what is good; so does Mr. Ruskin. But he takes the trouble to tell us what is good and why it is good, and we owe no gratitude to the artists and a very great deal to him.

Now to do all this, to read Nature, Poetry and Painting for us, and to continue doing it, was Ruskin's peculiar work, and the greater part of it was most nobly done. We ask, with sorrow, why he abandoned it? We have suffered no greater grief than when he left it and took up other labours, for which he was eminently unfitted, and the effect of which was to spoil his powers for his especial business. Sanitary reform, political economy, the dressing of England, manufactories, crime, poverty! *que diable allait-il faire dans cette galère?* A man must have iron nerves and little acute sense of beauty, to play his part in that battle-field, and the result on Ruskin has been like that which would follow on sending a poet like Shelley into one of the war hospitals. He ceases to be able to write poetry and he kills the patients.

This is one of the great mistakes which are scarcely ever remedied, and we trace its results in every one of these Lectures, which are weakened by the forced intro-duction of irrelevant matter, and by the hopeless tone which much musing on miserable subjects has brought into his temper and his style. We trace the latter in the very first page, where he says that it 'has chanced to him of late to be so little acquainted either with pride or hope that he can scarcely recover so much as he now needs of the one for strength, and of the other for foresight.' We appeal to him to throw by altogether the peculiar class of subjects of which we speak, and to believe that when God has given him so plainly a particular work to do, it is his first duty to stick to that work, and to put aside everything which interferes with it. Hope will return when he does his proper labour, and the noble pride of the workman in his toil will give him strength when a crowd of importunate duties outside his sphere are sternly shut out, and he concentrates himself on the one great duty of his life – the unveiling to men Truth and Beauty in Art and in Nature.

We trace this despondent tone, and the consequent false view of the world, still more pathetically in a passage in

the Catalogue of Examples, where he describes himself as
walking in his garden early in the morning to hear the
nightingale sing, and sees 'the sunlight falling on the
grass through thickets of the standard peach, and of plum
and pear in their first showers of fresh silver looking
more like much broken and far-tossed spray of fountains
than trees,' and hears the roar of the railroads sounding
in the distance, 'like the surf of a strong sea,' and
thinks that 'of all the myriads imprisoned by the English
Minotaur of lust for wealth, and condemned to live, if it
is to be called life, in the labyrinth of black walls and
loathsome passages between them, which now fills the
valley of the Thames - not one could hear, this day, any
happy bird sing or look upon any quiet space of the pure
grass that is good for seed.' It is so strongly expressed
and so prettily ended, and has so much of fact to bear it
out, that one at first is inclined to believe it all. But
it is very far from the whole truth. Every year sees more
grass in London, and more trees; the parks are more
crowded with children and working men and roughs, who with
all their rudeness respect the flowers and enjoy the
meadow; the song of the thrush is not quite gone from the
gardens of Kensington and Victoria Park; in spring and
summer time, owing to the very railways which Ruskin seems
anxious to abolish, thousands pour out of London every
week to Epping and Richmond and Hampton and the Downs, and
even drink the sea-breeze at Margate and Brighton. Our
poor see far more of the country and of lovely places than
they did in the past times which we glorify so foolishly;
and bad as London is, it is better now that we have proved
that we can actually stamp out the cholera, than it was in
the days when the Black Death strode unopposed through its
streets, and reaped a harvest in its filthy lanes and
reeking cottages, which it could not reap at the present
time, when the whole nation is ten times cleaner.

It is a picture by Cima of Conegliano, which he introduces to the students with this burst of sorrow, and he
bids them look upon it when they would be in the right
temper for work. 'It will seem to speak to you if you look
long: and say again, and yet again, Ἴδε ὁ αἴρων. His own
Alps are in the distance, and he shall teach us how to
paint their wild flowers, and how to think of them.' Professor Ruskin seems to infer from the whole of this
passage, and from others in the Lectures, that when these
delicate and beautiful pictures were painted by Bellini,
Cima, and others, there was more enjoyment of the country
and of lovely things by the poor, (as if our love of landscape was not ten times more wide-spread than that of the
Venetians!) and that the poor were better off, and lived

a cleanlier and healthier life, and had better dwellings
than they now possess in London. Neither Bellini nor
Conegliano, we imagine, troubled themselves as much about
the poor as even a vestryman of St. Pancras, and if we
take the city of Venice, to whose school Cima belonged,
the facts which speak of dirty disease, and ill living,
are appalling. In 1392 the Doge Morosini died of a great
plague which swept away 19,000 souls. Not quite a century
afterwards, in 1476, the Pest came again, and in 1484 it
was again raging with unremitting fury. In 1556 plague and
famine again devastated the city. Checked for a time, it
broke out again with desolating violence in 1576; and in
1630 the great church of S.M. della Salute, which guards
the entrance of the Grand Canal, was built by the vows of
the Senate to beseech the prayers of the Virgin to avert
another awful destruction from the people. We know now
pretty well, by our own sad experience, what these visita-
tions mean. They mean that the curse of darkness and low
living, and vile dwellings, and pestilential crowding was
as deep over the sun-girt city where Cima of Conegliano
worked, as it ever has been in England, as it is not now
in England. None of the other Italian cities were much
better off, though plague was naturally worse in Venice,
from its closer connection with the East, from its vast
population, and from its want of fresh-water and drainage.

This curious inability of seeing facts, when he is entangled with matters irrelevant to his proper work, has
spoiled some of Professor Ruskin's past labour, and
diminishes the influence of these Lectures. In another man
it would be culpable negligence. In his case, he is partly
blinded by his crowning mistake, to which we have alluded,
and partly swept away by his theory. But men should not be
blinded, and should not be swept away, and Ruskin's work
suffers in consequence. For by and by (and this is frequently the case) he is sure to see the other side of his
theory and to dwell on that with equal force. Both statements are set over one against each other, but in different
portions of his works; and the world of readers naturally
declares that he has contradicted himself. He denies this,
saying that he has stated both sides of the truth; but
stating both sides separately and with equal vehemence,
without having balanced them, he runs into exaggeration in
both, and, instead of distinctly defining one truth,
rushes into two mistakes. The result is that those who
admire and revere his teaching, as we ourselves most
sincerely do, are greatly troubled at times to defend him
and to understand him. They are wearied by the efforts
they have to make to set aside what is due to impetuosity,
and to find by a laborious comparison of passages what

the truth really is which he desires to tell.

We hoped, for example, that in the lecture on The Relation of Art to Morality he would have laid down plainly what he meant on this vext subject. But we are bound to say that he has done so in a confused manner. His first phrase is 'You must have the right moral State or you cannot have the Art.' He does not say you must have certain moral qualities in an artist or a nation, or you cannot have noble art:- he makes the immense requirement of a *right moral state*, which is either too vague a definition, or means that the whole state of any artist's moral character must be right or he will not produce good work. Everybody at once denies this, and brings examples to disprove it. Ruskin says that those who have misapprehended the matter have done so because they did not know who the great painters were, such as those 'who breathed empyreal air, sons of the morning, under the woods of Assisi, and the crags of Cadore.' Well, let us take him of Cadore. The life of Titian is not the life of a man in a right moral state, in our usual sense of the words; nor does it agree with Ruskin's sketch of a moral life, in which he includes 'any actual though unconscious violation of even the least law to which obedience is essential for the glory of life and the pleasing of its giver.' Titian lived the life of a noble natural character, but his morals were entirely unrestrained by any considerations belonging to high morality. He was the friend of Aretino, and that speaks volumes for his moral standard. Tintoret, a much higher moral character, despised Aretino. Titian dined with that vile person with the vilest of women. It does not say much for his reverence that he had no objection to chant the Magnificat over a dish of savoury partridges. He lived freely, he spent his money freely, he drank freely, though wisely. Nor was the society of his city in a right moral state. It had not sunk down into the faded baseness of Venice before the French Revolution. It had still a reverence for truth, and honour, and generosity, but these were combined with an audacious immorality of the body, with fiery jealousies, with the most headlong following of passions. A good deal of this is confessed by Professor Ruskin, but his confession only proves that his original phrase is far too large for his meaning. What he does mean, if we take the illustrations which follow as explanations, is this, that whatever is good in an artist's work springs from some corresponding element of good in his character, as, for example, truth of representation from love of truth. But this only predicates the existence in him of some moral qualities, not that he is in a right moral state, which means that the whole of his

character is moral. With these moral qualities may exist
immoral qualities, such as sensuality, and the evil influence of that will also be seen in his work. Stated thus,
Ruskin only means that a man's character is accurately
reflected in his art, and this, with respect to the *ideas*
of his work, we are by no means disposed to deny, seeing
it may be called a truism.

But in other places, in scattered phrases, he seems to
speak directly from the large statement, and to assume
that it is true in its entirety, though he has modified it
again and again. This is the element of confusion in the
lecture, and it is at times extremely provoking.

It is worth while, perhaps, to look at the subject more
closely. Noble art is the splendid expression, through
intense but subdued feeling, of noble ideas. Nobleness of
conception is its first element; but it is also necessary
that the ideas should be represented simply, directly, and
in a manner true to natural fact; that the harmony of the
work should be complete, and also its finish; that the
subordination of the parts to the whole, and their several
relations, should be clear in statement, unbroken by any
extravagance in any part, or any indulgence of mere fancy;
and that the technical skill employed should be almost
intuitive in absolute ease, accuracy, and knowledge.

Does all this presuppose a right moral state in the
Artist? The first element does partly do so, for it is not
possible that a base person can have noble thoughts or
express them nobly, - at least in the ear or to the eye of
a noble person: the imitation is at once detected; nor is
the feeling of a base person ever intense, and even should
he possess some passion, he cannot subdue it to the calm
in which a great thought can alone take its correspondent
form. Even that love of sensual pleasure which is so
characteristic of artist life, and which by no means
supposes a base character, though often an immoral one,
spoils, we think, the predominance of high imagination in
artistic work. No one who has studied Titian and Tintoret
can, in our opinion, compare the two, so far as moral
majesty of thought is concerned, and grandeur of imagination. In these points Tintoret as far excels Titian as his
life was simpler and purer than Titian's. The same may be
said of Raphael and Michael Angelo. But on the other hand,
a man like Angelico may be in a much more right moral
state than Titian, and yet never reach his nobility of
conception.

It is plain, after all, that the possession of Imagination is the first thing, and of Individuality the second,
and that the moral condition only influences and does not
secure or destroy the ideas of genius. What really reduced

the work of the later artists of the Renaissance to its
poverty of ideas while retaining exquisite technical
skill, was not their moral state, which was by no means so
bad as Ruskin says; but the way in which all individuality
was overridden by the predominance of the Past. They
became imitators, not inventors, and even Raphael's work
shows that this deadening influence had begun. The Renaissance began by intensifying individuality and setting it
free, in the case of Art, from the shackles of religious
conventionality; it ended by laying a heavier yoke of
convention on Art than even religion had done. Art could
not endure that, and it perished.

On the whole, then, noble conceptions in an artist's
work only presuppose *some* moral elements in his character,
and it is not seldom the case that when an artist's moral
state is absolutely right, there is a want in his work of
healthy naturalness, of fire and warmth, of bold representation of human life. He is liable to be overawed by his
own morality, he is likely to direct his work to a moral
end as his *first* aim; and that would be the ruin of Art.

But putting noble ideas aside, and taking up the other
qualities of great Art, such as preciseness of handling
and the rest, do these necessarily presuppose a right
moral state in the artist, or even analogous moral
qualities? Ruskin boldly declares that they do. The infinite grace of the words of Virgil is due, he says, to his
deep tenderness. The severity - severe conciseness, we
suppose - of the words of Pope, to his serene and just
benevolence. Both of these excellences may have been
influenced by the moral qualities mentioned; but we suspect they were mainly due to the literary work which preceded the 'Æneid' and the 'Essay on Man.' Pope was the
last great artist of that critical school which began, we
may say, with Dryden. Virgil developed into perfection the
gracefulness which the Roman world of letters had been
striving to attain for many years. They entered into the
labours of other men, and added to these the last touch.

Professor Ruskin goes still further with respect to
Art. After speaking in his best manner of the day's work
of a man like Mantegna or Veronese, and of the unfaltering, uninterrupted succession of movements of the hand
more precise than those of a skilful fencer; of the
muscular precision and the intellectual strain of such
movement, and of its being governed every instant by
direct and new intention, and of this sustained all life
long, with visible increase of power, - he turns round and
adds: 'Consider, so far as you know anything of physiology, what sort of an ethical state of body and mind that
means! Ethic through ages past! What fineness of race

there must be to get it; what exquisite balance of the
vital powers! And then, finally, determine for yourselves
whether a manhood like that is consistent with any
viciousness of soul, mean anxiety or gnawing lust, any
wretchedness of spite or remorse, any consciousness of
rebellion against law of God or man,' &c. &c. In this he
has left his modifications behind and swept back to his
large statement, and, without denying the portion of truth
in the sentence, it is plain that the inference is not at
all a necessary one. These qualities of the artist may be
the result, partly of natural gift, and partly of a previous art development, into the advantages of which he
steps at once. They presuppose that the artist has been
born into a school which has brought its methods up to a
certain point of perfection, from which a completer
development is possible. His genius adds to the past what
was needed to perfect it, and Titian or Turner orb their
special Art into its perfect sphere. The ethic state into
which Ruskin demands that he should be placed, because of
his precise hand, may not be an ethic state at all. His
absolute power of touch says, it is true, that neither the
artist himself nor his parents were desperate drunkards
nor imprudent sensualists, that they kept their physical
frame in fine order. But does that prove his morality or
that of his parents? A calculating sensualist, who is
prudent in his indulgence, may have a healthier body than
the man who has fought against sensualism all his life. A
man may be a liar or a thief, and his bodily powers be in
exquisite harmony. Fineness of race does not prove an
antecedent morality, nor perfection of handling an artist's
truth or honesty.

Again, he may have the patient power of a great master,
his government of the hand by selective thought, his perception of the just harmony of colour, and the man himself
be at the same time neither patient, nor temperate, nor
pure in his daily life. For all artists can lead a double
life, life in the world and life in their art; and genius
and morality are two things, not one. Their several
qualities resemble one another, but they are not identical. The intense industry of genius, its patience, its
temperance in the centre of passion, are of its very
nature; but outside the sphere of an artist's work, in
matters of common life, where these qualities would
become moral in resistance to sloth, to bad temper, and to
sensual indulgence, they may and do completely fail; nay,
even the restraint of the studio may lead directly to
absence of restraint in the world. One cannot argue as
Ruskin does from the possession of the one to the possession of the other, though we may with him distinctly argue

from the artist's search for lovely forms, and thoughts to
express, to his moral temper. We partly agree then and
partly disagree with our writer, but we have no hope that
people in general will ever know clearly whether they
agree or disagree with Mr. Ruskin on this subject till he
tells us plainly what he means by a moral state, for
surely the prevalence of kindness and order in a character
does not sum up the whole of its meaning.

With regard to the aim of Art, Ruskin is much clearer
than on the question of Art in relation to Morality. He
can no longer be attacked on the ground that he denies
that the first aim of Art should be to give a high
pleasure, for he states plainly that every good piece of
art involves essentially and first the evidence of human
skill and the formation of an actually beautiful thing by
it. We agree with him that, beyond this, Art may have two
other objects, Truth and Serviceableness. Mr. Ruskin has
done no work so well and so usefully as that in which he
has proved that great Art is always true, and that so far
as it does not represent the facts of things, it is
neither vital nor beautiful. The statement has naturally
to be modified when one comes to ideal pictures, but it
bears modification without the contradiction of its principle; and the mode in which, in the 'Modern Painters,'
these modifications are worked out within the sphere of
the original statement is equally subtile and true. The
necessity that there should be serviceableness as one
element of the artist's conception appears chiefly in the
Art of Architecture, and the general reception of the idea
that everything in a building should be *motivé* towards the
purpose of the building is largely due to the 'Stones of
Venice' and the 'Seven Lamps of Architecture.' In the
present lecture on The Relation of Art to Use, he goes, we
think, too far. The usefulness of truthful portraiture no
man denies, but we do not believe in Art being serviceable
to Geology, Botany, and History, except on the condition
of its ceasing to be art. The great artist can draw mountains accurately without knowing geology, and flowers
without knowing botany; but he cannot help either geologist or botanist by work which, if it is imaginative,
must generalize truth. Moreover, it is waste of time; as
great a waste of time as Ruskin himself makes when he
torments himself with business. A section of Skiddaw,
sufficient for all purposes, can be drawn by any pupil in
the School of Mines. Again, in the matter of history, it
is a very pretty pastime to illustrate Carlyle's
Frederick, to draw the tomb of Henry the Fowler, or the
battle-field of Minden; but so far as service to the
historian is concerned, a photograph of the tomb and a map

of the field by the Ordnance Survey would be far more
useful. The artist would paint his impressions of the tomb
and of the field of battle; the pictures would be delightful, but Turnerian topography would not assist the historian much.

Art is not to be handmaid to Science or History, but to
exist wholly within her own sphere and for her own ends.
Her utility is in the communication of beauty and the
giving of a noble enjoyment. She is the handmaid, not of
any particular class of men, but of mankind, and the best
advice to give to students who wish to make art useful is
this, 'Don't draw for the help of Science or History, draw
for your own delight in Nature and Humanity - and to
increase the delight of others. If your work lives to stir
or confirm an enduring energy, or to kindle a true feeling,
or to lead men to look more wisely, kindly, or closely at
the life of humanity or the world of nature, it will be of
more ennobling usefulness than all the labours of scientific or historical scholars. Let this be your aim, to give
high pleasure to men, and to sacrifice your life for that.
Then the usefulness of your art is secured.'

We have left ourselves but little space in which to
speak of the three last practical lectures on Line, Light,
and Colour. They go straight, with the inevitable digressions intermixed, to the objects of the Art School. The
conception which Ruskin has of those objects is different
from the usual one, but it is none the worse for that. It
is well that one professor at least should see that one of
the first aims of an art school at a university should be
to teach young men to see beautiful natural fact and to
love its beauty. In after-life they will demand it of
artists, and the demand will react with benefit both on
artists and art. They cannot learn this better than by
drawing natural objects with accuracy. Ruskin has given
himself to the teaching of this, and his method seems to
be admirable. We refer our readers to the Lectures, but
his main object, in his own words, is this, to teach his
pupils 'to draw spaces of their true shape, and to fill
them in with colours which shall match their colours.' He
is right in dwelling upon colour more than on light and
shade, and in his protest against the theory that shadow
is an absence of colour. No words in the whole Lectures,
considered not only as truth, but as establishing in his
hearers' minds a true ideal of Art, are more important
than these two sentences. 'Shadow is necessary to the full
presence of colour, for every colour is a diminished
quantity or energy of light, and, practically, it follows,
from what I have just told you, that every light in painting is a shadow to higher lights, and every shadow a light

to lower shadows; that also every colour in painting must
be a shadow to some brighter colour and a light to some
darker one, all the while being a positive colour itself.
And the great splendour of the Venetian school arises from
their having seen and held from the beginning this great
fact - that shadow is as much colour as light, often much
more ... while the practice of the Bolognese and Roman
schools in drawing their shadows always dark and cold
renders *perfect* painting impossible in those schools.'
That is one sentence; here is the other: 'Whether you fill
your spaces with colours or with shadows, they must be
equally of the true outline and in true gradations. Without perfect delineation of form and perfect gradation of
space, neither noble colour is possible nor noble light.'
Principles of these kinds worked out in teaching and
taught by personal superintendence will make some of his
pupils good workmen, and all good judges of the general
aspects of art. To illustrate these things and others, and
to inspire the students, Professor Ruskin, with a noble
generosity for which he has not been sufficiently thanked
- he has been so often generous that men have come to look
upon his gifts as they look upon the gifts of air and
light, so common that one forgets to be grateful - has
given to the School of Art a whole collection of examples,
many of them of great value and rarity, and many of them
his own personal work, the results of years of accurate
study and patient drawing. There are some artists who have
been impertinent enough to despise and even to deny the
artistic quality of Ruskin's work. But many of these drawings of flowers, of shells, of old buildings, and especially of such stonework as Gothic capitals, Venetian
doorways, the porches of cathedrals, are of the highest
excellence, and possess a quality of touch and an imaginative sympathy with the thing represented, combined with an
exquisite generalization of truth for which we look in
vain in the work of many artists whose names stand high.

We believe that by Ruskin's work at the Art School in
Oxford this result at least will be attained, that the
young men who afterwards will become, by their wealth,
patrons and buyers of art, will know good work when they
see it, and be able and willing to rescue from the ruin of
Italian restorers and destroyers pictures which are now
perishing, unpitied and unknown. They will cease to waste
their money. The expenditure, at present, of rich people,
on the most contemptible nicknacks, on Swiss cottages and
silver filagree, and Florentine frames and copies on china
at Dresden and pietra dura, is as pitiable as it is incredible. Room after room in large houses is filled with
trash which ought to be destroyed at once, for the demand

for it keeps a mass of men producing things which are only
worthy to pave roads with. The very production of copies
of pictures is in itself a crime, and the only thing which
is worse is the buying of them.

But we must close our paper. We have spoken with open-
ness of the faults which we find in Professor Ruskin's
work, and it has been difficult to assume the critic: for
our own gratitude to him has been and is so deep, and we
are so persuaded of the influence for good which he has
had on England, that blame had to become as great a duty
as praise before we could express it. And even in the
midst of our blame, we felt the blessing of contact with a
person of a strong individuality, the pleasure of meeting
in the middle of a number of writers cut out after the
same pattern, with one who cuts out his own pattern and
alters it year by year. His theories may, many of them, be
absurd, but we may well put up with the absurdity of some
for the sake of the excellence of others, more especially
for the sake of the careful work which hangs on to them
and can be considered apart from them. We should be dis-
mayed to lose the most original man in England. It is
quite an infinite refreshment to come across a person who
can gravely propose to banish from England all manufactories which require the use of fire, who has the quiet
audacity to contradict himself in the face of all the reviewers, and who spins his web of fancies and thoughts
without caring a straw what the world thinks of them. The
good which a man of so marked an originality does to us
all is great, if it is provoking; and we had rather
possess him with his errors than a hundred steady-going
writers who can give solemn reasons for all they say. The
intellectual excitement which he awakens, the delight and
anger which he kindles in opposite characters, and the way
in which his words create a stir of debate, marks the man
of genius whose mistakes are often as good as other
persons' victories, and who from this very quality of
individuality, united to the personal attractiveness of
his simple and sympathetic humanity, is calculated to be
of great and lasting good to Oxford.

We have read many lectures on Art Subjects, many books
on Art Criticism. They have their merits, merits which Mr.
Ruskin's work does not possess. They are formal, easily
understood, carefully arranged; all scattered thought, or
impetuous fancy, or wild theory is banished from their
pages. We walk through a cultivated garden, the beds are
trimly laid down, the paths are neat and straight, the
grass is closely shaven, the trees are trees of culture,
the very limes on the edge are kept in order, and walls
surround it on all sides. At last, on the very outskirts

of the garden, beyond the bounding wall, and looked down
upon by a row of pert hollyhocks who have in the course of
many seasons arrived at the power of producing double
flowers in an artistic manner, we catch a glimpse of a
wild bit of grassy land, full of grey boulders and some
noble trees growing as they like it, and below a brook
chattering pleasantly over the stones. Every flower of the
field blooms here and runs in and out among the rocks and
roots after its own sweet will. The woodbine, the wild
rose sprays, the ivy and moss, play the maddest and the
prettiest pranks by the brook-side. The sky is blue above,
with a world of drifting clouds, and the ground below is a
mystery of light and colour. It is true there are burnt
spaces of grass here and there, and clusters of weeds, and
now and then a decayed tree stem; but for all that, when
we see the pleasant place, we do not think twice about it,
we forget our garden, we leap the wall - and we live far
more than half of our art life with the books of Ruskin.

Ruskin 1872–1900

Charles Locke Eastlake (1836-1906), not to be confused
with his uncle, who bore the same names, was educated at
Westminster School and subsequently became a pupil of
Philip Hardwick. In 1854 Eastlake gained recognition for
his architectural drawings whilst showing promise as a
water-colourist as well. From 1866 to 1877 he was secretary of the Royal Institute of British Architects and in
1878 was appointed keeper and secretary of the National
Gallery, a post he held until 1898. Eastlake was a distinguished writer on art and on industrial design. One of
his well-known publications was 'Hints on Household Taste
in Furniture, Upholstery, and Other Details'; he also
produced a series of notes on several foreign galleries
and lectured on different facets of industrial workmanship.
See Introduction, p. 20.

It was suggested in the last chapter that during the ten
years which elapsed between the commencement and the completion of All Saints' Church, the public taste in architecture underwent a decided change. It would perhaps have
been more correct to say two or three changes, but undoubtedly the first and perhaps the most important one was
expressed by that phase in the Gothic Revival which has
since been distinguished - and in one sense honourably
distinguished - by the name of Ruskinism.
　　If the author of 'Modern Painters' had been content to
limit his researches, his criticism, and the dissemination

of his principles to the field of pictorial art alone, he
would have won for himself a name not easily forgotten. No
English amateur had measured so accurately the individual
merits and deficiencies of the old schools of painting, or
was so well qualified to test them by the light of reason.
No critic had educated his eye more carefully by observation of Nature. No essayist enjoyed the faculty of expressing his ideas with greater force or in finer language. But
Mr. Ruskin's taste for art was a comprehensive one. He
learnt at an early age that painting, sculpture, and
architecture are intimately associated, not merely in
their history but in their practice, and in the fundamental
principles which regulate their respective styles. His
love of pictures was not that of a mere collector or
dilettante, who buys them to hang up in gilt frames to
furnish his drawing-room, but that of an artist who considers no noble building complete without storied walls
and sculptured panels, and who believes that even in an
ordinary dwelling-house there might, under a proper condition of things, be found scope for the carver's handiwork
and limner's cunning.

Mr. Ruskin looked around him at the modern architecture
of England and saw that it not only did not realise this
ideal but was diametrically opposed to it. He found the
majority of his countrymen either profoundly indifferent
to the art or interested in it chiefly as antiquarians and
pedants. He saw public buildings copied from those of a
nobler age, but starved or vulgarised in the copying. He
saw private houses – some modelled on what was supposed to
be an Italian pattern, and others modelled on what was
supposed to be a Mediæval pattern, and he found too often
neither grandeur in the one nor grace in the other. He saw
palaces which looked mean, and cottages which were tawdry.
He saw masonry without interest, ornament without beauty,
and sculpture without life. He walked through the streets
of London and found that they consisted for the most part
of flaunting shop fronts, stuccoed porticos, and plaster
cornices. It is true there were fine clubs and theatres
and public institutions scattered here and there; but
after making due allowance for their size, for the beauty
of materials used, and for the neatness of the workmanship, how far could they be considered as genuine works of
art? Mr. Ruskin was by no means the first person who asked
this question; but he was the first who asked it boldly,
and with a definite purpose....

Mr. Ruskin is one of the most accomplished art critics,
and perhaps the most eloquent writer on art that England
has seen, in this or any other age. He is also, if any
man ever was, a theoretical philanthropist. His views on

the subject of art may in the main be sound; his philanthropical intentions are, we doubt not, sincere; but, considered in combination as they are usually associated,
they present a scheme which is utterly impracticable.

On the Gothic Revival, as it was ordinarily understood,
Mr. Ruskin himself did not look very hopefully. He had
seen the fitful variations of taste to which modern architecture had already been exposed, and perhaps he foresaw
other and more radical changes by which it was threatened.
He was impatient of the tame and spiritless formality
which distinguished too many specimens of contemporary
design; but, on the other hand, he was sick of the cant
which continually demanded novelty and freedom from pre-
cedent.

> A day never passes without our hearing our English
> architects called upon to be original and to invent a
> new style: about as sensible and necessary an exhorta-
> tion as to ask of a man who has never had rags enough
> on his back to keep out the cold to invent a new mode
> of cutting a coat. Give him a whole coat first and let
> him concern himself about the fashion of it afterwards.
> We want no new style of architecture. Who wants a new
> style of painting or of sculpture? But we want *some*
> style.

This is not exactly one of the happiest of Mr. Ruskin's
similes, but it serves to illustrate his meaning. What he
meant was that a style of national architecture should be
definitely selected for adoption, and universally practised. The choice of a style he limited to four types:
(1) Pisan Romanesque; (2) Florentine of Giotto's time;
(3) Venetian Gothic; and (4) the earliest English Deco-
rated. Of these he considered that the last would, on the
whole, be the safest to choose; but it was to be 'well
fenced' from the chance of degenerating again into Perpendicular, and might be enriched by the introduction of a
French element.

To ensure conformity of taste to this standard when
once settled, Mr. Ruskin proposed that an universal system
of form and workmanship should be everywhere adopted *and
enforced*. How it was to be enforced and by whom he did not
venture to explain. Whether it was to become the law of
the land; what provision was to be made for its fulfilment;
what penalties were to be attached to its neglect or
violation, whether the architect of a Jacobean mansion
would be subject to a fine, or how far any decided tendency to Flamboyant design could be considered as a mis-
demeanour; all these were details of his scheme which he

left others to determine. That the scheme presented a difficulty he was aware, but he did not consider that any difficulty could affect the value of his proposition.

It may be said that this is impossible. It may be so. I fear it is so. I have nothing to do with the possibility or impossibility of it. I simply know and assert the necessity of it. If it be impossible, English art is impossible. Give it up at once. You are wasting time and money and energy upon it, and though you exhaust centuries and treasuries, and break hearts for it, you will never raise it above the merest dilettanteism. Think not of it. It is a dangerous vanity, a mere gulf in which genius after genius will be swallowed up, and it will not close.

It was wild and impetuous reasoning such as this which broke the spell of Mr. Ruskin's authority and robbed his eloquence of half its charm. People began to ask themselves whether a man gifted, even as they knew him to be gifted, with a keen appreciation of the beautiful in art and nature, with intellectual faculties of a high order, with a moral sense which revealed itself in the minutiæ of æsthetics – whether even such a guide as this was to be trusted when he allowed his theories to waft him into dreamland, or to culminate in plans which would have been considered unfeasible in Utopia.

In so far as the author of 'The Seven Lamps of Architecture' confined himself to strictures on all that was false or mean or meretricious in bad art, or pointed out the truth, the purity, and grace of noble art (and on the whole no one was better qualified to draw these distinctions), he did excellent service to national taste. In so far as he allowed his prejudices to get the better of his judgment, in so far as he attempted to form – what never will be formed – a perfect and universally acceptable test of architectural excellence, or pursued fanciful theories at the expense of common sense, he exposed himself to the obvious charges of unfairness and inconsistency, and damaged the cause which he had most at heart.*...

And, for all his errors and failings, Mr. Ruskin *was* heard. Never, since the days of the English decadence – never, since the Pointed arch was depressed into Tudor ugliness – never, since tradition lost its sway in regulating the fashion of structural design – has the subject of Gothic Architecture been rendered so popular in this country, as for a while it was rendered by the aid of his pen. All that had been argued – all that had been preached on the subject previously, was cast into the shade by the

vigour of his protest. Previous apologists for the Revival
had relied more or less on ecclesiastical sentiment, on
historical interest, or on a vague sense of the picturesque
for their plea in its favour. It was reserved for the
author of 'The Stones of Venice' to strike a chord of
human sympathy that vibrated through all hearts, and to
advocate, independently of considerations which had hitherto only enlisted the sympathy of a few, those principles
of Mediæval Art whose application should be universal.
There are passages in this work recording nobler truths
concerning architecture than had ever before found expression in our mother tongue. The rich fertility of the
author's language, his happy choice of illustrative
parallels, the clear and forcible manner in which he
states his case or points his moral, and, above all, the
marvellous capacity of his descriptive power, are truly
admirable. No finer English has been written in our time.
It is poetry in prose.

That he made many converts, and found many disciples
among the younger architects of the day, is not to be
wondered. Students, who but a year or so previously had
been content to regard Pugin as their leader, or who had
modelled their notions of art on the precepts of the
'Ecclesiologist,' found a new field open to them, and
hastened to occupy it. They prepared designs in which the
elements of Italian Gothic were largely introduced:
churches in which the 'lily capital' of St. Mark's was
found side by side with Byzantine bas-reliefs and mural
inlay from Murano; town halls wherein the arcuation and
baseless columns of the Ducal Palace were reproduced;
mansions which borrowed their parapets from the Calle del
Bagatin, and windows from the Ca' d'Oro. They astonished
their masters by talking of the Savageness of Northern
Gothic, of the Intemperance of Curves, and the Laws of
Foliation; and broke out into open heresy in their abuse
of Renaissance detail. They went to Venice or Verona – not
to study the works of Sansovino and San Michele – but to
sketch the tomb of the Scaligers and to measure the front
of the Hotel Danieli. They made drawings in the Zoological
Gardens, and conventionalised the forms of birds, beasts,
and reptiles into examples of 'noble grotesque' for decorative sculpture. They read papers before Architectural
Societies, embodying Mr. Ruskin's sentiments in language
which rivalled the force, if it did not exactly match the
refinement, of their model. They made friends of the Pre-
Raphaelite painters (then rising into fame), and promised
themselves as radical a reform in national architecture as
had been inaugurated in the field of pictorial art. Nor was
this all. Not a few architects who had already established

a practice began to think that there might be something
worthy of attention in the new doctrine. Little by little
they fell under its influence. Discs of marble, billet-
mouldings, and other details of Italian Gothic, crept into
many a London street-front. Then bands of coloured brick
(chiefly red and yellow) were introduced, and the voussoirs
of arches were treated after the same fashion.†

But the influence of Mr. Ruskin's teaching reached a
higher level than this, and manifested itself in unexpected quarters. Years afterwards, in the centre of the
busiest part of our busy capital - the very last place one
would have supposed likely to be illumined by the light of
'The Seven Lamps' - more than one palatial building was
raised, which recalled in the leading features of its
design and decoration the distinctive character of
Venetian Gothic.

The literature of the Revival was sensibly affected by
the same cause. It is impossible not to recognise even in
the title of Mr. Street's charming volume, 'The Brick and
Marble Architecture of North Italy,' a palpable echo from
'The Stones of Venice,' while in some of his theories -
as, for instance, that the undulation in the pavement of
St. Mark's was intended to typify the stormy seas of life
- we find a reflex of Mr. Ruskin's tendency to natural
symbolism.

For a considerable time, indeed, the principles enunciated by this accomplished author and critic gained
ground even in spite of violent opposition. It was perhaps
while they were most vigorously attacked on one side that
they received the staunchest support from the other. But
the current of public taste, even in the artistic world,
is capricious in its course, and is subject to constant
deviation. Of late years other influences have been at
work - for good or evil one can scarcely yet say, but
certainly to some purpose. If the Gothic Revival has lost
Mr. Ruskin as a leader, it is to be trusted that he may
still watch its progress as a counseller and a friend.

Notes

* It is but fair to state here that Mr. Ruskin has since
expressed himself dissatisfied with the form in which many
of his early opinions were recorded at this period of his
life.
† In the suburbs this mode of decoration rose rapidly into
favour for cockney villas and public taverns, and laid the
foundation of that peculiar order of Victorian Architecture which has since been distinguished by the familiar

but not altogether inappropriate name of the Streaky Bacon
Style.

40. J.J. JARVES, SIGNED ARTICLE, JOHN RUSKIN, THE ART-SEER,
'ART-JOURNAL'

January 1874, vol. 13, n.s., 5-6

____

James Jackson Jarves (1818-88) was born in Boston, and was
said to be the first American to write a sustained study
of art: this was 'Art-Hints' (1855), a volume strongly
Ruskinian in tenor. After a business and journalistic
career in the Hawaiian islands, Jarves settled in Florence
in 1852, where he was briefly US vice-consul, and became
a member of its Anglo-American circle. He formed a collection of paintings singularly representative of his own
spiritual and historical views and, with the help of
Charles Eliot Norton, endeavoured to sell them to the
Boston Athenaeum but without success. They subsequently
were acquired by Yale University. Jarves also possessed a
fine collection of glass which he gave to the Metropolitan
Museum of Art (New York) in 1881. He was a voluminous
writer who recorded his travels in Hawaii, Central America,
and California; he also produced various autobiographical
volumes. See Introduction, p. 21.

____

If there be any one writer to whom the Anglo-Saxon mind
is especially indebted for directing its attention anew to
Art, it is Mr. Ruskin. Many others had preceded him as
critics and teachers; but in the tame old way, which
edified few. Pictures, also, had greatly multiplied in
England, without developing any special comprehension of
their æsthetic merits in their collectors, whose regard
for mere names was as fluctuating as any other caprice of
fashion. At this juncture there suddenly appeared in the
æsthetic horizon a youthful critic of remarkable flow of
language, startling novelty of ideas, and redundant powers
of illustration, who, at one assault, firmly established
himself in the field of Art as a radical inonoclast. Old
reputations were shivered at a blow, new ones made in a
breath, time-honoured systems and rules overturned at the
first bout - in fine, Art, as commonly accepted in England, was sent flying in craven panic before the literary
lance of this fresh Don Quixote of the quill.

Nor was the panic wholly unreasonable or unseasonable.
'The Oxford graduate,' John Ruskin (for he is our knight-
errant), had the keenest of scents for the artistic
foibles and vices of the hour, a chivalric loyalty to
truth in the abstract, an unselfish love of Art, honesty
of purpose, and religiosity of soul that savoured of the
spirit which defies even martyrdom for liberty of praise
or denunciation. His strong belief in himself led him to
conclude it to be the final proof of error and wrong-
mindedness for another to differ from him. This is as
heroically as bluntly affirmed in unmistakable language
in his earlier controversies, and we have seen nothing in
his later writings to indicate any modification of this
opinion. Acutely learned, subtilely dexterous of diction,
magnificently rhetorical, intensely hostile to cants and
deceptions of every species, penetrating the very marrow
of æsthetic right and wrong by his moral chemistry; as
fiercely prophetic of tongue as a maddened seer, impla-
cable as a savage in his hates, yet tender-hearted and
sympathetic as a maiden in his loves; illogical (yet we
have read a letter of his to a distinguished poet in which
he says, of himself, referring to a critical charge of
this sort in one of the Reviews, if there be any one
faculty which I possess above all others, it is the logical one), having no faculty of generalization, always
seeing things apart in minutest detail and from closest
vision, the natural sight running to one extreme of
material observation, and his imaginative sight to its
opposite; as bitterly ingenious in fault-finding as eloquently extravagant in laudation and conclusion; the most
sincerely impressible of theorists and fervid demolisher
of false gods, with the loftiest ideas of man's duty and
his own pet idealisms; vehemently publishing his intui-
tions and observations as immutable principles of life;
rejoicing, like Job's war-horse in the battle, but easily
made despondent; with an unbalanced brain, running to fine
points and bent on Ruskinizing the world - the while most
inconsistently sad and angry because of failure - despite
himself, John Ruskin has done much good work for us all in
his adopted cause. He has stirred anew the languid
currents of æsthetic thought both in England and America;
incited a deeper interest and investigation into the
motives as well as the methods of Art-education; suggested
beautiful and noble ideas; disclosed fresh sources of
enjoyment and inspiration; helped to reconcile Art with
Nature, and put us in better fellowship with both; and,
best of all, relentlessly exposed and denounced evils,
driving to bay the mean parasites that habitually infest
all good work and sound aims. In short, notwithstanding

his many entanglements of thought, eccentricities of pre-
sentment, incapacity of putting objects and ideas relatively right, or of accurately measuring the differences
between the little and the great, of seeing the world as
it actually exists, of curbing his own egoism, unphilo-
sophical turmoil of soul, foregone prejudices, constitutional irritability, restraining his passion for Utopias,
and of making intellectual allowance for his own defective
physical fibre, - notwithstanding all these drawbacks,
Ruskin has been a profitable as well as fascinating writer
for the general reader.

Perhaps even more: for he well-nigh founded a sect of
youthful followers, some of whom, enthusiasts of impressible, congenial proclivities, have turned his teachings
to practical account; while others, bewildered in trying
to follow him to the end, have fallen back on their own
independent judgments. In New York there arose a set of
writers, stimulated by his books into vehement and transient activity, who imbibed but little of his spirit
besides its destructiveness, which in them speedily
degenerated into butcher-like criticisms on the luckless
artist they selected for assault. Whatever there is sound
in Ruskin has come from his intuitive honesty, generosity,
and philanthropic aim, the absolute æsthetic conscience
of the man and sensitiveness to the spiritual basis of
being; whatever is erratic, disturbing, and unsound, from
his equally innate psychological and physiological deficiencies, which neither deeper culture nor wider experience seem to help, but rather to emphasize; so that,
as he has grown older, he has become more disposed to
inveigh against everything, including himself - to make
his life and ours one wailing Jeremiad, instead of bringing into relief its hopes and consolations.

Ruskin's egotism, which tries all truths and tests all
facts by their fitness to its intensity of conviction, is
the dry powder which propels his shots so straight and
hard at their mark. Sometimes they rebound on himself. His
target is the entire world. Art, religion, government,
social science, domestic life - each and all must be made
anew by his receipt, if humanity will be saved. The frankness with which he assails whatever irritates him, and the
sincerity with which he enunciates that the vulgar many
should humbly submit to be ruled by the select few, if not
altogether wise in action, are sure to be tied by some
threads of truth to fundamental principles which thinkers
might profitably investigate. It will not do to ridicule
or despise the wildest of Ruskin's sayings, simply from
their apparent absurdity. There is in him a faculty which
can probe through sore or sound flesh, into deeper currents

beneath, even if it cannot always turn its findings to
salutary account.

Indeed preachers make poor statesmen, because of concentrated narrowness of vision; but they often detect
symptoms overlooked by broad-eyed worldlings. However
foolish, therefore, any of Ruskin's wishes may read, there
is somewhere in them a sharp-cut truth; however impracticable his plans, suggestions of grave import.

But once hold of his specific idea or fact, Ruskin
finds no better way of using it than firing it off point-
blank against some weightier idea or fact. He says of the
American rebellion, 'that accursed war having washed all
the salt out of the nation in blood, left America to the
putrefaction and the morality of New York.' 'I should like
to destroy without rebuilding the city of New York.' Mark
his individual delight in destruction: '*I* should like to
destroy;' not that another should do the work. Lately, in
the 'Pall Mall Gazette,' he writes, - 'There are numbers
of the people I should like to *murder*.' In his 'Fors
Clavigera' it is gravely stated, 'that if upon the proclamation of war every woman in Europe would go into
mourning, war would become impossible;' an opinion on a
par in ratiocination with his theory of marriage as the
'reward of merit' only - all youthful couples and their
property to be under the tutelage of the State, and 'that
the wise and kind, few or many, shall govern the unwise
and unkind.' He thinks the world has more need of cursing
than blessing, and it will help forward the millennium if,
'when we want to go anywhere, we will go there quietly and
safely, and not at forty miles the hour, in risk of our
lives; when we want to carry anything anywhere, we will
carry it either on the backs of beasts or on our own.'

This way of writing saddens quite as much as it amuses,
and would justify the suspicions of his best friends, as
he himself confesses, that 'he has gone mad,' were it not
so consistent with the normal condition of his reasoning
powers, as shown in his whole career as an author. It
explains, too, why he is unknown among people not using
the English tongue. To all such he is simply and utterly
unintelligible. We who are accustomed to his eccentricities
of thought and expression, may trace the golden woof
which redeems them from absolute foolishness, showing that
however angrily and paradoxically Ruskin may denounce his
evils, it is ever done with the view of forcing men to
accept his freely proffered goods. When time shall have
fairly sifted the wheat from the chaff in his writings,
the world at large will have gained in its Art-literature,
and people will have grown wiser and happier, so far as
whatever proves thoroughly sound and good in them shall

become practically incorporated into their lives.

41. D.C. THOMSON, FROM A SIGNED ARTICLE, RUSKIN AS AN ART
CRITIC, 'ART-JOURNAL'

November 1879, vol. 18, n.s., 225-8

David Croal Thomson (1855-1930) was born and educated in
Edinburgh. Sometime editor of the 'Art-Journal', he was a
critic of considerable standing and wrote studies of
'Phiz' (Hablot K. Browne) and of the Barbizon School.

...Mr. Ruskin has had many evidences that he is appreciated
by the country. He is the one of the few authors of Fine
Art books the general public care to read. His earlier
works are at a premium, and his reprints have gone through
many editions. He was chosen by the nation, in 1857, to
inspect and arrange for public use the thousands of
sketches left by Turner. In 1869 he was elected first
Slade Professor of Art at Oxford, a post he has recently
resigned on account of ill-health. In 1874 he was offered
the gold medal of the Royal Institute of Architects, which,
however, he did not see his way to accept. At the end of
last year he was presented with the long-coveted drawing
by Turner of the 'Pass of Splügen,' and even his expenses
at the Whistler trial have been defrayed by public sub-
scription, merely to show the subscribers' regard and
esteem for him. The assertion is sometimes made by ignorant
and thoughtless writers that Mr. Ruskin is mad. No one
who has read any of his great books could truly say so.
Wildly enthusiastic he unquestionably is, but insane he
certainly is not. Enthusiasts have frequently been termed
maniacs by the foolish people of their time, but many a
so-called madman of one generation has been hailed as a
great and enlightened genius by another.
    In conclusion, we think we have a right to consider him
the best-qualified man to lead the public taste in Art,
and though he may sometimes be prejudiced in his judgment
of pictures, yet, on the whole, he is as impartial as ever
Art critic was - we would almost go the length of saying
as ever critic can be. He brings all the learning of the
age to bear on his subject - and nothing is more dull and
uninteresting than to read writers who know only one
subject - and he never hesitates to spend much labour in

ascertaining the exact truth regarding any of the points
under discussion. There can also be little doubt he has
done infinitely more good as an Art critic than ever he
could have accomplished as a painter. He himself admits
that he would never have been a great painter, although
possibly he would have been an original one. But all the
world has lost in losing his paintings is amply made up by
the benefit he has done in placing Art criticism in the
position it ought to and does hold, namely, of ability to
appreciate the highest works of artists, and adequately
interpret them for the benefit of the public and of
painters themselves.

42. ALEXANDER WEDDERBURN, FROM A SIGNED REVIEW BY AN
OXFORD PUPIL, THE PUBLIC LETTERS OF JOHN RUSKIN, D.C.L.,
'CONTEMPORARY REVIEW'

July 1880, vol. 38, 69-100

Alexander Dundas Ogilvy Wedderburn (1854-1931) was educated
at Haileybury and Christ Church, Oxford. He had a distinguished legal career as a barrister and, later, bencher of
the Inner Temple. Wedderburn became QC in 1897 and for
some years was Recorder of Gravesend. He was co-editor,
with E.T. Cook, of the Library Edition of Ruskin's
writings. See Introduction, p. 21.

In my first Paper upon these Letters I dwelt exclusively
upon such as treated of Art. I preferred to begin with
those - as I there pointed out - partly because most of
them preceded in chronological order those with which I
have now to deal, and partly because Art is still the
chief subject upon which Mr. Ruskin's authority is widely
recognized. He is still regarded, by the general public,
mainly as the author of 'Modern Painters,' 'The Stones of
Venice,' and 'The Seven Lamps of Architecture;' and the
works in which he himself now finds most to alter, are
those in which they see most to praise. Thus the book
'which, hitherto, remains their favourite,' is one which
he is 'resolved never to republish as a whole;' whilst the
volumes which he has written on other subjects, or in
later years, are, for various reasons, those upon which
they place a lower value, and by which he sets the highest
store. It is even possible to fix a date, 1860, when the

fifth and final volume of 'Modern Painters' was first
issued, by which to mark this difference in opinion between
the author and his public; the public practically ignoring
all that Mr. Ruskin has written since that date - whilst
he reverses their judgment. And so strong is his conviction
on this point that where, in a particular instance, he no
longer approved of some expressions in a chapter of one of
his books* published in 1865, he has still retained it in
a recent reprint of the volume, expressly in order to
leave no room for any one to say that he has 'withdrawn,
as erroneous in principle, so much as a single sentence of
any of his books written since 1860.'

This critical attitude of Mr. Ruskin towards one portion
of his writings, and this comparative ignorance in the public of another portion of them, must not, of course, be
exaggerated. It would be easy to quote recent passages in
which he endorses, with full approval, much that he wrote
before the date I have named; and it would be obviously
absurd to imagine that there are not very many people who
have made careful and continuous study of almost all his
books. Those who have done so may, indeed, be disinclined
to believe that others have not done the same, but that I
am convinced they are mistaken, and that Mr. Ruskin is
still most constantly congratulated, not on his latest, but
on his earliest work.

The reasons which weigh with him in this judgment of
the three books mentioned are clearly defined by their
author. In his brief preface to the last edition of
'Modern Painters,' in publishing which he yielded to a
general request, though with some violence to his own
feelings, he points out that he now objects to much of the
first two volumes of that work, as having been 'written in
a narrow enthusiasm, and that the substance of its metaphysical and religious speculation is only justifiable on
the ground of its absolute honesty.' Similarly, in the
introduction to the first volume of the whole series of
his revised works, commenced in 1871, after commenting on
the style in which he had first written, and on the
influence exercised over his language by his 'then
favourite in prose, Richard Hooker,' he continues thus:-
'What I wrote about religion was painstaking, and, I think,
forcible, as compared with most religious writing; especially in its frankness and fearlessness, but it was
wholly mistaken; for I had been educated in the doctrines
of a narrow sect, and had read history as obliquely as
sectarians necessarily must.' And of the predilection of
the public in favour of these early books of his he is
also well aware, for in the preface to the very recent re-
publication of 'The Seven Lamps of Architecture,' some two
months ago, he remarks that the public still like and
will read this book 'when they won't look at what would be

really useful and helpful to them.'

This predilection of the public, however, is interesting, because of the questions which it raises. Literary criticism has always refused to confess the same man to be supreme in more than one great department of Knowledge or of Art; and has ever distinguished the concentrated power of genius from the facile diversity of an accomplished mind. The universalist has never escaped the suspicion of charlatanry, and it is invariably doubted whether he who has attempted many matters can have pre-eminently succeeded even in one. And literary criticism has generally been right. But it is not enough to rest content with the fact that success in different pursuits has been rare; we must look for the cause of failure. We should go back, not to the one study or subject in which the man we may be considering is supreme, but to the qualities of mind which enabled him to be so; and we should then ask, not if of two subjects attempted by him one is inconsistent with the other, but whether both are, or are not, consistent with those qualities. Thus, where we see that an author's fame is based mainly upon a fine wit or a broad humour, we have support, even in the face of Shakespeare, for our refusal to applaud his attempting tragedy; but where we find that his writings are marked throughout by such characteristics as those of close observation and minute analysis, it were better to reflect whether these powers might not possibly be applied, with exceptional success, to very different branches of knowledge. A man cannot, indeed, serve two masters, but he may well render various services to one....

Note

* 'Ethics of the Dust,' Preface to the 1877 edition.

43. VERNON LEE, FROM RUSKINISM, 'BELCARO'

London, 1883, 198-229

Vernon Lee (1856-1935) was the pen-name assumed by Violet Paget. A long-time member of the Anglo-American expatriate circle in Florence, she wrote in several different literary forms: the poem, the novel, the play and, most frequently, the essay. Her assessment of Ruskin, although proliferating in philosophical reflections (another mode

of her literary expression), is impressively acute in its
detection of his flaws and strengths. See Introduction,
pp. 21-2.

...Many there must be, and every day more, who are harried
by their love of art and their sense of duty, who daily
ask themselves the question which first arose, nearly
forty years ago, in the mind of John Ruskin; and which,
settled by false answers, has recurred to him ever and
anon, and has shaken and shattered the very system which
was intended to answer it for ever.

John Ruskin has been endowed as have been very few men
as an artist, a critic, and a moralist; in the immense
chaotic mass, the constantly altered and constantly propped
up ruins of an impossible system, which constitute the
bulk of his writings, he has taught us more of the subtle
reasons of art, he has reproduced with his pen more of the
beauty of physical nature, and he has made us feel more
profoundly the beauty of moral nature, than has, perhaps,
been done separately by any critic, or artist, or moralist
of his day. He has possessed within himself two very perfect characters, has been fitted out for two very noble
missions:- the creation of beauty and the destruction of
evil; and of these two halves each has been warped; of
these two missions each has been hampered; warped and
hampered by the very nobility of the man's nature: by his
obstinate refusal to compromise with the reality of things,
by his perpetual resistance to the evidence of his reason,
by his heroic and lamentable clinging to his own belief in
harmony where there is discord, in perfection where there
is imperfection. There are natures which cannot be coldly
or resignedly reasonable, which, despite all possible
demonstration, cannot accept evil as a necessity and injustice as a fact; which must believe their own heart
rather than their own reason; and when we meet such
natures, we in our cold wisdom must look upon them with
pity, perhaps, and regret, but with admiration and awe and
envy. Such a nature is that of John Ruskin. He belongs, it
is true, to a generation which is rapidly passing away; he
is the almost isolated champion of creeds and ideas which
have ceased even to be discussed among the thinking part
of our nation; he is a believer not only in Good and in
God, but in Christianity, in the Bible, in Protestantism;
he is, in many respects, a man left far behind by the
current of modern thought; but he is, nevertheless, and
unconsciously, perhaps, to himself, the greatest representative of the highly developed and conflicting ethical and
æsthetical nature which is becoming more common in

proportion as men are taking to think and feel for themselves; his is the greatest example of the strange battles
and compromises which are daily taking place between our
moral and our artistic halves; and the history of his
aspirations and his errors is the type of the inner history
of many a humbler thinker and humbler artist around us.

When, nearly forty years ago, Ruskin first came before
the world with the wonderful book - wonderful in sustained
argument and description, and in obscure, half crazy, half
prophetic utterances - called 'Modern Painters,' it was
felt that a totally new power had entered the region of
artistic analysis. It was not the subtle sympathy with
line and curve, with leaf and moulding, nor the wondrous
power of reproducing with mere words the depths of sky and
sea, the radiancies of light and the flame and smoulder of
cloud; it was not his critical insight nor his artistic
faculty which drew to him at once the souls of a public so
different, in its universality, from the small eclectic
bands which surround other æstheticians; it was the feeling, in all who read his books, that this man was giving a
soul to the skies and seas; that he was breathing human
feeling into every carved stone and painted canvas; that
he was bidding capital and mosaic, nay, every rudest ornament hewn by the humblest workman, to speak to men with
the voice of their own heart; that for the first time
there had been brought into the serene and egotistic world
of art the passion, the love, and the wrath of righteousness. He came into it as an apostle and a reformer, but as
an apostle and a reformer strangely different from
Winckelmann and Schlegel, from Lessing and Goethe. For,
while attacking the architecture of Palladio and the
painting of Salvator Rosa; while expounding the landscapes
of Turner and the churches of Verona, he was not merely
demolishing false classicism and false realism, not merely
vindicating a neglected artist or a wronged school: he was
come to sweep usurping evil out of the kingdom of art, and
to reinstate as its sole sovereign no human craftsman, but
God himself.

God or Good: for to Ruskin the two words have but one
meaning. God and Good must receive the whole domain of art;
it must become the holy of holies, the temple and citadel
of righteousness. To do this was the avowed mission of
this strange successor, haughty and humble, and tender and
wrathful, of the pagan Winckelmann, of the coldly serene
Goethe. How came John Ruskin by this mission, or why
should his mission differ so completely from that of all
his fellows? Why should he insist upon the necessity of
morally sanctifying art, instead of merely æsthetically
reforming it? Why was it not enough for him that artistic

pleasure should be innocent, without trying to make it
holy? Because, for Ruskin's nature, compounded of artist
and moralist, artistic engagement was a moral danger, a
distraction from his duty - for Ruskin was not the mere
artist, who, powerless outside his art, may because he
can only, give his whole energies to it; he was not the
mere moralist who, indifferent to art, can give it a
passing glance without interrupting for a moment his work
of good; he felt himself endowed to struggle for righteousness and bound to do so, and he felt himself also
irresistibly attracted by mere beauty. To the moral nature
of the man this mere beauty, which threatened to absorb
his existence, became positively sinful; while he knew
that evil was raging without requiring all his energies to
quell it, every minute, every thought diverted from the
cause of good was so much gain for the cause of evil;
innocence, mere negative good, there could not be, as long
as there remained positive evil. Thus it appeared to
Ruskin. This strange knight-errant of righteousness,
conscious of his heaven endowed strength, felt that during
every half-hour of delay in the Armida's garden of art,
new rootlets were being put forth, new leaves were being
unfolded by the enchanted forest of error which overshadowed and poisoned the earth, and which it was his work
to hew and burn down; that every moment of reluctant fare-
well from the weird witch of beauty meant a fresh outrage,
an additional defiling of the holy of holies to rescue
which he had received his strong muscle and his sharp
weapons. Thus, refusing to divide his time and thoughts
between his moral work and his artistic, Ruskin must
absolutely and completely abandon the latter; if art
seemed to him not merely a waste of power, but an absolute
danger for his nobler side, there evidently was no alter-
native but to abjure it for ever. But a man cannot thus
abandon his own field, abjure the work for which he is
specially fitted; he may mortify, and mutilate and imprison his body, but he cannot mortify or mutilate his
mind, he cannot imprison his thoughts. John Ruskin was
drawn irresistibly towards art because he was specially
organised for it. The impossible cannot be done: nature
must find a vent, and the artistic half of Ruskin's mind
found its way of eluding the apparently insoluble difficulty: his desire reasoned, and his desire was persuaded.
A revelation came to him: he was neither to compromise
with sin nor to renounce his own nature. For it struck him
suddenly that this irresistible craving for the beautiful,
which he would have silenced as a temptation of evil, was
in reality the call to his mission; that this domain of
art, which he had felt bound to abandon, was in reality

the destined field for his moral combats, the realm which
he must reconquer for God and for Good. Ruskin had considered art as sinful as long as it was only negatively
innocent: by the strange logic of desire he made it
positively righteous, actively holy; what he had been
afraid to touch, he suddenly perceived that he was
commanded to handle. He had sought for a solution of his
own doubts, and the solution was the very gospel which he
was to preach to others; the truth which had saved him was
the truth which he must proclaim. And that truth, which
had ended Ruskin's own scruples, was that the basis of art
is moral; that art cannot be merely pleasant or unpleasant,
but must be lawful or unlawful, that every legitimate
artistic enjoyment is due to the perception of moral
propriety, that every artistic excellence is a moral
virtue, every artistic fault is a moral vice; that noble
art can spring only from noble feeling, that the whole
system of the beautiful is a system of moral emotions,
moral selections, and moral appreciation; and that the aim
and end of art is the expression of man's obedience to
God's will, and of his recognition of God's goodness.

Such was the solution of Ruskin's scruples respecting
his right of giving to art the time and energies he might
have given to moral improvement; and such the æsthetical
creed which he felt bound, by conviction and by the
necessity of self-justification, to develop into a system
and to apply to every single case. The notion of making
beauty not merely a vague emanation from the divinity, as
in the old platonic philosophies, but a direct result, an
infallible concomitant of moral excellence; of making the
physical the mere reflexion of the moral, is indeed a very
beautiful and noble idea; but it is a false idea. For -
and this is one of the points which Ruskin will not admit
- the true state of things is by no means always the
noblest or the most beautiful....

Such has been the case with John Ruskin; he shrank from
owning to himself what we have just recognized, with
reluctance, indeed, and sorrow, that the beautiful to
whose study and creation he was so irresistibly drawn, had
no moral value; that in the great battle between good and
evil, beauty remained neutral, passive, serenely egotistic.
It was necessary for him that beauty should be more than
passively innocent: he must make it actively holy. Only a
moral meaning could make art noble; and as, in the deep-
rooted convictions of Ruskin, art was noble, a moral meaning must be found. The whole of the philosophy of art must
be remodelled upon an ethical basis; a moral value must
everywhere sanction the artistic attraction. And thus
Ruskin came to construct a strange system of falsehood, in

which moral motives applied to purely physical actions,
moral meanings given to the merely æsthetically significant, moral consequences drawn from absolutely unethical
decisions; even the merest coincidences in historical and
artistic phenomena, nay, even in the mere growth of
various sorts of plants, nay even the most ludicrously
applied biblical texts, were all dragged forward and combined into a wondrous legal summing-up for the beatifica-
tion of art; the sense of the impossibility of rationally
referring certain æsthetical phenomena to ethical causes
producing in this lucid and noble thinker a sort of frenzy,
a wild impulse to solve irrational questions by direct
appeals for an oracular judgment of God, to be sought for
in the most trumpery coincidences of accidents; so that
the man who has understood most of the subtle reasons of
artistic beauty, who has grasped most completely the
psychological causes of great art and poor art, is often
reduced to answer his perplexities by a sort of æsthetico-
moral key and bible divination, or heads-win tails-lose,
toss-up decision. The main pivots of Ruskin's system are,
however, but few: first, the assertion that all legitimate
artistic action is governed by moral considerations, is
the direct putting in practise of the commandments of God;
and secondly, that all pleasure in the beautiful is the
act of appreciating the goodness and wisdom of God. These
two main theories completely balance one another; between
them, and with the occasional addition of mystic symbolism, they must explain the whole question of artistic
right and wrong....
   Again, the necessity of referring all good art to
morality and all bad art to immorality, obliges Ruskin to
postulate that every period which has produced bad art has
been a period of moral decay. The artistic habits which
displease him must be a direct result of a vicious way of
feeling and acting in all things: the decay of Venetian
architecture and sculpture must be distinctly referable to
the decay of Venetian morality in the 15th century; and
the final corruption and ruin of the state must be traced
to the moral obliquity which caused Venetians to adopt
pseudo-classic forms in the Riva façade of the Ducal
palace; moral degradation and artistic degradation, acting
and re-acting on each other, bring about, according to
Ruskin, political ruin; the iniquities of the men who
became apostates to Gothic architecture are visited upon
their distant descendants, upon the Venetians of the days
of Campo Formio. Now here again the ethical basis induces
a complete historical misconception, a misconception not
only in the history of art, but also in the history of
civilization. For, just as his system of moral sin and

artistic punishment blinds Ruskin to the necessities of change and decay in art, so, also, it prevents his seeing the inevitable necessity of political growth and decline. Ruskin seeks the cause of the fall of Venice in moral corruption manifested, or supposed to be manifested, in art; but the cause of the fall of Venice must be sought elsewhere. Look at this lagoon, this Adriatic, this Mediterranean: in the 14th century they are the source of the greatness of the Zenos and Pisanis; three or four hundred years later they will be the cause of the pettiness of the Morosinis and Emos. In the present, in this time of Dandolo, into which Ruskin has led us, it is to them that Venice owes the humiliation of Barbarossa in the porch of St. Mark's; to them in the future will be owed the triumph of Bonaparte and the tricolour waving from the flagstaff of the square....

In this way has Ruskin, one of the greatest thinkers on art and on ethics, made morality sterile and art base in his desire to sanctify the one by the other. Sterile and base, indeed, only theoretically: for the instinct of the artist and of the moralist has ever broken out in noble self-contradiction, in beautiful irrelevancies; in those wonderful, almost prophetic passages which seem to make our souls more keen towards beauty and more hardy for good. But all this is incidental, this which is in reality Ruskin's great and useful work. He has made art more beautiful and men better without knowing it - accidentally, without premeditation, in words which are like the eternal truths, grand and exquisite, which lie fragmentary and embedded in every system of theology; the complete and systematic is worthless and even dangerous, for it is false; the irrelevant, the contradictory, is precious, because it is true to our better part. Ruskin has loved art instinctively, fervently, for its own sake; but he has constantly feared lest this love should be sinful or at least base. Like Augustine, he dreads that the Devil may be lurking in the beautiful sunshine; lest evil be hidden in those beautiful shapes which distract his thoughts from higher subjects of good and God; he trembles lest the beautiful should trouble his senses and his fancy, and make him forget his promises to the Almighty. He perceives that pleasure in art is more or less sensuous and selfish; he is afraid lest some day he be called upon to account for the moments he has not given to others, and be chastised for having permitted his mind to follow the guidance of his senses; he trembles and repeats the praise of God, the anathema of pride, he mumbles confused words about 'corrupt earth' - and 'sinful man,' - even while looking at his works of art, as some anchorite of old may

instinctively have passed his fingers across his beads and
stammered out an *Ave* when some sight of beauty crossed his
path and made his heart leap with unwonted pleasure.
Ruskin must tranquillize his conscience about art; he must
persuade himself that he is justified in employing his
thoughts about it; and lest it be a snare of the demon, he
must make it a service of God. He must persuade himself
that all the pleasure he derives from art is the pleasure
in obeying God, in perceiving his goodness: that the
pleasure he derives from a flower is pleasure not in its
curves and colours and scent, but in its adaptation to its
work, in its enjoyment of existence; that the enjoyment he
derives from a grand view is enjoyment of the kindness of
God, and the enjoyment in the sight of a noble face is
enjoyment of the expression of harmony with God's will; in
short, all artistic pleasure must become an act of adoration, otherwise, a jealous God, or a jealous conscience,
will smite him for abandoning the true altar for some
golden calf fashioned by man and inhabited by Satan. And
to this constant moralising, hallowing, nay, purifying of
art, are due, as we have seen, the greater number of
Ruskin's errors; his system is false, and only evil can
spring from it; it is a pretence at a perfection which
does not exist, and which, like the pretence at the super-
human virtue of the anchorite and mystic, must end in
lamentable folly: in making men lie to their own heart
because they have sought to clothe all that is really pure
in a false garb of sanctity and have blushed at its naked
reality; because it makes a return to nature a return to
sin, since what is natural has been forbidden and what is
innocent has been crookedly obtained; because it tries to
make us think we are nothing but soul, and therefore turns
us to brutes when we remember that we are also body, and
devils when we perceive that we are also reason. Because,
in short, it is a lie, and only falsehood can be born of
it. For, in his constant reference to a spiritual meaning,
Ruskin has not only wasted and sterilised our moral
impulses, but has reduced art to mere foulness; in his
constant sanctifying of beauty he makes it appear impure.
Above all, in his unceasing attempt to attach a moral
meaning to physical beauty, he has lost sight of, he has
denied, the great truth that all that which is innocent is
moral; that the morality of art is an independent quality
equivalent to, but separate from, the morality of action;
that beauty is the morality of the physical, as morality
is the beauty of the spiritual; that as the moral sense
hallows the otherwise egotistic relations man to man, so
also the æsthetic sense hallows the otherwise brutish
relations of man to matter; that separately but in harmony,

equally but differently, these two faculties make our
lives pure and noble. All this Ruskin has forgotten: he
has made the enjoyment of mere beauty a base pleasure,
requiring a moral object to purify it, and in so doing he
has destroyed its own purifying power; he has sanctified
the already holy, and defiled with holy water, which
implies foulness, the dwelling of holiness.

   This is the lesson to be derived from the attempt at
noble self-delusion which Ruskin has practised upon himself....

44. WILLIAM MORRIS, SIGNED PREFACE TO THE KELMSCOTT PRESS
EDITION OF 'THE NATURE OF GOTHIC'

Hammersmith, 1892, i-v

William Morris (1834-96), poet, painter, prose writer,
authority on the decorative arts, printer, and sometime
Socialist, was educated at Marlborough and Exeter College,
Oxford. A man of many parts, Morris was much influenced by
Pre-Raphaelitism and, from his youth, by Ruskin's social
and artistic concepts. 'The Nature of Gothic' was the
fourth publication of the Kelmscott Press, of which Morris
was the founder and guiding spirit. See Introduction,
p. 22.

The Chapter which is here put before the reader can be
well considered as a separate piece of work, although it
contains here and there references to what has gone before
in 'The Stones of Venice.' To my mind, and I believe to
some others, it is one of the most important things
written by the author, & in future days will be considered
as one of the very few necessary and inevitable utterances
of the century. To some of us when we first read it, now
many years ago, it seemed to point out a new road on which
the world should travel. And in spite of all the dis-
appointments of forty years, and although some of us, John
Ruskin amongst others, have since learned what the equipment for that journey must be, and how many things must be
changed before we are equipped, yet we can still see no
other way out of the folly and degradation of Civilization.
For the lesson which Ruskin here teaches us is that art is
the expression of man's pleasure in labour; that it is
possible for man to rejoice in his work, for, strange as

it may seem to us to-day, there have been times when he
did rejoice in it; and lastly, that unless man's work once
again becomes a pleasure to him, the token of which change
will be that beauty is once again a natural and necessary
accompaniment of productive labour, all but the worthless
must toil in pain, and therefore live in pain. So that the
results of the thousands of years of man's effort on the
earth must be general unhappiness and universal degradation; unhappiness & degradation, the conscious burden of
which will grow in proportion to the growth of man's
intelligence, knowledge, and power over material nature.

If this be true, as I for one most firmly believe, it
follows that the hallowing of labour by art is the one aim
for us at the present day. If Politics are to be anything
else than an empty game, more exciting but less innocent
than those which are confessedly games of skill or chance,
it is toward this goal of happiness of labour that they
must make. Science has in these latter days made such
stupendous strides, and is attended by such a crowd of
votaries, many of whom are doubtless single-hearted, and
worship in her not the purse of riches and power, but the
casket of knowledge, that she seems to need no more than a
little humility to temper the insolence of her triumph,
which has taught us everything except how to be happy. Man
has gained mechanical victory over nature, which in time
to come he may be able to enjoy, instead of starving
amidst of it. In those days science also may be happy; yet
not before the second birth of art, accompanied by the
happiness of labour, has given her rest from the toil of
dragging the car of Commerce. Lastly it may well be that
the human race will never cease striving to solve the
problem of the reason for its own existence; yet it seems
to me that it may do this in a calmer and more satisfactory
mood when it has not to ask the question, Why were we born
to be so miserable? but rather, Why were we born to be so
happy? At least it may be said that there is time enough
for us to deal with this problem, and that it need not
engross the best energies of mankind, when there is so
much to do otherwhere.

But for this aim of at last gaining happiness through
our daily and necessary labour, the time is short enough,
the need so urgent, that we may well wonder that those who
groan under the burden of unhappiness can think of anything else; and we may well admire and love the man who
here called the attention of English-speaking people to
this momentous subject, and that with such directness and
clearness of insight, that his words could not be disregarded. I know indeed that Ruskin is not the first man
who has put forward the possibility and the urgent

necessity that men should take pleasure in Labour; for
Robert Owen showed how by companionship and good will
labour might be made at least endurable; & in France
Charles Fourier dealt with the subject at great length,
& the whole of his elaborate system for the reconstruction
of society is founded on the certain hope of gaining
pleasure in labour. But in their times neither Owen nor
Fourier could possibly have found the key to the problem
with which Ruskin was provided. Fourier depends, not on
art for the motive power of the realization of pleasure in
labour, but on incitements, which, though they would not
be lacking in any decent state of society, are rather
incidental than essential parts of pleasurable work; and
on reasonable arrangements, which would certainly lighten
the burden of labour, but would not procure for it the
element of sensuous pleasure, which is the essence of all
true art. Nevertheless, it must be said that Fourier and
Ruskin were touched by the same instinct, and it is
instructive and hopeful to note how they arrived at the
same point by such very different roads.

Some readers will perhaps wonder that in this important
Chapter of Ruskin I have found it necessary to consider
the ethical & political, rather than what would ordinarily
be thought, the artistic side of it. I must answer, that,
delightful as is that portion of Ruskin's work which
describes, analyses, and criticises art, old and new, yet
this is not after all the most characteristic side of his
writings. Indeed from the time at which he wrote this
chapter here reprinted, those ethical & political considerations have never been absent from his criticism of
art; and, in my opinion, it is just this part of his work,
fairly begun in the 'Nature of Gothic' and brought to its
culmination in that great book 'Unto this Last,' which has
had the most enduring and beneficent effect on his contem-
pories, and will have through them on succeeding generations. John Ruskin the critic of art has not only given
the keenest pleasure to thousands of readers by his life-
like descriptions, and the ingenuity and delicacy of his
analysis of works of art, but he has let a flood of daylight into the cloud of sham-technical twaddle which was
once the whole substance of 'art-criticism,' and is still
its staple, and that is much. But it is far more that John
Ruskin the teacher of morals and politics (I do not use
this word in the newspaper sense), has done serious and
solid work towards that new-birth of Society, without
which genuine art, the expression of man's pleasure in his
handiwork, must inevitably cease altogether, and with it
the hopes of the happiness of mankind.

45. GEORGE SAINTSBURY, FROM MR. RUSKIN, 'CORRECTED
IMPRESSIONS'

New York, 1895, 198-218

George Edward Bateman Saintsbury (1845-1933) was born at
Southampton and educated at King's College School, London,
and Merton College, Oxford. For some ten years he was a
journalist acting as critic for the 'Academy' and the
'Saturday Review'. His numerous essays were collected
under such titles as 'Miscellaneous Essays' (1892),
'Corrected Impressions' (1895), and 'Essays in English
Literature, 1780-1860' (2 vols, 1890-5). Saintsbury was
also a critic of French literature as manifest by his
'Essays on French Novelists' (1891). He revised Scott's
edition of Dryden, contributed to the English Men of
Letters series and to the 'Cambridge Bibliography of English Literature' and, in 1895, was appointed Professor of
Rhetoric and English Literature at the University of
Edinburgh, after which he wrote 'A History of Criticism
and Taste in Europe' (3 vols, 1900-4) as well as numerous
other studies in English prosody and criticism. See Introduction, pp. 22-3.

After the havoc that has been made during the last four or
five years in the ranks of the great seniors of English
Literature there is, perhaps, but one name left, if indeed
there be one, who shares the first class, in merit and
seniority combined, with that of Mr. Ruskin. There is
certainly none which has seen, during the lifetime of its
owner, such curious vicissitudes of popular repute. It
will soon be, if it is not already, fifty years since 'A
Graduate of Oxford' arose to admonish the British nation
of its sins and shortcomings in the matter of art and
appreciation of art. For some ten years or more after
that, Mr. Ruskin was a voice crying in the wilderness, but
attracting more and more younger voices to go and cry
after him. For about twenty years subsequent to this
first decade he was a power, in some of his innumerable
lines sweeping public taste more or less with or before
him. And then the inevitable reaction which generally
waits till after a man's death, but which in his case was
hastened by certain oddities of his own whereon more must
be said hereafter, set in with more than its usual
severity. Young England, once Mr. Ruskin's disciple in
art, has accomplished in regard to him the denial of St.
Peter without St. Peter's repentance. It knows not the

man; it will have none of him; it calls his favourite
ideas 'the Ruskinian heresy,' and labours to set up some
quite different thing from Ruskinism. And all the while,
to those outsiders who can look coolly at the game, it is
perfectly obvious that the blasphemers of Mr. Ruskin never
could, metaphysically speaking, have come into existence
but for Mr. Ruskin himself; and that they are, according
to the well-known custom of certain savage tribes, eating
their father.

I think I may speak without too great presumption for
these outsiders. I have never been a Ruskinite, though I
have always thought that nobody in our time has touched
Mr. Ruskin at his very best as an artist in the *flamboyant*
variety of English prose; and I have never been an anti-
Ruskinite, though I know perfectly well what the anti-
Ruskinites mean by their fault-finding, and even to a
certain extent agree with it. When Mr. Ruskin began, as
above remarked, to cry in the wilderness, it must be
admitted by every one who gives himself the trouble to
know, that he had a very great and terrible wilderness to
cry in. I have never, being as has been said a hopeless
outsider, been able to acquiesce in the stereotyped
opinion (accepted docilely by a dozen generations of young
would-be rebels) that Paris is an artistic Jerusalem, and
London an artistic Samaria. But in the second quarter of
this century we were in rather a bad way artistically. We
had Turner (who was certainly a host, though a very un-
disciplined host, in himself), we had Etty (who has always
seemed to me the prophet in art who has had least honour
in this his own country), and we had some others. But for
sheer ugliness and lack of artistic feeling in almost all
respects, the reign of William the Fourth and the first
twenty years of so of the reign of her present gracious
Majesty made what has been subsequently termed a 'record'
in English history. Architecture had begun to feel a well-
intentioned but by no means always wisely directed revival;
music, painting, most sculpture, almost all books, furniture, plate and domestic *supellex* generally exhibited a
perfectly hopeless level of middle-class banality. I do
not know that matters have in all ways improved since.
With some things that are much better we have had many
things that are much worse. We have had the vicious popu-
larisation of cheap machine-made art; we have had
execrable vulgarities, we have had cant and affectation
and *pastiche*. But, whereas from the thirties to the
sixties, it was almost impossible to buy anything new that
was not complacently hideous, from the sixties to the
nineties it has always been possible to buy something new
that was at least graceful in intention.

And this was more the doing of Mr. Ruskin than of any
single man. Of course, nothing of the kind is ever the
doing of any single man. The Oxford Movement, the Præ-
Raphaelites, the '51 Exhibition, - a horrid thing in
itself, - the increasing custom of travel abroad, and a
dozen other things not only helped, but did much more than
any man could do. But Mr. Ruskin did as much as any man
could do; and that is a good deal. He had perfect leisure,
a considerable fortune, a wonderful literary faculty, an
intense love for art. He was gifted by nature with what is
the most fortunate gift for a man of genius, the most unfortunate for another, an entire freedom from the malady
of self-criticism. It has never during his long career
ever troubled Mr. Ruskin to bethink himself whether he
knew what he was talking about, whether he was or was not
talking nonsense, whether he was or was not contradicting
flatly something that he had said before. This is a great
advantage for a prophet in these or any times; and Mr.
Ruskin had it.

With such gifts he set himself to work to beat up the
quarters of British Philistia, first in the department of
art, and then in many another. At first he used Turner and
the Præ-Raphaelites for his battering-rams; then he was
for a season wholly Venetian; then he spread himself
widely into political economy and philosophisings of all
kinds; then he erected a sort of private pulpit, and in
'Fors Clavigera' and other things made almost a religion
of his own idiosyncrasy; then, as all men know, he established himself at his own University and led men captive,
as an irreverent one phrased it, by 'road-making and
rigmarole.' Then a fresh band of Philistines, masquerading
as the circumcision of Art itself, set upon him and cried
shame upon his version of æsthetics, and found fault with
the imperfection of his technique, and urged Millet
against Turner, and flung studio jargon against lecture-
room mysticism. And meanwhile, oddly enough, his despised,
and I must say I think rather despicable, Political
Economy won the ground that his æsthetics had lost; and
all or half of our socialists and semi-socialist nowadays
talk 'Unto this Last,' without its mysticism or its eloquence, and with twice its unreason.

A most odd career: not exactly paralleled, so far as I
can remember, and chequered by many things which in this
rapid sketch I have had to leave out, such as the singular
and very important relations of Mr. Ruskin to Carlyle. A
career on which, no doubt, the anathema of the most distinguished of Mr. Ruskin's own Oxford contemporaries may
be pronounced to the effect that it is 'fantastic and
lacks sanity'; which may be called (if anybody likes) a

kind of failure; but which has influenced England in a
vast number of different ways as the career of no other
man living or lately dead has influenced it.

It is extremely difficult to criticise Mr. Ruskin, if
only for the very simple reason that, as has been remarked
already, he has never condescended to criticise himself.
He once characteristically boasted that he 'had never
withdrawn a sentence, written since 1860, as erroneous in
principle.' In 1860 Mr. Ruskin was nearly forty, and we
are to suppose (which, indeed, is self-evident from the
complete recasting of the earlier volumes of 'Modern
Painters') that there was a good deal to withdraw before
that. But the fact is that, disowned or not disowned, all
his work in reality bears the same marks, - an intense
love of beauty; a restless desire to theorise on beautiful
objects; a vivid imagination; a rather weak logical gift;
a strong but capricious moral sense; a knack of succumbing
to any tempting current theory; a marvellous command of
eloquent prose; and, as must be constantly repeated, an
utter absence of critical faculty properly so called.

Such a combination with such faculties of expressing it
must needs produce work as disconcerting as it is stimulating....

Discipline is what Mr. Ruskin has always lacked; as
well in methods of expression as in the serene self-
confidence which has enabled him to deliver himself on any
and every subject, without any suspicion that he is talking ill-informed nonsense. Discipline Oxford did not give,
had indeed no full opportunity of giving, to Mr. Ruskin;
but she gave him, there can be no doubt, additional
inspiration. She nourished in him that passion for architecture which no single city in the United Kingdom is so
richly dowered with the means of exciting and gratifying;
and she, no doubt, also strengthened in him the general
Romantic tendency of which he is so characteristic an
exponent.

For the other part of the matter it has long ago seemed
to me - I do not know that I have seen it noticed or
suggested by anybody else - that the central peculiarity
of Mr. Ruskin is a singular and almost unparalleled union
of two main characteristics, one of which is usually
thought of as specially French, the other as specially
English. The first is an irresistible and all-pervading
tendency to generalize, - to bring things under what, at
any rate, seems a law, to erect schemes, and deduce, and
connect. The other is the unconquerable ethical tone of
all his speculations. To follow out the ramifications of
this strangely crossed nature of his would take a very
great deal of space, and would partake more of the style

of abstract criticism than would perhaps be suitable to
this book and plan. But one or two applications and
corollaries of what has just been said may be indicated.

Thus it may be pointed out that Mr. Ruskin's extraordinary insensibility to the ludicrous hangs on to both
the un-English and the English sides of his intellectual
temperament. His mania for generalizing blinds him to the
absurd on the one side, as we constantly find it doing in
Continental thinkers; his insatiable appetite for moral
applications, and his firm belief in his moral mission
blind him, as we find these things do often in Britons.
When Mr. Ruskin says that a square leaf on any tree would
be ugly, being a violation of the law of growth in trees,
we feel at once that we are in the company of an intellectual kinsman of the learned persons whom Molière satirised.
He deprecates expenditure on plate and jewels (while admitting that 'noble art may occasionally exist in these')
because they are matters of ostentation, a temptation to
the dishonest, and so on, - a moral paralogism which would
be almost impossible to any one not of British blood.

But I must leave this key to Mr. Ruskin in the hands of
the ingenious reader, who will find it does a great deal
of unlocking. A man with an ardent sense of duty combined
with an ardent desire to do good; eager to throw everything into the form of a general law, but eager also to
give that general law, directly or indirectly, mystically
or simply, an ethical bearing and interpretation; extremely
fond of throwing his discourse into an apparently argu-
mentative form, but probably more prone than any man of
equal talents who has lived during this century to logical
fallacies and illicit processes of every kind, - grasp the
man as this, and the works will cease to be a puzzle or an
irritation, because the reason of them will at once be
plain.

And it would be a very great pity, indeed, if the Book
of Ruskin were to remain to any one merely a closed book,
as irritation or as puzzle. For, if these curious volumes
are taken with a due amount of rational salt, they cannot
fail to enlarge and exercise the tastes and powers of the
reader; while, if read simply for enjoyment, they will be
found to contain the very finest prose (without exception
and beyond comparison) which has been written in English
during the last half of the nineteenth century. The great
merit of this prose is that it is never, as most of the
ornate prose styles of a more recent day are, affected and
unnatural. Great pains have been spent on the writing of
English prose during the last twenty years - greater, I
think, than had been taken for several generations. But
the result has almost always had (to my taste at least)

something too much of the lamp....

   Now, Mr. Ruskin's purple patches - despite a rather too
great tendency to run not merely into definitely rhythmical, but into definitely metrical forms - are never
laboured, they never suggest effort, strain, or trick. He
warms to them naturally, he turns them out without taking
his coat off. They are to be found, it is true, mainly,
though by no means wholly, in his earlier books. The practice of alternately chatting and scolding, to which he unfortunately betook himself some five-and-twenty years ago,
is not favourable to the production of fine English,
unless the writer can rise to the level of a real *sæva
indignatio*. This Mr. Ruskin can seldom do; and, as has
been already noted, his weaknesses never betray themselves so much as when he is talking of what he does not
like.

   But in his early days of enthusiasm he was often magnificent - no lesser word will do....

   But I am outrunning my limits. To sum up the impression
side of the matter, - when I was young, Mr. Ruskin's
crotchets used to irritate me more than they ought; they
now irritate me hardly at all, and only bore me a little.
But I think I like his beauties more than ever; and I am
disposed to think, also, that he has brought more folk to
art than he has ever bitten with his own heresies about it.

46. EDMUND GOSSE, FROM 'A SHORT HISTORY OF MODERN ENGLISH
LITERATURE'

New York, 1897, 356-8

Edmund Gosse (1849-1928) was, with Saintsbury (see headnote to No. 45), another pillar of late Victorian literary
criticism. Son of the zoologist Philip Gosse, he held
various positions of librarianship in the British Museum,
the Board of Trade, and the House of Commons. He was also
an accepted translator of Ibsen. His contributions to
literary criticism, English and French, were as extensive
and far-reaching as Saintsbury's as the following titles
indicate: 'Seventeenth Century Studies' (1883), 'A History
of Eighteenth Century Literature' (1889), and 'French
Profiles' (1905). Gosse also wrote the lives of Gray,
Raleigh, Congreve, Donne, and others, and he wrote a
number of volumes of verse. His 'Father and Son' (published anonymously in 1907) is perhaps what he will be

best remembered by; it is a moving account of the dicho-
tomy between generations so characteristic of Victorian
middle-class England. Gosse's literary criticism is now
out of fashion, but his brief remarks on Ruskin are not
without pertinence.

It is impossible, while dealing with these glories of the
middle Victorian period, to omit, although he still lives,
all mention of one more glorious still. Full of intellectual shortcomings and moral inconsistencies as is the
matter of Mr. JOHN RUSKIN, his manner at its best is
simply incomparable. If the student rejects for the moment,
as of secondary or even tertiary importance, all that Mr.
Ruskin has written for the last forty years, and confines
his attention to those solid achievements, the first three
volumes of 'Modern Painters,' the 'Stones of Venice,' and
the 'Seven Lamps of Architecture,' he will find himself in
the presence of a virtuoso whose dexterity in the mechanical part of prose style has never been exceeded. The
methods which he adopted almost in childhood - he was a
finished writer by 1837 - were composite; he began by
mingling with the romantic freshness of Scott qualities
derived from the poets and the painters, 'vial-fuls, as it
were, of Wordsworth's reverence, Shelley's sensitiveness,
Turner's accuracy.' Later on, to these he added technical
elements, combining with the music of the English Bible
the reckless richness of the seventeenth-century divines
perhaps, but most certainly and fatally the eccentric
force of Carlyle. If, however, this olla-podrida of diver-
gent mannerisms goes to make up the style of Ruskin, that
style itself is one of the most definite and characteristic possible.

What it was which Mr. Ruskin gave to the world under
the pomp and procession of his effulgent style, it is,
perhaps, too early yet for us to realise. But it is plain
that he was the greatest phenomenal teacher of the age;
that, dowered with unsurpassed delicacy and swiftness of
observation, and with a mind singularly unfettered by convention, the book of the physical world lay open before
him as it had lain before no previous poet or painter, and
that he could not cease from the ecstasy of sharing with
the public his wonder and his joy in its revelations. It
will, perhaps, ultimately be discovered that his elaborate,
but often whimsical and sometimes even incoherent disquisitions on art resolve themselves into this - the rapture
of a man who sees, on clouds alike and on canvases, in a
flower or in a missal, visions of illuminating beauty,
which he has the unparalleled accomplishment of being able

instantly and effectively to translate into words.

The happy life being that in which illusion is most prevalent, and Mr. Ruskin's enthusiasm having fired more minds to the instinctive quest of beauty than that of any other man who ever lived, we are guilty of no exaggeration if we hail him as one of the first of benefactors. Yet his intellectual nature was from the start imperfect, his sympathies always violent and paradoxical; there were whole areas of life from which he was excluded; and nothing but the splendour and fulness of his golden trumpets concealed the fact that some important instruments were lacking to his orchestra. It is as a purely descriptive writer that he has always been seen at his best, and here he is distinguished from exotic rivals - at home he has had none - by the vivid moral excitement that dances, an incessant sheet-lightning, over the background of each gorgeous passage. In this effect of metaphysical temperament, Mr. Ruskin is sharply differentiated from Continental masters of description and art initiation.

47. FREDERIC HARRISON, FROM 'TENNYSON, RUSKIN, MILL AND OTHER LITERARY ESTIMATES'

London, 1900, 48-71

Frederic Harrison (1831-1923) was born in London and educated at King's College School, London, and Wadham College, Oxford. Harrison possessed an extraordinarily versatile intellect and excelled as jurist (he was called to the bar in 1858), historian (writing on Cromwell, William the Silent, and Chatham), and Positivist (as interpreter of the movement and of Compte in particular). Inevitably, Harrison wrote for some of the major magazines including the 'Westminster Review'. His interest in literature was abiding as is evinced by 'Early Victorian Literature' (1896) and numerous other studies. See Introduction, pp. 23-4.

Is it indeed beyond hope that our generation should at last do entire justice to our brightest living genius, the most inspiring soul still extant amongst us, whilst he may yet be seen and heard in the flesh?

The world has long been of one mind as to the great charm in the writings of John Ruskin; it feels his subtle

insight into all forms of beauty; and it has made familiar
truisms of his central lessons in Art. But it has hardly
yet understood that he stands forth now, alone and inimitable, as a supreme master of our English tongue; that as
preacher, prophet (nay, some amongst us do not hesitate to
say as saint), he has done more than as master of Art;
that his moral and social influence on our time, more than
his æsthetic impulse, will be the chief memory for which
our descendants will hold him in honour.

Such genius, such zeal, such self-devotion should have
imposed itself upon the age without a dissentient voice;
but the reputation of John Ruskin has been exposed to some
singular difficulties. Above all, he is, to use an Italian
phrase, *uomo antico*: a survival of a past age: a man of
the thirteenth century pouring out sermons, denunciations,
rhapsodies to the nineteenth century; and if Saint Bernard
himself, in his garb of frieze and girdle of hemp, were to
preach amongst us in Hyde Park to-day, too many of us
would listen awhile, and then straightway go about our
business with a smile. But John Ruskin is not simply a man
of the thirteenth century: he is a poet, a mystic, a
missionary of the thirteenth century - romantic as was the
young Dante in the days of his love and his chivalrous
youth, and his Florentine rapture in all beautiful things,
or as was the young Petrarch in the lifetime of his Laura,
or the young Francis beginning to dream of a regeneration
of Christendom through the teaching of his barefoot Friars.

Now John Ruskin not only is in his soul a thirteenth-
century poet and mystic: but, being this, he would
literally have the nineteenth century go back to the thirteenth: he means what he says: he acts on what he means.
And he defies fact, the set of many ages, the actual
generation around him, and still calls on them, alone and
in spite of neglect and rebuffs, to go back to the Golden
Ages of the Past. He would not reject this description of
himself: he would proudly accept it. But this being so, it
is inevitable that much of his teaching - all the teaching
for which he cares most in his heart - must be in our day
the voice of one preaching in the wilderness.

He claims to be not merely poet of the beautiful, but
missionary of the truth; not so much judge in Art as
master in Philosophy. And as such he repudiates modern
science, modern machinery, modern politics - in a sense
modern civilisation as we know it and make it. Not merely
is it his ideal to get rid of these; but in his own way he
sets himself manfully to extirpate these things in practice from the visible life of himself and of those who
surround him. Such heroic impossibilities recoil on his
own head. The nineteenth century has been too strong for

him. Iron, steam, science, democracy - have thrust him
aside, and have left him in his old age little but a solitary and most pathetic Prophet, such as a John the Baptist
by Mantegna, unbending, undismayed, still crying out to a
scanty band around him - 'Repent, for the kingdom of
Heaven is at hand!'...

The world has long been of one mind, I have said, as
to the beauty of Ruskin's writing; but I venture to think
that even yet full justice has not been rendered to his
consummate mastery over our English tongue: that it has
not been put high enough, and some of its unique qualities
have not been perceived. Now I hold that in certain
qualities, in given ways, and in some rarer passages of
his, Ruskin not only surpasses every contemporary writer
of prose (which indeed is obvious enough), but he calls
out of our glorious English tongue notes more strangely
beautiful and inspiring than any ever yet issued from that
instrument. No writer of prose before or since has ever
rolled forth such mighty fantasias, or reached such pathetic melodies in words, or composed long books in one sustained strain of limpid grace.

It is indeed very far from a perfect style: much less
is it in any sense a model style, or one to be cultivated,
studied, or followed. If any young aspirant were to think
it could be imitated, better were a millstone hung round
his neck and he were cast into the sea. No man can bend
the bow of Ulysses: and if he dared to take down from its
long rest the terrible weapon, such an one might give
himself an ugly wound. Ulysses himself was shot with it
wildly, madly, with preposterous overflying of the mark,
and blind aiming at the wrong target. Ruskin, be it said
in sorrow, has too often played unseemly pranks on his
great instrument: is too often 'in excess,' as the Ethics
put it, indeed he is usually 'in excess'; he has used his
mastery in mere exultation in his own mastery; and, as he
now knows himself, he has used it out of wantonness -
rarely, but very rarely, as in 'The Seven Lamps,' in a
spirit of display, or with reckless defiance of sense,
good taste, reserve of strength - yet never with affectation, never as a tradesman, as a hack....

It cannot be denied that Ruskin, especially in his
earlier works, is too often obtrusively luscious, that his
images are often lyrical, set in too profuse and gorgeous
a mosaic. Be it so. But he is always perfectly, trans-
parently clear, absolutely free from affected euphuism,
never laboriously 'precious,' never grotesque, never
eccentric. His besetting sins as a master of speech may be
summed up in his passion for profuse imagery, and delight
in an almost audible melody of words. But how different is

this from the laborious affectation of what is justly condemned as the 'poetic prose' of a writer who tries to be
fine, seeking to perform feats of composition, who flogs
himself into a bastard sort of poetry, not because he
enjoys it, but to impose upon an ignorant reader! This
Ruskin never does. When he bursts the bounds of fine
taste, and pelts us with perfumed flowers till we almost
faint under their odour and their blaze of colour, it is
because he is himself intoxicated with the joy of his
blossoming thoughts, and would force some of his divine
afflatus into our souls. The priestess of the Delphic god
never spoke without inspiration, and then did not use the
flat speech of daily life. Would that none ever spoke in
books, until they felt the god working in their heart.

To be just, we should remember that a very large part
of all that Ruskin treats concerns some scene of beauty,
some work of fine art, some earnest moral exhortation,
some indignant rebuke to meanness, - wherein passionate
delight and passionate appeal are not merely lawful, but
are of the essence of the lesson. Ruskin is almost always
in an ecstasy of admiration, or in a fervour of sympathy,
or in a grand burst of prophetic warning. It is his
mission, his nature, his happiness so to be. And it is
inevitable that such passion and eagerness should be
clothed in language more remote from the language of conversation than is that of Swift or Hume. The language of
the preacher is not, nor ought it to be, the language of
the critic, the philosopher, the historian. Ruskin is a
preacher: right or wrong he has to deliver his message,
whether men will stay to hear it or not; and we can no
more require him to limit his pace to the plain foot-
plodding of unimpassioned prose than we can ask this of
Saint Bernard, or of Bossuet, of Jeremy Taylor or Thomas
Carlyle....

But when, his whole soul aglow with some scene of
beauty, transfigured by a profound moral emotion, he
breaks forth into one of those typical descants of his,
our judgment may still doubt if the colouring be not overcharged and the composition too crowded for perfect art,
but we are carried away by its beauty, its rhythm, its
pathos. We know that the sentence is too long, prepos-
terously, impossibly sustained - 200 words and more - 250,
nay, 280 words without a single pause - each sentence with
40, 50, 60 commas, colons, and semicolons - and yet the
whole symphony flows on with such just modulation, the
images melt so naturally into each other, the harmony of
tone and the ease of words are so complete, that we hasten
through the passage in a rapture of admiration. Milton
often began, and once or twice completed, such a resounding

voluntary on his glorious organ. But neither Milton, nor
Browne, nor Jeremy Taylor, was yet quite master of the
mighty instrument. Ruskin, who comes after two centuries
of further and continuous progress in this art, is master
of the subtle instrument of prose. And though it be true
that too often, in wanton defiance of calm judgment, he
will fling to the winds his self-control, he has achieved
in this rare and perilous art some amazing triumphs of
mastery over language, such as the whole history of our
literature cannot match.

Lovers of Ruskin (that is all who read good English
books) can recall, and many of them can repeat, hundreds
of such passages, and they will grumble at an attempt to
select any passage at all. But to make my meaning clear,
I will turn to one or two very famous bits, not at all
asserting that they are the most truly noble passages that
Ruskin ever wrote, but as specimens of his more lyrical
mood. He has himself spoken with slight of much of his
earlier writing - often perhaps with undeserved humility.
He especially regrets the *purpurei panni*, as he calls them,
of 'The Seven Lamps' and cognate pieces. I will not quote
any of these *purpurei panni*, though I think that as
rhetorical prose, as apodeictic perorations, English
literature has nothing to compare with them. But they *are*
rhetorical, somewhat artificial, manifest displays of
eloquence - and we shall all agree that eloquent displays
of rhetoric are not the best specimens of prose composition.

I take first a well-known piece of an early book, the
old tower of Calais Church, a piece which has haunted my
memory for nearly forty years.

The large neglect, the noble unsightliness of it; the
record of its years written so visibly, yet without
sign of weakness or decay; its stern wasteness and
gloom, eaten away by the Channel winds, and over-grown
with the bitter sea grasses; its slates and tiles all
shaken and rent, and yet not falling; its desert of
brickwork, full of bolts, and holes, and ugly fissures
and yet strong, like a bare brown rock; its carelessness of what any one thinks or feels about it; putting
forth no claim, having no beauty, nor desirableness,
pride, nor grace; yet neither asking for pity; not, as
ruins are, useless and piteous, feebly or fondly
garrulous of better days; but useful still, going
through its own daily work, - as some old fisherman,
beaten grey by storm, yet drawing his daily nets: so it
stands, with no complaint about its past youth, in
blanched and meagre massiveness and serviceableness,

gathering human souls together underneath it; the sound
of its bells for prayer still rolling through its rents;
and the grey peak of it seen far across the sea,
principal of the three that rise above the waste of
surfy sand and hillocked shore, - the lighthouse for
life, and the belfry for labour, and this - for patience
and praise.

This passage I take to be one of the most magnificent
examples of the 'pathetic fallacy' in our language.
Perhaps the 'pathetic fallacy' is second-rate art; the
passage is too long - 211 words alas! without one full
stop, and more than forty commas and other marks of punc-
tuation - it has *trop de choses* - it has redundancies,
tautologies, and artifices, if we are strictly severe -
but what a picture, what pathos, what subtlety of observation, what nobility of association - and withal how complete is the unity of impression! How mournful, how
stately is the cadence, most harmonious and yet peaceful
is the phraseology, and how wonderfully do thought, the
antique history, the picture, the musical bars of the
whole piece combine in beauty! What fine and just images -
'the large neglect,' the 'noble unsightliness.' The tower
is 'eaten away by the Channel winds,' 'overgrown with
bitter sea grasses.' It is 'careless,' 'puts forth no
claim,' has 'no pride,' does not 'ask for pity,' is not
'fondly garrulous,' as other ruins are, but still goes
through its work, 'like some old fisherman.' It stands
blanched, meagre, massive, but still serviceable, making
no complaint about its past youth. A wonderful bit of
word-painting - and perhaps, word-painting, at least on a
big canvas, is not strictly lawful - but such a picture as
few poets and no prose-writer has surpassed! Byron would
have painted it in deeper, fiercer strokes. Shelley and
Wordsworth would have been less definite. Coleridge would
not have driven home the moral so earnestly; though
Tennyson migh have embodied it in the stanzas of 'In
Memoriam.'
    I should like to take this passage as a text to point
to a quality of Ruskin's prose in which, I believe, he has
surpassed all other writers. It is the quality of musical
assonance. There is plenty of *alliteration* in Ruskin, as
there is in all fine writers: but the musical harmony of
sound in Ruskin's happiest efforts is something very
different from *alliteration*, and much more subtle. Coarse,
obtrusive, artificial *alliteration*, *i.e.* the recurrence of
words with the same initial letter, becomes, when crudely
treated or overdone, a gross and irritating form of affectation. But the prejudice against alliteration may be

carried too far. Alliteration is the natural expression of earnest feeling in every form - it is a physiological result of passion and impetuosity:- it becomes a defect when it is repeated too often, or in an obtrusive way, or when it becomes artificial, and studied. Whilst alliteration is spontaneous, implicit not explicit, felt not seen, the natural working of a fine ear, it is not only a legitimate expedient both of prose and of verse, but is an indispensable accessory of the higher harmonies, whether of verse or prose.

Ruskin uses alliteration much (it must be admitted, in profusion), but he relies on a far subtler resource of harmony - that is *assonance*, or as I should prefer to name it, *consonance*. I have never seen this quality treated at all systematically, but I am convinced that it is at the basis of all fine cadences both in verse and in prose. By *consonance* I mean *the recurrence of the same, or of cognate, sounds*, not merely in the first letter of words, but where the stress comes, in any part of a word, and that in sounds whether vowel or consonant. Grimm's law of interchangeable consonants applies; and all the well-known groupings of consonants may be noted. The liquids connote the sweeter, the gutturals the sterner ideas; the sibilants connect and organise the words. Of poets perhaps Milton, Shelley, and Tennyson make the fullest use of this resource. We need not suppose that it is consciously sought, or in any sense studied, or even observed by the poet. But *consonance*, *i.e.* recurrence of the same or kindred sounds, is very visible when we look for it in a beautiful cadence. Take Tennyson's -

Old Yew, which graspest at the stones
   That name the under-lying dead,
Thy fibres net the dreamless head,
   Thy roots are wrapt about the bones.

How much does the music, nay the impressiveness, of this stanza depend on *consonance!* The great booming O with which it opens, is repeated in the last word of the first, and also of the last line. The cruel word 'graspest' is repeated in part in the harsh word 'stones.' Three lines, and six words in all, begin with the soft 'th': 'name' is echoed by 'net,' 'under-lying' by 'dreamless'; the 'r' of 'roots' is heard again in 'wrapt,' the 'b' in 'fibres,' in 'about,' and 'bones.' These are not at all accidental cases of *consonance*.

This musical *consonance* is quite present in fine prose, although many powerful writers seem to have had but little ear for its effects. Such men as Swift, Defoe, Gibbon,

Macaulay, seldom advance beyond alliteration in the ordinary sense. But true *consonance*, or musical correspondence of note, is very perceptible in the prose of Milton, of Sir Thomas Browne, of Burke, of Coleridge, of De Quincey. Above all, it is especially marked in our English Bible, and in the Collects and grander canticles of the Prayer Book; and is the source of much of their power over us. Of all the masters of prose literature, John Ruskin has made the finest use of this resource, and with the most delicate and mysterious power. And this is no doubt due to his mind being saturated from childhood with the harmonies of our English Bible, and to his speaking to us with religious solemnity and in Biblical tones.

This piece about the tower of Calais Church is full of this beautiful and subtle form of alliteration or colliteration - 'the large neglect, the noble unsightliness of it' - 'the record of its years written so visibly, yet without sign of weakness or decay' - 'the sound of its bells for prayer still rolling through its rents.' Here in a single line are three liquid double 'll'; there are six 's'; there are five 'r' in seven words - 'sound rolling through rents' is finely expressive of a peal of bells. And the passage ends with a triple alliteration - the second of the three being inverted: 'bel' echoing to 'lab' - 'the lighthouse for life, and the belfry for labour, and this - for patience and praise.'...

We may turn now to a passage or two, in which perhaps Ruskin is quite at his best. He has written few things finer, and indeed more exactly truthful, than his picture of the Campagna of Rome. This is in the Preface to the second edition of 'Modern Painters,' 1843.

Perhaps there is no more impressive scene on earth than the solitary extent of the Campagna of Rome under evening light. Let the reader imagine himself for the moment withdrawn from the sounds and motion of the living world, and sent forth alone into this wild and wasted plain. The earth yields and crumbles beneath his foot, tread he never so lightly, for its substance is white, hollow, and carious, like the dusty wreck of the bones of men. The long knotted grass waves and tosses feebly in the evening wind, and the shadows of its motion shake feverishly along the banks of ruin that lift themselves to the sunlight. Hillocks of mouldering earth heave around him, as if the dead beneath were struggling in their sleep. Scattered blocks of black stone, four-square remnants of mighty edifices, not one left upon another, lie upon them to keep them down. A dull purple poisonous haze stretches level along the

desert, veiling its spectral wrecks of massy ruins, on
whose rents the red light rests, like dying fire on
defiled altars; the blue ridge of the Alban Mount lifts
itself against a solemn space of green, clear, quiet
sky. Watch-towers of dark clouds stand steadfastly
along the promontories of the Apennines. From the plain
to the mountains, the shattered aqueducts, pier beyond
pier, melt into the darkness, like shadowy and countless troops of funeral mourners, passing from a nation's
grave.

Here is a piece of pure description without passion or
moralising; the passage is broken, as we find in all good
modern prose, into sentences of forty or fifty words. It
is absolutely clear, literally true, an imaginative picture
of one of the most impressive scenes in the world. All who
know it, remember 'the white, hollow, carious earth,' like
bone dust, 'the long knotted grass,' the 'banks of ruin'
and 'hillocks of mouldering earth,' the 'dull purple
poisonous haze,' 'the shattered aqueducts,' like shadowy
mourners at a nation's grave. The whole piece may be set
beside Shelley's poem from the 'Euganean Hills,' and it
produces a kindred impression. In Ruskin's prose, perhaps
for the first time in literature, there are met the eye of
the landscape painter and the voice of the lyric poet -
and both are blended in perfection. It seems to me idle to
debate, whether or not it is legitimate to describe in
prose a magnificent scene, whether it be lawful to set
down in prose the ideas which this scene kindles in an
imaginative soul, whether it be permitted to such an artist
to resort to any resource of grace or power which the
English language can present.
This magnificent piece of word-painting is hardly surpassed by anything in our literature. It cannot be said to
carry alliteration to the point of affectation. But the
reader may easily perceive by analysis how greatly its
musical effect depends on profusion of subtle *consonance*.
The 'liquids' give grace: the broad $\bar{o}$ and $\bar{a}$, and their
diphthong sounds, give solemnity: the gutturals and double
consonants give strength. 'A dull purple poisonous haze
stretches level along the desert' - 'on whose rents the
red light rests like dying fire on defiled altars.' Here
in thirteen words are - five r, four t, four d, three l, -
'Dark clouds stand steadfastly' - 'the promontories of the
Apennines.' The last clause is a favourite cadence of
Ruskin's: its beautiful melody depends on a very subtle
and complex scheme of *consonance*. 'From the plain to the
mountains, the shattered aqueducts, pier beyond pier, melt
into the darkness, like shadowy and countless troops of

funeral mourners, p̄assing from a nation's gr̄ave.' It is
impossible to suppose that the harmonies of this 'coda'
are wholly accidental. They are the effect of a wonderful
ear for tonality in speech, certainly unconscious, arising
from passionate feeling more than from reflection. And Mr.
Ruskin himself would no doubt be the first to deny that
such a thought had ever crossed his mind; - perhaps he
would himself denounce with characteristic vehemence any
such vivisection applied to his living and palpitating
words....

As a matter of fact, John Ruskin himself undertook to
curb his Pegasus, and, like Turner or Beethoven, distinctly
formed and practised 'a second manner.' That second manner
coincides with the great change in his career, when he
passed from critic of art to be social reformer and moral
philosopher. The change was of course not absolute; but
whereas, in the earlier half of his life, he had been a
writer about Beauty and Art, who wove into his teaching
lessons on social, moral, and religious problems, so he
became, in the later part of his life, a worker about
Society and Ethics, who filled his practical teaching with
judgments about the beautiful in Nature and in Art. That
second career dates from about the year 1860, when he
began to write 'Unto this Last,' which was finally published in 1862.

I myself judge that book to be not only the most original and creative work of John Ruskin, but the most original
and creative work in pure literature since 'Sartor
Resartus.' But I am now concerning myself with form: and,
as a matter of form, I would point to it as a work containing almost all that is noble in Ruskin's written prose,
with hardly any, or very few, of his excesses and mannerisms. It is true...we have a single sentence of 242 words
and 52 intermediate stops before we come to the pause.
But this is occasional; and the book as a whole is a
masterpiece of pure, incisive, imaginative, lucid English.
If one had to plead the cause of Ruskin before the Supreme
Court in the Republic of Letters, one would rely on that
book as a type of clearness, wit, eloquence, versatility,
passion.

From the publication of 'Unto this Last,' in 1862, John
Ruskin distinctly adopted his later manner....

48. ROBERT F. HORTON, FROM A SIGNED REVIEW, 'LONDON QUAR-
TERLY REVIEW'

April 1900, n.s., no. 6, 289-307

Robert Forman Horton (1855-1934) was born in London and
educated at Shrewsbury School and New College, Oxford. He
was a Nonconformist divine and, briefly, a university
lecturer in History. In 1880 he became pastor of a Congregational church in Hampshire and subsequently played an
important role in religious affairs. He published widely
in theology, criticism, biography, and history. The 'London
Quarterly Review' was a conservative, Methodist organ
appealing to educated middle-class readers of Nonconformist
bent.

...There were few who felt the music of his words, that
were not lured to explore the secret of his thoughts. And
whether he knew it or not, his teaching fell into a prepared soil. The object of the present article is to
indicate the extent of the influence which he wielded. And
this may be traced in art, in conduct, and above all in
economics. He supposed that his prophetic utterances on
the last subject were not taken seriously, but met by the
reproach *ne sutor ultra crepidam*. But it is quite conceivable that this was his most original contribution to the
thought of his time; and that when 'Modern Painters' is
read only for its beauty of diction, 'Unto this Last' will
be quoted as the renaissance of political economy.

But to approach these subjects in order: is it too much
to say that thousands in this generation owe all their
interior understanding of great art to Ruskin? It may be
true that Turner was already appreciated before Ruskin
became his interpreter; but the character and quality of
the appreciation are the fruit of his interpretation.
Until our eyes were anointed with that salve we did not
observe the miraculous insight which makes Turner's trees
and rocks nature, while the trees and rocks in a Gains-
borough were only a mannered convention. Nothing but a
patient analysis could reveal the unconscious science
which underlay Turner's art. That Turner's world is the
actual world, radiant, significant, steeped in the rainbow
of poetry, was not a fact so obvious that the majority of
us would have recognised it without a guide. Nay, the
reaction of realism has sufficiently shown that we could
easily drift back to the pre-Ruskinian days, but that the
words of the prophet are written in enduring letters of

gold.

Then what would Santa Croce and the Spanish Chapel have
been to us but for the 'Mornings in Florence'? And what
would some of our lives have been without the Spanish
Chapel and Santa Croce? The glamour of Raphael and
Leonardo, nay, even the dull sentimentalism of Guido and
Domenichino, held the world captive. No one had time or
thought for Simone Memmi and Taddeo Gaddi, or even for
Giotto, beyond his tower. But Ruskin taught us to penetrate
the spirit of those earlier and more serious masters. We
went with him in the early morning while the shafts of
light could pierce the low-vaulted chamber, and learnt the
noble thought of the great Florentine, that all wisdom,
science, and education are the outcome of Pentecost. Or we
passed reverently the prostrate form on the stone pillow
of the floor of Santa Croce, to make our first acquaintance with St. Francis, where Giotto stretched him for
ever, among the devout and sceptical followers, reclining
on the moveless bier, gazing on the vision of angels that
passes not away.

How many of us, but for the 'Stones of Venice,' would
have learnt to read the Bible of St. Mark's or to tread
the *calle* with the reverent memory of the great souls that
founded and maintained that republic in the sea? Should we
not have wasted all our time with Titian's gorgeous
canvases, and been blind to the modest marvels of
Carpaccio? A year ago I visited, Ruskin in hand, St.
Giorgio di Schiavone, and studied that picture in which
Carpaccio delineates the conquest of lust in the victory
of St. George over the dragon. Who but Ruskin would have
taken us to that dishevelled church, or gained for the
master a hearing from the modern world? And yet while
Titian intoxicates the eye with the lust of the world and
the vain glory of life, it is Carpaccio who finds that the
one delight of the world is to overcome it, and the one
glory of man is to seek the glory of God.

Or to take but one more instance, the Tombs of the
Scaligers were a subject of curiosity only until they
became in Ruskin's hands a great sermon in stone. Since
Ruskin spent his hours of meditation in that strait in-
closure it has become impossible for us to miss the meaning of the decline from Dante's Can Grande to that Can
Signorio, who, lustful and murderous, forestalled the
judgment of survivors by building his own gorgeous tomb in
all the glory of the warlike saints, and of the personified
virtues.

But it is not only that to thousands of us Ruskin gave
eyes to see and a heart to understand; his eloquent protests have largely transformed our architecture, our

domestic furniture, and our whole conception of our sur-
roundings, whether in nature or in cities, as a great unconscious influence in the moulding of character and the
ordering of life. It required no great insight to see that
Seven Dials was hideous, or that the Black Country was
like a blighted heart to England; but it required both
insight and courage to describe the Houses of Parliament
as 'the absurdest and emptiest piece of filigree - and as
it were eternal foolscap in stone - which ever human
beings disgraced their posterity by.' And we had no one
before Ruskin to tell us that 'if cottages are ever to be
wisely built again, the peasant must enjoy his cottage and
be himself its artist, as a bird is.' William Morris was a
pupil of Ruskin's. And if we are beginning to rediscover
the delight in handicraft, and to find a metal work, a
frieze work, a tapestry, an earthenware, which retains in
it the joy of the worker, instead of being the soulless
duplication of thoughtlessness and machinery, it is to
Ruskin that we must refer this return into the good old
ways.

No doubt there is a reaction from Ruskin's judgments in
art. Whistler, who was the object of his withering criticism, has attained recognition as a great and original
genius. It has become true in Ruskin's case, as in all
others, and even with peculiar force with one whose
language is so trenchant and final, that we can attach
more importance to a critic when he praises than when he
condemns. While the truth and beauty of all art can only
be recognised by the truth and beauty in the eye of the
observer, there may be defects or limitations in the eye
which render it incapable of recognising truth and beauty
in all places where they exist. But it may be conjectured
that Ruskin was prepared for a reaction. He had to save us
from abysmal depths of vulgarity and soullessness in our
art judgments; and he had to turn our attention to the
eternal springs of beauty. A certain vehemence, and even a
certain onesidedness, was necessary. Eyes which were captivated by Guido Reni and Guercino, or saw nothing painful
in the Houses of Parliament or the dome of the National
Gallery, could only be opened by vituperation of the
things they immoderately admire, while when once the eyes
were trained to the true admiration they might return to
give a modified approbation of the Aurora and of the Angel
of the Lily, and to find some picturesqueness in the
Houses of Parliament if not in the dome of the National
Gallery.

The revival of village industries and handicraft art
which has brought a new life into the dales round Keswick
is a result which may yet have a great future. Mr. Godfrey

Blount's 'Arbor Vitae' shows that Ruskin's teaching has called into being fresh and original thinkers on the subject. In the neighbourhood of Haslemere there is a little school of unostentatious workers, who, turning from drawing-room pictures which are painted for money, bought for vanity, and displayed for ostentation, are seeking for a national art at the sources; the object is to give the touch of individuality to objects of household furniture and to secure decorative effects, not by putting ornaments on things, but by making things themselves ornaments. This is but one of the many channels in which Ruskin's vast influence on modern art is at work.

Now to turn to the ethical and didactic influence of the dead master: there are many passages in his writings which betray the despondency of a lonely thinker and a contemned prophet. It seemed to himself that his exhortations were thrown to the winds; and one might have supposed that his work as a teacher was vanity. But this sense of failure arose from ignorance of the effect which he was producing. It is possible that particular precepts of his were ignored, or perhaps they passed underground to germinate by-and-by; for, to say truth, many of his particular precepts were vehement and exaggerated judgments seen without the relief and modifications which practice must take into account. If his hearers did not obey these requirements of the new Sinai, neither did the lawgiver himself. He denounced usury in unmeasured terms; and yet, as he admitted, he lived on it. Was it possible to expect that even the most reverent could accept as quite serious a principle which the teacher could not practise? I have heard it said, too, that some of the counsels given to girls in 'Sesame and Lilies,' regarding dress, reading religious work, etc., are not of the kind which can be accepted *au pied de la lettre*. Why should they? Did the master expect that they would be? For the ethical and didactic value of Ruskin did not lie in particular precepts, which, where they deviated from accepted standards, were apt to be eccentricities and even extravagances, but in that invigoration of the moral sentiment, in that magical light thrown on common life, in that insight into the connexion between religion and conduct, which the earnestness and inspiration of his writings produce. Like his predecessor, whom he acknowledged as his master, Thomas Carlyle, he acted upon his generation not so much by moral instruction as by moral stimulus. If one were to reduce Carlyle's definite instruction to concrete forms, the decalogue which resulted would be meagre; the whole law would seem to be summed up in a barbarous conviction that might is right. For the gospel of love seemed to be substituted

the gospel of force. But Carlyle as a writer and a sage
operated on his readers in a very different way. In the
stirring of the waters a healing power was exerted. There
was the rush of invisible wings, voices called out of the
upper air. And young, ardent souls sallied forth, not to
maintain the Carlylean dogma, but in dogmas of other
kinds, orthodox or heterodox, to prove the Carlylean
spirit, the love of work, the hate of lies, the earnest
confidence in God. It is not necessary to maintain that
all inspired teachers are of this kind, and that we
misuse them when we miss the spirit and cling only to the
letter. But certainly Ruskin was of this kind. His writings
are not a new Decalogue, but in them the old and venerable
Decalogue, the indefeasible laws of God, are uttered again
with the majesty of lightning and earthquake; again the
reverent soul stands in the mouth of the cave wrapped in a
mantle while the words of the still small voice are heard.
It would, of course, be preposterous to rank these words
of a modern prophet with Scripture; but it is not preposterous to compare his mode of instruction with that of
Scripture; it is not by a uniform and consistent presenta-
tion of ethical principles or requirements that the effect
is produced; but a spirit is at work which transfuses,
moulds, and employs materials of very different kinds, so
that the unity is not in the material but in the spirit.

As a young man in the second volume of 'Modern Painters'
he laid down a principle which is the key to all his subsequent work, and he followed it with one of those flexible
passages of harmonious words which are the secret of his
abiding charm. And this double value of the passage must
excuse the long quotation:

[Quotes from 'Man's use and function' to 'like His
eternity', 'Works' 4: 28-9.]

Surely we may say that there is something of the quality
of inspiration in such a passage as this. It is not argument, it is not the assertion of some new truth; it may be
doubted even whether the description of the Utilitarians
is absolutely just to Bentham and Mill. But there is in it
the power which stirs in a Hebrew prophet like Isaiah, or
in a Puritan poet like Milton. It has the faculty of revelation. A secret passion at its heart and a moving eloquence in its utterance attract and rivet the reader while
the heavens open, and the eternal truth becomes plain that
God is the only explanation of man, and the harmony of man
with God is the only rational object of human life....
...the last part of the subject [is] the influence which
Ruskin has exercised on our problems of social amelioration.

Before passing to it, however, it may be worth while to
pause and meet a note of disappointment which is sufficiently audible to-day. How can we talk of progress, it
may be asked, whether due to Ruskin or to others, when
books such as 'Liza of Lambeth,' or 'No. 5 John Street,'
or 'Tales of Mean Streets,' and 'The Child of the Iago,'
are among the most constant elements of our literary
production? How have the invectives availed, any more than
those of prophets and apostles before him; when this is
still the dismal feature of our crowded cities, a class
sodden with wealth and another class sodden with poverty,
at the one end of the scale thousands living the unclean
life of drink and lust and vulgar display, making no
serious effort except to find new pleasures, finding no
lasting delight in the pleasures purchased at such a
cost, and at the other end of the scale hundreds of
thousands who tremble on the line of starvation, finding
their one relief in sensual acts, and their one religion
in a dull hatred of the fortunate? But the reply to this
cry of despondency is to be found in this: that these
books are written and sold, is due to the awakening sense
that we are our brother's keeper. There is nothing new in
the selfish luxury of the rich and in the hopeless squalor
of the poor. What is new is that a large part of the
community, all the more thoughtful and earnest part, no
longer passes by the unsavoury facts as part of the inevitable order, but is determined to know, and knowing to
attempt a remedy. That is the element of truth in the
cheerful assurance of an eminent statesman, 'We are all
socialists to-day.' We are all, broadly speaking, conscious
that the extremes of wealth and poverty are a gangrene in
the community, and the community is committed to heal
itself of the disease. And if that conviction is now
practically universal, the main thanks are due to John
Ruskin, who, we have ventured to predict, will be remembered by posterity as the great writer who set in motion
the forces of social amelioration....

Ruskin challenged the economists even in their definitions. He declared that they had given a wrong account of
wealth and of value; he disputed their analysis of both
labour and capital; he showed that all their conclusions
were vitiated by these mistaken definitions. In place of
the economic man he insisted on restoring man, man that
was made in the image of God; and as a result economics
had to become human. We are not dealing with stars in
their courses or stocks and stones and trees, but with
flesh and blood, hearts that feel and can love, brains
that think, and wills that can act *against* the iron laws
of fate.

The form of his writings did not dispose economists to
take him seriously. The inimitable charm of 'Fors
Clavigera,' a work made up entirely of digressions, and
vivid with every colour and harmony of which writing
admits, did not suggest economic discussion. Was the poet
or the painter among the economists? He came there, his
pen dipped in the hues of the rainbow, and with the
apparent irresponsibility of a lark singing among the
clouds. And in the quaint richness of his half-legendary
proposal of a Companionship of St. George, the dry-as-dust
mind was not prepared to see the serious purpose, which
chose the name George not on legendary grounds but because
it means, or is supposed to mean, 'a worker of the earth.'
As Virgil sang his Georgics to save an empire that was
decaying because manhood was divorced from the soil, so
this inspired writer formed his Society of St. George for
the lowly purpose of leading young England back to the
wholesome ways of the earth and co-operation with the
productive forces of nature. But while Virgil, the laureate
of an artificial court, was poet and nothing else, Ruskin,
the mouthpiece of a great and free people, was only
formally a poet; he was materially an economic teacher,
trying to awake in young minds the sense of certain eternal
verities concerning man, society, and the earth on which
we live. Perhaps that 'Fors Clavigera,' Fortune bearing
the key, has only begun its work, and will yet apply the
key to some of our intractable locks.

Ruskin was an illustration of genius according to that
definition, 'Genius is a zigzag lightning in the brain
which other men have not.' His straightest course always
had an erratic appearance; and while one was delighted to
wander with him where he would, one often forgot where he
was going. One of my undergraduate recollections is seeing
the little group of men, from Corpus and Christ Church,
and from Balliol, for Alfred Milner was one of them, in
sweaters and flannels and boating-blazers, at work on a
road at Ferry Hinksey. The scoffer went out to observe,
and reported that the part of the road which Ruskin's
lambs were making was not materially more impassable than
the rest of the rutted track, which led no particular
whence or whither, and therefore could not affect for good
or ill the humblest traveller. What went ye out for to see?
Men clothed in soft raiment, and handling picks and
shovels as ill as they were ever handled? Nay, but it was
a prophet, and even more than a prophet. The dilettantism
was only on the surface; underneath was an immense seriousness. The whole action was merely symbolical, like a panel
of Simone Memmi's, or like St. Francis' building with his
own hands Santa Maria dei Angeli, or, for the matter of

that, like the baptism in Jordan or the Supper in the
upper chamber. Fools might laugh at the symbol, but the
wise accepted the truth.

That labour, and labour alone, is the foundation of
wealth; that wealth does not consist in material products,
but in healthy and happy human beings; that the wealth of
nations, therefore, is not to be estimated by its accumulated or floating capital, but by the number of wholesome,
clean, developed souls that compose it, - this was the
truth which the master was trying to teach in a parable.

In 'Unto this Last' he dropped the parabolic style and
spoke plainly, not prosaically but plainly, the truth
which was in his heart. Still economists disregarded him.
Here was the usual string of quixoticisms and paradoxes,
dressed in the familiar garb, which no one could resist.
But for their part they enjoyed reading it with the rest,
and returned refreshed to their economics as from a play
or a concert - he was 'unto them as a very lovely song of
one that hath a pleasant voice and can play well on an
instrument.' He, like Ezekiel, chafed under his inability
to convince the world that this was no paradox, but rather
a commonplace. True, he could not be dull, like the economists; but he was handling realities and arguing the
matter gravely, with the dullest of them. It was strange
that the brilliance and glory of his style should seem to
be a hindrance, but so for a while it was. Who made thee
an economist over us? was the question. He had to all
appearance been entirely occupied in art, studying the
composition of rocks and the contours of mountains, to
appraise Turner, or the first principles of architectural
utility, in order to appraise Venice. What attention could
he have paid to demand and supply, capital and labour,
production and distribution, the wage fund, the law of
diminishing returns, the theory of rent? Now, the truth
was that he had been poring over these things with intense
earnestness, impelled by the thought that until they were
rightly understood there could not be again any great art.
But his study had been, not in the text-books of the
science, but rather in the facts of life. He had claimed
the privilege of genius, the privilege which Adam Smith
claimed, though with how different an equipment, to go
straight to the facts again and look at them with serious
and reflecting eyes....

It is now recognised that hopefulness, freedom, change,
are elements in efficient work; and the sanctities of the
home and the careful protection of the mother are included
in the demands of political economy. The word of the
prophet is quick and powerful. It will go on and prosper,
until the first consideration of the State will be not

property, but men; not the security of those who are in
possession, but the claims of the dispossessed. Presently
a government, elected by the people and for the people,
will regard the presence of labour ill-paid, or not paid
at all, a national calamity, the swarms of houseless
tramps and city dossers a matter as pressing as the wrongs
of Englishmen in a foreign state, the overcrowding and
insanitary conditions of life a question of the first
public interest. The schools will not be made the sport of
sectarian bigotry, but developed to the highest possible
efficiency for making the children wholesome and happy,
because instructed and disciplined. The rights of labour
will be regarded as the primary rights - *viz*. the right of
every man to labour and to reap the full fruit of his
labour, and the right of labourers to refuse support to
those who do not labour; it will be seen that they who
have only their hands and brains to offer are at a disadvantage in bargaining with those who have accumulated
capital, and as the hands and brains are all important,
while the capital is mere brute force, the whole weight of
the community will be thrown in the scale of the more
helpless but more necessary side. With the freedom and
security of labour will come a new delight in it; and from
labour which men delight in will grow again, as always
before, a genuine art, the expression of the healthy human
spirit rejoicing in the work of its hands, and at liberty
to feel and therefore to produce what is beautiful.

'The condition of England question,' which to the
sombre forerunner was announced as the all-important question, will at last have found its right place, And the
solution of the question will have been found along the
lines of the great nineteenth-century prophet, whose love
of beauty led him to the search for truth, whose search
for truth brought him to the springs of beauty. His words
will never perish; they belong to the living word of God;
they will ring out as the prophetic herald until the dawn
of our economic redemption breaks....

49. LESLIE STEPHEN, FROM A SIGNED ARTICLE, JOHN RUSKIN,
'NATIONAL REVIEW'

April 1900, vol. 35, 240-55

Leslie Stephen (1832-1904), biographer, literary critic,
and historian of ideas, was educated at Eton and Trinity

Hall, Cambridge. He took holy orders and remained for
several years at Cambridge as a fellow. Subsequently, he
wrote for many major journals, among them the 'Pall Mall
Gazette', the 'Saturday Review', 'Fraser's', and the
'Fortnightly'. He edited (1871-82) the 'Cornhill' and
published many of his own articles - mainly from that
magazine - under the title 'Hours in a Library'. History,
philosophy, and literature are entwined in much of
Stephen's writing which includes 'History of English
Thought in the Eighteenth Century', 'Science of Ethics',
'Studies of a Biographer', and 'Life of Fawcett'. Stephen
was largely responsible for the founding of the 'Dictionary
of National Biography', and he was also an ardent
mountaineer. In 1865 he relinquished holy orders and later
published 'An Agnostic's Apology' (1893). He was knighted in
1902. He was twice married: first, to one of Thackeray's
daughters, and second, to Julia Prinsep by whom he had the
daughter later to become the novelist, Virginia Woolf.
Stephen stands as a major Victorian intellectual figure.
See Introduction, p. 24.

Ruskin's death, as we all agreed, deprived us of the one
man of letters who had a right to burial in Westminster
Abbey. We may rejoice that his representatives preferred
Coniston. The quiet churchyard in a still unpolluted
country was certainly more appropriate for him than the
'central roar' of what he somewhere calls 'loathsome
London.' But the general consent marks the fact that
Ruskin had come to be recognized as a compeer of our
greatest writers of the age. By many he is also revered as
one who did more than almost any contemporary to rouse the
sluggish British mind from its habitual slumber. His
career, indeed, suggests many regrets. His later writings
are too often a cry of despair and vexation of spirit. The
world is out of joint, and all his efforts to set it right
have failed. To those who cannot quite agree that we are
all driving post-haste to the devil, the pessimism may
seem to indicate the want of intellectual balance which
did much to waste surpassing abilities. But if his vagaries
are sometimes provoking, at any rate they are always
interesting. Though my intellectual idols in old days were
of a different school, I was never so dull as to be indifferent to the curious fascinations of his books. I have
been refreshing my memory of them lately, and if I cannot
profess myself an ardent disciple, I have at least read
with renewed or increased admiration of his literary power.
One excellence is conspicuous at first sight. The cardinal
virtue of a good style is that every sentence should be

alive to its fingers' ends. There should be no cumbrous
verbiage: no barren commonplace to fill the interstices
of thought: and no mannerism simulating emotion by fictitious emphasis. Ruskin has that virtue in the highest
degree. We are everywhere in contact with a real human
being, feeling intensely, thinking keenly, and, even when
rhetorical, writing, not to exhibit his style or his eloquence, but because his heart burns within him. In his
later moods, indeed, Ruskin held that he had been too much
given to the ornate: he had been seduced by his admiration
for Hooker to indulge in the elaborate long-winded
sentences: and he had certainly had a weakness for very
deliberate 'purple patches.' That was a venial fault as a
young man, and was sufficiently punished by misdirected
admiration. People, as he complained, would take him for a
coiner of fine phrases, instead of a real philosopher and
a serious critic of art. 'Modern Painters,' as even an
artistic ignoramus could see, was something much more than
rhetoric. It was an intellectual feat which becomes more
surprising the more one thinks of it. The first volume, we
remember, was not only written when he was twenty-three,
but when he had had, in some respects, a singularly narrow
education. Ruskin, we may note, was at Oxford during the
most exciting period of the 'movement.' His ablest contemporaries were all going through the Newman fever. Ruskin
seems never to have been aware that such a person as
Newman existed. He amused himself with geology and botany,
and seems to have been as blind as became the son of a
sound Evangelical wine-merchant to the very existence of
any spiritual ferment. That might seem to prove that he
cared nothing for intellectual speculations. Yet within a
year or two he was writing a book of which it may be said
that no work produced by an English author of the same
period of life has ever done so much to set people thinking in a fresh direction. The generous desire to do justice
to Turner, which prompted the book, led, I suppose, to the
most triumphant vindication of the kind ever published. In
any case the argument was so forcibly put as to fall like
a charge of lyddite into the camp of the somnolent critics
of the day. The book, whatever its errors, is, I fancy,
the only one in the language which treats to any purpose
of what is called æsthetics. It is amusing to notice what
difficulty the young critic has in finding any previous
authorities to confute. He goes back to Locke's essay, and
Burke on the Sublime and Beautiful, and Alison on Taste,
and the papers by Reynolds in Johnson's 'Idler,' which
have also, as he remarks, the high sanction of their
editor. In truth, English speculation on such matters was
nearly a blank. Untrammelled by any solemn professors of

æsthetics, Ruskin could be all the fresher; and perhaps
the better able to impress readers who were neither philosophical nor æsthetic. People who shared the indifference
to art of those dark ages (I can answer for one) were
suddenly fascinated and found to their amazement that they
knew a book about pictures almost by heart. They did not
foresee the day in which a comfortable indifference to
artistic matters, instead of being normal and respectable
would be pitiable and almost criminal. Ruskin, no doubt,
gave the first impulse to the change.

The popular reputation was partly due to passages which
a severe taste can only just approve. Yet the worst one
can say of such famous bits of rhetoric as the comparison
of Claude's skies with Turner's is, that they approach
Shelley's finest imagery too nearly for prose. The rhetoric
rests, in any case, upon some remarkable qualities. His
defence of Turner is mainly an exposition of Turner's
truthfulness to nature, and shows that his eulogist is
qualified to judge of his fidelity. Ruskin has watched sky
and sea and mountains so closely, that he is revolted by
the old conventional portraits and demonstrates his point
with extraordinary fulness of knowlege. He surpasses the
average critic in that respect as a scientific specialist
surpasses a mere popular observer. Ruskin, indeed, took
himself to have a specially scientific mind. So far as
aptitude for science means power of observation, the claim,
I imagine, was perfectly justified. He came in later
years to detest science 'in the lump,' and to speak of
leaders of science with unfortunate arrogance. But his
power of seeing the phenomena vividly was as remarkable as
his power, not always shared by scientific writers, of
making description interesting....

He has to make his theories - if theories he must have
- not by patient induction, but by flashes of intuition.
His theory of the beautiful simply formulates his own
childish instincts. Wordsworth had seen, we know, in his
own early feelings a proof of the soul's pre-existence
'with God, who is our home.' So Ruskin, though he somewhere calls this fanciful, regards the sense of beauty as
a revelation - as something like the inner light of
mystics. All natural beauty, he says, is 'typical of the
divine attributes'; and he tries to show in detail how the
sense of beauty corresponds to a perception of infinity,
order, symmetry, unity, and so forth, and how the external world is thus a divinely appointed system of symbols,
dimly recognized even in childhood. This theory, no doubt,
is as good as others. Like others, indeed, which present
themselves as a direct inspiration of the prophet, it may
fail to convince opponents; and the elaboration into a

symmetrical system must not be taken too seriously. Ruskin
quaintly remarks how hard he found it to prevent his
'Seven Lamps of Architecture' from becoming eight or nine
upon his hands. No doubt his first follower, if he had
found one, would have redistributed his symbols, and
interpreted various objects to mean entirely different
truths. It should be taken, as we take Wordsworth's ode,
not as a prosaic argument, but as an imaginative way of
expressing his own sentiments. If disputable as a general
theory, it shows what the love of nature meant for Ruskin.
To him it seemed to be a part of religion; and a description is for him not a mere catalogue of forms and colours
and sensations, but a divine language to be interpreted by
'high instincts' (if I may quote the inevitable ode again)
before which our mortal nature trembles like a guilty
thing surprised. To read the true meaning of these outward
and visible signs is the function of what he calls the
'theoretic faculty'; and, parenthetically, I may add that
his theory, good or bad in itself, leads him to very
interesting literary criticisms. I do not know whether the
chapters in which he discusses the 'theoretic' faculty or
imagination will pass muster with later psychologists
better than his theory of the beautiful with professors of
æsthetics. But I never read anything which seemed to me
to do more than these chapters to make clear the true
characteristics of good poetry. Ruskin's critical judgments are certainly not always right; no critic can always
judge rightly, unless at the cost of being thoroughly
commonplace, and Ruskin is often wayward and sometimes
extravagant. But his sense of what was excellent was so
keen and genuine, and he could often analyse his impressions so subtly that I have seemed to myself (perhaps it
was an illusion) to have really learnt something from his
remarks.

Ruskin's theory suggested many difficulties, which,
indeed, is the chief use of a theory. Contemporary critics
condemned him and his clients, the Pre-Raphaelites, as
'realists.' He was taken to hold, that is, that the merit
of a work of art was measureable entirely by the quantity
of 'truth' which it contained. In the 'Modern Painters' he
is constantly struggling against this interpretation,
though he never gets the point quite clear. There is a
difficulty in carrying out the theory consistently. The
painter, it seems, is to give the facts pure and simple,
but then it is just because the facts signify ideas. The
greater the realism, though it may sound paradoxical, the
greater the idealism. If, indeed, the 'love of nature' -
the intense joy and awe which Ruskin and Wordsworth felt
in their early days - be interpreted to mean that the

natural scenery which Turner painted is symbolic of divine
truths, the closer the imitation the fuller will be the
revelation. But when Ruskin is showing the marvellous
accuracy of Turner's perceptions, he seems to become simply
scientific or prosaic. Turner's merit is explained to be
that he instinctively grasped the laws of mountain
structure and saw what later geologists tried to explain.
It is only by a kind of after-thought that the scenery is
made to be somehow edifying and symbolic. There is a
greater difficulty behind. After all, is the 'love of
nature' so clearly a religious or moral sentiment? In a
chapter of 'Modern Painters' upon the Moral of Landscape,
Ruskin tries, with great ingenuity, to show that the passion is at any rate congenial to the highest moral feelings.
Yet he betrays some doubt. With Byron, the 'love of nature'
- if we are to take his word for it - was a corollary of
his misanthropy. He loved the deep and dark blue ocean precisely because it has a pleasant way of sending man shiver-
ing and howling to his gods. Is not that the logical view?
To love rock and stream precisely for their wildness surely
means that you dislike the garden and the field which are
useful to human beings. The love of nature, as interpreted
by Rousseau and his followers, meant, in fact, a condemnation of civilized man, not misanthropy, indeed, but a conviction of the thorough corruption of men as they are -
whatever we may hope for men as they are to be.
When, in the 'Modern Painters,' Ruskin tried to extend
his theory from the beauty of inanimate nature to the
beauty of organized beings, he felt this difficulty. Some
animals, and many men, are undoubtedly ugly. If they are
symbolic of anything, it is of something the very opposite
of divine - of sensuality, greed, and cruelty. In the
language of his Evangelical days, Ruskin regards this as a
result of the 'Adamite fall.' As the love of nature is
essentially a part of religion, he naturally comes to a
theory which identifies the 'æsthetic' with the moral or
religious instinct, and scandalized many people who did
not wish their love of art to be trammelled by any
crotchets of morality. The change from the Ruskin of the
'Modern Painters' to the Ruskin of the later days is, of
course, marked by the development of this feeling. The
vileness of man, instead of the beauties of nature, becomes his chief preoccupation. In the early volumes he is
not only enthusiastic, but seems to count upon the enthusiasm of his readers. He is exultingly smiting the
Philistine hip and thigh with a certain complacency; and
the good time is coming in which Turner and the Pre-
Raphaelites will be duly honoured. The fervid rhetoric is
the natural language of one who is leading a band of

followers to the promised land. Something gradually
changed, not his character, but his habitual tone of
feeling....

    About 1860 he began his warfare against the creed of
the modern world, which for him was represented by the
Political Economists. He was taken to be a dangerous
heretic. Thackeray had to stop 'Unto this Last' in the
'Cornhill' and Froude to decline 'Munera Pulveris' for
'Fraser.' The strength of the popular prejudice surprises
later readers. For some years we have been flouting the
old Political Economists with a scorn as unqualified as
the respect with which they were formerly greeted. Ruskin,
indeed, had precedents enough for identifying political
economy with the degrading and materializing tendencies of
modern society. The doctrine had been denounced from its
very birth by Conservatives, Socialists, and Radicals of
many types as heartily as Ruskin could wish. He declared
himself to be an interpreter of Carlyle, to whom, as he
said, he owed more than to anyone, and who had spoken the
whole truth about the matter in 'Past and Present.' No one
could acknowledge an intellectual debt more loyally and
heartily, and Carlyle's philosophy in general, as well as
his special denunciations of the 'dismal science,' had
clearly a potent influence upon his disciple. The Christian
Socialists, too, with whom Ruskin associated, were protesting against the old orthodox doctrine in the same
spirit - to say nothing of other critics who arose within
the ranks of the Economists themselves. There was nothing
new in the simple fact of a revolt. Carlyle, however, to
the ordinary Briton, passed for an eccentric old Diogenes
- a railer at things in general, or perhaps a humorist
whose misanthropy was half affectation. The Christian
Socialists might be amiable and excellent crotchet-
mongers, whose philanthropy wanted common-sense. And undoubtedly, there was a vulgar version of Political
Economy, which used the orthodox phrases ignorantly and
blatantly enough, preached an absolute and selfish 'indi-
vidualism,' and discovered that every scheme of social
reform was somehow condemned by inexorable scientific law.
Ruskin, therefore, resolved, he tells us, to come to close
quarters with pseudo-science; and to make it the 'central
work of his life to write an exhaustive treatise upon
Political Economy.' He began, apparently, by reading
Ricardo and Mill and such other authorities with attention;
though with a strong impression that they would turn out
to be humbugs. One result was that he attributed to some
of his opponents, to J.S. Mill in particular, a complicity
with a vulgar version of their doctrines which they altogether repudiated. He should have recognized that Mill

could speak as emphatically as himself of the injustice of
the actual social order; and sympathized quite as much
with the Socialist aspiration. There was, undoubtedly, a
radical antagonism of principle; but Ruskin was too
passionately eager to distinguish between the stupid and
selfish opponents, and men whose ability and genuine zeal
he ought to have appreciated.

Ruskin's assault on the Political Economists scandalized the public. The craftsmen still believed implicitly
in their Diana of the Ephesians. Carlyle's huge growls had
passed over men's heads like distant thunder, too vague to
be effective. Ruskin meant to be the lightning, striking
distinct and tangible points. He had, as he had showed in
his other works, a singular power of putting nasty questions, of hitting weak points, exposing loose and wordy
phrases, and generally making himself disagreeable to
self-complacent phrase-mongers. He succeeded in irritating
if not in convincing. For he was sure the respectable
world shut its ears and kept him out of correct periodicals. Naturally, he has now the credit which comes to the
earlier mouthpieces of a rising sentiment. I cannot
believe, indeed, that those 'arrows of the chace' - to
adopt his title for his occasional letters - really advanced economics. He could make special points, but not
construct a mere scientific theory. His moral sense was in
too great a hurry to step in. He could not look at the
facts quietly before fulminating his spiritual censures.
When, for example, he convinced himself that usury was
wicked, he jumped - most generously but most impatiently -
to rash and, as I think, absurd conclusions. To tell him
that his theory would be fatal to the whole structure of
modern industry might convince him that it must be true,
for modern industry is one mass of corruption. To me, I
confess, his doctrine seems to show that one's conscience
may be a dangerous guide unless it condescends to be enlightened by patient and impartial enquiry. We cannot
honour too cordially Ruskin's sensibility to social evils,
and the vehement hatred of baseness and brutality which
inspired his headlong assault. But one result of his
errors was that they gave some apparent excuse to the
infinitely commoner fault of cultivating indifference.

Ruskin's righteous indignation took, it must be admitted, some very queer forms. 'I will put up with this
state of things not an hour longer,' he says in the first
letter of the 'Fors Clavigera.' The singular series which
followed must always be one of the curiosities of literature. No man of genius, in the first place, ever treated
his public with such unceremonious frankness. One is often
inclined to accept his own view that his style had improved

by increased directness and sacrifice of rhetorical ornament. On the other hand, the incapacity for keeping to any
line of thought has reached its highest point. The twenty-
fifth letter begins, à *propos* to nothing, with a famous
receipt for a 'Yorkshire Goosepie,' a Brobingnagian pie,
which engulfs also a turkey, ducks, woodcocks, a hare, and
any quantity of spices and butter. He proceeds at once to
a description of the British penny, diverges into heraldry,
and ends by an account of Edward III.'s fight with the
French at Calais. Amazed correspondents, he tells, us,
enquired into the meaning of this pie, and his answer,
though it manages to introduce an assault upon Darwinism,
hardly clears the point. One can hardly doubt that the
discursiveness and eccentricity were indicative of a
morbid irritability of brain which was to cloud his intellect, and which is the best apology for certain utterances
which offended his readers. When a correspondent complained
of his speaking of Mill and Mr. Herbert Spencer as 'geese,'
he replied that he said so simply because he 'knew a goose
when he saw one.' Other phrases show a rudeness strange in
one who in personal intercourse was the most courteous of
men. When, indeed, he has said something specially sharp,
he generally proceeds to insist upon the extreme care and
moderation of his language. 'Whatever is set down for you
in "Fors,"' he says, 'is assuredly true, inevitable, trust-
worthy to the uttermost, however strange.' He quaintly
admits in a note that he may make a mistake or two upon
merely 'accessory points.' Such extravagancies, and there
are plenty of them, shocked the critic of well-regulated
mind. Matthew Arnold, if I remember rightly, refers to
some of them as instances of British crudity. We may forgive them if we take them as due to a physical cause. No
doubt, however, he had a tendency to such escapades: he
took a pleasure, as he admits somewhere, in a 'freakish'
exaggeration of his natural humour. Carlyle used often to
qualify his extravagant remarks by a huge guffaw, which
implied that he was only half serious; and Ruskin's sharp
sayings were entitled to the same allowance. He is partly
soothing himself by equivalents for a good 'mouth-filling'
oath, and partly amusing himself by the neatness with
which he can hit a weak point.

The 'Fors,' however, shows feeling deep and genuine
enough. It fully explains his enforced resemblance to
Swift. He is as vehement, if neither so coarse nor so
pithy. 'I perceive,' he says, 'that I live in the midst of
a nation of thieves and murderers; that everybody around
me is trying to rob everybody else, and that, not bravely
and strongly, but in the most cowardly and loathsome way
of lying trade; that "Englishman" is now merely another

word for blackleg and swindler; and English honour and
courtesy changed to the sneaking and the smiles of a
whipped pedlar, an inarticulate Autolycus, with a steam
hurdy-gurdy instead of a voice.' He only hopes to 'pluck up
some drowned honour by the locks' 'out of this festering
mass of scum of the earth and miserable coagulation of
frog-spawn soaked in ditchwater.' He follows an equally
bitter passage elsewhere by observing that his words are
'temperate and accurate - except in short-coming of blame.'
A few great teachers, he tells us, even Carlyle and
Emerson, accept too easily the comforting belief that
right will speedily become might. That is not the ordinary
view of Carlyle, who was gloomy enough for most of us.
Ruskin, in passages like the above, seems to be trying to
surpass his master. The attempt led him often enough to
overshoot the mark. It is not fair to say that we are
worse than Eccelin of Padua, who slew 2,000 innocent
persons to maintain his power, whereas we lately slew in
cold blood 500,000 persons by slow starvation - that is,
as he explains, did not prevent a famine in Orissa. The
cases are not strictly parallel. In spite of such feats of
logic, Ruskin's bitter utterances constantly made you
wince. His attacks on modern society might be caricatures,
but clearly there were very ugly things to caricature.
Whether he bewailed the invasion of country solitudes by
railways and the invasion of suburban villas, or the mean
and narrow life of the dwellers in villas, or went further
and produced hideous stories of gross brutality in the
slums of London or Manchester, he had an unpleasant
plausibility. If you tried to reply that such things were
not unprecedented, you felt that the line of defence was
rather mean, and that even if Ruskin was over angry you
had no business to be too cool. When I read 'Fors' I used
always to fancy that I could confute him, and yet to feel
uncomfortable that he might be essentially in the right.
The evils which had stung so fine a nature to such wrath
must at least be grievous.

How much Ruskin did to awaken people to a sense of
social diseases, or how far his diagnosis was correct, is
another question. I am only considering the literary
aspect. Ruskin is now often compared to his master, and
although attempts to compare great writers, and especially
to place them in order of merit, are generally vexatious,
the relation between the master and his disciple may
suggest certain points. In the twenty-five years which
preceded Ruskin's assault upon the Economists, Carlyle had
been, one may say, the leader of the intellectual opposition. He denounced the prevailing tendencies, one outcome
of which was in his dialect the 'pig philosophy' of

Utilitarians and Materialists. His disciples were few, and
even those who shared his antipathies were often shocked
by his rugged idiosyncrasies and what seemed to be his
deliberate mannerisms. Yet, considered as a prophet, it
seems to me that Carlyle had a far more potent influence
upon the more thoughtful young men of the time than Ruskin
ever possessed. He might be grotesque and extravagant, but
his influence embodied a more vigorous and coherent philosophy. He had the uncompromising thoroughness of the
Puritan, and this involved a quaint contrast. Carlyle, as
a descendant of John Knox, approved of the famous sentiment, 'May the devil fly away with the fine arts.' He
sympathized with Cromwell's view of the right method of
dealing with cathedrals, and would have been ready enough
to smash painted windows and deface the images of saints.
Ruskin, who drew his early religious impression from an
enfeebled version of Puritanism, was alienated from it
precisely by this iconoclastic tendency. Though he never
followed Newman, he came to admire mediæval art so warmly
that he has some difficulty in explaining why, at a later
period, he did not become a Catholic. There was a point of
contact, no doubt, in the hatred of the 'pig philosophy'
(the word does not represent my own prejudices) and
Ruskin's conviction of the desirable subordination of art
to morality. Ruskin saw, as he tells us, that art had
decayed as much in Catholic as in Protestant countries,
and fell back upon a religious creed, vague enough except
as expressing antipathy to scientific materialism. But his
version is curiously modified in the process of engrafting
the love of the beautiful upon Carlyle's sterner philosophy.

The arrogance of Ruskin's language was partly adopted
from Carlyle, and, indeed, is one of the awkward consequences of being an inspired prophet. It is implied in
your very position that your opponents are without an
essential mental faculty. You do not condescend to argue,
but have a direct vision of truth not perceptible to the
blind. Carlyle's famous conversion left him facing the
'Everlasting No' of Atheism in a humour of 'indignation
and grim fire-eyed defiance,' But he held equally that we
must disengage ourselves from the old creeds and legends
which were once the embodiment, but had now become mere
obstructions to the religious spirit. We must 'clear our
minds from cant,' and 'cant' included a great deal that
was dear to weaker brethren. Ruskin, without positively
dissenting, represents a different sentiment. He really
loved the old symbols which to Carlyle appeared to be
outworn rags of 'Hounsditch.' It is characteristic that
while professing his debt to Carlyle, he associates him

(of all people) with George Herbert, the Anglican divine.
He was affected, at times, not only by the sweetness of
sentiment of Herbert's poetry, but by the ingenuity in
finding everywhere symbols of religious truth. The method
becomes characteristic; as external nature is a divine
symbolism, the old religious art, and all great poetry and
philosophy, Shakespeare and Dante and Homer and the Book
of Genesis, are a kind of mystic adumbration of esoteric
truths. The 'Tempest' is an allegory; the labyrinths of
Crete and the legend of the Sirens contain profound wisdom.
Though he did not read German, he was impressed by the
second part of 'Faust,' just because it is intolerably
allegorical, and has, it appears, a bearing upon the
theory of usury. Quaintly enough, he complains that the
greatest men have found it necessary to wrap up their
truths in enigmas soluble only by the wise; and declares
that even the parables in the New Testament are 'necessarily misleading' to the profane. When a man interprets
books or, as sometimes happens, history by his fancy
instead of his understanding, he becomes simply absurd to
plain common-sense, unless one gives him credit for not
being quite in earnest. But if considered merely as products of graceful fancy, investing tender feeling or sharp
satire with the charm of poetical ingenuity, his discourses
sometimes make admirable literature. The very titles of
his books, the 'Sesame and Lilies' and 'Love's Meinie,'
and so forth, are promises that his moralizing shall be
transfigured into the most poetical forms. I do not know
that the promise is always kept: the fancies become too
palpably arbitrary, and aggravate the strange discursiveness. But the little book which seems to be his most
popular, the 'Sesame and Lilies,' deserved its success.
His style, I think, was at its best. He can still be as
eloquent as of old, though less ornate; and, though the
argument wanders a little, he manages to give a regular
and concentrated expression of his real convictions. The
last section in that volume, The Mystery of Life and its
Arts, is, to my mind, the most perfect of his essays.
Perhaps I am a little prejudiced by its confession, franker
than usual, of the melancholy conviction that, after all,
life is a mystery: and no solution really satisfactory. It
is a good bit of pessimism, especially if you omit the
moral at the end.

To most admirers, however, this would hardly be a
recommendation. Rather they were drawn to Ruskin because,
in spite of the gloomy views which he shared with Carlyle,
he did not give the same impression of 'grim fire-eyed
despair.' Carlyle, we used to say, though he could denounce the world, could suggest no remedy. Ruskin, hardly

more hopeful in fact, was yet always suggesting a possible
regeneration....

The real charm of Ruskin will perhaps be most perceptible to the future reader in a region less disturbed by
controversy. Ruskin's distaste for the actual world led
him often to look fondly to the days of his infancy, when
there were still honest merchants and unpolluted fields
even at Dulwich, and some people - especially his father
and mother - who could lead simple lives of reasonable
happiness. People, I observe, have lately acquired a habit
of insisting upon the extraordinary stupidity and selfishness of the last generation. They are good enough sometimes to make allowances for poor people born before the
Reform Bill, on the ground that it is unfair for the historian to apply to a rude age the loftier standards of
modern life. It is pleasant for the elderly to be reminded
that some of their fathers and mothers were really worthy
people, though Ruskin's estimate cannot be taken as unbiassed. To say the truth, one has a kind of suspicion
that the objects of his reverence would not have appeared
to us quite as they do to him. That does not prevent the
'Præterita' from being one of the most charming examples
of the most charming kind of literature. No autobiographer
surpasses him in freshness and fulness of memory, nor in
the power of giving interest to the apparently commonplace.
There is an even remarkable absence of striking incident,
but somehow or other the story fascinates, and in the last
resort, no doubt on account of the unconscious revelation
of character. One point is the way in which a singular
originality of mind manages to work out a channel for
itself, though hedged in by the prejudices of a sufficiently narrow-minded class and an almost overstrained
deference to his elders and his spiritual guides. But it
is enough to say here that the book should be acceptable
even to those to whom his social and artistic dogmas have
ceased to have much significance.

Index

The index is divided into two parts: I Works by Ruskin;
II General Index.

I   WORKS BY RUSKIN

II GENERAL INDEX

THE CRITICAL HERITAGE SERIES

GENERAL EDITOR: B. C. SOUTHAM

Volumes published and forthcoming

ADDISON AND STEELE	Edward A. Bloom and Lillian D. Bloom
MATTHEW ARNOLD: THE POETRY	Carl Dawson
MATTHEW ARNOLD: PROSE WRITINGS	Carl Dawson and John Pfordresher
W. H. AUDEN	John Haffenden
SAMUEL BECKETT	L. Graver and R. Federman
ARNOLD BENNETT	James Hepburn
WILLIAM BLAKE	G. E. Bentley Jr
THE BRONTËS	Miriam Allott
BROWNING	Boyd Litzinger and Donald Smalley
ROBERT BURNS	Donald A. Low
BYRON	Andrew Rutherford
THOMAS CARLYLE	Jules Paul Seigel
CHAUCER 1385–1837	Derek Brewer
CHAUCER 1837–1933	Derek Brewer
CHEKHOV	Victor Emeljanow
CLARE	Mark Storey
CLOUGH	Michael Thorpe
COLERIDGE	J. R. de J. Jackson
WILKIE COLLINS	Norman Page
CONRAD	Norman Sherry
FENIMORE COOPER	George Dekker and John P. McWilliams
CRABBE	Arthur Pollard
STEPHEN CRANE	Richard M. Weatherford
DEFOE	Pat Rogers
DICKENS	Philip Collins
JOHN DONNE	A. J. Smith
DRYDEN	James and Helen Kinsley
GEORGE ELIOT	David Carroll
T. S. ELIOT	Michael Grant
WILLIAM FAULKNER	John Bassett
HENRY FIELDING	Ronald Paulson and Thomas Lockwood
FORD MADOX FORD	Frank MacShane
E. M. FORSTER	Philip Gardner
GEORGIAN POETRY 1911–1922	Timothy Rogers
GISSING	Pierre Coustillas and Colin Partridge
GOLDSMITH	G. S. Rousseau
THOMAS HARDY	R. G. Cox
HAWTHORNE	J. Donald Crowley
HEMINGWAY	Jeffrey Meyers
GEORGE HERBERT	C. A. Patrides
ALDOUS HUXLEY	Donald Watt
IBSEN	Michael Egan